Architectural
Technology (CORE)

M I C H A E L   H A N N O N

eec direct

Published by
EEC Direct
Toomevara,
Co. Tipperary
Tel: (067) 26186

Editing and layout: Bookworks Ltd, Birr
Design: Brosna Press Printing & Design, Ferbane
Printed in Ireland by: Kilkenny People Printing Ltd

Artwork
Ute Rüter-Duggan
Michael Hannon
William Rood
Tony Sweeney
COFORD
Wood Marketing Federation

Photography
Scott Gilchrist
Michael Hannon
Modelworks

First edition published 2003
Reprinted 2004

ISBN 1-902148-03-7

About the cover

Cartwright Pickard Architects' contemporary and energy efficient design for a new operations centre for Phoenix Natural Gas in Belfast has won a number of major awards. The development was praised by the judges for its "innovative energy-saving features, use of natural light, external awareness and open configuration".

James Pickard of Cartwright Pickard Architects, said "Our principal objective was to design an efficient and attractive HQ building with a significantly reduced energy consumption, and to a tight cost plan to keep rent levels competitive. The finished building is a landmark office scheme that has achieved both environmental sustainability and economic viability".

The building has a bright modern appearance, with a full-height glazed entrance allowing the interior to be flooded with light during the day and glow attractively at night (see the *Options* cover). Large spans of glass create a bold visual statement and offer panoramic views from the inside.

Around half the building is glazed to optimise the cost of heating and cooling against savings on artificial lighting. Sunscreens shade the building in summer, while allowing beneficial winter sun to offset heat losses. Natural cross ventilation using openable windows was combined with mechanical ventilation to supply fresh air, with comfort cooling if required.

Contents

Foreword

CRH plc is one of the world's leading construction materials companies and is particularly pleased to be associated with the publication of this book.

Construction projects can have a profound impact on both the environment and the quality of life in the community. This textbook will help its readers to achieve an in-depth understanding of the materials, processes and other issues involved in domestic construction.

A key feature of this textbook is the way it addresses sustainable architecture, the conservation and responsible use of natural resources as well as the disposal of domestic waste. It covers the environmental and ecological issues relevant to the selection and use of raw materials and the importance of clean air and water.

Michael Hannon has produced a book that is specifically geared towards Irish conditions, drawing at the same time from international best practice. This leading-edge publication is sure to remain a valuable resource and reference manual for academics, students and practitioners of Architectural Technology for the foreseeable future.

Congratulations to Michael on the publication of this comprehensive and interesting work which readers are sure to find both useful and enjoyable.

Jack Golden, CRH plc
October 2003

Introduction

To the teacher

This book offers comprehensive coverage of all aspects of the Architectural Technology core material. This is the first Irish publication for this subject area, containing both higher level and ordinary level material. The material is totally up-to-date at the time of going to press and reflects current Building Regulations and trends in the construction industry.

This text was written with the student in mind, as is evident by the number of diagrams used and the design and layout of the book. Nevertheless, it will be necessary for you, the teacher, to guide your students through the material contained in each chapter. Some of the material will not be examinable until the syllabus is officially introduced. The Options will be published in a companion text prior to the introduction of the new syllabus.

I would like to get feedback from you on this publication. My aim is to keep this resource current and up-to-date, which will involve the publication of revised editions to reflect changes in the construction sector and in the Building Regulations. You can be a part of this process by contacting me at: michael@eecdirect.ie

I look forward to hearing from you.

To the student

Welcome to the study of Architectural Technology. This course concentrates on domestic construction, beginning with an architectural appreciation of the past and moving on to the many processes and procedures involved in domestic construction.

The text used is clear and concise to encourage you to read it outside of class times. Diagrams and photographs are used extensively to further help your understanding of key details and concepts. Sidebars are used throughout the text to explain new and sometimes difficult terms when they are used for the first time. Every effort has been made to make the material interesting, enjoyable, relevant and up-to-date. I hope you enjoy your study of Architectural Technology and that on completion it will open up new opportunities for you.

I would like to hear your comments on this book. You can contact me at: michael@eecdirect.ie

I look forward to hearing from you.

Michael Hannon
October 2003

Acknowledgements

I would like to acknowledge the following for their assistance in the preparation and production of this book:

Diarmuid Guinan, Ann Quinlan and all the team at Brosna Press

Warren Yeates for editorial and origination work

Ute Rüter-Duggan, Ciaran Hynes, William Rood and Tony Sweeney for artwork

Jim O'Connor, Charlie Mullen and Richard Murphy for proofing the text.

Jack Golden and Ruaidhri Horan at CRH

Mark Cahalane of Drury Communications

Noel Duggan and his staff at EEC Direct

Joe O'Carroll, COFORD

Donal Magner, Wood Marketing Federation

Barry Murphy and his team at MODELWORKS

Joanne Bridges, BRIDGES Communications

Cartwright Pickard Architects

Grace Keeley Michael Pike Architects

Department of the Environment and Local Government

Joe Beggan and Colm McAvinchey, Kingspan

Radiological Protection Institute of Ireland

Sustainable Energy Ireland

Bord na Mona Technology

Scott Gilchrist, Archivision

Paul Clerkin, Irish-Architecture.com

Record Hand Tools; Spear & Jackson

Met Eireann

Velux Roof windows

A final word of thanks to Regina and Adrian for their patience and understanding.

Michael Hannon
October 2003

Architectural Awareness

The remarkable preservation of some of our oldest stone buildings proves the value that lime putty plays in making good mortar. Lime mortar reduces the absorption of water by other walling materials and allows the wall to breathe. It helps mortar to penetrate into fine crevices, forming a strong even bond and ensures joints of adequate strength in tension and compression. Lime has been used for thousands of years and has many varied and important uses from its traditional uses in the building industry to new, more high tech uses in environmental pollution control systems.

☞

☞
The Anglo-Normans needed
strong fortresses and stone was
the natural choice for castles
such as Trim and Belgard
(pictured), which has become
the corporate headquarters
for the CRH group.

Company History

CRH was formed through a merger in 1970 of two leading Irish public companies, Cement Limited (established in 1936) and Roadstone Limited (1949). The newly formed group was the sole producer of cement in Ireland, and the principal producer of aggregates, concrete products and asphalt.

Since that time, CRH's strategic vision has been to become an international leader in building materials, delivering superior and sustained shareholder returns, while reducing its dependence on individual markets and achieving a balance in its geographic presence and portfolio of products.

CRH has developed formidable local, regional and national leadership positions across its three core businesses of primary materials, value-added building products and specialist distribution.

Chapter 1

Architectural appreciation

What is architecture?

Marcus Vitruvius, an architect and engineer of the first century BC, once described in his *Ten Books of Architecture* that any truly effective design must fully and equally satisfy three basic conditions: **firmness**, **commodity** and **delight**. 'Firmness' referred to the buildings capacity to stand up, 'commodity' to its usefulness, and 'delight' to its beauty.

Five influences on architecture that can be traced back in time include:

- **Needs.** People need shelter and a place to live. Natural shelters such as caves were used in the Stone Age.
- **Technology.** The environment influences building technology. Local stone and timber was used for buildings. Technology influenced how tools were made and how buildings were constructed.
- **Culture.** Architecture reflects the culture and history of a people and the region in which they live.
- **Climate.** climatic influences on architecture concentrate on keeping the rain out, letting light, air and sun in, keeping the heat in and the cold out. These influences vary in significance in different regions of the world.
- **Society.** Technology and society are intertwined. As technology evolved, civilisations formed in towns and cities under the control of rulers, emperors, priests etc. Monumental architecture dominated the best sites and represented the power of the rulers.

Architecture exists all around us, in our homes, our neighbourhoods, our communities, towns and cities. Architecture is about all of us, and how we interact with the buildings and structures we come in contact with on a daily basis. Architecture is part of everyone's daily experience.

This chapter will explore the history of architecture and related issues to give an understanding of how the past has influenced the present.

Shelter

Architecture began as protection from the elements. The early huts and refuges of caves and cliffs, though practical, also had a cultural dimension. The surroundings were decorated with paintings of animals and figures.

People began building homes during the Ice Age. These dwellings were designed in direct response to climate, local materials, and hunting patterns.

Archaeologists have discovered that some of the earliest Ice Age structures were supported by gigantic bones and tusks and covered in mammoth hides. This skin and bone tradition survived for thousands of years. A variation of this construction involved covering sapling frames with bark, reeds and animal skin.

Native Americans developed a portable version of this shelter called the **tipi**. It consisted of covering poles with buffalo hides and contained an entrance and smoke flaps. The parts were dismantled and packed when it was time to move and pulled by dogs and horses.

1-1 Native American tipi showing poles, buffalo hide covering, entrance and smoke flap

The nomads built temporary dwellings of sticks and animal hides that were easily transported (Fig. 1-2 overleaf).

1-2 Brushwood hut. 300,000 years ago our ancestors created simple shelters from closely packed brushwood held in place by rocks. Huts like this were only occupied for part of the year as the people moved about in search of food.

Farming led to more permanent structures to guard the crops and protect the animals.

One of the earliest settlements is the city of Jericho in Jordan, which dates to about 8000 BC. The people lived in stone houses with plaster floors, surrounded by high walls and towers. In the Indus river valley, early civilisations date back between 4500 and 2500 BC. These sheltered communities gradually developed into cities.

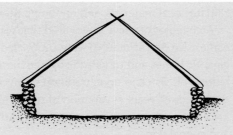

1-3 Round houses like this were built by the people of coastal Israel, Syria and Lebanon in c. 10,000 BC

Monuments to civilisation were the next type of architecture to develop. Egyptian civilisation built some of history's greatest monuments, such as the Great Pyramids at Giza (2723–2563 BC) and the Temple at Karnak (2133–1992 BC).

1-4 The Great Pyramid at Giza, Egypt, built around 2550 BC. This structure is approximately 144 m tall with each side of a square base measuring 226 m.

Architectural history

This overview of architectural history begins with early civilisations and moves quickly through the ages to modern architecture. The language of architectural history designates different styles of architecture. These styles are associated with different places and times. This text deals with the following styles:

- Early Civilisations
  - Early civilisations
  - Classical Greece and Rome

- Middle Ages (Medieval Period)
  - Medieval Vernacular
  - Romanesque Architecture
  - Gothic Architecture

- European Renaissance
  - Baroque Architecture

- Industrial Age

- Modern Architecture

Early civilisations

The first towns and cities appeared around 8000 BC when people began to live in communities. The people were often ruled by powerful leaders who lived in palaces. Some form of organised religion usually existed, which meant that temples had to be built. The palace and the temple were the largest buildings in the early civilisations. Strong walls with gatehouses and watchtowers defended the cities from invasion.

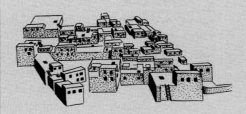

1-5 An example of one of the first towns in Turkey, c. 6000 BC. The mud brick houses were built close together. Access was through trap doors in the flat roofs. The flat roofs were used as work areas when it was not too hot.

Some of the most important early civilisations developed c. 4300 BC in Mesopotamia (now part of Iraq). The settlements were based around the Tigris and Euphrates rivers, and some of these early cities evolved into empires.

Everything from houses to temples was built from bricks moulded from straw and mud.

Stepped structures called ziggurats were built with staircases on the outside and a temple or shrine at the top for worshipping the gods of nature. Artisan workshops, storehouses and housing were located in clusters around the base of the temple.

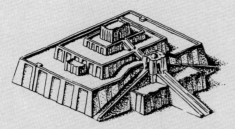

1-6 *Ziggarut at Ur c. 2100 BC. This temple, like many others, was designed to bring the priests closer to the heavens. It stands some 21 metres above the ground.*

The ancient Egyptians built approximately 80 pyramids along the banks of the Nile from 2700 to 1640 BC. Many of these were tombs for the Pharaohs (kings).

The pyramids took years to construct. Limestone was quarried from the banks of the Nile, transported on boats and dragged to the building site. It is not known exactly how the pyramids were built, but the blocks of stone were probably dragged up a ramp. The ramp was extended as the pyramid rose in height. The exterior of the pyramids were covered with a better quality stone. Gold was often used to cover the summit of the pyramid.

1-7 *Three pyramid styles existed. The Step pyramid (left), the Bent pyramid of 2723 BC (centre) and the Great or Straight-sided pyramid of 2528 BC (right), which was the most common type.*

Capital refers to the upper part of a column or pier that supports the entablature (see Fig. 1-8). Entablature is the part of a classical temple above the columns, having an architrave, a frieze, and a cornice. A colonnade is a set of evenly spaced columns.

Classical Greece and Rome

The building elements of this highly defined style of architecture consisted of columns, capitals and colonnades. The Greeks developed this architecture for temples in the seventh century BC.

The proportions in Greek architecture were based on mathematical ratios. The Romans copied ancient Greek architecture after they conquered Greece, while developing their own designs.

Classic is Latin for elite. Latin was the language of the Romans.

This ancient Greek and Roman architecture came to be known as **Classical** and continued for 2500 years.

Greek temples were not only a place to worship gods, but also stood as symbols of Greek society and culture. They were built on the highest point in every city. Surrounding the temples were civic buildings, stadiums, theatres and houses.

The Greeks built their temples and other major public buildings with limestone and marble. The stone was held in place by bronze or iron pins set into molten lead. This proved to be a flexible system that could withstand earthquakes and last for centuries.

The Greeks of the Classical era developed an elegant style of architecture with three main orders or styles. Each order consists of a column that extends from a base at the bottom to a shaft in the middle and a capital at the top. The diameter of the shaft is normally greater at the bottom, and tapers towards the top.

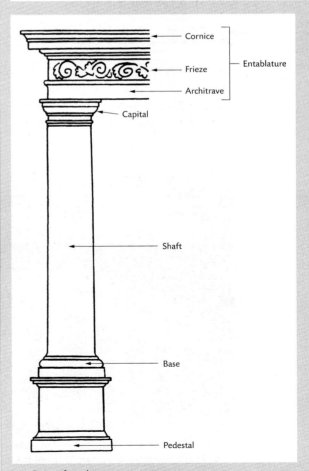

1-8 *Parts of a column*

The capital supports a horizontal element called the entablature. The entablature is made up of three parts, the architrave is the lowest part, the frieze is the middle part and the cornice is the top part. The parts of the column are sometimes named after the human body (feet, body and head).

The proportions of the orders were developed over hundreds of years. Over time they became lighter and more refined. The three orders are the Doric, Ionic and Corinthian.

THE DORIC ORDER is the oldest and the simplest of the orders. Columns are placed close together. The shafts are sculpted with concave curves called flutes. The capitals are plain with a rounded section at the bottom and a square section at the top. The Doric column represents the proportions of a man's body. The Doric order was used in the Parthenon.

THE IONIC ORDER was developed in the Ionian islands in the sixth century BC. It is taller than the Doric order. The Ionic column represents femininity. The Ionic order is easily recognised due to the two scrolls, called **volutes**, on its capital. The volutes may have been based on shells or animal horns.

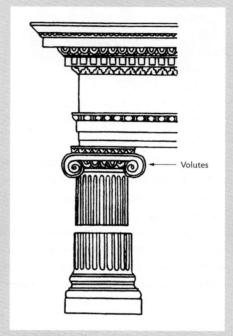

1-11 *The Ionic order*

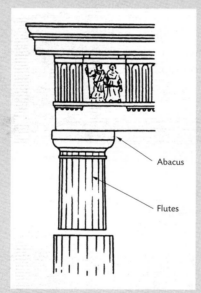

1-9 *The Doric order*

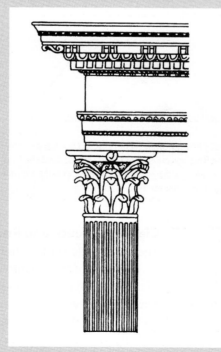

1-12 *The Corinthian order*

1-10 *The Parthenon – a temple to the Greek goddess Athena, built between 447 and 432 BC*

THE CORINTHIAN ORDER Corinthian is the third order, named after the city of Corinth, where it was developed at the end of the fifth century BC. It is similar to the Ionic order, except that its capital is more ornate. The capital is generally carved with two layers of curly acanthus leaves. Corinthian is the tallest of the three orders and represents the slight figure of a maiden.

The order in which a temple was built complemented the gender of the god or goddess celebrated.

The Greeks demonstrated a mastery of geometry, attention to symmetry and an understanding of proportion in their architecture. Greek architecture strived to create the perfect form, consequently the surviving buildings are referred to as 'timeless'.

ROMAN ARCHITECTURE

The Romans eventually conquered Greece. They learned about Greek architecture from the Etruscans, a cultured people who came from Asia Minor c. 800–700 BC. The Etruscans invented an order of their own known as the Tuscan. This was a simplified version of the Doric order and it became a favourite of the Romans.

The huge Roman Empire stretched from Britain to Asia and Africa. The Romans adapted the classical style of Greek architecture and added domes, vaults, arches and brickwork. Romans used concrete for the first time. These changes were revolutionary and changed architecture forever.

With such a large empire, the Romans had the labour force and the resources to construct enormous public buildings. These consisted of temples, markets, and places of entertainment such as ampitheatres. These large buildings were symbols of the power and status of the emperors.

> **Amphitheatre**
> a building, usually circular or oval, in which tiers of seats rise from a central open arena.

1-14 The Pantheon, 118–128 AD, built for the Emperor Hadrian. This is one of the most revered examples of architecture of this time. The temple is built of concrete and faced with bricks on the outside and marble on the inside. It has a large domed roof with a central unglazed window to let in sunlight.

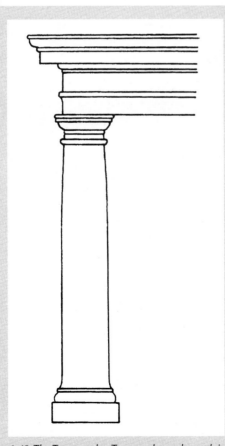

1-13 The Tuscan order. Tuscan columns have plain bases and capitals, and shafts without flutes.

Colosseum – interior

Colosseum – exterior

Colosseum – model

1-15 *The Colosseum was the largest amphitheatre of its time (70–80 AD). This vast arena measures 189 m across and could hold over 50,000 spectators. A large canopy protected the spectators from the heat and the sun.*

The Middle Ages

Architecture in the Middle Ages was linked to the rise of organised religion. Churches were the dominant architectural form, with interiors that promoted a sense of mystery. New churches were planned on the axial basilicas of Rome and new construction techniques were employed to build cathedrals that could accommodate large gatherings.

MEDIEVAL VERNACULAR In the middle ages, everyday dwellings were built with whatever materials were available. The local materials and climate, rather than the latest architectural fashion, influenced the simple style builders used. These vernacular buildings were built in the same style for hundreds of years.

Basilica
A rectangular early Christian or medieval church, usually having a nave with clerestories, two or four aisles, one or more vaulted apses, and a timber roof.

Clerestory
A row of windows in the upper part of the wall of a church that divides the nave from the aisle, set above the aisle roof. It may also refer to the part of the wall in which these windows are set.

1-16 *An early vernacular building was the cruck-framed house. The main beams formed an inverted V-shape, visible at both ends of the building. Wattle and daub was used between the beams.*

MEDIEVAL CASTLES The nobility of the middle ages often lived in castles. These were military strongholds as well as homes.

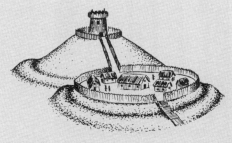

1-17 *A motte-and-bailey castle. Wooden towers were built on the motte. The bailey contained wooden huts for people and animals.*

Castles were designed to withstand sieges and were self-sufficient, with workshops, kitchens and stables. Wooden towers were constructed on earthen mounds called **mottes**. Later stone towers called **keeps** replaced the wooden ones.

1-18 *The Tower of London (1087–1097 AD) replaced a motte-and-bailey.*

ROMANESQUE ARCHITECTURE of the middle ages imitated Roman architecture. It started around 1000 AD. This style of architecture used round arches, simple vaults and Corinthian capitals in some places. New features of this era included façades with rows of arches and twin towers added to frontages.

1-19 *The famous 'Leaning Tower of Pisa' (1174–1271) was built as the bell tower for Pisa Cathedral in Italy. It is circled with decorative arches called arcading and leans about 5 m to one side. A new foundation was laid recently to stabilise the leaning tower.*

Gothic architecture

The Gothic style emerged in the 12th century. Its features included pointed arches, large windows, stone tracery, stone vaulted ceilings, and flying buttresses.

By 1200 Christianity had become a major force in the civilised world. Cathedral architecture became larger and more magnificent, reflecting a more stable and affluent society. The aim of Gothic architecture was to build as high and as light as possible.

Innovative construction techniques were employed to capture the expressive qualities of light in the church because it was believed that light represents Christ's presence. These techniques included the pointed arch with diagonal ribs, which freed the floor from heavy bearing walls. The ribbed vault eliminated the need for walls. Flying buttresses on the exterior carried the weight and thrust of the pointed vaults. This technique allowed greater heights and thinner structures. Gothic cathedrals became thin shells of stone and glass.

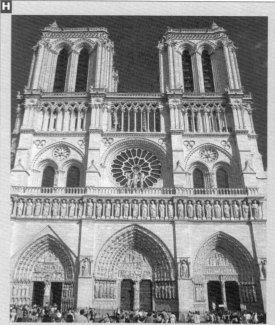

1-20 Notre Dame Cathedral (1163 – c. 1250) is a landmark in Paris. It has all the characteristic features of the Gothic style, including the west front with its two imposing towers and rose window. The west front contains the three main entrance doorways, decorated with rows of statues.

1-21 Gothic windows in the 12th century were lancets (top left). Lancets were paired in the 13th century to make two-light windows (top right). Later, windows were filled with tracery – geometric and perpendicular (bottom left and bottom right).

The Renaissance

The Renaissance refers to a 're-birth' or revival of ancient classical values. Reason took its place alongside religious teachings. Architects viewed themselves as individuals, capable of creating buildings in harmony with nature and the human body. They no longer viewed themselves as servants of God.

Italian architects in the 15th century were the first to be influenced by the Renaissance. They applied new theories, based on science and mathematics, to create ideal proportions based on geometric shapes.

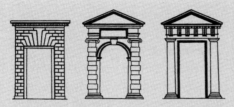

1-22 Italian Renaissance doorways may be decorated and sometimes topped with a triangular pediment. They may have classical columns and carved stonework.

Leonardo da Vinci (1452–1516) is probably the most famous individual associated with the Renaissance. He painted the Mona Lisa and the Last Supper. His drawing of man, inscribed in the circle and the square, illustrates the proportions of the human body. He was also an engineer, designer, scientist and philosopher.

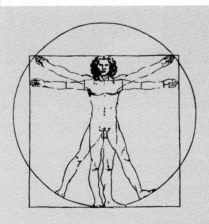

1-23 Leonardo da Vinci's drawing of the male figure illustrates the proportions of the human body.

During the Renaissance, buildings were based on simple geometric shapes, the square and the circle. These were meant to symbolise ultimate perfection. Renaissance buildings are smaller than Gothic cathedrals. This is because they are meant to represent the human intellect as much as the power of God.

CATHEDRAL OF FLORENCE

The first building in which the designer and the builder were separate persons was the Campanile, or bell tower, of the cathedral of Florence. The design was made by the painter Giotto and constructed by cathedral masons from 1334 to 1359.

1-24 Florence Cathedral

The dome of this cathedral was not built until the early 15th century, when Filippo Brunelleschi, a goldsmith and sculptor, began to make statues for the cathedral. Gradually he became interested in the building itself and built some smaller parts of it. In about 1415 he prepared a design for the dome that he daringly proposed to build without the aid of formwork, which had been essential in all previous Roman and Gothic construction. Brunelleschi studied the Roman Pantheon before planning this dome.

After building a 1:12 model of the dome in brick to demonstrate his method, the design was accepted and built under Brunelleschi's supervision from 1420 to 1436. Along the way, he invented a crane to lift stone to the top of the structure for the masons. He was thus the first real architect to conceive a building's form, its construction methods, and to guarantee its performance.

1-25 Filippo Brunelleschi (1377–1466), a Florentine architect, is considered the father of Renaissance architecture. He studied science and maths and in 1415 he discovered linear perspective.

ST PETER'S BASILICA The next great dome of the Renaissance was that of St. Peter's Basilica in Rome, begun by Pope Julius II in 1506. The technology was very similar to that of Brunelleschi, and the diameter is nearly the same. The dome's design went through many changes and extended over a period of nearly 80 years. The major contributors to the design were the painter and sculptor Michelangelo, who served as architect from 1546 to 1564, and the architects Giacomo della Porta and Domenico Fontana, under whose direction it was finally built during the 1580s.

The dome was considerably thinner than Brunelleschi's and was reinforced by three tie rings made of continuous iron chains. It developed numerous cracks, and in the 1740s five more chains were added to further stabilise it. Since the dome used a proven technology, most of the design was done on paper with drawings, rather than by building models.

1-26 St. Peter's Basilica, Rome

Baroque architecture

The Baroque style emerged during the 17th century. It was based on curved forms, rich materials, complex shapes and dramatic lighting.

The Baroque philosophy was to show that architecture could reach all levels of society. Buildings were no longer designed in isolation but were integrated into the urban surroundings. Baroque began in Italy, but the style spread to many parts of Europe.

The Baroque style is strongly evident in London. Christopher Wren was the architect responsible for rebuilding the city following a devastating fire in 1666. His major task was to replace the Gothic cathedral of St. Paul's.

1-27 The Palace of Versailles (1661–1756), France, is an excellent example of Baroque architecture. It contains galleries, staterooms, a chapel, an opera and the spectacular Hall of Mirrors.

The industrial age

The production of iron and steel in the 18th century forced many countries to move to an industrial economy from an agricultural one.

This change brought a need for different types of buildings. People moved from rural areas to the cities, so more houses were required for them. Factories were required to house the machinery for the manufacturing industries.

1-28 Iron bridge, (1777) Coalbrookdale, England. This bridge has a 30 m span over the river Severn. It was the first large-scale cast iron structure of the industrial age. A town called Ironbridge grew up around it.

The infrastructure of roads, canals, bridges and tunnels brought new building types such as mills, warehouses, factories and docks, as well as hotels and banks in the cities. Steam engines replaced water power.

The demand for new buildings led 19th century architects and engineers to experiment with new ways of building with iron and steel. They devised structures in which the skeleton of steel is the main structure. Steel could span vast interiors, and allowed very tall buildings to be constructed for the first time. This new material and techniques allowed huge buildings to be constructed at lightning speed.

The Crystal Palace (1851) is regarded as the first architectural monument of the Industrial Age. It omitted references to past architectural styles. The palace was enormous in scale, measuring 555 m with an internal height of 32 m. It only took three months to construct.

1-29 The Crystal Palace (1851) was designed as a prefabricated structure. It was destroyed by fire in 1936.

1-30 The 320 m high Eiffel Tower (1889) was the tallest building in the world when it was built.

Modern architecture

By the 20th century architects began to turn away from old styles and were ready to embrace new technology with new architecture. The availability of new materials and new techniques of construction influenced them.

Architects found inspiration in nature and from machines, instead of imitating past styles. The motivation for this shift was a rapidly transforming world. Cities were springing up everywhere, nationalism was on the increase, and the role of women in society was changing.

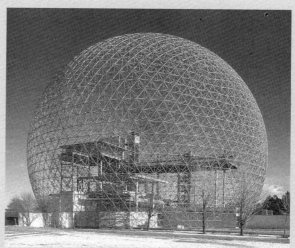

1-31 The Geodesic Dome by Richard Buckminster Fuller, used in the Montreal Expo 67. They are a means of enclosing large space in a structure with a small surface area.

Architects created tall glass and steel towers, white concrete houses with flat roofs and long strips of windows. The buildings had no additional or unnecessary decoration. These features became known as the International Style of architecture. It began in Europe and spread to many of the cities in the United States.

The Bauhaus is considered one of the greatest influences on modern architecture. (Bauhaus comes from 'Bau' meaning 'building' and 'haus' meaning 'house'.)

The Bauhaus movement was founded in 1919 by Germany's leading architect, Walter Gropius (1883–1969), he believed that art, design and construction should be united. The philosophy of the Bauhaus was 'form follows function'.

Bauhaus architecture consisted of ultra-modern shapes of concrete, glass and steel that were simple, functional and unadorned. The Bauhaus building at Dessau, Germany, is a perfect example.

1-32 Bauhaus school, Dessau, Germany (1925–26), by Walter Gropius. The glass walls reveal a structure of steel and concrete.

Le Corbusier (1887–1965), played a key role in the development of 20th century modernism with his writings as well as his architecture.

1-33 Villa Savoye (1929–31), built in France by Le Corbusier. It is constructed of lightweight concrete slabs and plastered brickwork.

Le Corbusier's design for a modern building was a new structural system of stilts that lifted the building off the ground to allow people and traffic to travel underneath. The interior could be treated as what he called a 'free plan', with rooms enclosed by non-load-bearing partitions.

Ludwig Mies van der Rohe (1886–1969), is best known for developing boxy, steel-and-glass architecture for everything from houses to skyscrapers. He was the designer of the 20th century landmark building, the Barcelona Pavilion (1929). This building marked the end to European dominance of the International Style. 'Mies' buildings were reduced to their simplest structure, in keeping with the famous Miesian idiom 'Less is more'.

1-34 Barcelona Pavilion (1929) by Mies van der Rohe

Frank Lloyd Wright (1885–1959), was the greatest American architect. Wright was inspired by a love of nature and based his ideas on what he called 'organic architecture'. He used local wood and stone in his buildings, generally leaving them exposed. His buildings look like they belong in their setting, as though they have evolved from the landscape rather than been imposed upon it.

His greatest masterpiece is *Falling Water* at Bear Run, Pennsylvania (1935–37). In this building a series of floors cantilever over a waterfall, elements appear to grow out of the landscape. Wrights definition of a good building is 'one that makes the landscape more beautiful than it was before'. *Falling Water* exemplifies this definition.

1-35 Falling Water (1930s) by Frank Lloyd Wright. It has thick stone walls with sweeping roofs and balconies of concrete.

Modern buildings reflect the freedom of design that is achievable through better technology and new materials. The International Style is still applied by some architects, who are building tall steel-and-glass office blocks and apartments. Many architects have explored the sculptural qualities of concrete, while others have turned buildings inside out, placing pipes, air-conditioning, and services on the outside.

1-36 *Lloyds Building (1979–84) London, by Richard Rogers. A high-tech modern corporate headquarters of steel frame construction with glass curtain walling. The services are exposed on the exterior.*

Architectural design

Architecture is characterised by its usefulness to human activity, its stability and degree of permanence, and its expression of ideas. Different techniques have been developed throughout history for defence and protection from the elements. All have taken note of the human environment. Architecture is the result of societal needs. The architect's role is to adapt design to serve the culture of a community.

Design is the basis of all architecture. Architecture provides shelter and privacy. It creates symbols of social status in a community. Architecture is involved in religion and mythology. It endeavours to create a sense of place.

*The word **design** comes from the Italian verb **disegnare**, which means to create.*

In design, the architect assesses the needs, devises solutions and implements the solutions. Information about a project is collected through research, observation, written documentation

and/or oral interviews. Architects use form, space, composition, and scale, light, texture and colour in the design process.

Drawings and models are generated to present the design solutions. Evaluation and alternatives evolve, ensuring that the design process is open and dynamic, until eventually all parties are satisfied.

Scale and proportion

Scale

Scale is the ratio between the size of something real and that of a model or representation of it. In architecture two types of scale are in use.

- **Generic scale** determines size by referring to other forms, such as the size of a window relative to the height of the building.
- **Human scale** refers to the size of space relative to the dimensions of the human figure, known as anthropometry.

Anthropometric data is used in the design of chairs, stairways, tables, furniture, doorways, etc. In ancient architecture the height of the human figure was taken to be the same as the width of the outstretched arms.

The human figure influenced the development of the Classical orders. The masculine Doric order had a ratio of 6:1 or 7:1 of height to width. The feminine Ionic order was scaled between 8:1 and 9:1. The Corinthian order was the largest of the three having a ratio greater than 9:1.

The impact of colour on walls and ceilings and floor patterns can have a profound effect on the scale of space. Light, shape and colour of a space affect its scale and inform its size. Objects placed within a space also help to inform on scale and size. Changes in ceiling height affect the experience of the interior volume.

Proportion

Proportion may be described as the mathematical relationship between the dimensions of a form or space. All materials have inherent constraints in terms of proportion due to structural ability, shape or manufacturing processes. It is the role of the architect to organise a building's space and form.

Many proportioning systems have been developed through the ages. These include Euclidean geometry, the Golden Section, the Classical Orders, and Anthropometrics.

Composition

Composition arranges meaningful ideas into architecture. It may be defined as the arrangement of the parts of a work in relation to each other and to the whole. Composition arranges ordered, useful and aesthetic space. A number of ordering systems aid the architect in achieving composition.

AXIS This is a linear system for organising form and space. The axis leads to the idea of symmetry.

SYMMETRY was the basis for all planning in classical architecture. It may be axial (organised about an axis), or radial (organised about a central point).

RHYTHM in architecture is the harmonious sequence of masses alternating with voids, of light alternating with shade, of alternating colours, etc. Rhythm is set up by the reoccurrence of an element, as in line, shape, or colour. Strongly related to repetition, which is fundamental to all architecture.

TRANSFORMATION An earlier solution may be transformed, modified or adapted to contemporary needs.

Elements of design and principles related to communication of design are dealt with in later chapters.

Urban planning

Urban planning is strongly related to architecture. It is little more than 100 years old as a profession, but as an art or a science it can be traced back to the first planned cities of Mesopotamia. Some Egyptian cities grew to 20,000 people during the great pyramid construction era. This demanded some sort of civic and urban organisation. Town planning principles of transportation, agriculture and defence were evident along the Indus river valley.

Rectangular grids were used in Greek city-states to give geometric form to the urban landscape. Roman engineers left a legacy of aqueducts and a network of roads all over the Roman Empire.

Planning in the ancient world was based on physical properties, politics, economies, and social structures. Buildings related to worship, commerce and government were located in the centre of the city, with housing on the periphery.

Large towns did not appear until the 15th century. Architects extended the architecture of individual buildings around a street or a square in an ordered manner.

Planned European cities sprang up in the 19th century. Overcrowding necessitated new planning systems to deal with housing, streets, water supply, and transportation. These included replacing the irregular and winding, narrow streets of medieval times with broad, well-lit streets that efficiently connected the inner and outer suburbs of the city.

Preservation

Preservation in an architectural context means to protect from decay or dissolution, to maintain and sustain the existing form, integrity and materials of a building.

Preservation presents architects with new challenges. How much or how little should the existing architecture be changed in the name of preservation and restoration? Should the original be repaired to look like it did when it was first built, or should it be preserved in its found state?

The preservation architect needs to know how to change a structure without violating its integrity and identity. Buildings require constant repair and maintenance. Additions and alterations are natural phenomena in the life of a building.

Elements of preservation include conservation, restoration, reconstruction, replication and rehabilitation.

- **Conservation** of buildings simply means caring for them. The principle cause of deterioration in historic buildings is neglect and lack of maintenance. The vulnerable locations are where water can enter the building, in particular the gutters and the roof. No conservation should take place without a prior survey and analysis of the building. Conservation is further dealt with from an Irish perspective in Chapter 3.
- **Restoration** involves removing or replacing fragments or elements of a building and putting back the architectural form and details. Restoration achieves completeness and restores the original aesthetics of a building.
- **Reconstruction** relates to the reproduction of a building, when an historic building has been destroyed. The reconstruction takes place on the original site. Demolition with the intention of reconstruction is not allowed.

- **Replication** is making an exact copy of the building. It is the most radical form of preservation.
- **Rehabilitation** is finding a new use for the building while preserving its historic and architectural character.

Architecture represents who people are and what they value. Civilisation loses a little bit of history with every building that is demolished.

A recent preservation technique is to demolish all but the façade of a building. A new interior is built behind the façade. Some preservationists claim that this is better than total demolition while others claim that it gives the building a superficial image and that the building loses its architectural integrity.

Sustainability

The World Commission on Environment and Development has defined **sustainability** as

'meeting the needs of the present without compromising the ability of future generations to meet their own needs.'

From 'Our Common Future'
(London, Oxford University Press, 1987)

There are three dimensions to sustainability; environmental, social and economic. Environmental dimensions of sustainability include:

- reduced waste, effluent generation, and emissions to the environment
- reduced impact on human health
- use of renewable raw materials
- reduction or elimination of toxic substances

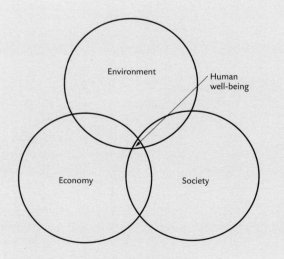

1-37 Three dimensions of sustainability

The principle of environmental sustainability is to leave the Earth in as good or better condition for future generations as we found it. Human activity is only environmentally sustainable when it can be performed without depleting natural resources or degrading the natural environment.

Sustainable design

'Architecture presents a unique challenge in the field of sustainability. Construction projects typically consume large amounts of materials, produce tonnes of waste, and often involve weighing the preservation of buildings that have historical significance against the desire for the development of newer, more modern designs.'

The Earth Pledge (www.earthpledge.org)

Sustainably designed buildings aim to lessen their impact on our environment through energy and resource efficiency. The following principles for sustainable architecture are based on the objectives of the BRE's Environmental Assessment Method

- Demolish and rebuild only when it is not practicable or economical to reuse, adapt or extend an existing building or structure
- Reduce the need for transport during demolition and construction.
- Control all processes to reduce noise, dust, vibration, pollution and waste.
- Study the site and make the most of the prevailing winds, weather patterns, solar orientation, services including public transport, and the form of surrounding buildings.
- Design the building to minimise its impact on the environment over its life span. Make it easy to maintain by incorporating techniques and technologies for conserving energy and water and reducing emissions to land, water and air.
- Use construction techniques that are indigenous to the area, and follow local traditions in materials and design.
- Place greater emphasis on the function of the building and the comfort of the occupants than on any statement it is intended to make about its designer or owner.
- Make the building secure, flexible and adaptable to meet future requirements.
- Build to meet the current Building Regulations. The longevity of a building depends on form, finishes and the method of construction employed, as much as on the materials used.
- Avoid using materials from non-renewable sources or that cannot be reused or recycled.

Sustainable buildings are often referred to as **Green buildings**. Green buildings are high-quality buildings. They last longer, cost less to operate and maintain, and provide greater occupant satisfaction than standard buildings. Green buildings often cost less or no more to build than conventional designs.

Some facts related to sustainable architecture:
- 40% of the world's energy consumption is required to operate buildings.
- Buildings are responsible for a considerable amount of the world's waste production.
- The building industry is depleting natural resources beyond sustainable levels.

Measures to improve sustainability of architecture include:
- responsible use of natural resources
- specifying materials according to life cycle analysis
- reducing construction and demolition (c and d) waste
- reducing water consumption – recycling grey water and collecting rainwater (**grey water** systems refer to both recovered wastewater and rainwater)

Sustainability must consider the complete construction cycle of:
- the legal framework
- design
- construction
- use, and
- reuse

Chapter 2
History of building technology

Introduction

The history of building is marked by a number of trends. Improvements in the durability of materials, tool technology, interior environment control techniques and construction machinery continue to influence building design and construction.

A tent illustrates the basic environmental elements that building designers attempt to control.

The tent creates a membrane to shield its occupants from rain and snow. It controls heat transfer by keeping out the hot rays of the sun and confining heated air in cold weather. It also blocks out light and provides visual privacy.

Because the membrane must be supported against the forces of gravity and wind, a structure is necessary. While membranes made of hides are strong in tension, poles must be added to make the structure rigid.

2-1 The principles of the tent are still used in construction

Much of the development of building construction concerns the search for more sophisticated solutions to the basic problems the tent set out to solve.

The earliest buildings were made from readily available materials such as leaves, branches, animal hides, turf, stones and mud. These materials could be cut and shaped with primitive tools like stone axes and knives made from sharpened bones.

2-2 Stone Age axe head

Later, more durable natural materials were used— such as clay, stone, and timber—and, in modern times, synthetic materials—such as brick, concrete, metals, and plastics. The development of stronger materials and improved knowledge of their behaviour fuelled the quest for buildings of ever greater height and span.

The degree of control exercised over the interior environment of buildings has become increasingly precise. Regulation of air temperature, light and sound levels, humidity, odours, air speed, and other factors that affect human comfort, has improved enormously.

The energy available to the construction process, which began with human muscle power, and now involves powerful machinery, has greatly reduced construction times.

Primitive building: the Stone Age

The hunter-gatherers of the late Stone Age, who roamed wide areas in search of food, built the earliest known temporary shelters. They may have braced crude huts made of wooden poles, or weighted down the walls of tents made of animal skins, presumably supported by central poles. Excavations at a number of sites in Europe dated to before 12,000 BC show circular rings of stones that are believed to have formed parts of such shelters.

2-3 *Crude huts made from wooden poles*

2-4 *Huts covered with animal skins*

Early peoples often inhabited caves, but if there were no caves they improvised by roofing holes in the ground. Evidence from wall paintings suggests that these may have been up to 3 metres deep.

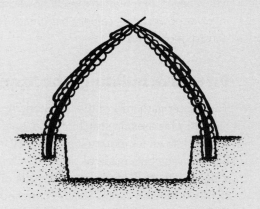

2-5 *Roofed holes in the ground may have been up to 3 metres deep*

In the early days of Egypt there is evidence of a type of framed house made from overlapping planks held together with hide. These structures were designed to be dismantled and re-erected in the desert during the annual flood.

The beginnings of agriculture in about 10,000 BC, gave a major impetus to building construction. People no longer travelled in search of game or followed their herds, but stayed in one place to tend their fields. Dwellings began to be more permanent.

WATTLE AND DAUB Evidence of composite building construction of clay and wood, called wattle-and-daub, has also been found in Europe and the Middle East.

The walls were made of small saplings or reeds, which were easy to cut with stone tools. The saplings were driven into the ground, tied together with vegetable fibres, and then plastered over with wet clay for rigidity and weatherproofing. The roofs have not survived, but were probably made of crude thatch or bundled reeds. Both round and rectangular forms have been found, usually with central hearths.

2-6 *Wattle and daub—a form of wall construction consisting of interwoven twigs plastered with a mixture of clay, lime, water, and sometimes dung and chopped straw*

NEOLITHIC TIMBER STRUCTURES

Heavier timber buildings also appeared in Neolithic cultures, although the difficulties of cutting large trees with stone tools limited the use of sizable timbers for frames.

These frames were usually rectangular in plan, with a central row of columns to support a ridgepole and matching rows of columns along the long walls. Rafters were run from the ridgepole to the wall beams.

Stability of the frame was achieved by burying the columns deep in the ground. The ridgepole and rafters were then tied to the columns with vegetable fibres.

The usual roofing material was thatch—dried grasses or reeds tied together in small bundles. The bundles of thatch were tied in an overlapping pattern to light wooden poles that spanned the rafters. Horizontal thatched roofs leak badly, but, if they are built at the proper angle (pitch), the rainwater runs off before it has time to soak through. Primitive builders soon determined the roof pitch that would shed rainwater but not the thatch.

Many types of infill were used in the walls of these frame houses, including clay, wattle and daub, bark (favoured by American Woodland Indians), and thatch. In South-East Asia, where such houses are still built, they are raised above the ground on stilts for security and dryness, the roofing is often made of leaves and the walls are largely open to allow air movement for natural cooling.

Another variation of the frame was found in Egypt and the Middle East, where bundles of reeds were substituted for timbers.

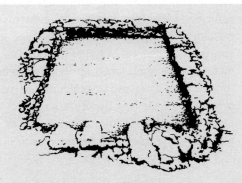

2-7 An early Neolithic building, showing the rectangular plan

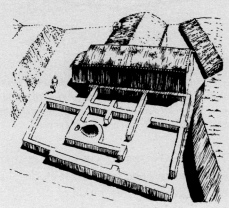

2-8 A Neolithic house, Iraq

Bronze Age and early urban cultures

The first communities large enough to be called cities were developed in the world's great river valleys—including the Nile, the Tigris and Euphrates, the Indus, and the Huang Ho—where intensive agriculture based on irrigation was practised.

Bronze Age brick construction

These cities were built with a new technology, based on the clay available in the riverbanks. Packed clay walls of earlier times were replaced by those constructed of prefabricated units—mud bricks. This represented a major conceptual change. The free-form shapes made possible with packed clay were replaced with the geometric regularity imposed by the rectangular brick. Building plans became strictly rectangular.

Bricks were made from mud and straw formed in a four-sided wooden frame, which was removed after evaporation had sufficiently hardened the material. The wet bricks were then thoroughly dried in the sun. The straw acted as reinforcing to hold the brick together when the inevitable shrinkage cracks appeared during the drying process.

The bricks were laid in walls with wet mud mortar, or sometimes bitumen, to join them together. Wall openings were supported by wooden lintels. In the warm, dry climates of the river valleys, weathering action was not a major problem, and the mud bricks were left exposed or covered with a layer of mud plaster.

The roofs of these early urban buildings have disappeared, but it seems likely that they were supported by timber beams and were mostly flat, since there is little rainfall in these areas. Such mud brick or adobe construction is still widely used in the Middle East, Africa, Asia, and Latin America.

Later, about 3000 BC, the first fired bricks appeared, in Mesopotamia (now part of north-eastern Iraq). Ceramic pottery had been developing in these cultures for some time, and the techniques of kiln-firing were applied to bricks, which were made of the same clay.

Step 1 Winning, or mining, the clay

Step 2 Preparation of the clay

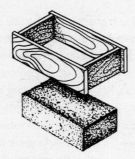
Step 3 Moulding

Step 4 Drying

Step 5 Burning

2-9 Brickmaking is a five step process

Because of their high cost in labour and fuel, fired bricks were used at first only in areas of greater wear, such as pavements or the tops of walls that were subject to weathering.

Fired bricks were also used to build sewers, which drained wastewater from cities. It is in the roofs of these underground drains that the oldest surviving true arches in brick are found, a humble beginning for what would become a major structural form.

Bronze Age timber construction

The development of bronze, and later, iron technology in this period led to the making of metal woodworking tools, such as axes and saws. Less effort was required to fell and work large trees, which led to new developments in building techniques—timbers were cut and shaped extensively, hewn into square posts, sawn into planks, and split into shingles. Log cabin construction appeared in the forested areas of Europe, and timber framing became more sophisticated.

Shingle
a thin piece of timber used like a tile for covering roofs or walls. It usually reduces in thickness from tail to head. Shingles were used in ancient Rome and split shingles (or shakes) were common in medieval Britain.

Bronze Age stone construction

When tools and building technology had advanced sufficiently, it became practical to construct buildings from quarried stone. The stone construction process began at the quarries. Most quarries were open-faced, although in some cases tunnels were extended several hundred metres into cliffs to reach the best quality stone.

For extracting sedimentary rock such as limestone, the chief tool was the mason's pick.

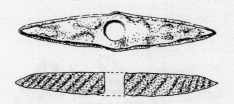

2-10 An iron mason's pick head found during excavations at Dalton Parlours, Yorkshire, England. As with a modern pickaxe, a wooden shaft would have been inserted through the hole in the centre of the metal head and wedged in place.

The picks were used to cut vertical channels as wide as a person around rectangular blocks of stone, to expose five faces. Separation of the sixth face was achieved by drilling rows of holes into the rock with metal bow drills. Wooden wedges were driven into the holes to fill them completely. The wedges were doused with water, which they absorbed and which caused them to expand, breaking the stone free from its bed.

In the extraction of igneous rock such as granite, which is much harder and stronger than limestone, the mason's pick was supplemented by balls of dolerite weighing up to 5 kilograms, which were used to break the rock by beating and pounding.

Granite was also drilled and sawed with the help of abrasives, and split with expanding wooden wedges.

Dolerite
an extremely hard and tough igneous rock. It makes an excellent monumental stone and is one of the dark-coloured rocks known commercially as black granite.

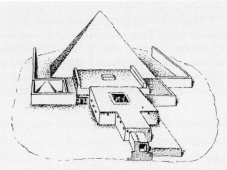

2-11 *The pyramid of Sahure, built c. 2400 BC, is 45 metres higher than St Paul's Cathedral. Though it covers approximately 5.25 hectares it deviates from a perfect square by only 15 mm.*

2-12 *St Paul's Cathedral, London*

Roman construction

Roman stone construction

The Romans adopted Etruscan stone construction based on the arch and built many spectacular examples of what they called *opus quadratum*, or structures of cut stone blocks laid in regular courses.

The surviving Roman buildings with stone arches or vaults have typical spans of only four to seven metres; small stone domes with diameters of

The Etruscans
An ancient people of central Italy whose civilisation greatly influenced the Romans.

four to nine metres were built in Roman Syria. Such arches and domes imply the existence of sophisticated timber formwork to support them during construction, as well as advanced lifting machinery, but there are no exact records of either.

Roman brick construction

Brickmaking, particularly in the region of Rome itself, became a major industry and finally, under the empire, a state monopoly. Brick construction was cheaper than stone due to the economies of scale in mass production and the lower level of skill required for bricklaying. The brick arch was adopted to span openings in walls, precluding the need for lintels.

2-13 *Early example of a brick arch*

Mortar was at first a mixture of sand, lime, and water, but a new ingredient was introduced at the beginning of the 2nd century BC. The Romans called it *pulvis puteoli* after the town of Puteoli (now Pozzuoli), near Naples, where it was first found. The material, formed in Mount Vesuvius and mined on its slopes, is now called pozzolana.

When mixed with lime, pozzolana forms a natural cement that is much stronger and more weather-resistant than lime mortar alone, and will harden even under water. Pozzolanic mortars were so strong and cheap, and could be used by labourers of such low skill, that the Romans began to substitute it for bricks in the interiors of walls.

Finally, the mortar of lime, sand, water, and pozzolana was mixed with stones and broken brick to form a true concrete, called *opus caementicium*. This concrete was used first with brick forms in walls, and later was poured into wooden forms, which were removed after the concrete had hardened.

An early large-scale example in Rome of brick-faced concrete is the plain rectangular walls of the Camp of the Praetorian Guard, built by Sejanus in AD 21–23. But the possibilities of plastic form suggested by this initially liquid material, which could be worked easily into curved shapes in plan and section, soon led to the creation of a series of remarkable interior spaces, spanned by domes or vaults and uncluttered by the columns required by horizontal stone beam construction.

The domed form was rapidly developed in a series of imperial buildings that culminated in the emperor Hadrian's Pantheon of about AD 118–128. This huge circular structure was entered from a portico of stone columns and was surmounted by a dome 43.2 metres in diameter, lighted by an oculus (round opening) at the top.

The walls supporting the dome are of brick-faced concrete 6 metres thick, lightened at intervals by internal recesses. The dome is of solid concrete 1.5 metres in average thickness and rises 43.2 metres above the floor. This magnificent structure has survived in good condition to modern times. The diameter of its circular dome was unsurpassed until the 19th century.

2-14 Hadrian's Pantheon 118–128 AD (note the huge circular structure). See also Fig. 1-14.

Roman timber and metal construction

The Romans also made major advances in timber technology. Reliefs on Trajan's Column show the timber lattice truss bridges used by Roman armies to cross the Danube.

2-15 Trajan's twenty-pier timber lattice bridge, c. AD 99, from a relief on Trajan's Column

2-16 Trajan's Column is a unique monument to the Roman Emperor Trajan. Three novel features of this monument include the chamber carved in its base to house Trajan's ashes, the spiral staircase which winds upwards within its otherwise solid marble shaft to a viewing platform at its top, and the continuous sculpted frieze which decorates the exterior of the column.

The truss, a hollowed-out beam with the forces concentrated in a triangulated network of linear members, was apparently a Roman invention. No evidence of their theoretical understanding of it exists, but nevertheless they were able to master the design of trusses in a practical way.

The notion of the truss was extended from timber to metal. Bronze trusses, running over three spans of about 9 metres each, supported the roof of the portico of the Pantheon.

Metals were used extensively in Roman buildings. In addition to bronze trusses, the Pantheon had bronze doors and gilded bronze roof tiles. Lead was another material introduced by the Romans for roofing—it was waterproof and could be used at very low pitches.

Roman building support systems

WATER SUPPLY Perhaps the most important use of lead was for pipes to supply fresh water to buildings and to remove wastewater from them. The Romans provided generous water supply systems for their cities, all of which worked by gravity and many used aqueducts and syphons.

Although most people had to carry their water to their homes from public fountains, there was limited distribution of water to public buildings (particularly baths) and some to private residences and apartment houses. Private and semiprivate baths and latrines became fairly common.

2-17 Aqueducts are structures, often bridges, that carry conduits used to convey water over long distances.

The wastewater drainage system was limited, with no treatment of sewage, which was simply discharged into a nearby river. But even these fairly modest applications of public sanitation far exceeded those of previous cultures and were not surpassed until the 19th century.

LIGHTING Another material that the Romans applied to buildings was glass, which had been developed by the Egyptians who used it only for jewellery and small ornamental vessels. The Romans devised many kinds of coloured glass for use in mosaics to decorate interior surfaces. They also made the first clear window glass, produced by blowing glass cylinders that were then cut and laid flat.

Seneca (c. 4 BC–AD 65) described the sensation caused by the appearance of glazed sun porches in the villas near Rome. Although no Roman glass installations have survived, glass apparently became fairly common in public buildings and was even used in middle-class apartment houses in the capital.

HEATING In most Roman buildings, the central open fire remained the major source of heat—as well as annoying smoke—although the use of charcoal braziers made some improvement. A major innovation was the development of **hypocaust**, or indirect radiant heating.

In Roman hypocaust heating, an open space below a floor was heated by gases from a fire or furnace below, which allowed the passage of hot air to heat the room above. Heated air passed through flues in floors and walls.

The heated masonry radiated a pleasantly uniform warmth, and smoke was eliminated from occupied spaces.

The Basilica of Constantine at Trier has a well-preserved example of hypocaust heating, where the

Brazier
a portable metal receptacle for burning charcoal or coal, used for cooking and heating.

stone slabs of the floor are supported on short brick columns, creating a continuous heating space beneath it.

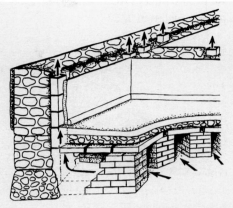

2-18 Hypocaust—an ancient Roman heating system in which hot air circulated under the floor and between double walls

Romanesque and Gothic construction

The disappearance of Roman power in western Europe during the 5th century led to a decline in building technology.

Brickmaking became rare and was not revived until the 14th century. Pozzolanic concrete disappeared entirely, and it would not be until the 19th century that manufactured cements would equal it. The use of domes and vaults in stone construction was also lost.

Building techniques fell to Iron Age levels, exemplified by log construction, packed clay walls, mud brick, and wattle and daub.

Advanced building technologies were developing in China in this same period during the Sui (AD 581–618) and T'ang (AD 618–907) dynasties. In the 3rd century BC the completion of the Great Wall, about 6,400 kilometres in length and following a sinuous path along the contours of rugged terrain, had demonstrated remarkable achievements in masonry technology, logistics, and surveying methods.

2-19 The Great Wall of China

The An-Chi Bridge, built about AD 610 in Hopei province, had a stone arch with a span of 37.5 metres, far exceeding the Roman bridge at Alcantara, built in AD 866, washed away and reconstructed in 1257.

2-20 *The An-Chi Bridge is renowned for its stone arch.*

Extensive work was also done in the development of heavy timber framing, which was used primarily for temples. Stone tower pagodas up to 60 metres high were built and fired brick was also widely used.

Romanesque and Gothic stone construction

Beginning in the 9th century there were the first stirrings of the revival of stone construction in Europe. The Palatine Chapel of Charlemagne at Aachen (consecrated 805), with its octagonal segmented dome spanning 14.5 metres, is an early example of this trend.

2-21 *The Palatine Chapel of Charlemagne*

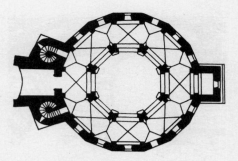

2-22 *Plan of the Palatine Chapel*

Despite this early revival, the true Romanesque style—building 'in the Roman manner' with stone arches, vaults, and domes to span interior spaces—did not really begin until the later part of the 11th century.

From 1050 to 1350 more stone was quarried in France alone than in the whole history of ancient Egypt—enough to build 80 cathedrals, 500 large churches, and tens of thousands of parish churches. The great building campaign of medieval times has been called the 'cathedral crusade'.

The basic tools of the medieval masons had changed little from those of Egypt, but they did have large saws driven by waterwheels to cut stone as well as machinery for raising and moving materials.

Romanesque masons had two main employers, the state and the church. The state built mostly for military purposes. But the church had other interests, which propelled the development of stone construction in new and daring directions.

St. Augustine had written that light is the most direct manifestation of God. It was this idea that led the search for ways to introduce more and more light into churches, opening ever larger windows in the walls until a new kind of minimal stone skeleton evolved.

Medieval masons found that there was a more efficient form for the arch than the classical circle—the **catenary curve**. This is a curve formed by a chain when it hangs under its own weight from two points.

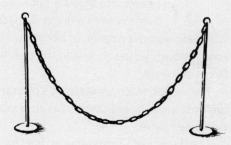

2-23 *Catenary curve— the curve assumed by a heavy uniform flexible cord hanging freely from two points*

The masons' belief in geometry and the perfection of circular forms led them to approximate the catenary shape with two circular segments that met in a point at the top, the so-called Gothic arch.

2-24 *Gothic arch—a narrow acutely pointed arch with two centres of equal radii*

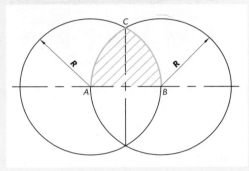

2-25 *Geometry of Gothic arch*

2-26 *Spire, or steeple: a tall structure that tapers upwards to a point. The spire appeared after the cathedral crusade.*

The revival of brick construction

Fired bricks began to be made again in Europe in the 14th century, preceded in many areas by the use of salvaged Roman brick. Fourteenth-century bricks were not as precise as the Roman ones and were often distorted in firing. Therefore, large lime-mortar joints were needed for regular course lines.

Bricks became nearly standardised at something close to the present size, about $20.3 \times 9.5 \times 5.7$ centimetres, and bonding systems based on this approximately 2:1 proportion were developed. These bonding patterns reduced continuous vertical mortar joints, which were prone to cracking because the mortars were of substantially lower strength than the bricks.

Brick remained quite expensive because of the cost of the fuel needed to fire it, and it was used mainly where there was no readily available stone. In the late medieval period and mostly in northern

Nave
the central space in a church often flanked by aisles.

Europe, brick was adapted to Gothic stone forms to build so-called hall churches, with naves and aisles of equal height.

Masonry fireplaces and chimneys

Although Roman hypocaust heating disappeared with the empire, a new development in interior heating appeared in western Europe at the beginning of the 12th century—the masonry fireplace and chimney—which began to replace the central open fire.

2-27 *The masonry fireplace and chimney replaced the central open fire in the 12th century.*

The large roof openings over central fires let in wind and rain, so each house had only one and larger buildings had as few as possible. Therefore, heated rooms tended to be large and semi-public, where many people could share the fire's warmth. The roof opening did not effectively remove all the smoke, some of which remained to plague the room's occupants.

The chimney did not let in much air or water and could remove most of the smoke. Although much of the heat went up the flue, it was still a great improvement, and, most significantly, it could be used to heat both small and large rooms, and multi-storey buildings as well.

Houses, particularly large ones, were broken up into smaller, more private spaces each heated by its own fireplace, a change that decisively altered the communal life-style of early medieval times.

Romanesque design

From 1350 until 1750 much of building technology was focused on the domed church, which developed as a symbol not only of religious belief but also of national and urban pride. There was a conscious rejection of Gothic forms in favour of the ideological appeal of Rome.

This attitude led to a split between the processes of design and construction and to the appearance of the first architects (a word derived from the Greek *architekton*, meaning a chief craftsman), who conceived a building's form, as opposed to the builder, who constructed it.

Development of Roman techniques and materials

TIMBER TRUSSES Giorgio Vasari used king-post timber trusses for a 20-metre span in the roof of the Uffizi, or Municipal Office Building, in Florence in the mid-16th century.

At the same time, the Venetian architect Andrea Palladio used a fully triangulated timber truss for a bridge with a span of 30.5 metres over the Cimone River.

Palladio clearly understood the importance of the carefully detailed diagonal members, for in his diagram of the truss in his Four Books on Architecture he said that they 'support the whole work'. The tension connections of the timber members in the truss were joined with iron cramps and bolts.

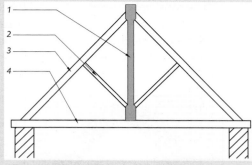

1 King post   2 Strut   3 Principal rafter   4 Tie

2-28 *Components of a typical king post truss*

2-29 *Uffizi—an art gallery in Florence built by Giorgio Vasari in the 16th century and opened as a museum in 1765*

GLASS Another Roman material that was revived and much improved in the Renaissance was clear glass. A new technique for making it was perfected in Venice in the 16th century. It was known as the crown glass method and was originally used for making dinner plates. Glassblowers spun the molten glass into flat disks up to a metre in diameter. The disks were polished after they had cooled and were cut into rectangular shapes.

The first record of crown glass windows is their installation in double-hung counterweighted sliding-sash frames, at Inigo Jones's Banqueting House in London in 1685. Large areas of such glass became common in the 1700s, pointing the way toward the great glass and iron buildings of the 19th century.

HEATING The efficiency of interior heating was improved by the introduction of cast-iron and clay-tile stoves, which were placed in a free-standing position in the room. The radiant heat they produced was uniformly distributed in the space, and they lent themselves to the burning of coal—a new fuel that was rapidly replacing wood in western Europe.

The industrial age

The Industrial Revolution brought new materials and the demand for new building types that completely transformed building technology.

Standard iron building elements soon appeared, following the Industrial Revolution, pointing the way to the development of metal buildings. Early applications of iron in construction are found several centuries prior to the industrial age.

There are records of iron chain suspension bridges with timber decks in China from the early Ming dynasty (1368–1644). The iron tension chains in the domes of St. Peter's and St. Paul's cathedrals are other examples. But the first large cast-iron structure of the industrial age was the bridge over the River Severn at Coalbrookdale, Shropshire, England (see Fig. 1-26).

The first use of wrought-iron trusses, which were made of flat bars riveted together, was in a 28-metre span for the roof of the Théâtre-Français in Paris in 1786 by the architect Victor Louis; there iron was used not so much for its strength as its noncombustibility, which, it was hoped, would reduce the hazard of fire.

2-30 *Theatre Francais, Paris 1786*

The completely independent iron frame without masonry adjuncts emerged slowly in a series of special building types. The first modest example was Hungerford Fish Market (1835) in London.

The next type to use the full iron frame was the greenhouse, which provided a controlled, light and warm environment for exotic tropical plants in the cold climate of northern Europe. Among the first of these was the Palm House at Kew Gardens near London, built by the architect Decimus Burton in the 1840s.

2-31 *Palm House, London. An example of a full iron frame structure*

Brick manufacture

The production of brick was industrialised in the 19th century. The laborious process of hand-moulding, which had been used for 3,000 years, was superseded by 'pressed' bricks. These were mass-produced by a mechanical extrusion process in which clay was squeezed through a rectangular die as a continuous column and sliced to size by a wire cutter.

Periodically fired beehive kilns (stoked by coke) continued to be used, but the continuous tunnel kiln, through which bricks were moved slowly on a conveyor belt, had appeared by the end of the century.

The new methods considerably reduced the cost of brick, and it became one of the constituent building materials of the age.

Timber processing

Timber technology underwent rapid development in the 19th century in North America, where there were large forests of softwood fir and pine trees that could be harvested and processed by industrial methods.

Steam- and water-powered sawmills began producing standard-dimension timbers in quantity in the 1820s. The production of cheap machine-made nails in the 1830s provided the other necessary ingredient that made possible major innovations in building construction.

Building science

A significant achievement of the first industrial age was the emergence of building science, particularly the elastic theory of structures. With it, mathematical models could be used to predict structural performance with considerable accuracy, provided there was adequate quality control of the materials used.

Although some elements of the elastic theory, such as the Swiss mathematician Leonhard Euler's theory of column buckling (1757), were worked out earlier, the real development began with the English scientist Thomas Young's modern definition of the modulus of elasticity in 1807.

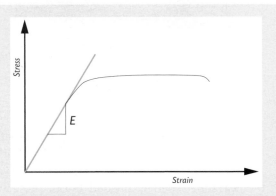

2-32 *Young's modulus of elasticity: the ratio of the stress applied to a body or substance to the resulting strain within the elastic limit.*

Building services

The development of the steam engine and its associated boilers led to a new technology in the form of steam heating. James Watt heated his own office with steam running through pipes as early as 1784.

During the 19th century, systems of steam and later hot-water heating were gradually developed. These used coal-fired central boilers connected to networks of pipes that distributed the heated water to cast-iron radiators and returned it to the boiler for reheating. Steam heat was a major improvement over stoves and fireplaces because all combustion products were eliminated from occupied spaces.

Plumbing and sanitation systems in buildings advanced rapidly in this period. Public water-distribution systems were the essential element. The widespread use of cast-iron pipes in the late 18th century made higher pressures possible, and they were used by Napoleon in the first steam-powered municipal water supply for a section of Paris in 1812.

Gravity-powered underground drainage systems were installed along with water-distribution networks in most large cities of the industrial world during the 19th century. Sewage-treatment plants were introduced in the 1860s. Permanent plumbing fixtures appeared in buildings with water supply and drainage, replacing portable basins, buckets, and chamber pots.

In England during the 1870s Thomas Twyford developed the first large one-piece ceramic washdown water closet. At first these ceramic fixtures were very expensive, but their prices declined until they became standard, and their forms remain largely unchanged today.

The second industrial age

Steel building technology

If the first industrial age was one of iron and steam, the second industrial age, which began in about 1880, could be called one of steel and electricity. Mass production of this new material and of this new form of energy transformed building technology.

Caisson
a watertight chamber open at the bottom and containing air under pressure, used to carry out construction work under water.

By 1895 a mature high-rise building technology had been developed: the frame of rolled steel I-beams with bolted or riveted connections, diagonal or portal wind bracing, clay-tile fireproofing, and caisson foundations.

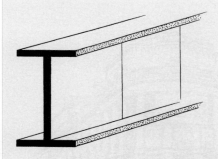

2-33 *I-beams are also referred to as RSJs (rolled steel joists).*

Environmental technologies

The electric-powered elevator provided vertical transportation, but other environmental technologies were still fairly simple. Interior lighting was still largely from daylight, although supplemented by electric light. There was steam heating but no cooling, and ventilation was dependent on operating windows; thus these buildings needed narrow floor spaces to give adequate access to light and air.

The race for higher buildings came to an abrupt halt with the Great Depression and World War II, and high-rise construction was not resumed until the late 1940s.

Reintroduction of concrete

The second industrial age also saw the re-emergence of concrete in a new composite relationship with steel, creating a technology that would rapidly assume a major role in building construction. The first step in this process was the creation of higher-strength artificial cements.

Lime mortar—made of lime, sand, and water—had been known since ancient times. It was improved in the late 18th century by the British engineer John Smeaton, who added powdered brick to the mix and made the first modern concrete by adding pebbles as coarse aggregate.

Joseph Aspdin patented the first true artificial cement in 1824, which he called Portland Cement. The name implied that it was of the same high quality as Portland stone. To make Portland cement, Aspdin burned limestone and clay together in a kiln. The clay provided silicon compounds, which when combined with water, formed stronger bonds than the calcium compounds of limestone.

In the 1830s Charles Johnson, another British cement manufacturer, saw the importance of high-temperature burning of the clay and limestone to a white heat, at which point they begin to fuse. In this period plain concrete was used for walls, and it sometimes replaced brick in floor arches that spanned wrought-iron beams in iron-framed factories. Precast concrete blocks also were manufactured, although they did not effectively compete with brick until the 20th century.

REINFORCED CONCRETE The first use of iron-reinforced concrete was by the French builder François Coignet in Paris in the 1850s. Coignet's own all-concrete house in Paris (1862), with roofs and floors reinforced with small wrought-iron I beams, still stands.

But reinforced concrete development began in earnest with the French gardener Joseph Monier's 1867 patent for large concrete flowerpots reinforced with a cage of iron wires. Another French builder, François Hennebique, applied Monier's ideas to floors, using iron rods to reinforce concrete beams and slabs.

Shell construction in concrete began in the 1920s. The first example was a very thin (6 centimetres) hemispherical shell for a planetarium (1924) in Jena, Germany, spanning 25 metres.

In 1927 an octagonal ribbed shell dome with a span of 66 metres was built to house a market hall in Leipzig. Many variations of thin shells were devised for use in industrial buildings. The shell emerged as a major form of long-span concrete structure after World War II.

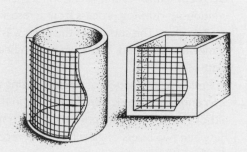

2-34 *Details of Monier's iron wire cages used in concrete flower pots which led to the development of reinforced concrete*

2-35 *Planetarium in Jena, Germany*

Lighting

In the second industrial age, environmental technologies developed rapidly. Most of these technologies involved the use of electricity, which declined in cost during this period.

The carbon-filament bulb, developed by Thomas Edison 1879, was inefficient, but banished the soot and fire hazards of coal-gas jets and soon gained wide acceptance. It was succeeded by the more efficient tungsten-filament incandescent bulb, which first appeared in 1908. The double-coiled filament used today was introduced about 1930.

Incandescent
emitting light as a result of being heated to a high temperature.

Light intensity increased in all buildings as electricity costs decreased.

Glass as a building material

Glass underwent considerable development in the second industrial age. The making of clear plate glass was perfected in the late 19th century, as were techniques of sandblasting and etching.

Clear plate glass is made by casting and rolling and characterised by its excellent surface produced by grinding and polishing.

In 1905 in the United States the Libbey Owens Glass Company began making sheet glass by a continuous drawing process from a reservoir of molten glass. The surface of this glass was somewhat distorted, but it was much cheaper than plate glass.

Prefabricated panels of double glazing about 2.5 centimetres thick were first made in the 1940s, although the insulating principle of air trapped between two layers of glass had been recognised much earlier.

In 1952 the Pilkington Brothers in England developed the float glass process, in which a continuous 3.4-metre-wide ribbon of glass floated over molten tin and both sides were fire finished, avoiding all polishing and grinding. This became the standard method of production.

High-rise buildings (multi-storey buildings)

A high-rise building is generally defined as one that is taller than the maximum height which people are willing to walk up, thus it requires mechanical vertical transportation. This limits the range of possible building uses to residential apartments, hotels and office buildings, though occasionally retail and educational facilities are high-rise.

The first high-rise buildings were constructed in the United States in the 1880s. They arose in urban areas where increased land prices and high population densities created a demand for buildings that rose vertically rather than spread horizontally, thereby occupying less precious land area.

High-rise buildings were made practicable by the use of steel structural frames and glass exterior sheathing (curtain walling). By the mid 20th century, such buildings had become a standard feature in most countries in the world.

Curtain walls
non-load-bearing sheets of glass, masonry, stone, or metal that are affixed to the building's frame through a series of vertical and horizontal members called mullions and muntins.

Chapter 3

Architectural and craft heritage

Vernacular architecture

Vernacular architecture refers to local building styles and building materials. It is a type of community architecture, not the work of individual architects. Vernacular architecture responds to practical problems, such as providing shelter and human comfort, with simple tools and craft skills passed down from generation to generation.

The construction techniques and technologies employed were in response to the local climate, topography and the socio-economic class of the artisans (craftspeople). Use of local materials, natural and manufactured, prefabrication of building parts and the standard form of building are the fundamentals of vernacular architecture.

Innovative techniques were used for air control, moisture control, heat gain and cooling in this style of architecture built 'without architects'. The architect of today can learn much from the wisdom of the past.

Vernacular houses

Over the centuries, house styles evolved in response to the local environment. They had distinctive regional forms passed on to successive generations as part of a community tradition.

In contrast, formal buildings were influenced by national or international trends, were more substantial and were designed by architects.

The Irish vernacular house is a thatched building. The house is rectangular in plan and no more than one room wide. Each room opens into the next with no corridor or hallway. The doors and windows are placed along the front and the back but not on the end walls. Vernacular houses are one storey high.

The houses are of a simple construction. The walls support the roof. Stone or mud is used for walls; straw, reed or rushes is used for thatch. All materials are sourced locally.

Irish vernacular houses derive their aesthetic appeal from the use of simple proportions.

Recent housing styles in Ireland have contrasted with the vernacular tradition. Nevertheless, that tradition serves as a model of inspiration for future generations and as a record of how Irish people lived over past generations.

3-1 A typical Irish vernacular house

Vernacular styles

Variations in vernacular styles are found in different parts of the country. In the west and the north, houses with exposed gable-ends and hearths in the gable walls are common. Stone was the main material used in walls. The ground plan consisted of three rooms, with the kitchen in the centre and bedrooms on each side.

This house form evolved from 'long-houses' also known as 'byre-dwellings'. (A byre is a shelter for cows.)

Byre dwellings contained both byre and dwelling in the one building, without division walls, and were common in the west of Ireland until the nineteenth century. When cattle were evicted from the houses, the former byre-end was divided from the kitchen and used as a bedroom or a store.

In older houses the kitchen had two doors, directly opposite each other. This was useful for the removal of smoke from the turf fire and for moving livestock in and out of the house.

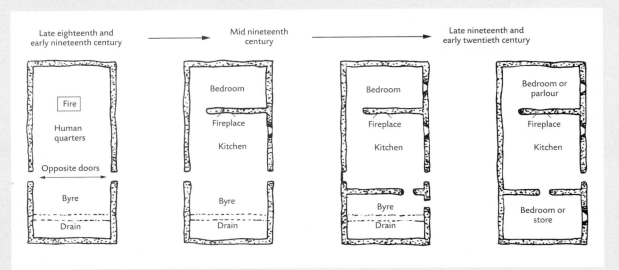

Late eighteenth and early nineteenth century → Mid nineteenth century → Late nineteenth and early twentieth century

3-2 *The evolution of the Irish vernacular house*

In the east of Ireland the basic features of vernacular houses were the hearth located in the centre, hipped roofs and a lobby entrance. Stone or mud was used to make the walls. There is no evidence that animals and humans were housed together. Farm outbuildings were more specialised than in the west.

There are very few, if any, cottages that date back to the Middle Ages. This scarcity reflects the social structure of the time. At that time only the gentry and the upper classes had substantial and permanent dwellings.

The traditional rural cottage can be traced back to the plantations of the sixteenth and early seventeenth centuries. The social and economic structure of that time produced the landless rural worker, who lived and worked in the countryside but had little interest in the economic or social structures.

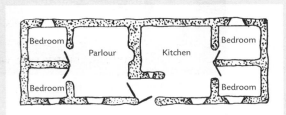

3-3 *Plan of a lobby entrance farmhouse, typical of the south-east*

3-4 *Hipped roofs and a central hearth are features of homes found in the east of Ireland. This example has been reconstructed in Bunratty Folk Park.*

The Great Famine of the 1840s seriously impacted on farm labourers. Their numbers were reduced rapidly due to emigration and death. As a result their homes fell into disuse and decay. The cottages either became ruins or were used as outhouses by neighbouring farmers.

Following this period new houses were built throughout the country. The traditional cottage of this time was owner-built and owner-occupied. It provided a home for families who worked and lived in the countryside. These people owned very little land, no more than a small patch of ground beside the house.

Improvements were made to rural housing of the late nineteenth and early twentieth centuries by enlarging old houses. This process evolved gradually and did not lead to a break with vernacular architectural form. Enlargement often consisted of simply incorporating the byres and sheds into the house. Additional fireplaces and chimneys were required following enlargement.

As an alternative to elongation an upper storey was added. Sometimes only a portion of the house were raised, either an end room or a centre portion. The new addition might have a slated roof as opposed to thatch. Windows and doors were sometimes symmetrically arranged. The constant feature that remained was that houses were still one room in width. Window sizes were generally smaller at the rear than at the front.

Sleeping accommodation varied depending on the wealth of the cottier. There were no beds in the poorest one-room cabins and the occupants slept 'in stradogue'. This means that they lay on a bed of rushes under a large blanket with their feet to the fire. An improvement was to have a wooden or stone bench used as a seat during the day and as a bed at night.

An alcove or recess is often found near the fire in older houses along the western coast. This feature sometimes formed part of the external structure and sometimes was contained within the thick boundary wall. The main purpose of this feature was to accommodate a bed and hence became known as a bed-outshot. While it allowed some privacy, it was a poor substitute for a separate bedroom.

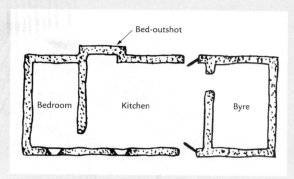

3-5 Bed-outshot forming part of the external structure of the house

Cottage furniture

Traditional cottage furniture was homemade and functional. The low wooden stool was the most common item found. It had three legs to give stability on the uneven clay floors. A rough dresser, low tables and a rope mattress bed were other furniture items of this era. Good quality furniture was only found in the houses of the wealthiest Irish farmers from the end of the 19th century onwards.

Building materials

Houses were built with materials from the local area. Local variations are found both in methods and materials for roofing, construction, walling and thatching.

Roofs

The main form of roof was the couple truss, supported by the wall. Purlins were used in Northern Ireland, which rested on the gable walls and had no supporting trusses. Evidence of cruck construction is found in the north. Crucks consist of pairs of curved timbers that span from ground level up to the apex. They carry the weight of the roof.

Timber houses were built for a time in the early seventeenth century. They quickly deteriorated, as they were unsuited to the damp Irish climate.

The craft of thatching and the materials used vary around the country. A layer of sods (scraws) is fixed to the roof timbers to provide support for the thatch. The materials used varied from wheaten straw, the most common, to oaten straw to reed. Flax was common in Donegal and Fermanagh. Rushes and tough grasses were also used. The thatch is held in place by pinning the straw to the scraws with scallops (thin, flexible pegs of briar or hazel.)

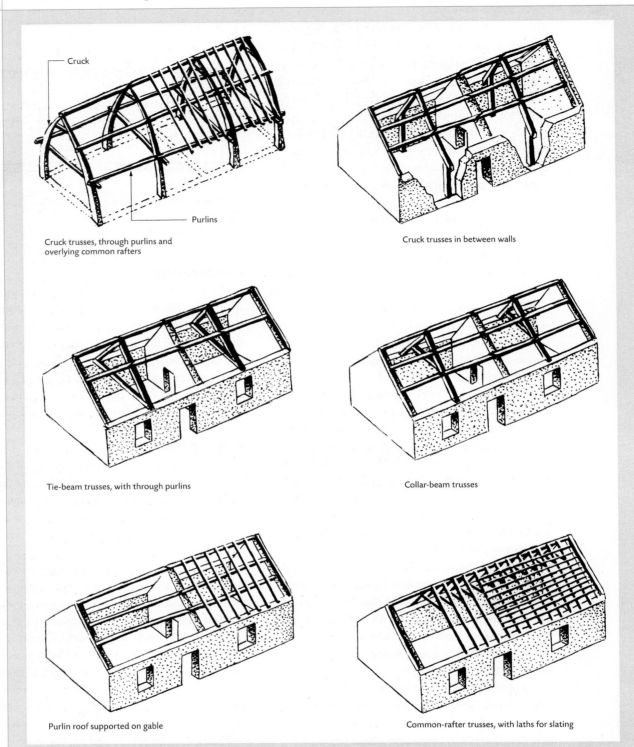

Cruck

Purlins

Cruck trusses, through purlins and overlying common rafters

Cruck trusses in between walls

Tie-beam trusses, with through purlins

Collar-beam trusses

Purlin roof supported on gable

Common-rafter trusses, with laths for slating

3-6 *Traditional roof timbering systems*

In northern and western regions a rope net was tied to pegs in the house walls to secure the thatch. This was to protect the thatch from strong winds. Another method used to protect the roof was to allow the gable to project above the level of the thatch.

Stone gables were common along the western coasts. Elsewhere the two-room hip-roofed cottage with a central chimney was the norm. The reason for the variation in the design of cottages between east and west is that hipped cottages were introduced into Ireland by the Normans in the Middle Ages. The thatch gabled cottage is an older, more authentic Irish type (refer also to Figs. 3-1).

3-7 The thatch is protected by the gable projecting above the level of the thatch

Slate gradually replaced thatch, appearing first on the higher-class buildings of the middle ages. It was not until the second half of the nineteenth century that slate was widely used on vernacular houses. The transition to slate is not yet complete as Ireland still has approximately 2600 thatch houses.

3-8 A slated vernacular house

Corrugated iron sheeting often replaced thatch and was a cheaper option to slate. Thatch roofs are very fragile and need to be maintained and renewed on a regular basis. If thatch buildings are neglected they quickly pass beyond the point of recovery.

The skill of thatching and the number of thatched roofs is in decline and has disappeared from many areas. A grant scheme is in place to assist with upkeep and replacement of thatch roofs and also to promote the skill of thatching.

3-9 Tin roofs of corrugated iron, which were originally thatched, are still found in Ireland.

Walls

Stone is the most common material used in the walls of vernacular buildings. The stone was randomly laid and finished with layers of whitewash. Clay or lime mortar served as external rendering.

Ashlar refers to a block of hewn stone with straight edges for use in building.

Wattle and daub is a form of wall construction consisting of interwoven twigs plastered with a mixture of clay, lime, water, and sometimes dung and chopped straw.

Dry stone walling is evident in the west. Good quality ashlar stonework is seldom found in vernacular buildings.

Timber and wattle (or wattle and daub) were important building materials of earlier generations. Their importance and use declined as the forests and woods were cut down. Timber was then used only for roof construction.

Mud was used in the east when timber resources became scarce. Stone was less common in the east than in the west. Mud walls were made from a mixture of wet clay and rushes. The walls were built without any support or mould and were trimmed with a spade.

Turf was used to build temporary farm buildings, and in some cases dwellings for the poor. Sometimes the entire house was built from turf; sometimes it was used just to build the gables. The gables were more protected than the front and rear of the house as they generally had outbuildings joined to them, or they would be positioned to take advantage of the topology of the site.

Windows were small in size and small in number for two reasons. Glass was a luxury item and house owners were taxed by window size up until the 1850s.

3-10 A small window in the gable indicates the presence of a loft.

The half door was the main entrance door found in traditional cottages. The lower part could remain closed and the upper part let in air and light when open. The half door compensated for the poor quality of windows.

3-11 A small cottage showing the half door and small windows

Before the introduction of chimneys the hearth was left open and smoke escaped through the thatch, windows and doors. This made living conditions very uncomfortable. A design consequence of this was stools and furniture were made low to allow the occupants sit below the thick clouds of smoke.

3-12 Early vernacular houses of the 1700s did not have chimneys. The smoke escaped through the door and thatch and through the windows if they were present.

However, benefits of smoke permeating through the thatch were it kept vermin away and also distributed heat throughout the house.

Bricks were first used in vernacular construction in the late eighteenth century, but were not widely used until the late nineteenth century.

Rural Irish dwellings

Buildings are scattered throughout the Irish landscape due to the high proportion of people who still live in the country. The form, materials and construction techniques of older buildings demonstrate the ability to adapt to various environments.

Newer buildings demonstrate the rapid pace of change in society with their break from earlier forms and non-use of local building materials. This has resulted in a fusion of style and a lack of regional distinctiveness.

The rural cottage

Three types of country cottage existed at different periods in this country. The first is the small vernacular cottage that has already been described.

The second type is the estate cottage. The landlord built these for his labourers in the eighteenth and nineteenth centuries, using stone walls and slated roofs. These houses were built individually or in small groups around the estate. In large estates these groups of houses were often mini-villages.

3-13 Estate cottages in Birr, Co. Offaly

Estate cottages are of a higher quality than vernacular dwellings. Roofs have a high pitch and were slated. They have ornamental bargeboards and projecting porches. Their distinctive architectural features meant that this type of rural cottage has experienced less change than other types.

3-14 The ornamental bargeboard is a characteristic feature of estate cottages.

The plan forms of the estate cottage were simple. The accommodation consisted of a kitchen, a parlour, and one or two bedrooms. Like the vernacular cottage, they were single storey, although examples of two-storey and one-and-a-half-storey cottages also exist.

The third type of cottage had its origins in the late nineteenth century. The Labourer's Acts allowed local authorities to construct approximately 50,000 new cottages for landless labourers. These were built between 1883 and 1921 under the remit of the Congested Districts Board.

The Congested Districts Board *purchased estates with the objective of returning them to tenants and the enlargement of holdings.*

The style of these cottages changed over time and between regions. They consisted of masonry or concrete walls with slated roofs. There were detached and semi-detached versions built along roadsides on one acre of ground, enough land to feed a cow or two and to grow some vegetables.

The Land Commission, the Congested Districts Board, and the County Councils continued cottage building in rural areas after independence.

The Land Commission *took over the duties of the Congested Districts Board in 1927, and was dissolved in 1992.*

3-15 *A typical Congested Districts Board house. The porch may have been added later.*

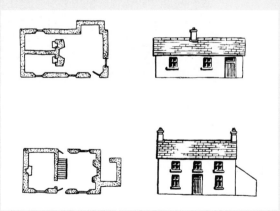

3-16 *Single-storey and one-and-a-half storey Congested Districts Board Houses*

3-17 *Land Commission houses were slated originally (top). Later styles used tiles (bottom).*

Rural cottages continued to be built over the years, the design reflecting changes in architectural style and materials. During the 1920s and 1930s tiles were used on occasions instead of slates, cement plaster instead of lime plaster, and steel windows instead of timber windows.

Changes from the 1950s onwards included a small entrance hall, casement windows instead of the traditional up-and-down sash type, tiled roofs, and piped water and sewage.

The early County Council house of the 1920s was hipped and slated.

A short time later the Council used tiles.

A typical County Council cottage of the 70s and 80s

Present day rural Council cottages

3-18 County Council cottages from the 1920s to the present

Architecturally these cottages, erected by public organisations, are superior in terms of design and aesthetics to many recent bungalow types erected by individuals. These cottages blend very well with the landscape and are an important part of our architectural heritage.

Two-storey houses

The first examples of two-storey houses date from the early eighteenth century, but the majority are from much later into the nineteenth century. The ground plans are similar to the one-storey dwellings, and retain the door and hearth locations.

Towards the end of the nineteenth century ordinary farmers were building two-storey slated houses. Two styles from this period are evident, the first has the chimneys on the gable ends and the door is positioned centrally. The second style has a hipped roof with the chimney stacks positioned in the centre.

3-19 Two styles of late nineteenth century two-storey houses

Features from formal houses are evident in both styles, such as a 'Georgian' fanlight above the front door and large windows. They contained little evidence of the vernacular influence other than the width of the house, which was still only one room wide.

Formal buildings

House styles vary from region to region depending on the social class of the owners. Large houses seldom have vernacular features. Instead they are influenced by national and international trends.

A formal house falls between the great house (Westport House, for example) and the vernacular dwelling. Both formal and vernacular features are evident in the building. The symmetrical arrangement of doors, windows and chimneys in the front of the building show the influence of formal models, while the vernacular influence is evident from the ground plan.

3-20 *An example of a formal house showing symmetry of windows, doors and chimneys*

These houses are associated with large farms and date to the seventeenth and eighteenth centuries.

In the nineteenth century, prosperous farmers, professional people and the gentry replaced their thatched houses with formal Georgian style houses. These houses had slated, hipped roofs. The front door, with a Georgian fanlight, is a distinguishing feature, located in the centre of the house. Windows and chimneys are also arranged symmetrically. Though two storey was the norm, some Georgian houses were three storey.

3-21 *Formal Georgian style house of the nineteenth century*

Bungalows

Bungalows have spread across the countryside since the 1960s. They are replacing traditional dwellings and demonstrate a clear break with vernacular architecture. Bungalows are now so common that some regard them as a new vernacular. They are not just sited in towns and villages but in isolated areas of the countryside as well.

The general profile of people living in bungalows in rural areas is of people with urban occupations. This is a particular Irish occurrence, not evident in European countries. Reasons for it might include:

- the rural background of many people
- the increased use and ownership of cars
- the difficulty of obtaining sites in urban areas
- the ease with which farmers are prepared to sell sites

There are many controversial aspects to bungalows, not least a disregard for rural traditions. They face directly onto main roads, often on highly visible sites, some in contempt of the landscape and often showing little regard for their impact on it. They lack design features and are aesthetically bland, often reflecting the influence of off-the-shelf books of plans.

Precursor to the bungalow, bay windows with flat concrete roofs

Similar to above design but with hipped bay windows

3-22a *The evolution of the bungalow (continued overleaf)*

The common bungalow, lacking any design features

Particular decades adopted specific design features. This example shows arched windows of the 1980s

Modern bungalows come in many different designs

3-22b *The evolution of the bungalow (continued)*

3-23 *Quality Irish cottages are still being built that reflect the vernacular tradition*

The present trend is in favour of two-storey houses. They appear to be challenging and replacing the bungalow. Clear guidelines are required from the planning authorities to ensure that future buildings are in harmony with the landscape and reflect local building traditions and materials.

Traditional thatched house with gabled roof

Traditional thatched house with hipped roof

The 'long farmhouse', with slated roof or sometimes thatch or iron

Two-storey farmhouse, originally single-storey

Two-storey farmhouse for the more prosperous farmer

3-24a *Traditional rural house types found in Ireland*

Estate cottage, built in single,
one-and-a-half and two-storeys.

First County Council cottages

County Council cottages 1920s – 1950s

Bungalow 1930s - 1960s, the precursor to the modern bungalow

Modern bungalow 1960s - present. Horizontal window form.

3-24b *Traditional rural house types found in Ireland*

Towns and villages

The origin of Ireland's towns, cities and villages has been strongly linked with colonisation and revolutions. Three different phases of town creation can be identified. These are the Norman period, the plantation period and the reign of the landlords (estate towns and villages).

The Norman influence

The Normans arrived towards the end of the twelfth century and built on the earlier Viking foundations. The market place and the town wall were the key features of the Norman town. Walled towns are dominated by a river. Their average size is between six and fifteen hectares. Examples include Kilkenny, Athenry, New Ross and Drogheda.

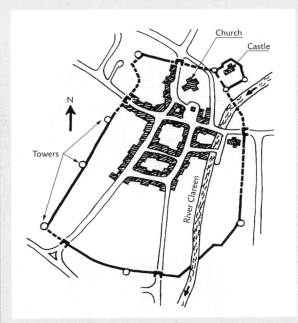

3-25 *Athenry, Co. Galway, has the best-preserved medieval town walls in Ireland. They date from about 1310 AD.*

Small manor villages developed outside these towns. The focus of these villages was the parish church, the castle and the manorial mill. Another type of agricultural village developed later on called 'clachans', which had no nucleus and consisted only of clusters of houses.

The plantation era

The seventeenth century saw the existing village system collapse. The impact of the Reformation resulted in protestant landlords occupying new sites and promoting the Anglican church as the centre of their new town.

A change in farming patterns from tillage to pasture resulted in the labour force no longer congregating in the villages.

While many villages died and were lost, approximately 400 new ones were created by new landlords. These were set up as focus points for their estates. Towns and villages are the main features of the plantation era. A triangular green is often found at the centre of these villages.

Elaborate walled grid

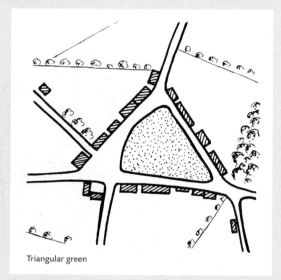

Triangular green

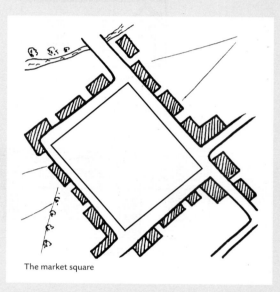

The market square

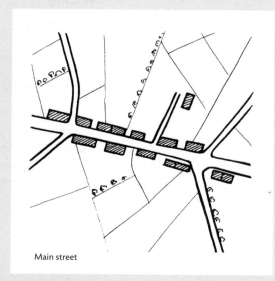

Main street

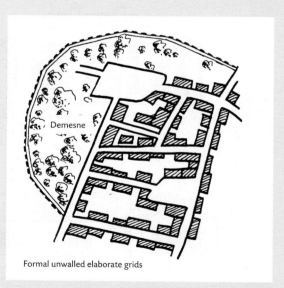

Formal unwalled elaborate grids

3-26a *Common design layouts for towns and villages*

The octagon plan

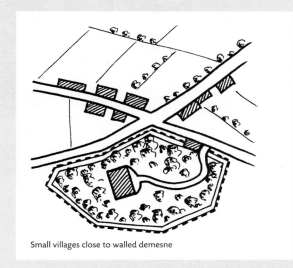

Small villages close to walled demesne

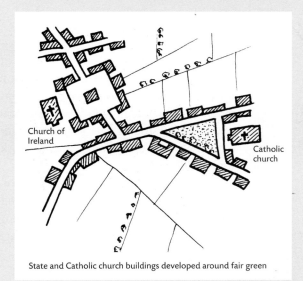

Church of Ireland

Catholic church

State and Catholic church buildings developed around fair green

3-26b Common design layouts for towns and villages (continued)

Estate towns and villages

The period from 1720 to 1740 saw a dramatic increase in the number of estate villages. These villages were planned and designed around a wide street, to accommodate the market. Examples include Ballina, Summerhill, Sixmilebridge and Ballycastle.

The octagon was a common design shape used at this time, as at Slane.

A significant number of estate towns was created in the 1780s as a result of a policy to relocate textile industries outside Dublin. Towns of this era included Balbriggan, Prosperous and Cheekpoint in Waterford. Road building at the time had a major impact on the creation of towns, particularly in the west.

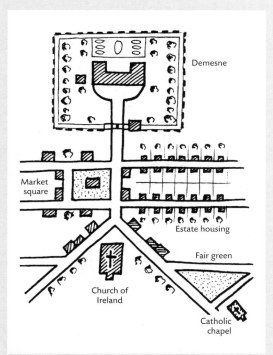

Demesne

Market square

Estate housing

Fair green

Church of Ireland

Catholic chapel

3-27 A typical estate village shows a considerable amount of architectural unity. The 'big house' and demesne was the principal focus.

The landlord was the most significant figure of this era in relation to urban development. The estate house and demesne were an important part of the town structure, in some towns they still are. The landlord specified the standards for new buildings, street improvements and other changes.

Many urban streets were widened during this era, new urban spaces were created and public buildings were carefully positioned.

Modern urban development really began in the eighteenth century and continued until the middle of the nineteenth century. Over a forty-year period the layout of many towns, as they exist today, was created.

The creation of estate villages and towns came to an end by the Famine of the 1840s. Following this era many towns were remodelled, with the assistance of a town planner, known at the time as a 'projector'.

Little progress was made in the nineteenth century. Towns around seaside resorts sprung up in the second half of the century. The improvement in transport, especially the railways, had an impact on urban development by increasing the availability of building materials. In the late nineteenth century developments, brick was used instead of stone, especially in smaller towns.

The Republic of Ireland promoted a rural ethos following independence. This reflected disaffection for towns created under colonisation.

The influence of the Catholic Church led to the creation of parishes around the church. The church became the nucleus for the community, soon attracting a pub, school, shops, post office and barracks. Catholic towns soon became the focus of the new Ireland.

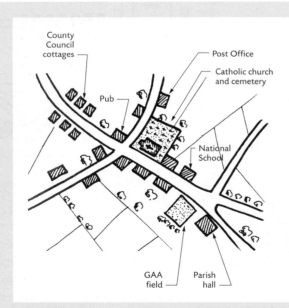

3-28 *The Catholic parish network of the early twentieth century. Small villages were created around the chapel at the crossroads.*

Structure of towns

From the beginnings of urbanisation the main feature in towns is the street or square.

The street is characterised by a group of buildings that face onto a main street. The buildings are connected to each other and may be similar in design with minor variations. In some streets the buildings are different in size, design, shape and use. In the middle ages the street was only a narrow path suitable for pedestrians and wheeled vehicles.

3-29 *A variety of building types in Nenagh, Co. Tipperary. These buildings are quite old and some may have been thatched originally.*

The square encompasses a broad area, where the street in effect becomes wider. This wide space was used principally for a market but may also have been created to mark an important event or to celebrate a great person.

Urban Irish dwellings

When Irish towns were created there was little or no distinction between place of residence and place of work. Shopkeepers lived over their shops, crafts-people lived over their workshops, and doctors and lawyers were in rooms. This trend no longer exists and it is now the exception to live and work in the same building.

Pre-1700 domestic urban buildings were most likely built of mud and wattle. The roofs made of thatch or possibly grass sods. These buildings would have been similar to the countryside cottages of the same era.

The period 1700 to 1850 was the most important urban development phase in our architectural history. The houses vary in size and shape from the large mansion to the small single-storey cabin. Terraced houses make up the majority of residential buildings from this era. Terraced houses were of two or three storey and sometimes four storey.

3-30 Terrace houses in Galway

The architectural characteristics of houses of this period are simplicity of design and construction. Walls were constructed of stone and finished with lime plaster. Brick was only used in the cities. Timber was used for floors and roofing. Originally many two-storey houses were thatched, later they were slated. Elevations were bland except for the doorway, which exhibited considerable detail. Doric or Ionic columns were constructed in timber or stone around the doorway.

3-31 Doorways often exhibit greater detail in terrace housing

Eventually lime plaster gave way to cement plaster, the twelve pane Georgian window was replaced by the two-pane type and thatch roofs gave way to slates.

Towards the end of the nineteenth century the lower basement floor became less common. External steps provided a distinction between the main entrance and the lower floors. Brick mouldings and bay windows became more common.

The traditional building unit was still the terrace. Later the detached and the semi-detached house became more popular.

The arrival of the motorcar, from the 1920s onwards, had an impact on the type and style of housing. The car was responsible for breaking down the distinction between the town and the country. Modern housing estates of detached and semi-detached houses were built considerable distances from existing town centres.

The Garden City movement influenced the layout of housing estates from the 1930s onwards. The aim of this movement was to develop a new concept of urban living. These new towns would have schools, libraries, community halls and playing fields, as well as open space, fresh air and natural landscaping. The Mount Merrion estate in Dublin is a typical example.

This period also witnessed a significant change in the use of building materials. Concrete blocks were used and finished with plaster, tiled roofs became more popular than slates, and steel replaced timber windows.

Housing styles have undergone considerable change since the 1960s. The book of plans became popular even though they were rarely based on sound architectural principles. Little attention was paid to site planning, orientation and the impact on the landscape. Architects became less involved in private house design. Private housing estates became the commonest from of housing in the cities and in many towns. Both houses and plot size reduced in size. Little distinction existed between densities in private estates and public sector estates.

The present trend in Ireland is for housing densities to continue to rise. In city centres house sizes are getting smaller and two-bedroom houses are now a starting and finishing point for many. The three-bed semi-detached is on the decline in Dublin, and being replaced by two bed apartments. Apartment blocks are now common in all major towns and cities.

3-32 *Apartment blocks vary widely in design*

3-34 *A common feature of new urban developments is to integrate semi-detached and longer housing blocks with apartment blocks, all of a similar design.*

Detached houses are disappearing in built-up areas outside Dublin in favour of 3-bed semi-detached houses. Building methods are also changing, as new building regulations further drive up the cost of building. Such building regulations are necessary to make houses more sustainable and energy efficient.

3-33 *Access to upper apartments is either through a connecting internal services shaft (top), or an external stairs. Buildings consisting of two or more apartments, directly above each other are also referred to as duplex buildings.*

Classical Georgian house

Cottage, may originally have been thatched

Street house, one storey over basement

Large town house, usually built in terraces

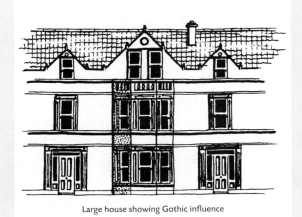

Large house showing Gothic influence

3-35b **Common urban house types (continued overleaf)**

Smaller town house

3-35a **Common urban house types**

Estate house

Early public housing

Terrace public housing

Semi-detached private housing with attached garage

3-35c Common urban house types (continued)

Architectural conservation

Protection of the built heritage

A significant change in attitude to our built heritage has come about in recent decades. A more active approach is now taken to safeguard this heritage.

Ireland ratified the Granada convention in 1997. The Granada convention seeks to protect architectural heritage, which is defined as monuments, groups of buildings and sites.

Historic buildings are an intrinsic part of our cultural heritage and national identity. They are a finite resource, and once lost or damaged cannot be replaced. Our architectural heritage comprises the large buildings of national importance, as well as vernacular buildings of the past, which have acquired cultural significance over time.

The 1999 Planning and Development Act introduces a range of new measures for the protection of the architectural heritage. Two new measures of particular interest are the Record of Protected Structures (RPS), and Architectural Conservation Areas (ACAs).

Responsibility for the protection of built heritage rests with the planning authorities at local level, and with the Minister for the Environment, Heritage and Local Government at central government level.

The main functions of the planning authorities include:

- The compilation and maintenance of a Record of Protected Structures
- Evaluation by conservation officers of proposed works that may affect the character of a protected structure and thereby require planning permission.
- The power to prevent a protected structure from becoming a danger by requiring the owner to carry out specific works.
- The administration of a grant scheme.
- The power to acquire the property, if deemed necessary to protect the structure.

Conservation

Conservation of historic buildings is the action taken to prevent decay, and to prolong the life of our national architectural heritage. The conservation process should be carried out without damaging the building, and without destroying or falsifying historical evidence.

There is now a significant public interest in and awareness of our built heritage, from thatched cottages, great country houses and shopfronts to bridges, mills and stone walls.

Restoration and reconstruction

- **Restoration** is the process of returning a heritage object to a known earlier state, without introducing new material.
- **Reconstruction** is altering a heritage object by introducing new or old materials into the fabric to produce a work that respects the original.

The two processes are often interwoven and both must be approached with the utmost care.

Work is often undertaken on an old building with the best of intentions and enthusiasm, but causes a great deal of unintentional damage, both aesthetic and technical. This arises through lack of information, or by using inappropriate or incorrect procedures. In many cases intervention may have been unnecessary in the first instance.

In new work, in a conservation context, the use of well-designed modern forms and materials, carefully chosen and respectful of the older environment is acceptable.

Conservation principles

Retention or restoration of historical significance

The aim of conservation is to retain, recover or reveal as much of the historical significance as is possible of the heritage object (building or artifact). Provision for its security, maintenance and future must be part of this aim. The end use of the restored or conserved building is of vital importance, as the new use has to be compatible with the needs of the building.

Conservation process based on research

It is important to know and understand the history of the building, and its current physical condition prior to commencing work. Otherwise costly errors can be made.

Minimum physical intervention

This is the basic guiding principle of conservation. It means making the minimum change to an historic building, in order to retain, wherever possible, the original fabric and character. Examples include repairing windows and shopfronts instead of replacing them.

An extension of this principle is to 'repair rather than replace'. Too often original features are binned. Initially the window frame or cornice may look totally beyond repair to the untrained eye. On further examination the original joinery or plaster can be retained or repaired. The result is a more authentic building, which preserves the feeling of age and history, and respects the fabric and original craftsmanship.

Accurate replacement

Any necessary replacement should copy the original exactly, if possible. The procedure is:

- Determine if the damaged or rotten portion is original.
- Keep a sample of any existing moulding.
- Get a reputable craftsperson to make an accurate copy.

Emphasise to the craftsperson the importance of accurate replication. Poorly detailed imitations are unacceptable. Make a particular effort to match the type and colour of the original for stone and brick replacement work. Use traditional and local materials in repair work, where possible.

Maintenance of visual setting

The setting of an historic building is integral with the whole and should be dealt with accordingly. This means that the demesne lands of a country house, the original frame of a painting and the historic streetscape of a town are all elements that should be conserved or restored where possible.

Maintenance of the setting may prove difficult in some instances. Nonetheless respect for the setting is important in conservation and restoration work.

New work

Record all new significant new work by documentation and photographs.

Reversibility

The concept of reversibility is applied, where possible, where any intervention in an historic building is planned. Reversibility entails that no work is undertaken which precludes the possibility of returning to the original state.

Conservation zones

The fabric of buildings that have undergone considerable decay require evaluation to determine conservation zones within the building. Conservation zones may extend throughout the whole building and include its surroundings.

> **Conservation zones** specific areas of a building that must be preserved. The whole building may not necessarily be included in a conservation zone.

Other buildings may not warrant such a rigorous conservation approach. There may be areas where intervention can be tolerated and the need for accurate restoration lessened.

For conservation to be sustainable it is important to direct resources towards preservation and repair rather than replication. The establishment of conservation zones within buildings is an important part of this process.

Modern solutions should not be ruled out when considering the above principles. Examples include the change of use for a building in order to ensure its survival.

Sequence of conservation work

1. Research and analyse history and fabric
The history of the building can be uncovered through old papers, maps, registers etc. The fabric of the building will also give clues to the past.

2. Survey building
An overall and accurate measured survey of the building is necessary. This applies whether it is a cottage, castle or shop front. The survey should include plans, elevations and sections. This will prove invaluable in identifying the building's history. A photographic record is also recommended. Identification of original material is very important.

3. Plan restoration with minimum intervention
Refer to the principles of conservation, and ensure that the least intervention possible takes place. Apply the guiding principle of repair rather than replace.

4. Implement under experienced supervision
Employ a professional, with experience of conservation and restoration, at the early stages. This will minimise the risk of costly error or unintentional damage being done.

5. Record work
Keep a written and photographic record during the course of the work. This is useful for future reference and for information.

6. Implement regular maintenance procedures
For the building to remain in a good condition it must be inspected and maintained on an ongoing basis. It makes economic sense to maintain and repair on a regular basis rather than face major and costly work when a crisis arrives.

Install and implement safety and security procedures as the need arises.

Current housing issues

Current housing policy encompasses provision for social and voluntary housing, shared ownership and affordable housing, including rented accommodation options. Provision is also included for homeless people, the elderly and Travellers.

The housing market is very complex. It must serve different needs of people in the market from the mobile employed individual to family or other households and to the investor. It must also serve the needs of the more vulnerable people in our society who depend on the State to intervene on their behalf.

It is important that all stakeholders work together to provide the best possible national housing infrastructure across the full range of society's needs, and to do this in a sustainable manner. The key stakeholders are those in Government departments, local authorities and industry.

Sustainability relates not just to the environment issues in terms of efficient land use and sustainable building types and materials used, but also to the delivery of housing in a cost-efficient manner with regard to social inclusion.

Housing is a key influence on people's life opportunities and quality of life. Delivering housing in a sustainable manner, which respects the environment, social and economic aspects of development, can improve quality of life for all sections of the community.

Housing demand
The number of houses in Ireland in 2020 could be double the number in 1992 because of changes in population. In recent years we have seen an unprecedented demand for houses due to the surge in economic growth and the demographic changes. Other contributing factors include increases in real disposable income and historically low interest rates.

The Irish population grew by about 8% between 1996 and 2002, while there has been greater growth in the key household formation age group, 25–34, which rose by an estimated 18%. At the same time the average household size (number of occupants) in Ireland has been steadily declining.

The impact of population growth and societal change, including marital breakdown and more elderly people living alone, means that Irish household sizes are declining. In 1991, there were, on average, 3.28 people per household in Ireland, that had declined to 2.97 by 2002.

Traditionally Ireland had larger household size than our EU partners but it is now converging towards EU norms. It is anticipated that household size will reach EU levels by 2011, which is about 2.63 people per household.

In the three year period between 2000 and 2002, more than 160,000 houses were built in Ireland. This high level of supply needs to be maintained to meet the demographic trends.

Low-density suburban development vs. traditional urban terraces

The current pattern of suburban development has a number of disadvantages when compared to traditional urban terraces.

In other countries, such as the United States and the United Kingdom, the cost of providing infrastructure and services for low-density developments is approximately twice the cost of providing for terraced developments. The direct cost in time and money for the average family are enormous. The average suburban family owns two cars and drives between 30,000 and 50,000 kilometres annually. After housing, suburban dwellers spend more on cars than on anything else.

A strong argument against the current suburban patterns of development is that environmental costs are considerable and irreversible. The health damage from car-related ozone pollution causes economic losses, which are on the increase. Run-off pollution is a serious threat to water quality, affecting a high percentage of the country's rivers, lakes and estuaries.

The increasing trend to move to the suburbs has created dis-investment in the city centres. The designated area legislation in Ireland has balanced this trend in recent years. The future prediction is that there will be a continual threat to investment in the city centre. This will increase demand for services, schools, utilities, and refuse collection in the expanding suburbs.

The planning regulations encourage single-use zoning. This makes it very difficult, if not impossible, to incorporate urban-design qualities associated with existing towns and cities. For example, few planning codes facilitate the creation of public spaces which characterise admired towns such as Galway, Kinsale and Kilkenny.

Suburbia is now the dominant form of settlement in Ireland, as in most western cultures. Unless this reality is confronted, 'urban sprawl' will continue. Suburbs have a hold on the imagination of most of the population and will therefore continue to dominate developing urban forms. Architects need to be aware and plan for how urban spaces work.

Ribbon development

Ribbon development refers to a built-up area on a secondary road linking to a major artery into the city centre. Cheaper land away from the city centre is the usual attraction. The line of buildings on each side of the road may be only one plot deep.

3-36 A recent example of ribbon development off a main road leading into Galway

Ribbon development is a particular problem in Ireland. It is in danger of turning the countryside into one long suburb. It is in danger of destroying the village tradition. Designs used in ribbon development are uncoordinated and raise questions about the planning process.

This trend in residential rural development is having a negative impact on the landscape. It is depopulating tertiary roads and leaving people behind in isolation. There is a strong need for long-term planning to deal with this issue.

Accessibility standards for all housing

According to Eurostat figures the average life expectancy in Ireland will have increased from 76 to 82 over the next 7 years.

Presently only 11.4% of the population is over 65, but by 2025 this will have risen to 17.25%. The gap with our EU neighbours is rapidly closing. In most of Europe and in Japan 25% of the population will be over 65 by 2025.

More than 80% of over-65s currently live in their own homes, while 11% live with their families. Only 4% are cared for in nursing homes and this figure is expected to remain constant. The proportion of this cohort living independently or with assistance within the community, is expected to increase to 90%, despite the longer life expectancy.

A policy for Lifetime Adaptable Housing needs to be developed to cater for these demographic changes. This policy needs to integrate special needs housing into mainstream housing. The question needs to be asked is how adaptable is the housing and neighbourhoods currently being built?

A mistaken belief is that inclusive design is only for disabled people. There are currently over 1.5 million people in Ireland who would directly or indirectly benefit from inclusive access to buildings, housing and public spaces. These include older people, families with young children, carers, and the friends and relatives who accompany people with disabilities.

The Building Regulations provide one set of standards for accessibility standards but higher lifetime standards are also needed. Standards need to be developed that can be applied to the upgrading of existing houses. A system of monitoring and control is essential during all stages of design and construction.

In addition to policies, regulations and controls, incentives need to be devised to encourage private sector developers in particular, to build to lifetime adaptable standards and to integrate wheelchair accessible dwellings into all housing schemes.

Urban redevelopment

Planning and development mistakes have been made in the past across Europe as well as in Ireland. The correction of such mistakes is termed 'redevelopment'. A current example of this in Ireland is the Ballymun redevelopment project.

The redevelopment of the Ballymun local authority housing estate has been underway since 1998. The aim of the redevelopment of Ballymun is to create a self-sustaining socially mixed town in contrast to the original 1960s scheme, which planned the area to be apart from the rest of the city with a 100% public housing scheme and no social mix.

The overall objective of the Ballymun Masterplan is to change Ballymun into an attractive, viable and self-sustaining town, with a projected population of 30,000 inhabitants.

The key features that the new Ballymun hope to achieve are:

- quality homes with a good social mix - architecturally designed 2, 3 and 4 storey homes are replacing the existing apartment blocks.
- planned town centre with a mix of commercial activity

- vibrant local economy with sustainable local employment
- five identifiable neighbourhoods with a range of community facilities
- well-defined top quality parks and suitable amenities effective local administration

Housing associations have been partnered with local self-help groups to provide necessary supports to vulnerable sectors. Some of these initiatives include integrated residential developments for people requiring additional supports, homeless hostels, sheltered accommodation, and specialist after-school and pre-school projects.

Housing on its own will not be successful unless the necessary community supports are in place. These include social and community services, such as childcare facilities, schools, health services and employment-generating activities.

The National Spatial Strategy (NSS) – rural development and rural settlement

The NSS is a 20 year planning framework for all parts of Ireland. It aims to achieve a better balance of social, economic and physical development across Ireland, supported by more effective planning.

It will mean better quality of life, due to less congestion and less long-distance commuting, more regard to the quality of the environment and increased access to services like health, education and leisure.

There are five elements to the future spatial structure of Ireland:

- a strong and internationally competitive Greater Dublin Area (GDA) driving both its own economy and national development
- strategically placed, national scale urban areas, acting as gateways, which will deliver a more spatially balanced Ireland and drive development in their own regions
- strategic medium to large size towns, which will act as hubs linked to the gateways, and also reach out to the more rural parts
- a strengthened county and large- to medium-sized town structure
- diversified and vibrant rural communities, which contribute to and benefit from the development of larger centres such as gateways and hubs

3-37 *The National Spatial Strategy requires that areas of critical mass and sufficient scale be built up through a network of gateways and hubs. Existing gateways include Dublin, Cork, Limerick/Shannon, Galway and Waterford. New gateways include Dundalk and Sligo. Letterkenny/(Derry), and Athlone/Tullamore/Mullingar, will act as linked gateways.*

The NSS identifies nine, strategically located, medium sized 'hubs'. The hubs include Cavan, Ennis, Kilkenny, Mallow, Monaghan, Tuam and Wexford. Ballina/Castlebar and Tralee/Killarney will act as linked hubs to promote regional development in their areas.

Gateways act at national level. Hubs act at regional and county level, partnered by county towns and other larger towns.

The strength and integrity of many rural communities is challenged as a result of declining population. Rural populations in other areas are increasing while community life in small towns and some villages declines. This decline is mainly due to long distance commuting to main cities and towns.

The NSS and rural settlement

The NSS supports sustainable rural settlement and sets out four objectives to achieve this

1 To sustain and renew established rural communities
2 To strengthen the established structure of villages and smaller settlements. This will help to accommodate additional population in a manner that supports the viability of public transport and local services such as schools and water services.
3 To ensure that key assets in rural areas are protected to support quality of life and economic vitality.
4 To ensure that rural settlement policies respond to the differing local circumstances in different regions.

The NSS makes a distinction between rural generated housing and urban generated housing.

- **Rural generated housing** is housing needed in rural areas within the established rural community by persons working in rural areas or in nearby urban areas. Rural generated housing needs arise for persons who are an intrinsic part of the rural community by way of background or the fact that they work full-time or part-time in rural areas.

- **Urban generated housing** is housing in rural locations sought by people living and working in urban areas, including second homes. Development driven by cities and towns should take place in their built areas. For those seeking a rural lifestyle, while working in a larger city or town, smaller towns and villages can cater for this type of housing demand in a sustainable manner.

Chapter 4

Acquiring a dwelling

Location

Many factors influence determining the location of domestic buildings. These include:

- the choice between a rural or urban location
- deciding whether to build or buy a house
- choosing a house design that will complement the site and be allowed by the planning authority
- environmental and ecological considerations of building a house in a particular location
- methods of financing the house

Choosing a site

Sites within city boundaries and those within easy driving distance of facilities such as schools, shops and amenities, cost more than sites in rural locations.

Mountain, sea or woodland views add to the value and give a site a pleasant outlook.

Ideally locate a site on slightly sloping, well-drained land. A serviced site is desirable but will be more expensive. On an un-serviced site, water, electricity, sewerage and telephone connections will have to be organised.

Consider the following conditions when choosing a site for a house:

- **Location.** Consider: urban or rural life, small estate or large housing scheme, convenience to work, public transport, shops, family, friends, schools, hospitals, churches and amenities, etc. Check local authority future plans (development plans) for the area.
- **Style of house.** Will the intended house design suit the site? Will it be necessary to modify the preferred house style to comply with local planning regulations?
- **Cost.** Sites are more expensive within and close to town boundaries. Location therefore affects cost. If the cost of the site is excessive, will this influence the style of house to be built and/or the amount of money to be borrowed?

- **Services.** Is the site serviced with water, electricity, sewage and telephone connections? While serviced sites are more expensive, the cost of providing each of the services on a non-serviced site can be expensive and needs careful consideration.
- **Soil type.** Subsoils have an effect on the building work.

  Hard rock provides a good foundation.

  Gravel is probably the most suitable subsoil for foundations and drainage.

  Sand is unsuitable for foundations, but is good for drainage.

  Clay, if stiff, is suitable for foundations but is usually poor for drainage.

  Filled or made ground is unsuitable for normal foundations and will require specialist detailing.
- **Planning legislation.** Does Outline Planning Permission exist for the site? If not, will there be any obstacles to permission being granted?
- **Aspect.** This refers to the direction the site is facing. Aspect is an important design consideration because it will affect the positioning of the rooms in order to maximise the amount of sun received during the normal period of use. While it is not possible to have every house facing south, the main rooms can be positioned at the rear of a north-facing house.

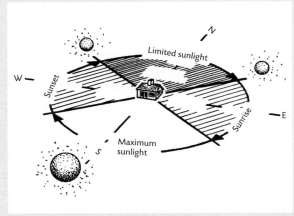

4-1 Aspect refers to the direction a house faces.

■ **Elevation**. Raised or elevated sites are more aesthetic and easier to drain than low-lying ones.

4-2 *Elevation refers to the height of the site, generally above road level.*

■ **Prospect**. Prospect refers to the natural view. The view may include some mature trees or some natural scenic views.

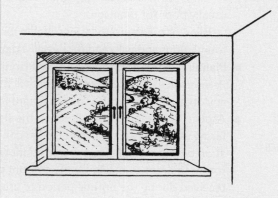

4-3 *Prospect refers to the natural view.*

■ **Site investigation**. All sites need to be investigated to determine their suitability for building.
   This investigation is usually concentrated on the load-bearing capacity of the soil and its drainage ability. Different types of trial holes are used for each test.

■ **Contamination**. Contamination may arise from sources outside the site, e.g. landfill. Previous uses of the site should be investigated and considered.

■ **Trees**. Note the location of large trees. Do not plant trees too near the house because in time roots could interfere with the house foundations.

4-4 *Large trees near houses can cause foundation problems*

■ **Natural surroundings**. Where possible retain the natural character of the surroundings. Avoid building beside main roads. A house is less obtrusive if it has access off a small side road.

■ **Wind**. Ideally the site should be sheltered from the prevailing winds.

Local development plans

Local development plans for a region may be viewed and/or purchased at the offices of the County Council or Urban Council. Local development plans are generally drawn up to cover a five-year period.

   Development plans exist for each county as a whole, and smaller ones may exist for individual towns or regions within the county.

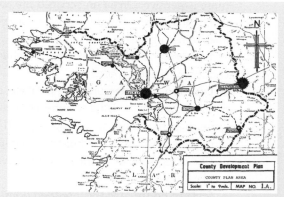

4-5 *Local Development Plans generally cover a five-year period. The above drawing shows the area covered by the Galway County Development Plan. Other drawings in the plan show areas designated for residential and commercial use; community facilities; agriculture; amenity; industry; and access to be preserved.*

The main aims of local development plans are:
1 To comply with the requirements of the Local Government Acts.

2 To participate actively in the economic growth of the region by planning for the provision of the demographic, infrastructural, environmental protection and land use planning needs of the region.

3 To provide detailed information for prospective investors, property owners, and developers in the region, which will assist them in the preparation of applications for planning permission.

4 To provide the public at large with an information base on the major activities of the County Council.

Consult local development plans prior to making any decision on choosing a location for a house. They contain information on guidelines and standards for:

- housing development
- septic tank and waste drainage systems
- heritage areas and buildings
- archaeological conservation
- environment impact studies
- industrial and commercial development

Guidelines for rural housing development

These guidelines are designed to help the individual make informed decisions at the early stages of the proposed development, particularly if it is a new house.

The first step is to respect the quality and integrity of the countryside. The primary objective for new development is to ensure that it blends into the landscape and does not detract from it. The landscape is Ireland's basic tourism resource. Tourism is the third-largest sector in the national and local economy.

Work with an architect or other competent designer. Consult with the planning staff in the planning authority at the earliest stage. This will ensure that the house fits into the landscape and that individual requirements are allowed in the design.

There are four main considerations involved in the development of rural areas:

LOCATION The general location of new development must be directed away from areas that cannot satisfactorily assimilate it.

SITING The siting of the house on the site requires sensitivity so that the building will not be obtrusive.

DESIGN The house must be designed in a manner appropriate to the countryside rather than an imitation of suburban styles.

DEVELOPMENT Completion of site development, including the necessary landscaping and planting, is vitally important, if the desired assimilation of the development is to be achieved.

Location principles

- The general policy of the planning authority is to locate new development in towns and villages where most of the services and community facilities are readily available.
- The ideal rural location is a relatively flat site with good hedge and tree cover and a wide access road.
- Avoid building in open areas where there are no existing buildings.
- Avoid building on the crests of hills in order to obtain panoramic views.
- Select sites on the gentlest part of slopes or in folds or indentations in the contours of the landscape.

Siting principles

- The objective of proper siting is to 'fit' the building into its immediate surroundings, and not to make it conspicuous.
- A house located on the most elevated part of the site will be obtrusive and will detract from the landscape.
- The fall in gradient required at the rear of the site for the functioning of the waste systems will place an additional constraint on site selection.

House design principles

- Architectural design requires professional expertise.
- Engage an architect or other competent designer and consult with the planning authority.
- Copying designs from books of plans or copying existing houses is not recommended. Many of them have basic defects, which may not be obvious to the inexperienced.
- Every house must be designed for its own site or area.
- The basic design and house type should harmonise with adjoining development, especially in open landscapes, e.g. number of storeys, external elements, colours and materials, etc.

- Avoid gable-fronted designs, which produce a visually unsympathetic form.
- In open and scenic landscapes, single-storey, low-profile simple designs are more appropriate.

Site development

A well-designed and well-sited house will still not be assimilated satisfactorily into its surroundings unless site development work is fully completed.

It is recommended that a survey of existing site conditions together with proposals for site development works including fencing, planting, landscaping and ground modelling, be included with all planning applications.

Obtaining permission to build

Planning permission is required for any development of land or property unless the development is specifically exempted from this need.

Development includes carrying out works (building, demolition, alteration) on land or buildings and making a material change of use of land or buildings.

Types of planning permission

There are four types of planning permission. An application may be made for:
- permission
- outline permission
- permission following the grant of outline permission
- retention

There is a time limit of eight weeks from when a valid planning application is made to a decision being given.

Developments by local authorities also need to comply with certain procedures.

Any development should comply with building regulations, which are legal requirements for good practice in the design and the construction of buildings.

FULL PLANNING PERMISSION

A completed application form must be submitted with certain documents attached. These documents are described below, and are the minimum requirements for full planning permission.

Substandard or incomplete documentation will result in the planning authority returning all of the documentation, and the planning application will not be accepted as a valid application.

Full planning permission expires five years after date of grant.

Documents required for full-planning permission
- **site notice** (number of copies varies from Council to Council, generally from one to three copies required)
- **newspaper notice** (full newspaper page containing the ad. plus one or two A4 copies of the ad.)
- **planning application form** (one copy)
- **site location map** (six copies)
- **site layout drawing** (six copies)
- **drawings and specifications** (six copies)
- **a schedule** of contents
- **description** of development
- **percolation/water table test results**
- **planning fee**

OUTLINE PLANNING PERMISSION

Outline planning permission is permission **in principle only**. It does not permit the carrying out of any work. Formal application for 'permission consequent on the grant of outline permission' must be sought and granted before commencing work. An outline application cannot be made if an EIS (Environmental Impact Statement) is required.

Outline permission expires three years after the date of grant.

See Table 4-1 for minimum documents required.

PERMISSION CONSEQUENT ON THE GRANT OF OUTLINE PERMISSION

This type of planning permission can only be applied for in cases where outline permission was previously granted. The outline permission must still be effective, and within the three years from the date when outline permission was granted.

The duration of permission consequent on the grant of outline permission is five years. When combined with outline permission the overall duration may extend to eight years.

See Table 4-1 for minimum documents required.

RETENTION

Retention relates to permission to retain an unauthorised development, i.e. a building built without planning permission.

If a development does not comply with planning regulations the planning authority have the right to refuse retention and issue a demolition order.

The fee for retention is, in general, three times the fee for full-planning permission. Minimum documents for retention are the same as for full permission.

Summary of documents required for the different types of planning permission

Documents required	Full planning	Outline planning	Permission following outline	Retention
Site notice*	3 copies	3 copies	3 copies	3 copies
Newspaper notice*	Full page plus 3 A4 copies of ad.	Full page plus 3 A4 copies of ad.	Full page plus 3 A4 copies of ad.	Full page plus 3 A4 copies of ad.
Planning application form	3 copies	3 copies	3 copies	3 copies
Site location map	6 copies	6 copies	6 copies	6 copies
Site layout drawing	6 copies	6 copies	6 copies	6 copies
Drawings and specifications	6 copies	not required	6 copies	6 copies
Schedule of contents	1 copy	1 copy	1 copy	1 copy
Description of development	Yes	Yes	Yes	Yes
Percolation/water test results	Yes	Yes	Yes	Yes
Planning fee	Yes	Yes	Yes	Yes

* Requirements vary depending on planning authority.

Table 4-1 *Documents required for planning applications*

Making a planning application

Application forms are available from the planning authority for the area. This can be the County Council or the Urban District Council/Corporation.

The person making the application, if not the owner, should have the written consent of the owner.

A fee is payable with the planning application, the amount depends on the type of development proposed and the type of permission being sought. A flat rate fee is payable for an application to construct a new house. Details should be sought from the planning authority.

Community-based developments may be exempt from planning fees. These include schools, churches and community centres. Check with the planning authority in advance.

Required documentation details

The following documents are required for some or all types of planning permission applications.
- newspaper notice
- site notice
- completed application form
- appropriate fee
- drawings
- schedule of contents

NEWSPAPER NOTICE
- A newspaper notice must be published in the two-week period immediately preceding the making of the application, and the planning authority must receive applications within two weeks of publication of a newspaper notice.

- Each planning authority will provide a list of approved newspapers to applicants.
- The type of application must be specified.
- In the case of permission following the grant of outline permission, the Outline Reference must be given.
- The location where the application may be inspected or purchased must be stated.
- Notice must indicate that an observation or comment can be made on payment of a fee within five weeks of receipt of the application by the planning authority.
- Planning authorities must allow Irish language newspapers where Gaeltacht areas are within their boundaries.

………….. COUNTY COUNCIL
Full planning permission sought for dwelling house, septic tank and effluent treatment plant at Address 1. Address 2.

This may be inspected or purchased at the Planning Office. A submission or observation in relation to the application may be made in writing on payment of €……. within 5 weeks of receipt of application.
Signed: Joe Bloggs

4-6 *Sample public notice for local paper*

SITE NOTICE

A site notice must be erected on site in the two-week period immediately preceding the making of an application, and must be kept in position for five weeks after the planning authority receives the application.

The following information must be displayed on a site notice:

- the date that the site notice was erected
- name of the planning authority
- townland name and postal address
- type of permission sought
- a description of the proposed development
- details of where and when the application can be inspected or purchased
- notice that observations or comments can be made on payment of a fee within 5 weeks of receipt of application by the planning authority
- the applicant's signature or signature and address of the agent

The planning authority may require that more than one site notice be erected.

The notice should be A4 size and less than 1.5 m above ground level. It should be located near the main entrance and must not be concealed.

A notice relating to a second application within 6 months of the previous one must be on a yellow background (where the application refers to the same site or part thereof).

The site notice must be replaced if it is damaged or becomes illegible.

DESCRIPTION OF DEVELOPMENT

Documents are required to show the development proposals, what the development will look like when finished, how it will relate to the site and to adjoining structures and property, etc.

PERCOLATION/WATER TABLE TEST RESULTS

If a septic tank or other waste disposal system is being installed it will be necessary to submit trial hole and percolation test results.

SPECIFICATION

A specification is a written description of the workmanship and materials for a particular project. It is one of a number of contract documents that have to be read in relation to each other, such as the drawings and bills of quantities.

*A **bill of quantities** is prepared by a quantity surveyor. It estimates the cost of the materials and labour necessary for a construction job.*

Specifications are written by an architect or a consulting engineer and are directed at the contractor.

SITE LOCATION MAP (1:2500)

The site location map must show:

- the outline of the site in red
- the OS sheet no.
- the north point
- the scale of the map (1:2500)

The site location map must be an original copy or else copyright permission must be obtained from the Ordnance Survey office.

.... COUNTY COUNCIL

1. I, Joe Bloggs intend to apply for permission for development at this site: Address 1, Address 2.

2. The development will consist of a four-bedroom bungalow, septic tank and effluent treatment plant.

3. The Planning Application may be inspected at the offices of the Planning Authority at the Planning Office, Address 1, Address 2, during office hours 9.00am to 4.00pm Monday to Friday.

4. A submission or observation in relation to the application may be made in writing to the planning authority on payment of a fee of €...............

5. Signed: Joe Bloggs

6. Date of erection of site notice: 17-05-2015

4-7 Sample site notice for erection on the site

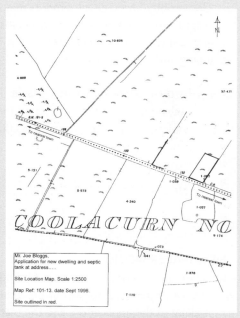

4-8 Sample site location map at a scale of 1:2500

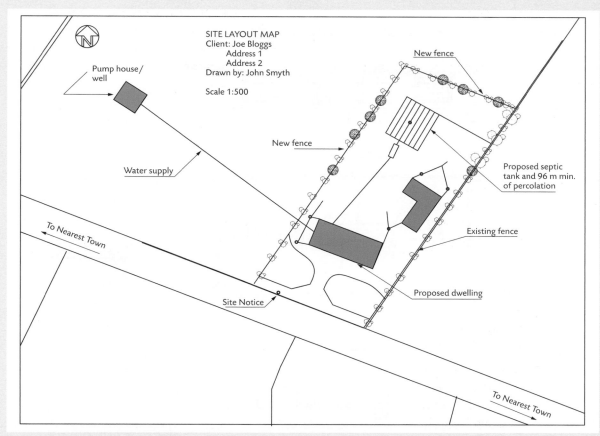

SITE LAYOUT MAP
Client: Joe Bloggs
Address 1
Address 2
Drawn by: John Smyth

Scale 1:500

Pump house/well

New fence

New fence

Water supply

Proposed septic tank and 96 m min. of percolation

To Nearest Town

Existing fence

Site Notice

Proposed dwelling

To Nearest Town

4-9 Sample site map at a scale of 1:500

SITE MAP (1:500)

The site map (scale 1:500) must show:

- the proposed and existing buildings, roads and site boundaries
- distances from existing and proposed structures to roads and site boundaries
- the ground floor level in relation to adjoining road levels
- existing and proposed water supply and sewage disposal systems
- existing and proposed access to the public road
- position of site notice
- the north point and scale of the map
- the name and address of the person responsible for preparing the map

DRAWINGS AND SPECIFICATIONS

The main plans and drawings must include the floor plans, elevations and sections of the proposed development (see Fig. 4-10 overleaf for a typical example).

The detail drawings must include the principal dimensions and overall height.

Elevations must include the main features, such as window patterns, roof slopes, materials, finishes and colours.

- six copies of plans, drawings and maps to appropriate scale
- showing site boundaries in red
- adjacent land in applicant's control in blue
- wayleaves in yellow (Wayleave is permission to cross land, sometimes involving payment. Examples would include allowing a contractor access to a building site, or allowing a person access to services outside a site boundary.)
- levels and contours
- site visibility distances: maximum achievable sight distances must be illustrated at the present access point for all new roadside developments. The minimum sight distance for a local county road is 70 metres. Full details are available from your local planning authority.
- new extensions/alterations clearly distinguished from existing building
- overall dimensions including distance of building from boundaries
- Ordnance Survey sheet nos. and north points (on maps)
- name and address of person who prepared the plans

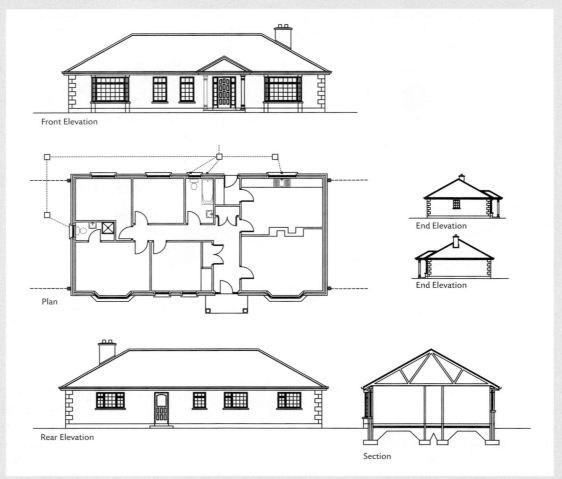

Front Elevation

Plan

End Elevation

End Elevation

Rear Elevation

Section

4-10 Typical plans, elevations and sections of house required for planning permission. Dimensions and text omitted for clarity.

SCHEDULE OF CONTENTS

- Schedule listing all of the contents submitted in the planning application. The name of each drawing should be listed along with the drawing number using the notation drawing 1 of 12, drawing 8 of 12 etc.

Contacting other bodies/organisations

It is recommended the ESB are contacted to determine if the proposed site can be supplied with electricity, and at what cost. It may not be enough to choose a site because it is near existing electricity lines.

The ESB must be consulted if there are overhead lines within 23 metres of the construction works.

Timescale for planning permission applications

The planning authority will deal with a properly completed application within 3 months from the date of application to the final grant of permission, though this period may vary if the planning authority requests further information.

Table 4-2 gives an example of the timescale involved in most cases.

How the decision is made

When making a decision, the planning authority takes a number of matters into consideration, including:

- the proper planning and development of the area
- their own development plan
- submissions and observations made by members of the public on the application

Non-planning issues, such as boundary or other disputes, will not be considered by the planning authority.

Any person can inspect or purchase a copy of the application and make written submissions or observations to the planning authority on any aspect of it, on payment of the appropriate fee.

Planning permission application timescale

Timescale	Action
Start	Notice published in paper and site notice erected
14 days later	Latest date for lodging application
Subsequent 2 weeks	Assessment of validity of application by planning authority
Within 5 weeks of receipt of application by planning authority	Observations or submissions by third parties
	Site notice must stay in place for full period
	Decision cannot be made by planning authority
Within 8 weeks of receipt of application by planning authority	Decision to grant or refuse must be reached
Within 3 days of decision	Planning authority issue copies of decision to applicant and those who have made submissions or observations.
Within 4 weeks of date of decision	Any appeal to An Board Pleanála must be lodged.
Anytime during the process	Application may be withdrawn by notice in writing
	Request for further information
	Request for revised plans (should be submitted within 4 weeks. If not submitted within 6 months, the planning application is withdrawn).

Table 4-2

Duration of planning permission

The standard duration for full planning permission is five years from the date of the grant of permission by the planning authority or An Bord .

The duration for Outline Permission is 3 years.

Application for the grant of full permission consequent to the grant of outline permission must be made within 3 years of the grant of outline permission. This period may be extended by application.

The period of validity of permission may be extended, provided that:

- the development has commenced;
- the application to extend is made in the last year of the validity of the application;
- the time frame required is reasonable;
- an explanation as to why the development was not completed on time is supplied.

Appeals procedure

An Bord Pleanála is responsible for the determination of appeals and certain other matters under the Local Government (Planning and Development) Acts, 1963 to 1999. The Board is also responsible for dealing with appeals under the Building Control Act, 1990, the Local Government (Water Pollution) Acts, 1977 and 1990 and the Air Pollution Act, 1987.

Appeals usually referred to as *normal planning appeals* constitute the principal task of the Board and account for most of the decisions made by it.

These appeals arise from decisions by the planning authorities on applications for permission for the development of land (including applications for the retention of structures or the continuance of uses).

An Bord Pleanála may review any planning decision made by a planning authority.

All individuals, interest groups, etc., who made observations or comments on a planning application within the specified time period have the right to appeal to An Bord Pleanála.

An appeal can be made against a refusal of an application for planning permission or against conditions attached to the granting of planning permission.

Members of the public may also appeal against the granting of permission for developments to which they are opposed (this is known as a third party appeal).

An Bord Pleanála must receive appeals within 4 weeks beginning on the date of the making of the decision by the planning authority.

An appeal must include:

- the name and address of the person or body making the appeal;
- details of the nature and site of the proposed development;
- the full grounds of appeal with supporting material and arguments;
- the correct fee.

Any party to the appeal may request an oral hearing provided the correct non-refundable fee is paid in addition to the appeal fee.

Where a third party appeal is made, a copy of it will be sent to the developer.

The Bord sends a copy of the appeal to the planning authority and, in the case of a third party appeal, to the developer.

These have one month to submit their views. The Bord's objective is to dispose of appeals within four months.

The Bord has discretion to dismiss an appeal where it is satisfied that it is without foundation.

Some general points regarding appeals:
- The Bord may require revised plans (and may grant permission on the basis of these revised plans).
- All documents are available for inspection:
  - during the decision period at the planning authority offices;
  - at an Bord Pleanála for 5 years from decision date;
  - for copying as for planning authority.
- Notifications from An Bord Pleanála are sent:
  - to the relevant planning authority;
  - to those who made observations to the planning authority.
- The Bord's objective is to make decisions within 18 weeks.
- The Bord may grant permission where development is a material contravention of the development plan.
- The Bord can dismiss vexatious, frivolous or insubstantial appeals.

Commencement

A **commencement notice** is necessary to inform the local Building Control Authority that a particular project is starting, in light of the duration of planning permission. It should be issued between 14 and 28 days before starting the works.

A commencement notice must be issued to the local building control authority in respect of work that requires Planning Permission or a Fire Safety Certificate.

A standard form of commencement notice requires the provision to the local building control authority of information on the proposed works, the project location, the building owner, designer and builder, foundations and drainage, and the name of the person from whom information on the proposals may be obtained.

A commencement notice must be accompanied with the appropriate fee.

Enforcement

The planning authority's function is to enforce that developments are carried out in line with planning permission. The planning authority has the right to stop and rectify any unauthorised development.

H Environmental and safety control

Environmental Impact Assessments (EIA) and Environmental Impact Statements (EIS) control this area.

Environmental Impact Assessment (EIA) is a procedure for:
- the examination of the likely effects on the environment of a proposed development;
- ensuring that adequate consideration is given to any effects; and
- avoiding, reducing or offsetting any significant adverse effects.

Planning authorities, as part of the process of planning applications, carry out the procedure.

The Environmental Protection Agency (EPA) assesses the environmental pollution aspects where an application has to be made for an integrated pollution control licence. Generally, large-scale developments require an EIA.

An Environmental Impact Statement (EIS) forms the basis of EIA. An EIS must include:
- a description of the proposed development;
- data necessary to identify and assess the main effects it is likely to have on the environment, and a description of these effects;
- a description of the measures envisaged avoiding, reducing or remedying these effects, where this is deemed necessary.

The Environmental Protection Agency (EPA) is responsible for preventing and controlling environmental emissions from certain activities with potential for significant impact on the environment.

Planning authorities are responsible for assessing the planning issues.

The EPA is concerned with emissions to air and water, the treatment and disposal of waste and the control of noise.

Acquiring a house

There are two ways to acquire a house, buy or build.

Buying a home

Buying a house, for most people, is the largest investment they will ever make. It is important to understand the factors involved, for instance:

- How much can I afford to pay?
- What is the best way to repay the mortgage?
- What type of mortgage should I choose?
- What should I look for when choosing a suitable property?

*A **mortgage** is a conditional conveyance of property, as security for the repayment of a loan. It is registered on the deed of property. The property cannot be sold without the mortgage being cleared. **Conveyance** refers to the transfer of the legal title to property.*

How much can you borrow?

The first thing to consider is how much can you comfortably afford to repay.

As a general guide, banks and lending institutions will allow you to borrow up to three times your annual salary, and in the case of a joint application, add on once the second income. Guaranteed bonuses and overtime can be included when calculating this figure.

Most lenders will not grant a borrower a mortgage of more than 90 per cent of the cost of their new home. The borrower is expected to provide a deposit of approximately 10 per cent of the purchase price, from his/her own resources.

Fees and charges associated with taking out a mortgage also need to be considered:

- **Mortgage application fee.** This is charged by the bank or building society when it grants a mortgage. The amount can be around 0.5 per cent of the value of the loan.
- **Stamp duty on the purchase deed.** This is a government tax that is charged on second-hand homes. New homes are only subject to stamp duty if their floor area is greater than 125 square metres. While this figure has remained constant for some time, it may change in some future Budget.
- **Stamp duty on the purchase price.** The government charges stamp duty to first time residential buyers if the purchase price is greater than €190,000 (2003) and provided that the property is used as the main property. Stamp duty is charged to second time buyers or purchasers of investment property if the

purchase price is greater than €127,000 (2003). These figures may change in future Budgets.
- **Legal fees.** There is a significant amount of legal work involved in buying a home. Legal fees may amount to 2 per cent of the purchase price. Always check the costs with the solicitor beforehand.
- **Valuation report.** The lender will require a professional valuation of the property, to check that the property is good security for the mortgage. It is important to choose a firm that belongs to a recognised professional body. The lender may carry out their own valuation using their own surveyor. This saves the client having to employ an independent surveyor.

   A valuation report indicates what a property is worth. It will not show if it is structurally sound, if the wiring is safe and so on.
- **Structural survey.** A structural survey is necessary for homes that are not new.

   A structural survey indicates the likely cost for any repairs or renovations that are needed.
- **Registration of title.** The solicitor will register the property in your name.

Other costs might include:
- decoration
- furniture
- carpets and curtains

Fortunately, buying a home is not all fees and costs; one financial incentive still exists. Income tax relief is available on the interest paid on the mortgage provided that the property is the main residence of the applicant. The amount of tax relief allowed may change from Budget to Budget.

Choosing the right mortgage

There are two basic types of mortgage:

1. ANNUITY OR REPAYMENT MORTGAGE

This is the most straightforward type of mortgage. Part of the loan is paid off each month, plus the outstanding interest. In the early years, the amount of the principal repaid is low, because interest charges account for most of each payment.

Annuity mortgages suit first-time homebuyers because the current income tax legislation allows tax relief on mortgage interest.

2. ENDOWMENT MORTGAGE

This is a means of combining mortgage repayment with savings through a life assurance policy. Interest is paid on the full loan throughout the mortgage term and this qualifies for tax relief.

Monthly contributions are also paid to an endowment policy, which will pay off the loan in the event of death.

By the end of the mortgage term the value of the policy should be sufficient to repay the mortgage in full and, perhaps return a cash surplus to the borrower as well.

VARIABLE AND FIXED-RATE MORTGAGES

Irrespective of the type of mortgage, the borrower can choose either a variable or fixed rate of interest. Both have advantages and disadvantages.

A variable mortgage rate will fluctuate in line with general interest rate movements.

A fixed rate mortgage provides stability and makes budgeting easier.

However, if interest rates go down, borrowers with a variable mortgage rate will benefit whereas borrowers with fixed interest rates will not benefit from a reduction in their repayments.

Finding the right house

Consider the following factors in the search for the right house:

- Where do you want to live? Do you want to be close to work, friends and/or family?
- Do you prefer to live in the country or the town?
- How many rooms do you want in the house (or, more realistically, how many do you need)?
- Do you want a garden?
- Do you want an old or new house?

It is a good idea to visit the area at different times of the day to check on traffic and noise.

Evaluate neighbouring properties. Do they enhance the value of your chosen property?

Check on the development plans for the area to see if they include further housing.

Contact an estate agent or auctioneer and inform them of the type of property you are interested in and the price range you are considering.

How to buy your new home

Once a suitable house has been located and the survey is satisfactory, it is time to make an offer.

Consult with the estate agent on what he/she thinks would be a reasonable offer. No offer is legally binding until the contracts have been signed.

Be aware of the possibility of 'gazumping' – that is the seller agreeing to sell a property at the stated price, and then reneguing on the agreement by selling to a higher bidder before the legally binding contract is signed.

For a new property, it is normal to be asked for a booking deposit before the builder has actually started work. The money is usually paid either to the builder's agent or to the auctioneer handling the sale on behalf of the builder.

When purchasing a new house it is important to be aware of HOMEBOND. This is a service provided by the National House Building Guarantee Company, through registered builders, to purchasers of new privately built houses and apartments. It provides a guarantee under three headings as follows:

1 Against loss of deposit in the event of bankruptcy or liquidation of the builder.
2 A Two-Year Defects Warranty against water and smoke penetration for two years after completion.
3 A Ten-Year Defects Warranty against major structural defects occurring within 10 years after completion and certification by HOMEBOND.

Before entering into a purchase arrangement check if the house is registered with HOMEBOND.

GETTING A VALUATION   A valuation/surveyor's report is required to make sure that the property is good security for the mortgage loan and that it is worth at least what is being borrowed.

A valuation is only an inspection of the visible and accessible interior and exterior of a property. It is advisable to pay for a more detailed structural report, particularly if it is an older property that is being purchased.

LEGAL MATTERS   A solicitor should be used for the 'conveyance'. This is the legal work attached to buying a property.

The solicitor will check the title to the property and also that there are no restrictions on the seller's rights – such as rights of residence.

Other checks will include that there are no boundary disputes with neighbours and that the previous owners have complied with planning permission for extensions, for example.

The solicitor will also check that the documentation is acceptable to the mortgage lender, see that the stamp duty is paid and oversee the exchange of contracts.

It is good practice to get an estimate of fees before engaging a solicitor and perhaps to contact two or three solicitors to check and compare their estimates of the probable costs.

Building a house

In recent years it has become popular for people to buy a site and organise the planning and building of a house that serves their requirements.

The most important consideration is to ensure that the rooms are of adequate size. After size comes character, whether this is in sympathy or in contrast with existing rooms.

Different people can help with the various aspects of the building project.

Architect

An architect is probably essential whatever the project size. The architect will provide advice on choosing the site, on the best design to suit individual requirements, on building costs, running costs and the building regulations.

The architect will develop a project brief with the client and make the designs.

If instructed he/she will make planning applications, advise on building contractors, obtain competitive quotations, monitor and certify the quality of construction work on site.

Builder

The services of a good builder are essential so as to ensure good quality work at a fair price.

A builder may be selected by the architect or by reference to previous clients. A single builder may be employed as the main contractor, who may in turn subcontract some of the more specialist work.

This procedure makes it easier to control the overall cost and reduce the time required to complete the building work.

Before appointing a contractor, check that the builder is registered with HOMEBOND, the scheme operated by the Construction Industry Federation.

Once the builder has been selected, the architect will prepare the contract documents and forward them along with the drawings and specifications to the builder for completion. At this stage the builder will be able to provide projected start and finish dates.

Direct labour

Direct labour is when the client decides not to employ a builder and instead employs the tradespeople and labourers directly. This practice is time consuming and necessitates a good understanding of the steps involved in the construction process by the client.

Work on site

The architect or his/her agent visits the site on a regular basis to check that work is carried out in accordance with the Contract Documents.

The architect will also value the work as it proceeds and will advise by way of Architect's Certificates that money is owed to the builder.

Payments may be made at fixed stages (for example, on completion of the external walls, the roof, the wiring and so on) but more often work is valued and paid for at fixed intervals, perhaps monthly.

A percentage (usually 10%) of the value of the work is retained for approximately twelve months as a surety against the proper completion of the job.

In addition to the architect's inspections HOMEBOND inspectors will require to see the work at certain stages to check the construction from the point of view of their guarantees.

Social and affordable housing

Access to affordable housing is an essential element of economic and social policy. Failure to address the housing needs of a growing population would impose significant costs and constraints on economic growth, competitiveness and social development.

The general principle of the housing policy objective by the State is that those who can afford to do so should provide for their own housing needs, either through home ownership or private rented accommodation. Those who are unable to provide for their own housing needs should have access to social housing.

The overall aim of public housing policy is to *enable every household to have available an affordable dwelling of good quality, suited to its needs, in a good environment and as far as possible at the tenure of its choice.*

This aim is pursued through five approaches:

- Overseeing and maintaining an appropriate national housing programme.
- Facilitating home ownership for the greatest number of households who desire and can afford it.
- Developing and supporting a responsive social housing sector.
- Developing and maintaining a framework for an efficient private rented sector.

- Developing and maintaining appropriate measures to secure conservation and improvement of the housing stock.

The demand for social and affordable housing is increasing in parallel with the increase in house prices. Social housing needs were traditionally met by the provision of local authority housing for rent. A number of new schemes are now in place and include the following.

Social housing

The social housing policy focuses on addressing the housing needs of eligible persons under Part V of the Planning and Development Act, 2000. A number of important principles have been recognised in this housing strategy, namely:

- The planning authority will engage in active dialogue with developers in relation to the transfer of lands or sites.
- The planning authority would prefer to reach agreement with the developer for the provision of houses (rather than sites or land).
- The design and mix of social and affordable housing will be determined through negotiating agreements with developers under Part V of the Planning and Development Act.

Changes to the Planning and Development (Amendment) Bill, 2002 were introduced to allow more housing for those in greatest needs. The 20% provision for social and affordable housing remains.

The new arrangements will allow for land, houses or sites to be provided at alternative locations, land exchanges between developers and authorities or make a payment to a local authority fund to provide social and affordable housing. All arrangements agreed must be fully in compliance with local housing strategies and development plans and must ensure social integration.

Shared ownership

The Shared Ownership System offers home ownership in a number of steps to those who cannot afford full ownership in one step in the traditional way. Initially, ownership of the house is shared between the shared owner and the local authority.

Affordable housing scheme

The Affordable Housing Scheme provides for the building of new houses in areas where house prices have created an affordability gap for lower income house purchasers. The houses will be offered for sale to eligible first-time purchasers at cost price, and, accordingly, at a significant discount from the market value of comparable houses in the area.

Disabled persons grant

Local authorities may pay a grant for the provision of additional accommodation or necessary works of adaptation to a house to meet the needs of a disabled member of the household.

Chapter 5

What is a dwelling?

Introduction

The first dwellings can be traced back to the Stone Age. The designs of this era do not compare well with present-day designs, but the basic structure was evident. These dwellings consisted of a floor, walls, a roof and a way to get in and out.

Over time, architects and designers re-designed some of the early building elements, but the basic design structure remains the same.

A dwelling is best described as a place of residence. It is a place of comfort and security, a place where the occupants feel 'at home'.

These attributes are achieved through proper planning and design, which includes:

- Planning the relationship of living spaces within the dwelling to suit individual needs.
- Designing for life as well as for living (in other words, ensuring that the dwelling will serve the future needs of the occupants).
- Designing for inclusion. Dwellings must be accessible to everyone, including people with disabilities.

Designing a dwelling

A dwelling is a building based on individual needs. Its design requires a particular approach if it is to accommodate properly the needs of its occupants.

Modern buildings are often described as being soulless or dehumanised. This is a result of the modern formal approach to architecture. People are rarely taken into account in building design. Formal architectural practice makes no room for the individual, but only for the notional 'standard' human being that might use the finished building.

Project brief

The first stage in designing a dwelling is to prepare a project brief. The brief is a written description of the dwelling to be designed. It covers all aspects of the building, from the relationship of rooms to one another, location, orientation, size, cost, heating, insulation, construction methods and so on.

Balancing the various considerations identified in the brief is the process of design. Writing a brief is the best way to plan the sort of house you want and decide how best to achieve it.

Planning interiors

The external aspect and view have a direct bearing on how a dwelling is inhabited. The plan layout of any dwelling is as much influenced by what is outside as what is needed inside.

Take advantage of south-westerly aspect for rooms that might be inhabited in the evening. Locate bedrooms on the east-facing side of the house for people who like to wake to the morning sun.

The location of adjacent dwellings or external views influences the siting and facing direction of a new dwelling. The relationships between rooms or living spaces may also influence the form a dwelling takes.

The kitchen

In the Middle Ages, the kitchen, with its fireplace, was the central room in a house. Later, closed fireplaces were constructed in the form of stoves. Cupboards, sinks, and plate racks were fixed to the wall.

The kitchen in a modern house is a busy room filled with equipment. In some situations it is combined with a dining area.

Kitchens are categorised according to their shape and size. They fall into one of the following basic arrangements:

- **Galley:** units and appliances are positioned on opposite walls. This style is only suitable for one or two people.

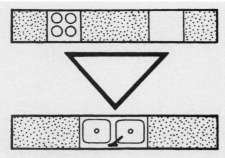

5-1 Galley kitchen layout

- **L-shaped:** appliances and units are on two adjacent walls.

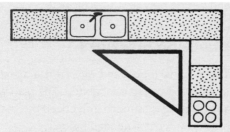

5-2 L-shaped kitchen layout

- **U-shaped:** appliances and units are arranged on three walls. This is considered the best arrangement because it is safe and efficient.

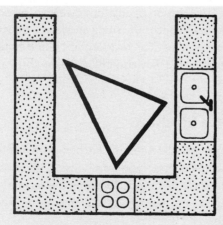

5-3 U-shaped kitchen layout

- **Line-a-wall:** units and appliances are placed on one wall. This style is only suitable for one or two people.

WORK TRIANGLE

Position the fridge, cooker and sink close together to form an invisible work triangle. This makes for an efficient kitchen and reduces the amount of unnecessary walking between appliances.

The smaller the work triangle, the more efficient is the work area. The recommended total length of the perimeter of the work triangle is between four and seven metres. Do not have doors interfering with the work triangle.

LIGHTING, SAFETY AND ERGONOMICS

Lighting (both natural and artificial), and ventilation are important in a kitchen to maintain a comfortable environment.

Switches, controls, means of escape and safety measures must accommodate all users.

Heights and locations of appliances and units must suit the user.

5-4 Designing and positioning kitchen units to suit human needs is referred to as ergonomics.

Kitchen types

The function of the kitchen determines what type of kitchen it is. There are a number of ways to determine the type of kitchen:

THE KITCHEN FOR COOKING The kitchen is designated solely for cooking and is separate from the dining area. The work triangle is particularly important in this situation.

THE KITCHEN/LIVING ROOM The kitchen is combined with the living room to become the heart of the dwelling, and the centre for gathering, cooking and dining. Such a room has many requirements and several spaces may need to be defined within the room.

THE KITCHEN/DINETTE This combination is used in conjunction with a formal dining room or as an alternative to it. If there is a dining room and it is used on a regular basis then the dinette area of the kitchen can be kept to a minimum, perhaps restricted to a breakfast bar.

The dining room

The dining room may form part of the kitchen or be a separate room. Its function is to cater for all family meals, and on occasions, entertaining family and friends.

Approaches to dining and use of the dining room vary throughout the world. The ideal that the family meal is a daily social event is fast-disappearing, with people rarely at home for meals at the same time.

Rooms for entertaining guests are best with a south-westerly aspect, to avail of evening light. A view of the garden, or doors opening onto an external patio area, might be appropriate to facilitate barbecues on summer evenings.

Dining areas located near the kitchen facilitate quick serving of food and speedy removal of dirty dishes. A serving hatch can divide the kitchen from the dining area. Sliding doors allow the kitchen to be separated from the dining area when entertaining.

Dining room style

A simple style that blends with the kitchen is best. Informal furniture in natural materials adds cosy warmth.

Formal dining rooms with expensive tables and chairs, a sideboard and a display cabinet are unlikely to be for everyday use.

Focus lighting in the dining area on the dining table. A rise-and-fall fitting is sometimes used to ensure that people see what they are eating.

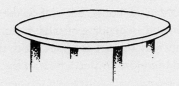

5-5 *A rise-and-fall light fitting*

Carpet is not essential in dining areas. Parquet flooring, cork tiles, finished wood or quarry tiles can be more effective and interesting. Durability is the main consideration when choosing a floor covering or finish.

Typical wall finishes consist of vinyl emulsion paint or wallpaper. They are durable and yet look sophisticated.

Central heating will create a comfortable temperature, but do not position the table too near radiators. Some people might find it too warm.

The living room

The living room is the gathering space in the home. Also called sitting room, lounge, family room, drawing room or parlour, it has many functions and styles. The lifestyle of the occupants of the dwelling dictates the type of room it becomes. The choice rests between a room in impeccable condition or a clean, comfortable, stylish room reflecting a well-lived in, relaxing room for people to enjoy.

Careful planning is required to create a successful living room. Consider the following:

- What activities will take place in the room – relaxation, study, TV, conversation, music, reading, hobbies?
- What other rooms will be connected to the living room?
- Will it be used as an access route and have lots of people walking through it?
- Will there be convenient access to the connecting rooms, to windows, doors, lighting etc.?
- How can the furniture be best arranged to allow easy flow patterns to be established?

The majority of living rooms are multi-purpose rooms. The most desirable living room consists of a well-proportioned large room with sufficient floor space and a window or French door overlooking a patio or garden area.

Traditionally, the heart of the living room is the fireplace, which acts as the room's focal point. Do not underestimate the appeal of a fire in winter for comfort and warmth.

5-6 *The fireplace is the focal point of the living room.*

Apply a floor covering that is comfortable, durable, stain- and dirt-resistant.

Provide direct lighting with moveable table lamps and standard lamps. Wall fittings provide background lighting. Dimmer switches allow light intensity to be controlled. Special lights focused on paintings create points of interest in the room.

An open fire or flame-effect fire is the key to a comfortable room. Central heating is ideal to maintain even temperatures throughout the room.

The bedroom

Bedrooms have different requirements, depending on who the user is and what their preferences are. Bedrooms are primarily somewhere to sleep, and so must be relaxing, but may also have other functions such as study, hobbies, etc.

There are no rules dictating where bedrooms are located within the house. Some people wish to sleep at the top of their homes while others like the idea of being able to open French doors onto a garden area.

More practical requirements may influence sleeping arrangements, like the need to be near a bathroom or childrens' rooms at night.

Master bedrooms usually contain an en-suite bath or shower room, and perhaps a walk-in-wardrobe.

The bathroom

Bathrooms in large private homes were not unknown in the 18th century. Splendidly equipped marble bathrooms are still preserved in several European palaces and mansions.

Bathrooms did not become commonplace until the 19th century. Fixtures may include a toilet, bidet, washbasin, bath, mirror, and shelves.

The equipping of bathrooms became a separate industry in the 20th century with a wide variety of special forms of bathroom furniture and fixtures. The materials used are porcelain, enamel, plastic, wood, and stainless steel.

The planning of a bathroom depends on its relationship with other rooms and on what other washing facilities are provided elsewhere in the home. A bathroom may not be required if each of the bedrooms have en-suite shower rooms.

The bathroom is increasingly treated as a place of relaxation and leisure. Many bathrooms incorporate saunas and jacuzzi features. It is important to finalise the bathroom layout at

the planning stage, because once the sanitary fittings are positioned they cannot be easily moved unlike other furniture.

The traditional bathroom layout consisted of the bath along one wall and the basin and toilet on the other. Consider alternatives, for instance, a long narrow bathroom would allow the basin, shower and bath to be built into one wall.

A bath takes on added appeal if either raised above or sunk into the floor.

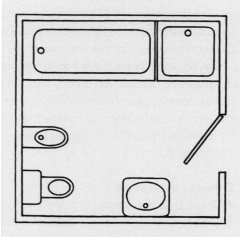

5-7 *Traditional bathroom layout would not have included a shower or a bidet.*

The utility room

A utility room is usually found in larger homes. The washing machine and tumble dryer are most likely located here, but any of the following may also be located in the utility room: a boiler, a sink for vegetable preparation, a WC area, clothes drying area, ironing space with permanent or collapsible ironing board, built-in shelves or wall-mounted units.

Consider exactly which items are to be stored in the utility room. The utility room is usually the smallest room in the house, but is often the room in greatest demand, depending on what is stored there.

The utility may also act as a back porch to the kitchen and therefore conserve heat to the kitchen.

Hallways and porches

The function of a hall or porch is to create an area between inside and outside, to allow visitors to shed their coats and also to prevent draughts entering the rest of the house. Consider which other rooms it would be desirable to enter from the hall.

Human comfort

Comfort is subjective. No set of conditions will satisfy all occupants simultaneously.

In designing for comfort it is usual to take account of people's adaptive behaviour and to allow them some degree of control over their immediate environment.

What makes people feel comfortable inside buildings?

People have a more relaxed attitude to variations in the interior climate if conditions in a building are natural rather than artificial. People need some degree of control over their own environment.

Glare caused by the sun is less offensive than glare from a light fitting. The 'breeze' from the window opened by oneself is more acceptable than if it had come from a central air-conditioning system.

Thermal comfort

Thermal comfort depends on the balance between heat gains from the internal metabolism of the body and heat losses to the environment.

People get uncomfortable if the body loses heat too quickly or too slowly. Some of the variables are environmental – air temperature, air speed, mean radiant temperature and humidity. Others are personal – clothing, body weight, activity level, subjective factors and adaptation.

> **Humidity** is a measure of the amount of moisture in the air.
> **Relative humidity** is the mass of water vapour present in the air expressed as a percentage of the mass that would be present in an equal volume of saturated air at the same temperature.
> **Absolute humidity** is the humidity of the atmosphere expressed as the number of grams of water contained in 1 cubic metre of air.

The **mean radiant temperature** of room surfaces is as important for comfort as the air temperature.

An increase in mean radiant temperature allows comfort conditions to be achieved at lower air temperatures.

A reduction of 1°C in room temperature can save up to 10 per cent in energy consumption.

Poorly insulated buildings have cold interior surfaces. They need higher air temperatures to compensate. Therefore, insulation saves energy not only by reducing building heat loss, but also by increasing air temperatures.

People can be made very uncomfortable by radiant asymmetry. This relates to where one surface has a radiant temperature considerably different from others in the room.

Single-glazed windows, cold floors and overhead heat sources are often to blame.

Abnormal differences in air temperature between head and feet also cause discomfort.

A difference of more than 30°C should be avoided. People generally feel comfortable if their feet are slightly warmer than their heads.

The higher the air speed, the greater is the rate of body heat loss through convection and evaporation.

Ireland's high relative humidity is a problem only in under-heated buildings in winter, where 'dampness' increases discomfort.

Visual comfort

Poor lighting may cause eyestrain, headaches, fatigue and irritability. It can also cause accidents.

For visual comfort, people need the right intensity and direction of illumination for the task they are engaged in, together with ambient lighting.

> **Ambient** refers to the immediate surroundings.

They also need good colour rendering, freedom from glare and some variety in lighting quality.

Acoustic comfort

High noise levels are very irritating. Very high noise levels cause distress and permanent damage to hearing. Natural ventilation implies open windows, which may result in obtrusive traffic noise or loss of sound privacy. If carpeting is omitted to limit the

> **Impact noise** sources include footsteps, slammed doors, vibrating machinery etc.

problem of house dust mites, or to allow the structure to act as a thermal store, consider taking other measures to reduce the transmission of impact noise.

Air quality

Compared with the other comfort variables, this is the one about which there is the most uncertainty.

The traditional problems of stuffiness and odour can be resolved by ventilation provided that the outdoor air is of acceptable quality.

> **Radon** a colourless, odourless, tasteless gas generated by the radioactive decay of radium.

Prevent radon build-up, in areas where it is known to be a risk, by sealing solid floors or providing sub-floor ventilation.

Energy rating

Most homes are poorly insulated. Much of the heat escapes into the outside atmosphere, resulting in higher than necessary energy usage to keep the home at a comfortable temperature.

An average poorly insulated house in Ireland typically consumes 600 kilowatts of energy per year for every square metre of floor area occupied. This level is required to maintain reasonable comfort levels. It includes all heating, cooking, lighting and power requirements.

Increasing insulation can reduce energy costs.

Sustainable Energy Ireland has introduced a system of energy ratings for all buildings. This Energy Rating will serve as a benchmark for the energy performance of a building.

An Energy Rating indicates the amount of energy required in a home for space and water heating to maintain a high standard of comfort.

The rating is given in terms of the number of kWh of energy required per square metre per year. The lower the energy rating, the less fuel required. This saves money and benefits the environment.

The Energy Rating of a house is influenced by its construction (insulation levels, types of windows, walls etc.) and other factors such as the type of heating system and controls.

Many older Irish houses have a rating at over 1000 kWh/m². Lower energy ratings are recorded in homes with an efficient heating system or in properties built with superior insulation levels.

It is possible to achieve an energy rating of less than 250 kWh/m² with proper detailing and an efficient heating system

In the future all buildings will need to be energy audited to establish their Energy Rating and their effect on the environment.

Heat energy rating software and energy audits are available to download from the internet. These tools allow a room-by-room analysis, identifying the home improvement projects that will make the greatest energy savings and reduce energy bills.

Solar heat gains

A building gains heat energy as well as losing it, and it is usual for both processes to occur at the same time.

In a country like Ireland, the overall gains are less than the losses, but the gains may still give useful energy savings.

The heat gained in a building by heat radiation from the sun depends on the following:
- latitude of the site
- season of the year
- orientation of the building on the site
- local weather
- type of windows
- type of roof and walls
- angles between the rays of the sun and the building surfaces.

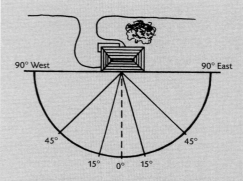

5-8 *Orientation. A house can be angled as much as 15 degrees east or west of true south and still be energy efficient.*

5-9 *Trees and overhangs on the south side of a house may block the high summer sun, while allowing the low winter sun to passively heat the house.*

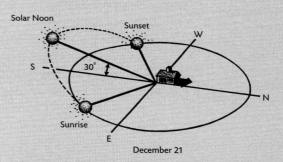

5-10 *Angle of winter sun is 30 degrees from horizon at solar noon*

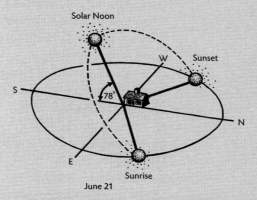

5-11 *Angle of summer sun is 78 degrees from horizon at solar noon*

The rate at which heat from the sun falls on a surface varies throughout the day and the year.

Most solar heat gain in Irish buildings is by direct radiation through windows. The maximum gains occur through south-facing windows in spring and autumn when the lower angle of the sun causes radiation to fall more directly onto vertical surfaces.

This type of heat gain is useful for winter heating, but it can cause discomfort at other times.

Sun controls are parts of a building that help prevent excessive heat gain and glare (very bright and intense light) caused by direct sunshine. The main types of device used include:

- External controls which consist of shutters, projecting eaves or floor slabs. These are the most effective form of sun control.
- Internal controls typically consist of curtains and blinds. These give protection against glare and direct radiation but they can re-emit heat inside the room.
- Special glass is now available that prevents the transmission of most heat radiation with only some loss of light transmission.

Casual heat gains take account of heat given off by various activities and equipment in a building, which were not designed to give off heat. Casual heat sources include:

- Heat from cooking and water heating
- Heat from people
- Heat from equipment, such as refrigerators and electrical appliances.
- Heat from lighting.

This type of heat gain can be considerable in industrial or public buildings. It must be considered when designing the heating and cooling systems.

Casual heat gain in houses is useful in winter. As houses become better insulated, it forms a higher proportion of the total heat needed.

Fire safety

Part B of the Building Regulations specifies the general requirements for fire safety in all buildings, including housing.

Conventional housing is exempt from the requirements for a Fire Safety Certificate under Building Control Regulations. However, in the case of apartments and bed-and-breakfast type accommodation, a Fire Safety Certificate is usually required.

Means of escape

The Building Regulations have been prepared on the basis that the occupants of any part of a building should be able to escape safely from a building in an emergency without external assistance.

The design of means of escape from a building must be based on an appreciation on the probable behaviour of fire. Fire may break out in any part of the building and then spread to other parts.

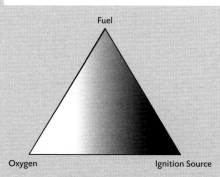

5-12 The fire triangle. If any one of these is missing, a fire cannot start. Taking steps to avoid the three coming together will reduce the chances of a fire occurring.

Fires do not normally start in two different places in a building at the same time.

Initially a fire will create a hazard only where it starts. Subsequently it may spread to other parts, usually along the circulation routes of the building.

Furnishings, equipment, services and plant are among the usual sources of origin.

Smoke and noxious gases produced by the fire are the primary danger associated with fire in its early stages. Most of the casualties in fires are caused by smoke. Smoke also obscures the way to escape routes and exits.

Measures designed to provide safe means of escape must include provisions to limit the spread of smoke and fumes.

In single-storey and two-storey dwellings, the internal layout usually provides an acceptable level of escape routes for the occupants.

The following points should be noted:
- Stairs should discharge within 4.5 m of an external door.
- Stairs should not discharge into a kitchen.
- Detection/alarm system to be provided.
- All habitable rooms in the upper storey should be provided with windows (or doors) suitable for escape or rescue.

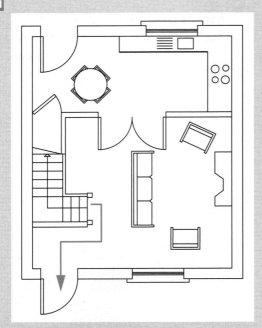

5-13 *Stairs should discharge within 4.5 m of an external door.*

In all houses, regardless of plan form, windows (or doors) suitable for escape or rescue must be provided from inner rooms and bedrooms.

A window designed for escape or rescue must provide an unobstructed opening of not less than 850 mm high by 500 mm wide. The bottom of this opening to be between 800 mm and 1100 mm above floor level. It should be located above an area of ground that is:

- free from permanent obstruction which may impede escape or rescue;
- suitable for the use of a ladder to provide rescue from the window; and
- readily accessible for ladder access to windows by fire brigade personnel.

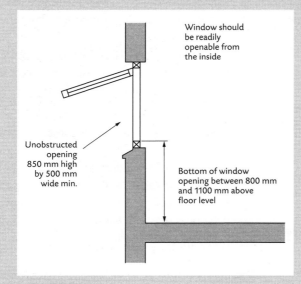

5-14 *Escape window*

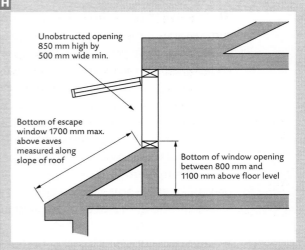

5-15 *Escape through a dormer window*

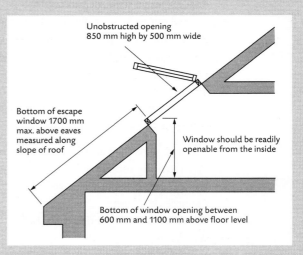

5-16 *Escape through a roof-light*

The installation of a fire detection and alarm system is considered essential to ensure early escape in the event of a fire.

A detection and alarm system should be installed in all houses in accordance with the following guidelines:

- The number and location of detectors will depend on the type and layout of the house.
  - In a typical two-storey, three–four bedroom house, locate detectors in the hallway and above the first floor landing.
  - In bungalows, the corridor between living and sleeping accommodation is a suitable location.
- Locate detectors on ceilings at least 300 mm from walls and light fittings.
- Locate detectors where they are readily accessible for testing and maintenance.
- Locate detectors in circulation areas so that no door to a habitable room is more than 7.5 m from a detector.

Wall and ceiling linings

Plastered surfaces are acceptable for both wall and ceiling linings. Other materials are restricted in use.

Untreated timber sheeting, for example, may only be used in small panels of 5.0 m² or less in wall linings only. Where two or more of these panels are used they must be separated from each other by a minimum of 2 m. The total area of untreated timber panels in any room must not exceed 20 m² or half the floor area of the room, whichever is less.

Alternatively, sheeting may be treated by a fire retardant varnish or paint, to give it a 'Class 1' Surface Spread of Flame rating.

Timber sheeting fixed directly to the underside of floor joists will not provide the recommended level of fire resistance for ceilings. The ceiling should be formed by plasterboard in the usual way with the timber sheeting fixed to the plasterboard.

Polystyrene tiles are not permitted as a ceiling finish.

> **Class 0** recognises the highest level of fire protection.
> **Class 10** recognises the lowest or no level of fire protection.

Fire resistance

The nature of conventional house construction is such that the standard requirements for fire resistance for floors and walls are automatically met by such construction.

Doors forming direct connections between garages and areas within houses should be of the self-closing type FD 30 (a fire door of 30 minute integrity), and should open over a 100 mm upstand or step down from the house to the garage.

Any garage attached to a house must be separated from the rest of the house by walls, floors or ceilings having full half-hour fire resistance.

> **Party wall** the wall separating two houses in a block of semi-detached houses.

Fire-stopping of party walls is essential to ensure that fire does not spread from house to house.

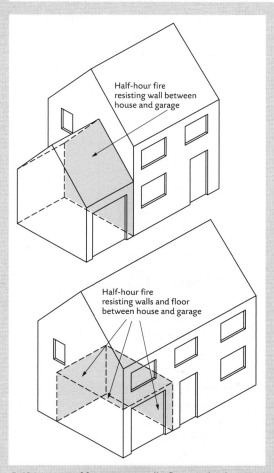

5-18 *Location of fire-resisting walls, floors and ceilings*

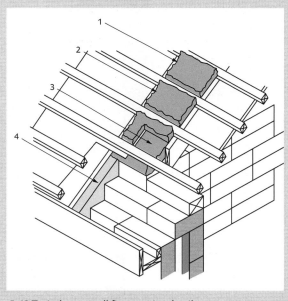

5-19 *Typical party wall fire-stopping detail*

1 cavity fire stopping to underside of roof covering
2 mineral fibre quilt
3 mineral fibre quilt along top of wall to underside of felt
4 50 mm thick wire reinforced mineral quilt

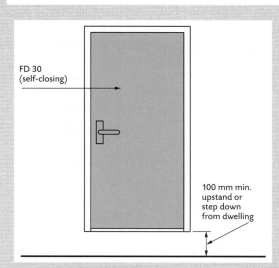

5-17 *Firedoor separating garage from rest of house*

FD 30
(self-closing)

100 mm min. upstand or step down from dwelling

In houses of masonry construction, it is not required to provide fire stopping in the form of a vertical cavity barrier at the junction of the party wall and the external wall, provided that the cavity wall around the doors and windows is closed.

The typical details employed to close the cavity at these points are shown in Figs. 5-20 to 5-23.

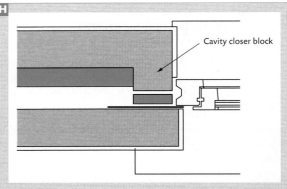

5-22 *Cavity closer block used to close the vertical jamb*

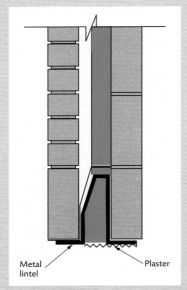

5-20 *Cavity closed at head using a metal lintel. A lintel that incorporates insulation is better.*

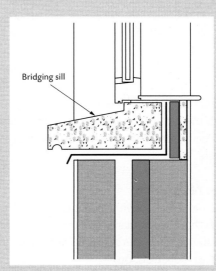

5-23 *Cavity closed at sill by means of a bridging sill*

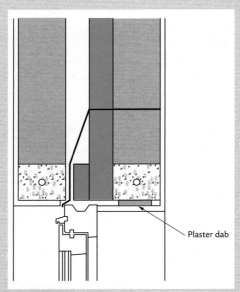

5-21 *Plasterboard fixed by dabs is required to close the cavity when using a pre-stressed concrete lintel.*

Roof coverings are required to prevent penetration of fire and flame spread on their surfaces.

The common roofing materials, such as concrete tiles and fibre cement slates, readily meet these requirements.

Flat roofing materials may need additional protection to achieve compliance. Bituminous felt, for example, needs to be covered with bitumen-bedded chippings when used as a roof finish close to boundaries.

Design for inclusion

Equality of access for everybody to the built environment is an essential prerequisite of equal opportunity and the development of an inclusive society.

Normal health, **normal height** and other similar concepts mean different things depending on gender, age and many other factors.

There is a significant proportion of the population whose faculties and abilities, whether physical, intellectual or emotional, are impaired, either temporarily or permanently.

Impairment refers to a condition of the body or mind that limits or makes impossible someone's ability to undertake a particular task.

The environment contributes to impairment. For example, a polished circular doorknob may prevent a person with poor grip from opening a door, while a lever handle may make the task easier. Alternatively, automatic doors cancel the poor grip condition.

Therefore, it is environments, not impairments, that enable or disable.

A report* asserts that 'access is the gateway to full participation in society for people with disabilities' and recommends that 'the universal right of access for all citizens becomes the over-arching principle which guides all relevant legislation, policy and practice in Ireland'.

*The report of the Commission on the Status of People with Disabilities – 1996

Technological advances provide useful solutions, but it is attitude to inclusive design and building management that makes the real difference.

The Building Regulations state that housing built from 2000 onwards must be 'socially accessible', i.e. both visitable and habitable by people with disabilities.

Implications of the Building Regulations in relation to access for people with disabilities will be dealt with under the following headings:

- Approach to a dwelling
- Access into a dwelling
- Circulation within a dwelling
- Use of facilities in a dwelling

Approach to a dwelling

For people with disabilities, the route from a site boundary or car park to the building entrance can be difficult to negotiate.

A building should not present hazards on circulation routes immediately adjacent to it.

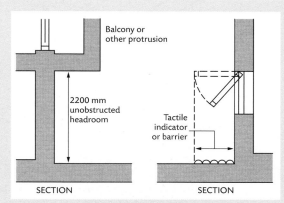

5-24 *Avoid external hazards so that people with disabilities may safely and independently access and use a building.*

Provide steps or ramps where it is not possible to make the approach level. Follow the Building Regulations' specific conditions in relation to external steps.

Design distances to be travelled from the road, public footpath or car park to the building entrance to be as short as possible. Some people with poor mobility move very slowly and may need rest periods of up to 2 minutes after travelling a distance of 30 metres.

Windows and doors in general use should not open out, nor should any section of the building protrude so as to cause a hazard on a path along the face of the building.

At least one entrance on the boundary of the dwelling should have a minimum clear opening of 800 mm.

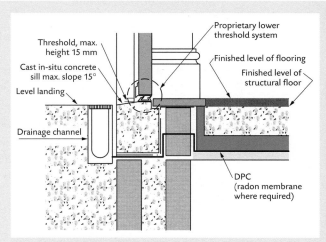

5-25a *Typical threshold detail at wheelchair accessible entrance*

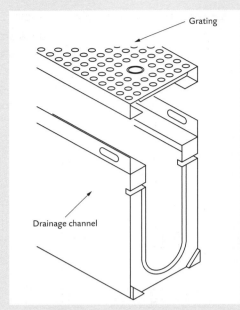

5-25b *Typical proprietary drainage channel assembly*

At least one entrance to the dwelling, preferably the main entrance, should be accessible to wheelchair users. There should be a clear area of at least 1.2 m × 1.2 m in front of every such entrance.

The approach to the entrance from the adjacent road, carpark or other area accessible to motor vehicles should be level (i.e. gradient less than 1:50). If a gradient is required, e.g. to remove surface water, make sure it is as gentle as circumstances allow.

Provide a clear unobstructed approach to the building of at least 1.0 metre wide. Ensure that this approach has a surface that is suitable for wheelchair traffic.

Access into a dwelling

Design an accessible entrance to meet the following regulations:

- Provide a doorway with a minimum clear opening width of 800 mm.
- Provide 300 mm of minimum unobstructed space on the side next to the leading edge of a single-leaf door (Fig. 5-26).
- Incorporate a glazed vision panel in the door (where feasible and practicable). See Fig. 5-27.
- Use **ironmongery** suitable for people with disabilities. See Fig. 5-28.
- Ensure that doors fitted with self-closing devices are suitable for people with disabilities.

Ironmongery
builders' hardware generally used on doors and windows. Examples include handles, locks, hinges and closers, mostly made of steel but also of aluminium, nylon, brass, or bronze.

Design lobbies to allow sufficient space to enable the wheelchair user and a person assisting the wheelchair user, to move clear of one door before using the next one. Allow space for a person to pass in the opposite direction. See Fig. 5-29.

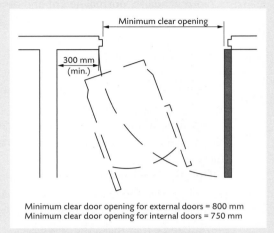

Minimum clear door opening for external doors = 800 mm
Minimum clear door opening for internal doors = 750 mm

5-26 *Minimum clear openings and clearances*

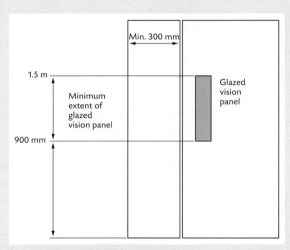

5-27 *Glazed doors – visibility to opposite side*

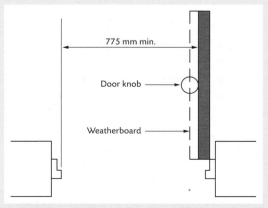

5-28 *Wheelchair accessible entrance – minimum width*

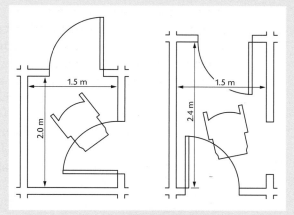

5-29 Examples of suitable entrance lobbies

Circulation within a dwelling

Design internal doors so that:

- They provide a minimum clear opening width of 750 mm.
- There is an unobstructed space of at least 300 mm on the side next to the leading edge.
- A glazed vision panel is incorporated (where feasible and practicable). The glazed panel should extend from 900 mm to 1.5 m above finished floor level (see Fig. 5-27).
- A single-pane fully glazed door or fixed panel is permanently marked within the area 1.2 m to 1.5 m above floor level. This is necessary to visually indicate the presence of a door or panel (see Fig. 5-30).
- The ironmongery is suitable for people with disabilities.

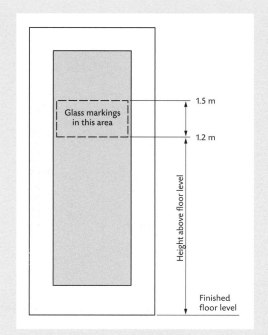

5-30 Glazed doors – visibility of side

Design corridors and lobbies accessible to wheel-chair users to have a clear unobstructed width of at least 1.2 m.

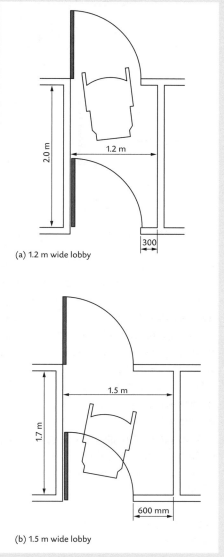

(a) 1.2 m wide lobby

(b) 1.5 m wide lobby

5-31 Suitable internal lobbies

Use of facilities in a dwelling

Design each storey of a building to allow for independent circulation by people with disabilities and independent access to the range of services and facilities provided on that storey.

Include a WC at entry level. Locate the WC so that it can be easily accessed from the accessible entrance, without the need to negotiate steps.

Locate the WC in a bathroom or separate WC compartment.

Provide a clear space of 750 mm × 1200 mm adjacent to the WC to facilitate sideways transfer from the wheelchair to the WC.

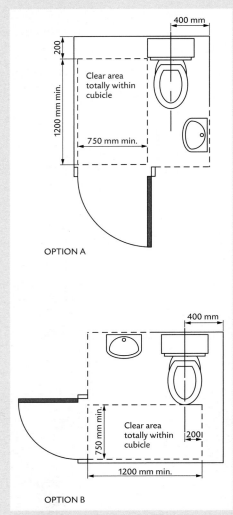

OPTION A

OPTION B

5-32 *Examples of WC cubicles for visitable housing*

The general recommendation for a WC compartment is to allow the wheelchair be fully contained within the compartment and the door closed with the wheelchair inside.

Give careful attention to the selection and location of ironmongery, taps, light switches, power points, communication facilities etc. so that they can be operated by light pressure and without unnecessary stretching, or stooping, by wheelchair users and the ambulant disabled.

Ambulant
refers to walking or being in a walking position.

Consistency of building detailing is an important part of good design for everybody. Consider the following points when detailing for people with disabilities:

- selection of wall and floor coverings;
- siting of power and plumbing outlets;
- siting and design of controls for lifts and domestic appliances;
- changes in floor finish at the top and bottom of a flight of stairs.

It can be argued that the conventional design of the home disables the very young, the elderly and people with disabilities.

Some people sell the family home when they get older and move to a 'more convenient' home or apartment. Perhaps the real reason for moving is that their home has become unusable with small bathrooms, narrow corridors, etc.

The Structure & Fabric

of Buildings

The bearing capacity of sedimentary rock depends on the angle of stratification. In Feltrim limestone quarry an inclinometer was used to find the dip of the beds to be 35 degrees in a southern direction. The beds were also found 1–2 m thick.

☞

The Boyne Bridge is a 350m long, cable-stayed, high-level bridge that carries the M1 Northern Motorway across the river Boyne to the west of Drogheda. It was the largest bridge construction project in this country in recent years. Roadstone commenced surfacing of the Boyne Bridge deck on 14 February, 2003 with the application of red sand asphalt to the southbound carriageway. The red sand asphalt layer provides protection for the waterproofing on the concrete to facilitate surfacing and also acts as a warning layer for any future work on the deck where cutting or drilling is involved.

Good foundation design is not only imperative for buildings. Sports surfaces such as Croke Park, where drainage as opposed to live loads is one of the main issues to take into consideration whilst designing foundations. The overall design of Croke Park consists of a central main drain down the centre of the pitch, with lateral drains feeding into it. A 150 mm layer of 10 mm washed pea gravel was placed on the base of the pitch, supplied by Roadstone.

Then a 250 mm layer of Sport Sand was placed on the pitch followed by a 50 mm layer of organic peat mix. These combined layers were stitched together by a very fine fibre thread, to bind the sand and peat mix together. Approximately 6,500 tonnes of sand was used in the construction of the pitch.

Farrans

Farrans Limited is a wholly owned subsidiary of CRH plc, based in Dunmurry, Belfast. The construction division specialises in building and civil engineering projects (railways, bridges, water distribution, roads etc.). The materials division produces the full range of building materials and products for the local market. Farrans is the largest building materials and contracting employer in Northern Ireland and played an important part in the construction of the impressive Odyssey Arena in Belfast.

Chapter 6

Elements of structure

Introduction

This chapter deals with the structural principles associated with buildings and their components. Many structural principles evolved from the study of natural forms and structures. We will examine the principles associated with forces and their impact on the design of structures. Examples of significant structural forms will demonstrate how new methods, materials and technologies have developed.

Natural forms and structures

By examining naturally occurring structures the structural principles behind their design becomes clear. It is easy to see how these principles are incorporated into modern day structures.

Inert
having no inherent ability to move or to resist motion.

Natural structures use live materials, whereas manufactured structures use **inert** materials. The two are unlikely to behave in the same manner.

We can learn a lot from nature. Nature has had a long time to perfect its designs, and living things have evolved into structures that are so complex and so efficient that humans' best efforts do not stand up in comparison.

Natural forms and structures may be divided into three categories:
1. structure in plants
2. structure in animals
3. structures built by animals

Structure in plants

A leaf is a perfect example of a lightweight natural structure. The main rib tapers from the base, the point where all the weight of the leaf is borne.

The other ribs emerge from the centre rib in a regular pattern and taper from the centre to the edge. A leaf is a cantilever structure, i.e. part of a structure projecting outwards beyond its support. This principle is echoed in building construction.

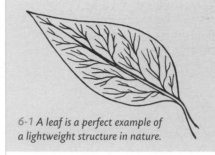

6-1 A leaf is a perfect example of a lightweight structure in nature.

Structure in animals

The structure of an insect's eye displays many parts, which are all held together and supported.

The outside surface of the eye takes the shape of a hemisphere. The modern day equivalent structure of the insect's eye is the **geodesic dome**. The geodesic dome is made up of a network of triangles.

GEODESIC DOMES are fractional parts of geodesic spheres. Geodesic spheres and domes come in various frequencies. The frequency of a dome relates to the number of smaller triangles into which it is subdivided. A high-frequency dome has more triangular components and is more smoothly curved.

A one-frequency icosahedron consists of 20 equilateral triangles. Each of these triangles can be divided into smaller triangles. A two-frequency dome results from dividing each of the icosahedron base triangles into four triangles. The side of the face of the base triangle is divided into two, thus 'two-frequency'.

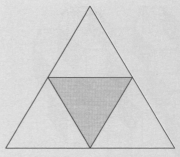

6-2 The base equilateral triangle of a 'two-frequency' dome is divided into four triangles.

Geodesic domes give the maximum amount of strength and rigidity from the minimum amount of materials. The higher the frequency, the greater the resistance of the structure to collapse.

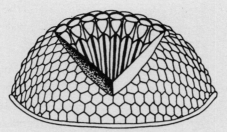

6-3 *An insect's eye is similar in structure to the geodesic dome, below.*

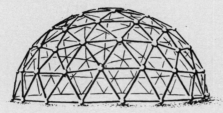

6-4 *The geodesic dome by Buckminster Fuller (see also Fig. 1-29)*

Structures built by animals

Insects and animals have developed a high level of skill in building their homes. The spider's web, the honeycomb cell structure of a beehive and the dam or lodge of a beaver are just some examples.

6-5 *The silk from which spiders' webs are spun has a higher tensile strength per cross-sectional area than steel.*

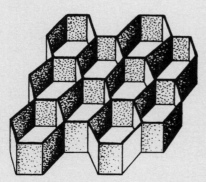

6-6 *Honeycomb cell structure of a beehive*

Spiders' webs are formed from 100% natural silk, which has a tensile strength per cross-sectional area that exceeds structural steel.

The honeycomb cell in a beehive is constructed so that it can contain the maximum amount of honey for the minimum amount of wall surface. As a result, the bees expend the minimum amount of energy when constructing the beehive.

Basic structural forms and concepts

Structures may be divided into three different forms: solid, skeletal and surface.

Solid structures

Caves and stone huts are early examples of solid structures.

Solid structures rely on solid construction such as masonry to support loads and safely transfer the loads to the ground.

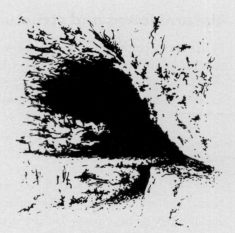

6-7 *A cave is a solid structure.*

6-8 *A stone hut is also a solid structure.*

Skeletal structures

Skeletal structures developed in response to the discovery of new materials and new methods of using existing materials.

Early examples include the tent and tent-like structures; modern examples include the geodesic dome, steel-framed and reinforced concrete-framed buildings.

Surface structures

Surface structures are a relatively new development in architecture. One of the best-known surface structures in nature is the eggshell.

Modern surface structures include the hyperbolic paraboloid and a variety of pneumatic structures.

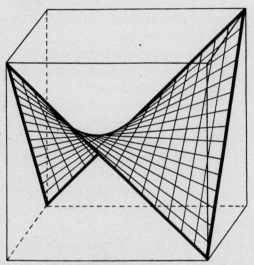

6-9 The hyperbolic paraboloid surface is a warped surface generated by a straight line moving along two straight-edged surfaces. The diagram shows a double hyperbolic paraboloid.

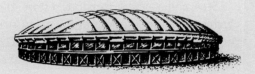

6-10 Pneumatic structures are the most cost-effective type of structure for long spans.

BC Place, Vancouver, Canada was built for the 1986 World's Fair as a multi-purpose stadium with seating for 60,000 people. The structure is a 190 m x 231 m super-ellipse in plan, and at the time of construction the world's largest air supported dome stadium. An air-supported roof consisting of two translucent teflon-coated fiberglass membranes and a two-way steel cable system is anchored to the 700 m U-shaped concrete compression beam at the top of the structure. The roof has a rise of 30 m when inflated.

Components of basic structural forms and concepts

Walls

Walls may be either **load-bearing** or **non-load-bearing**. A load-bearing wall supports the weight of floors and roofs. A non-load-bearing wall at most supports its own weight.

LOAD-BEARING WALLS A load-bearing wall of masonry construction is thickened in proportion to the forces it has to resist. These include its own weight, the load of floors, roofs, people, etc., and the lateral forces of arches, vaults, wind, etc. Its thickness can be reduced at the top, because loads accumulate toward the bottom.

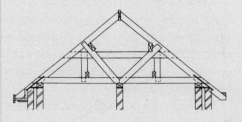

6-11 Loadbearing walls

Walls that must resist lateral forces are thickened either along the whole length or at particular points where the force is concentrated. The latter method is called **buttressing**.

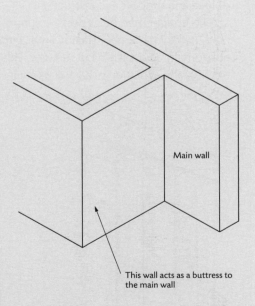

Main wall

This wall acts as a buttress to the main wall

6-12 Buttressing is a mass of masonry built against or projecting from a wall to stabilise the lateral thrust of an arch roof or vault.

Doors and windows weaken the resistance of the wall and divert the forces above them to the parts on either side. The walls on either side must be thickened in proportion to the width of the opening.

The number of openings that can be used depends on the strength of the wall material and the stresses in the wall.

The type of support required for floors and roofs determines the positions of walls in the building. The most common support is the beam. It must be jointed to walls at both ends. The maximum permissible length of the beam establishes the distance between bearing walls.

NON-LOAD-BEARING WALLS A non-load bearing wall carries no loads, except its own weight.

Modern steel and reinforced concrete frame buildings require exterior walls only for shelter. Exterior walls are sometimes dispensed with on the ground floor to permit easier access to a basement car park or to a service area, depending on the function of the building.

The wall rests or hangs upon members of the frame. It becomes a curtain, or screen, and may consist of any durable weather-resisting material.

Traditional materials may be used, but light walls of glass, plastic, metal alloys, wood products, etc., are equally efficient.

Post-and-beam

The post-and-beam system is the simplest method of load and support in construction.

Two upright members (posts, columns, piers) hold up a third member (beam, lintel, girder) laid horizontally across their top surfaces. This is the basis for the evolution of all wall openings.

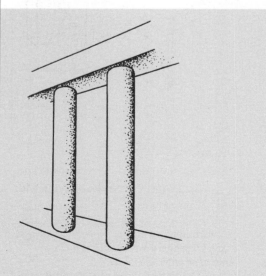

6-13 Example of the post-and-beam system

The beam must carry the loads that rest on it (and its own load) without deforming or breaking. Failure occurs if the material is too weak or if the beam is too long.

Beams composed of materials that are weak in bending, such as stone, must be short. Beam of materials that are strong in bending, such as steel, may span far greater openings.

In masonry construction, beams of monolithic (single-slab) stone, wood, and stronger materials are used.

The post must support the beam and its loads without crushing or buckling. Failure occurs, as in beams, from excessive weakness or length.

The difference with the post is that the material must be especially strong in compression. Stone, which has this property, is more versatile as a post than as a beam. Stone is superior to wood under heavy loads, but is not as strong as iron, steel, or reinforced concrete.

Masonry posts, including those of brick, are highly efficient. The loads compress the joints and add to their cohesiveness.

From prehistoric times to the Roman Empire, the post-and-beam system formed the basis of architectural design. The interiors of Egyptian temples and the exteriors of Greek temples are characterised by columns covered by stone beams. The Greeks opened their interior spaces by substituting wooden beams for stone. The wood required fewer supports.

Ancient uses of the post-and-beam were refined but not fundamentally altered until the production of cast-iron columns. These offered greater strength and smaller circumference and greatly reduced the mass and weight of buildings.

Much construction in modern materials is based on the post-and-beam system of the past.

Steel and concrete skeletons restore to modern architecture the simplicity of the oldest structures known. They abandon the fundamental concept of the duality of post-and-beam by fusing them into a unit throughout which stresses are distributed evenly. In the case of steel structures, beams are welded or mechanically jointed to columns. In reinforced concrete structures, beams and columns are mechanically jointed to act as a single unit.

Vaults

The evolution of the vault began with the discovery of the arch. The basic 'barrel' form first appeared in ancient Egypt and the Near East. It is simply a deep, or three-dimensional, arch.

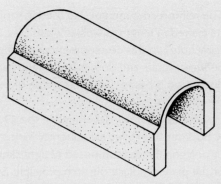

6-14 *The barrel vault can be compared to an extruded arch.*

The **barrel vault** exerts thrust in a similar way to the arch. It must be buttressed along its entire length by heavy walls. Openings must be limited in size and number. Gothic builders developed the **flying buttress** to reduce the thickness of the walls required in a barrel vault.

Thrust
is a push forward, upward or outward.

The flying buttress counteracts vault thrust not by continuous wall mass and weight, but by counterthrust. This is created by exterior half-arches placed at the height of the vaults at the points of greatest stress. These buttresses conduct stresses to heavier wall buttresses below the window level.

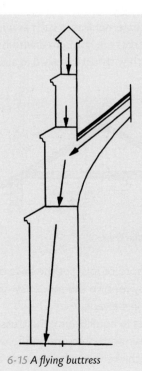

6-15 *A flying buttress*

The next important development in vaults, as in arches, came with 19th-century materials. Great iron skeleton vaults were constructed as a frame-work for light materials such as glass (Crystal Palace, London).

6-16 *Crystal Palace, London, 1851*

The elimination of weight and excessive thrust, the freedom in the use of materials, and the absence of **centring** problems favoured the simple barrel vault. It made more complex types obsolete.

Centring
refers to the curved temporary supports for an arch or dome during construction.

One of the most important innovations in the history of architecture is the reinforced-concrete shell vault. It is based on the principle of the bent or moulded slab.

The reinforced-concrete shell vault has all the advantages of load distribution of the concrete floor slab, plus the resistance to bending provided by its curved form.

The shell is reinforced so that it exerts no lateral thrust. It may be supported as if it were a beam or truss. The form no longer necessitates the conducting of loads into the wall, allowing the vault to be designed with great freedom.

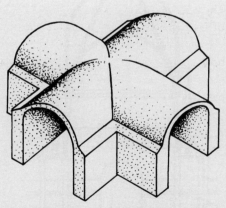

6-17 *A groined vault is a combination of simple barrel vaults.*

Domes

Domes appeared first on round huts and tombs in the ancient Near East, India, and the Mediterranean region only as solid mounds. They became techni-cally significant with the introduction of the large-scale masonry hemispheres by the Romans.

Domes, like vaults, evolved from the arch. In their simplest form they may be thought of as a continuous series of arches, with the same centre. The dome exerts thrusts all around its perimeter. The earliest monumental examples required heavy walls.

The dome was unsuited to the lightness and verticality of late-medieval styles, but was widely used in the **Renaissance** and **Baroque** periods.

Renaissance builders adapted the Gothic rib system to dome construction and found new ways to reduce loads and thrust (concentric chains, etc.). These permitted high drums and variations in the curvature of the dome.

The interior of high, domed buildings produced an awkward tunnel-like effect (as at Florence Cathedral and St. Paul's Cathedral, London).

Principally the symbolic character of the form explains the effort and ingenuity devoted to doming rectangular buildings. Vaulting is a simpler alternative.

Renaissance
the period of European history marking the waning of the Middle Ages and the rise of the modern world: usually considered as beginning in Italy in the 14th century.

Baroque
a style of architecture and decorative art that flourished throughout Europe from the late 16th to the early 18th century, characterised by extensive ornamentation.

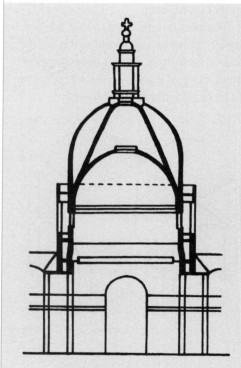

6-18 Internal shell of St. Paul's Cathedral

It was the desire to observe tradition that preserved the dome in the early era of iron and steel construction, and, with rare exceptions (Halle aux Blés, Paris; the Coal Exchange, London), nineteenth-century examples retained masonry forms without exploiting the advantages of metal.

The reinforced-concrete slab used in vaulting can be curved in length as well as width (like a parachute). In this development the distinction between vaults and domes loses significance. The distinction is based only on the type of curvature in the slab.

Geodesic domes, developed in the 1940s by R. Buckminster Fuller, are spherical forms. Triangular or polygonal faces composed of light skeletal struts or flat planes replace the arch principle. Stresses are distributed within the structure itself, as in a truss.

Geodesic domes can be supported by light walls and are the only large domes that can be set directly on the ground as complete structures.

Trusses

The trussed roof is the most common type of covering used throughout history.

It is constructed of triangular sections spaced at intervals, and made rigid in length by beams. Trusses formerly were made of wood and were used to cover masonry as well as framed structures.

The truss is based on the geometric law that a triangle is the only figure that cannot be changed in shape without a change in the length of its sides.

A triangular frame of strong pieces firmly fastened at the angles cannot be deformed by its own load or by external forces such as wind pressure. The forces are contained within the truss itself. In a vault they thrust outward against the walls.

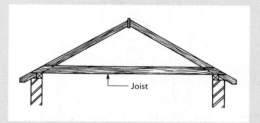

6-19 Simple triangular truss

The piece (chord or joist) at the base of the truss triangle resists by tension the tendency of the two sides to behave like a vault.

With its forces in equilibrium, the truss exerts only a direct downward pressure on the walls. They do not need be thickened or buttressed. This explains why most roofs are triangular in cross section.

A complex system of small triangles within the frame replaces the simple triangle for trusses that are too large to be constructed of three members of moderate size.

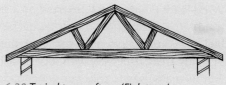

6-20 Typical truss rafter – 'Fink truss'

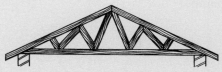

6-21 More complex truss rafter for larger spans – 'double-W truss'

Not all pitched roofs are trusses. In primitive building, in ancient Greece, and in much Chinese and Japanese wood architecture the chord (joist) is omitted and the sides exert thrust.

Trusses are not all triangular. The principle may be modified (as in modern steel and heavy timber construction) to apply to arches and vaults if chords of sufficient strength can be found.

Framed structures

A framed structure in any material is one that is made stable by a skeleton. It is able to stand by itself as a rigid structure without depending on floors or walls to resist deformation.

Materials such as wood, steel, and reinforced concrete, which are strong in both tension and compression, make the best materials for framing.

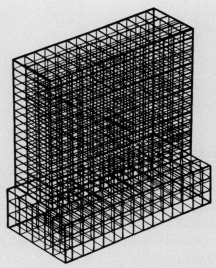

6-22 A framed structure consists of a rigid skeleton.

The heavy timber frame, in which large posts spaced relatively far apart support thick floor and roof beams, was the most common type of construction in eastern Asia and northern Europe from prehistoric times to the mid-19th century.

The American light wood frame (balloon frame), replaced the heavy timber frame. It was easier to handle and quicker to assemble (by nailing instead of by the slow joinery and dowelling of the past).

Construction is similar in the two systems. They are both based on the post-and-beam principle.

Posts rest on a level, waterproof foundation, usually composed of masonry or concrete, on which the sill (base member) is attached. Each upper storey is laid on crossbeams that are supported on the exterior wall by horizontal members.

Interior walls give additional beam support. In the heavy-timber system, the beams are strong enough to allow the upper storey and roof to project beyond the plane of the ground-floor posts. This increases the space to the upper storey and provides greater weather protection to the ground storey. The members are exposed on the exterior.

The light frame is sheathed with vertical or horizontal boarding or shingles. These are jointed or overlapped for weather protection.

Sheathing helps to brace as well as to protect the frame. The frame is not structurally independent as in steel frame construction.

The light-frame system has not been significantly improved since its introduction. It lags behind other modern techniques. Prefabricated panels designed to reduce the growing cost of construction have not been widely adopted.

Modern heavy-timber and laminated-wood techniques provide a means of building up compound members for trusses and arches. These challenge steel construction for certain large-scale projects in areas where wood is plentiful.

Steel framing is based on the same principles. It is

6-23 Portal frames can be made from steel, concrete or timber.

much simpler due to the far greater strength of the material.

Steel provides more rigidity with fewer members. The load-bearing capacity of steel is adequate for buildings many times higher than those made of other materials.

Riveting or welding fuses the column and beam. Stresses are distributed between them. Both can be longer and lighter than in structures in which they work independently as post-and-beam.

Four columns and four beams can span large cubic spaces. Joining cubes in height and width can produce buildings of almost any size.

Structural steel must be protected from corrosion and fire. To achieve this the skeleton is covered by curtain walls, surfaced in concrete or, occasionally, painted.

The steel frame is also used in single-storey buildings where large spans are required.

The greater rigidity and continuity of steel frames make them more versatile than timber frames. Steel is favoured for very tall structures for reasons of economy in construction and space.

An example is the system called box frame construction. Each unit is composed of two walls bearing a slab (the other two walls enclosing the unit are non-load bearing curtain walls); this type of construction extends the post-and-beam principle into three dimensions.

Structural principles associated with buildings and their components

A building may be defined as a static structure. When a structure is at rest no significant movement occurs as a result of the action of a number of forces.

Force
a dynamic influence that changes a body from a state of rest to one of motion, or changes its rate of motion.

All objects exert force due to their own weight. This force is usually in a downward direction. In order to prevent movement, this downward force must be resisted by an equal and opposite upward force.

Some principles associated with the study of forces include:

- **strength** – the ability of a material to resist forces by applied loads
- **stability** – the ability of a structure to resist overall movement, such as overturning.

Loading is the term used to describe forces acting on a building. These are divided into dead loads, live loads and wind loads.

Dead loads are made up of the weight of the building. **Live loads** are made up of the weight of anything that can be moved or that moves. Examples include people, furniture and equipment.

Wind loads are the forces exerted on a structure by wind. Wind loads affect the structural behaviour of building components, and great care must be taken in windy areas, especially with roof detailing. Formulas are used to calculate wind loads, and Ireland has two classified wind zones for this purpose.

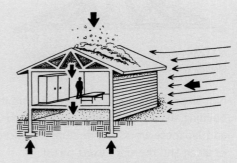

6-24 *Primary loads on a building consist of dead, live and wind loads.*

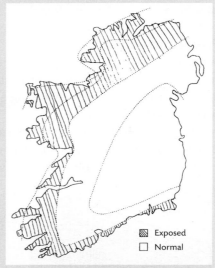

Exposed
Normal

6-25 *Ireland can be divided into two zones on the basis of wind speeds (Met Eireann).*

Stress

When designing a structure, estimate all the forces acting on the structure and its component parts. Make component parts strong enough to fulfil their particular requirements. The forces that need to be considered will depend on the type and purpose of the building.

The component parts of a structure or building are put into a state of stress by the forces they have to resist. The main forms of stress are tension, compression, shear and torsion.

TENSION   A tensile stress is produced when the forces acting upon it stretch a member.

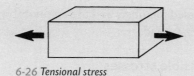

6-26 *Tensional stress*

COMPRESSION   A compressive stress is produced when a member is squeezed or compressed by the forces acting upon it.

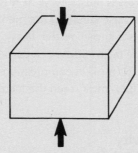

6-27 *Compressional stress*

SHEAR   A shear stress is produced when sliding occurs as a result of the application of forces.

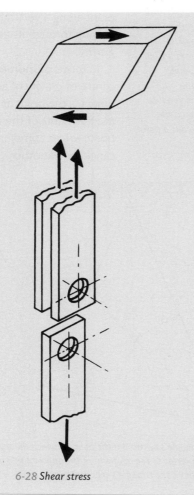

6-28 *Shear stress*

TORSION   A torque stress is produced when the forces acting upon it twist a member.

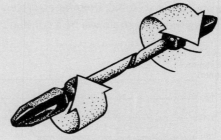

6-29 *Example of torsion*

COMBINED STRESSES   A component member of a structure may be subjected to several different stresses at any one time. It may be stretched and twisted at the same time, or bent and stretched.

Strain

Strain is the deformation or dimensional change in a member that occurs as a result of forces acting upon it. It is found by dividing the change in length by the original length. The dimensional changes that occur are usually very slight.

A member stressed in tension becomes longer and thinner, and a member stressed in compression becomes shorter and fatter.

A material cannot be subjected to stress without being strained.

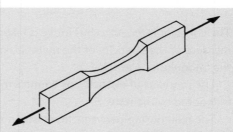

6-30 *Stress and strain go hand-in-hand. Members are strained as a result of tensional stress.*

Stiffness and elasticity

Some building materials, such as timber and steel, have elastic properties. When they are stretched or shortened by force they immediately return to their original dimensions when the force is removed, (provided, of course, that the force is not too great).

In elastic material, stress is proportional to strain. For example, if a tensile stress of 30 N/mm^2 in a steel bar produces a strain of 0.00015 mm, then 60 N/mm^2 will produce a strain of 0.00030 mm and so on, provided that the material remains elastic.

This relationship was first discovered by Robert Hooke and is now known as **Hooke's law**. Hooke's law states that if stress (tensile or compressive) is proportional to strain, then for any given material, stress divided by strain will be a constant.

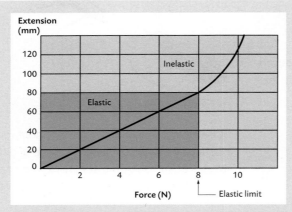

6-31 Hooke's law. *The graph shows the increase in length of an elastic wire as the stretching force on it increases.*

Over the straight-line part of the graph there is a 10 mm increase in length for every extra Newton (N) of applied force.

The change in length (strain) is proportional to the force (stress), a relationship called Hooke's law.

The wire begins to stretch disproportionately beyond an applied force of 8 N, which is the wire's elastic limit. When this force is removed, although the wire will decrease in length somewhat, it will not go back to its original length.

The constant referred to by Hooke is taken as a measure of the elasticity of the material, known as the 'modulus of elasticity'.

The modulus of elasticity, or **Young's modulus**, is denoted by the letter *E*.

The relationship between stress, strain and Young's modulus can be summarised by:

$$\frac{\text{Stress}}{\text{Strain}} = \text{Modulus of elasticity} = E$$

The values of *E* for various building materials can be calculated by applying tensional or compressional loads to sample materials in a testing machine, and recording the stresses and strains they produce.

E for mild steel is approximately 200 kN/mm² and *E* for timber is approximately 10 kN/mm². These figures do not relate to the strength of materials, only to their stiffness.

If a material has a high value of *E*, it will be difficult to stretch or shorten. Conversely, if a material has a low value of *E*, it will be easy to stretch or shorten it.

The modulus of elasticity of a material is important for calculating elongations of structural tension in members, the amounts of shortening in compressed members and the amounts by which beams may bend.

Permissible stresses

Permissible or working stresses are based on the knowledge of the failing strengths of the materials. These are obtained by testing them under the different forces and on research into the properties and behaviour of materials.

Permissible stresses must always be less than the stress that would cause failure of the members of the structure. This is known as the 'factor of safety'. For example, if the failing stress of a particular type of concrete is 32 N/mm² in compression and the working stress is 8 N/mm², then the factor of safety is 4.

Centre of gravity

The centre of gravity, or centroid, of any object is the point within that object from which the force of gravity appears to act.

Moments are the product of a physical quantity, such as force or mass, and its distance from a fixed reference point. Moments have a tendency to produce motion, especially rotation about a point or axis.

An object will remain at rest if it is balanced on any point along a vertical line passing through its centre of gravity.

In terms of **moments**, the centre of gravity of any object is the point at which the moments of the gravitational forces completely cancel one another.

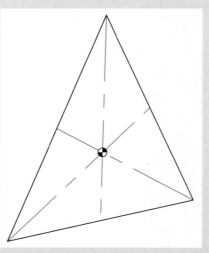

6-32 *A triangle's centroid is the point at which the segments from each vertex to the midpoint of the opposite side intersect. The centroid is the triangle's centre of gravity.*

The position of the centre of gravity for some simple shapes is easily determined by inspection. The centroid of a circle is at its centre and that of a square is at the intersection of the diagonals. A circle has an infinite number of lines of symmetry and a square has four.

The centroid of a section is not always within the area or material of the section. Hollow pipes, L-shaped and some irregular-shaped sections all have their centroid located outside of the material of the section.

This is not a problem since the centroid is really only used as a reference point from which distances are measured.

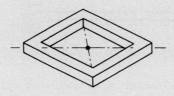

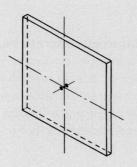

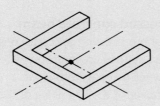

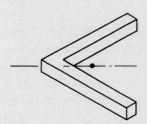

6-33 *The centre of gravity (centroid of area) is not always within the area of the section.*

The development of beams

A beam is a structural member that carries loads. These loads are most often perpendicular (at right angles) to its longitudinal axis, but they can be of any geometry.

A beam supporting a load develops internal stresses to resist the applied load. These internal stresses are bending stresses (Fig. 6-34), shearing stresses, and normal stresses.

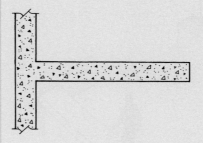

6-34 *Bending occurs when the tendency to rotate is resisted.*

Beam types are determined by method of support, not by method of loading. Below are three types of beams.

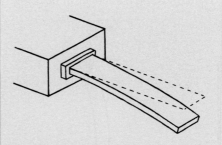

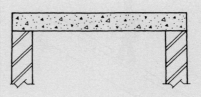

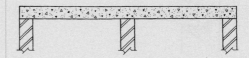

6-35 *Three main types of beam: simply supported beam, cantilever beam and continuous beam.*

The following points should be considered when designing a beam to be strong enough to safely carry its loads and make economical use of material:

- The beam must have sufficient bending strength to resist bending moments.
- The amount the beam bends must not be excessive.
- There must be no danger of failure due to shear forces.
- There must be no danger of buckling.

6-36 Buckling results when vertical forces on thin walls or columns make them bend in their height.

Beams in buildings bend very little. The amount is usually undetectable by the human eye. The diagrams explaining bending in beams are therefore exaggerated.

Beams in buildings are usually of elastic material (timber or steel). When a load is applied to such beams the top becomes shorter as a result of the bending. This part of the beam is in compression. The bottom of the beam becomes longer as it is in tension.

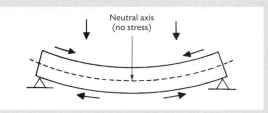

6-37 Principles of bending in beams: the top of the beam is in compression, whereas the bottom of the beam is in tension.

The simple reinforced concrete beam

The strength of concrete in compression is approximately 10 times greater than its strength in tension.

Placing steel in the areas of tensile stresses takes full advantage of the high tensile strength of steel. Fig. 6-38 shows steel placed at the bottom of a beam.

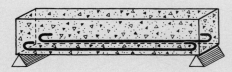

6-38 Bending reinforcement for concrete beam

When concrete sets, it shrinks slightly and grips the steel bars. This allows the concrete and the steel to bend as one unit when a load is applied to the beam.

The pre-stressed concrete beam

The process of pre-stressing concrete consists of putting it into a state of compression by tensioning steel bars or wires that pass through it.

It was conceived at the beginning of the 20th century and came to be recognised as the most important advance to have taken place in bridge construction since reinforced concrete came into general use.

The economies in material that pre-stressing made possible led to its rapid development in the period of shortages during and after World War II.

Concrete of high quality and strength is necessary to obtain the full benefits of the process. Rapid advances in concrete technology have resulted in its strength being doubled and its surface greatly improved since World War II.

The use of precast units have led to a marked increase in the length of simple or continuous spans, which can now be built economically up to lengths of 120 metres or more.

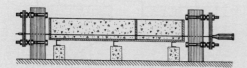

6-39 Principles of pre-stressing a concrete beam. The steel bars are placed in the lower third of the beam.

A wide variety of designs, including simple or continuous beams, cantilevers, arches, and girders, are possible with pre-stressed concrete. For spans of up to 43 metres, simply supported beams are the most economical.

Cantilever
refers to a beam, girder, or structural framework that is fixed at one end only.

Because of the thinness of the wire used in pre-stressed work, it is essential that it should be completely protected against corrosion.

It is of prime importance not to have cracks in the concrete and to produce a dense, flawless surface. The compression induced in the concrete tends to eliminate cracks. New materials for forms, such as hardboard, have enabled the surface of the concrete, whether flat or curved, to be of good texture, free from imperfections, easy to clean, and pleasing to the eye.

Before the concrete is cast, thin-gauge, flexible sheathing is fixed permanently in position in the moulds for the bars or wires to pass through. The bars or wires are tensioned after they have been placed in position.

The tension in the bars is created by screwing nuts on the ends of the bar against steel anchor plates.

For wires, the tensioning is done by means of hydraulic jacks, after which the wires are held by wedges.

Cement is then forced into the sheaths under pressure to grout in the wires or bars and prevent corrosion or slip.

The amount of pre-stress is usually greater than the tension stress that would otherwise be induced under full dead load and live load.

These methods can be applied to concrete, whether it is poured at the site or precast.

The development of the arch

The arch can be called a curved lintel. Early masonry builders could span only narrow openings because of the necessary shortness and weight of monolithic stone lintels.

6-40 Corbelling out masonry blocks would have been a forerunner to the development of the true arch.

6-41 Two inclined stone beams was the next step in the development of the arch.

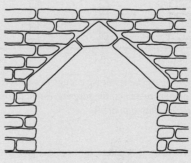

6-42 The introduction of a third stone accommodated greater spans. The stones support each other by their mutual compression.

6-43 The use of more bricks or stones eventually led to the arch.

Arches were used in Egypt and Iraq centuries before the birth of Christ. They were also used by the Romans for the construction of bridges and aqueducts built from approximately 300 BC.

Two problems were solved with the invention of the arch:

- Wide openings could be spanned with small, light blocks, in brick as well as stone.
- The arch was bent upward to resist and to conduct into its supports the loads that tended to bend the lintel downward.

Because the arch is curved, its upper edge has a greater circumference than the lower edge. This means that each of its blocks must be cut in wedge shapes that press firmly against the whole surface of neighbouring blocks and so conduct loads uniformly.

The arch creates problems of equilibrium that do not exist in lintels. The stresses in the arch tend to squeeze the blocks outward radially. Loads divert these outward forces downward to exert a resultant diagonal force, called thrust. This will cause the arch to collapse if it is not properly buttressed.

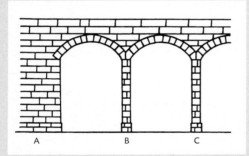

6-44 *If the abutment is not big enough it will overturn. With a number of arches, the supports B and C can be made smaller than support A.*

An arch cannot replace a lintel on two freestanding posts unless the posts are massive enough to buttress the thrust and to conduct it into the foundations (as in ancient Roman triumphal arches).

Arches may rest on light supports where they occur in a row. The thrust of one arch counteracts the thrust of its neighbours. The system will remain stable as long as walls, piers, or earth buttresses the arches at either end of the row.

The size of arches is limited only by economy; large arches exert large thrusts, and they are hard to buttress and to build.

The form may be varied to meet specific problems; the most efficient forms in masonry are semicircular, segmental (segment of a circle),

and pointed (two intersecting arcs of a circle). Non-circular curves also can be used successfully.

6-45 *Semi-circular arch*

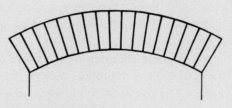

6-46 *Segmental arch*

6-47 *Circular arch*

6-48 *Pointed or Gothic arch*

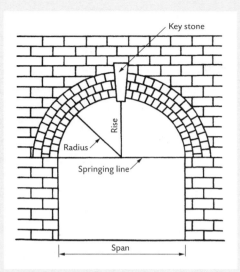

6-49 **Parts of an arch**

6-50 A latticed truss is more economical than a deep beam.

Arches were known in Egypt and Greece but were considered unsuitable for monumental architecture. In Roman times the arch was fully exploited in bridges, aqueducts, and large-scale architecture. New forms and uses were found in medieval and particularly Gothic architecture (flying buttress, pointed arch).

Steel, concrete, and laminated-wood arches of the 20th century have changed the concept and the mechanics of arches.

Their components are completely different from wedge-shaped blocks. They may be made entirely rigid so as to require only vertical support. They may be of hinged intersections that work independently. They may be thin slabs or members (in reinforced concrete) in which stresses are so distributed that they add the advantages of lintels to those of arches, requiring only light supports.

These innovations provide great freedom of design and a means of covering great spans without a massive substructure.

Struts, ties and triangulation

Deep beams are more efficient and stiffer than shallow beams. But over wide spans, deep beams may be uneconomical due to the amount of material required.

A solution to this is to reduce the beam's weight by replacing a solid mat with a web, joining the top and bottom by separate members placed along the diagonal lines of tension and compression. Fig. 6-50 shows an example of this type of structure. It is known as a lattice, framed or trussed girder.

However, lattice girders are not normally used because sufficient strength and stability may be obtained by using just one set of members as shown in Fig 6-51. The top members are in compression while the bottom members are in tension.

The diagonal members are in either compression or tension depending on whether they lie on the lines of compressive or tensile stresses.

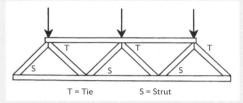

6-51 The lattice truss is not normally used because strength and stability may be obtained by using only one set of members as shown above.

The members in compression are called struts, and the members in tension are called ties. The struts must be rigid enough to resist buckling and consequently are larger than ties. Ties can be quite thin.

Spans requiring a considerable pitch, such as those for roofing slates, take the triangular form of the roof truss. These may be framed or trussed in various ways in order to keep compression members short.

The number of **purlins** required and the need to prevent deflection at the bottom tie are other considerations.

Purlin
a horizontal beam that provides intermediate support for the common rafters of a roof construction.

Structural materials in buildings

The main structural materials are brick, stone, concrete, timber and steel. Aluminium alloys and some plastics have been used structurally in recent years.

Bricks
Bricks have been used for thousands of years. In ancient times bricks were made of mud, mixed with

chopped straw for strength and to prevent crumbling after they were dried in the sun.

Brick compares favourably with stone as a structural material for its fire- and weather-resisting qualities, and for ease of production, transportation, and laying.

The size of bricks is limited by the need for efficient drying, firing, and handling. The shape of bricks along with the techniques of bricklaying, have varied little throughout history. Today bricks are made from clay, which is pressed into moulds by machine.

Clays used in brick-making represent a wide range of materials that include varying percentages of silica and alumina. They may be grouped into three classes:

1 Surface clays – found near or on the surface of the Earth, typically in river beds.

2 Shales – clays subjected to high geologic pressures and varying in hardness from a slate to a form of partially decomposed rock

3 Fireclays – mined deep beneath the surface. Fireclays have a more uniform chemical composition than surface clays or shale.

After moulding, clay bricks are 'fired' in a kiln to a temperature of about 1000°C. This crystallises the constituents into a rock-like material.

The many types of bricks available results from the many types of clay. Engineering bricks are the strongest. They are very hard, dense and strong.

All bricks are stronger in compression than in tension. This makes them unsuitable for resisting tensile forces.

Concrete blocks

Concrete blocks are generally made of 1:3:6 cement-sand-aggregate mix with a maximum size aggregate of 10 mm, or a cement-sand mixture with a ratio of 1:7, 1:8 or 1:9. These mixtures give concrete blocks a compression strength well above what is required for domestic buildings. The blocks may be solid, cellular, or hollow. Cellular blocks have cavities with one end closed. In hollow blocks the cavities are open at both ends.

Blocks are made to a number of coordinating sizes. Actual block sizes are about 10 mm less than the designated size to allow for the thickness of the mortar at joints.

Blocks are made using a simple block-making machine operated by engine or by hand. Water is sprinkled on blocks the day after they are made, and this continues for two weeks during curing. The blocks are removed for stacking after 48 hours, but the wetting is continued. The blocks are dried after curing. If damp blocks are laid in a wall, they will shrink and cause cracks.

Stone

Stone is favoured over other materials for monumental architecture. Its advantages are durability, adaptability to sculptural treatment, and the fact that it can be used in modest structures in its natural state.

Stone is difficult to quarry, transport, and cut. Its weakness in tension limits its use for beams, lintels and floor supports.

Rubble is the simplest and cheapest form of stonework. It consists of roughly broken stones of any shape bonded in mortar.

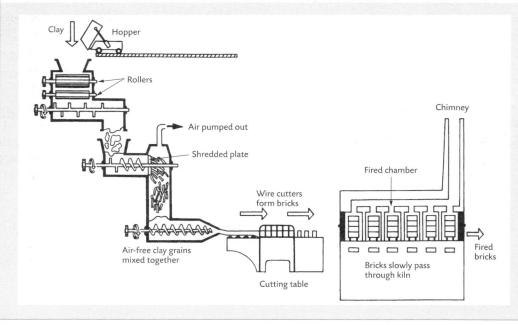

6-52
Brick manufacture

6-53 *Uncoursed random rubble wall*

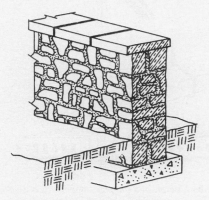

6-54 *Coursed random rubble wall*

Ashlar is the strongest and most suitable stonework for monumental architecture. It consists of regularly cut blocks (usually rectangular).

Stone masonry (in contrast with brick) does not depend on strong bonding for stability. It supports only direct downward loads.

The weight of stone creates problems of stability when loads push at an angle. Stone vaults and arches require more support and buttressing than equivalent forms in other materials.

Stone has been consistently used for building since the Stone Age, as exemplified by Stonehenge, in England.

6-55 *The most famous Neolithic monument, Stonehenge, was built in several phases on a sacred site on Salisbury Plain, England. Stonehenge is a series of concentric rings of standing stones surrounding a central altar stone.*

Stone has been replaced as a structural material by cheaper and more efficient manufactured products. Nevertheless, it is still widely used as a surface veneer for its practical and aesthetic qualities.

Timber

Timber, like stone, has been used for centuries for carrying and supporting loads. The load-carrying capacities vary depending on the species of timber.

Timber, unlike brick and stone, is fibrous and elastic. It is strong in tension as well as in compression.

Strength varies for each species and is dependent on the direction of the grain in relation to the direction of the load applied.

Softwoods are more commonly used in houses for structural applications such as floor-supporting joists. In recent times, portal frames have been constructed of laminated timber.

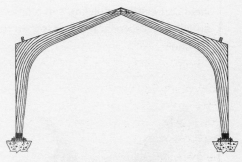

6-56 *Laminated timber portal frame*

Glue-laminated timber is used as a long-span material. It is prefabricated using metal connectors into trusses that span up to 45 metres.

Concrete

Concrete is a manufactured mixture of cement and water, with aggregates of sand and stones. It hardens rapidly by chemical combination to a stone-like, water- and fire-resisting solid of great compressive (but low tensile) strength.

It provides an economical substitute for traditional materials. It can be poured into forms while liquid to produce a great variety of structural elements. It has the advantages of continuity (absence of joints) and of fusing with other materials (steel).

The components of concrete are cement, coarse aggregates such as crushed stone, fine aggregates such as sand, and water.

In the mix, water combines chemically with the cement to form a gel structure that bonds the stone aggregates together.

In proportioning the mix, the aggregates are graded in size so the cement matrix that joins them together is minimised.

The upper limit of concrete strength is set by that of the stone used in the aggregate. The bonding gel structure forms slowly. The design strength is taken as that occurring 28 days after the initial setting of the mix. There is a one-month lag between the time in situ concrete is poured and the time it can carry loads. This can significantly affect construction schedules.

In situ concrete is used for foundations and for structural skeleton frames.

Concrete columns are usually of rectangular or circular profile and are cast in plywood or metal forms.

Three 20th-century developments in production had a radical effect on concrete architecture:

- **Concrete-shell** construction permits the erection of vast vaults and domes with a concrete and steel content. The thickness in relation to length and width is comparatively less than that of an eggshell.

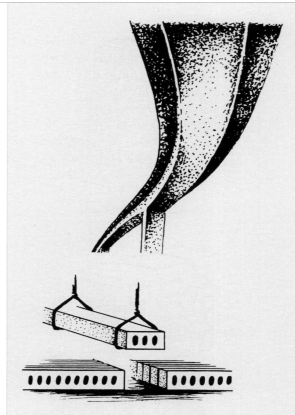

6-59 *Both simple and complex components are easily manufactured using precast concrete. Shown are a curved section of a road bridge (top) and hollow-core floor slabs.*

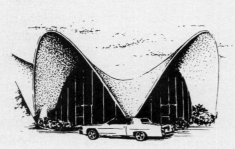

6-57 *Motel entrance, Las Vegas. This small shell is made in the form of two components of a monkey saddle.*

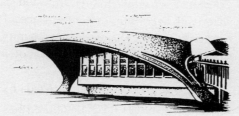

6-58 *Terminal building, Las Vegas Airport*

- **Precast-concrete** construction uses bricks, blocks, slabs, and supports made under factory conditions to increase waterproofing and solidity. Precast concrete decreases time and cost in erection.

- **Pre-stressed** concrete provides bearing members into which reinforcement is set under tension. This produces a live force to resist a particular load. The member acts like a spring. It can carry a greater load than an unstressed member of the same size.

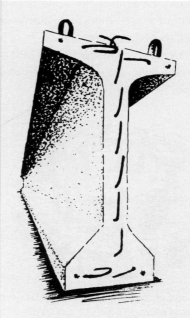

6-60 *Prestressed concrete members showing the steel reinforcement set under tension.*

Steel

Steel is a major structural material. It is a strong and stiff material and yet relatively inexpensive. It can be quickly fabricated and erected, which saves construction time.

Steel is non-combustible. It starts to lose strength when heated above 400°C (750°F). Building codes require it to be fireproofed in multi-storey buildings. In small and low-hazard buildings it can be left unprotected.

Steel is, by definition, an alloy of iron and carbon. The carbon content ranges up to 2 percent (with a higher carbon content, the material is defined as cast iron).

Steel is the most widely used building material for the world's infrastructure and industries. It is used to fabricate everything from sewing needles to oil tankers. The tools required to build and manufacture all these articles are also made of steel.

As an indication of the relative importance of this material, in 1989 the world's steel production was about 770 million tonnes, while production of the next most important engineering metal, aluminium, was about 18 million tonnes.

The relatively low cost of manufacturing steel is the main reason for its popularity. The abundance of its two raw materials (iron ore and scrap) and its unparalleled range of mechanical properties are other reasons for its popularity.

The major component of steel is iron, a metal that in its pure state is not much harder than copper. In its pure form, iron is soft and generally not useful as an engineering material. The principal method of strengthening it and converting it into steel is by adding small amounts of carbon.

Adjusting the carbon content is the simplest way to change the mechanical properties of steel.

Another way to change the properties of steel is by adding alloy elements other than carbon that produce characteristics not achievable in plain carbon steel. Each of the approximately 20 elements used for alloying steel has a distinct influence on its microstructure.

Checking the hardness of steel demonstrates its properties. Hardness is measured by pressing a diamond pyramid or a hard steel ball into the steel at a specific load.

TYPES OF STEEL There are several thousand steel grades published, registered, or standardised worldwide. All of them have different chemical compositions. Special numbering systems have been developed in several countries to classify the huge number of alloys.

Fortunately, steels can be classified reasonably well into a few major groups according to their chemical compositions, applications, shapes, and surface conditions – see Chapter 14.

CONNECTING STEEL The connections of steel shapes are of two types: those made in the workshop and those made at the building site.

Shop connections are usually welded, and site or field connections are usually made with bolts. This is due to the greater labour costs and difficulties of quality control in field welding.

Steel columns are joined to foundations with base plates welded to the columns and held by anchor bolts embedded in the concrete. The erection of steel frames at the building site can proceed very rapidly. Cranes can handle all the pieces and all the bolted connections made swiftly by workers with hand-held wrenches.

A large proportion of steel structures are built as prefabricated, pre-engineered metal buildings.

The development of iron and steel construction methods was the most important innovation in architecture since ancient times. These methods provide far stronger and taller structures with less expenditure of material than stone, brick, or wood. They can produce greater unsupported spans over openings and interior or exterior spaces. The evolution of steel frame construction in the 20th century entirely changed the concept of the wall and the support.

Steel structural members are rolled in a variety of shapes, the commonest of which are plates, angles, I-beams, and U-shaped channels.

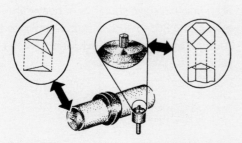

6-61 Steel hardness test, and tooling used for test

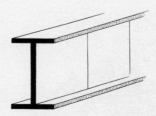

6-62 I-beams, also known as RSJs (rolled steel joists), are common structural steel members.

Steel bolts or rivets may join these members. The development of welding in the 20th century made it possible to produce fused joints with less labour and materials.

Steel must be protected against corrosion by surface coverings. Alloys such as stainless steel have been developed for exposed surfaces. Aluminium and other light metal alloys have come to be favoured for exterior construction because of their weather resistance.

Examples of significant structural forms

A tent illustrates a basic structural form that continues in use to the present. The tent contains a membrane to shed rain and snow. It controls heat transfer by keeping out the hot rays of the sun and confining heated air in cold weather. It blocks out light and provides visual privacy. The membrane must be supported against the forces of gravity and wind. A structure is necessary.

Much of the history of architectural technology is the search for better solutions to the same basic problems that the tent was set out to solve.

About 3000 BC in Mesopotamia, the first fired bricks appeared. The well-developed masonry technology of Mesopotamia was used to build large structures of great masses of brick, such as the temple at Tepe Gawra and the ziggurats at Ur and Borsippa, which were up to 26 metres high. These symbolic buildings marked the beginnings of architecture in this culture.

A new technology of cut-stone construction emerged in the temples and pyramids of the 4th dynasty (c. 2575–c. 2465 BC). The great Pyramids of Giza, the tallest of which rose to a height of 147 metres, are a marvelous technological achievement. Their visual impact is stunning even today. Taller structures were not built until the 19th century.

Stone construction moved in the direction of lighter and more flexible stone frames and the creation of larger interior spaces. Freestanding stone columns supporting stone beams appeared for the first time in the royal temples associated with the pyramids of about 2600 BC.

6-63 *The great Pyramids of Giza employed cut-stone construction.*

A fine surviving example of glazed brick is the Ishtar Gate of the Palace of Nebuchadnezzar at Babylon. It contains a true arch spanning 7.5 metres and dated to 575 BC.

6-64 *The Ishtar Gate, 575 BC, is a fine example of glazed brick.*

Perhaps the most spectacular building achievement of the age was the Pharos of Alexandria – the great lighthouse built for Ptolemy II in the 3rd century BC. It was a huge stone tower nearly as high as the Great Pyramid but much smaller at the base, perhaps 30 metres.

6-65 *The Lighthouse at Alexandria was built in 279 BC on the small island of Pharos by Sostratus of Cnidus for Ptolemy II. The lighthouse was over 100 metres high.*

Scandinavian stave churches of heavy timber were built in the 8th to 10th centuries, prior to the triumph of the stone church, and a few have survived to the present day.

6-66 *Stave churches embody a unique architectural style, and remain Norway's most important contribution to European architecture.*

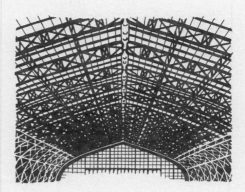

6-68 *This reproduction, from a viewbook of the sights and buildings at the 1889 Exposition Universelle in Paris, illustrates the interior of the Galerie des Machines, designed by Ferdinand Dutert. This enormous iron and glass structure – measuring 484 metres long, 126 metres wide, and 49 metres high – was intended to complement the Eiffel Tower.*

The Industrial Revolution brought new materials and a demand for new building types that completely transformed building technology.

The production of brick was industrialised in the 19th century. 'Pressed' bricks superseded the laborious process of hand moulding, which had been used for 3,000 years.

Steel was chosen as the principal building material for two structures built for the Paris Exposition of 1889: the Eiffel Tower and the Gallery of Machines.

The first use of iron-reinforced concrete was by the French builder François Coignet in Paris in the 1850s. Coignet's own all-concrete house in Paris (1862), still stands. The roofs and floors reinforced with small wrought-iron I-beams.

Reinforced concrete development began with the French gardener Joseph Monier's 1867 patent for large concrete flowerpots, reinforced with a cage of iron wires.

The Hallidie Building (1918) in San Francisco is an example of the earliest all-glass curtain wall. It was only on a single street façade.

6-67 *The Eiffel Tower*

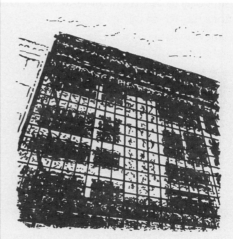

6-69 *The Hallidie building is an early example of all-glass curtain walling.*

The first multi-storey structure with a full glass curtain wall was the A.O. Smith Research Building (1928) in Milwaukee by Holabird and Root. In it aluminium frames held the glass, an early use of this metal in buildings.

6-70 *A.O. Smith Research Building, 1928. A highly unusual and modern building for its day, it is a powerful example of the International Style. It is made of aluminium and black stone.*

The dome and the shell vault continued to be the major forms of long-span structures after 1945.

The geodesic dome employs ribs placed in a triangular or hexagonal pattern on the geodesic lines, or great circles, of a sphere. Fuller's own patented forms were used in 1958 to build two large hemispherical domes 115.3 metres in diameter using steel tube members. Fuller's design was also used at the Expo 67 in Montreal. This dome is considered to be the most beautiful ever built.

The concrete dome or shell developed rapidly in the 1950s. The St. Louis Lambert Airport Terminal (1954) has a large hall 36.6 metres square. Four intersecting thin-shell concrete barrel vaults supported at the four corners span it. The thickness of the shell varies from 20 centimetres at the supports to 11.3 centimetres at the centre.

6-71 *The St. Louis Lambert Airport Terminal, 1954*

New forms of the long-span roof appeared in the 1950s based on the steel cables that had long been used in suspension bridges.

One example was the US Pavilion at the 1958 Brussels World's Fair, designed by the architect Edward Durell Stone. It was based on the familiar principle of the bicycle wheel. Its roof had a diameter of 100 metres. It had a steel tension ring at the perimeter from which two layers of radial cables were tightly stretched to a small tension ring in the middle. The double layer of cables gave the roof stability against vertical movement.

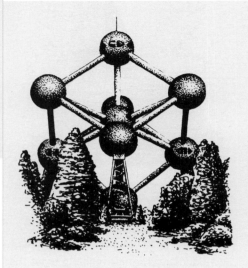

6-72 *The US Pavilion at the 1958 Brussels World's Fair*

Air-supported plastic membranes (pneumatic structures) are another form of long-span roof structures in tension. These were devised by Walter Bird of Cornell University in the late 1940s and were soon used for swimming pools, temporary warehouses, and exhibition buildings.

The Osaka World's Fair of 1970 included many air-supported structures. The largest was the U.S. Pavilion designed by the engineers Geiger Berger Associates. It had an oval plan of 138 × 79 metres. The inflated domed roof of vinyl-coated fabric was restrained by a diagonally intersecting network of steel cables attached to a concrete compression ring at the perimeter.

The system of the Osaka Pavilion was adapted for two large sports stadiums built in the 1980s, the Silverdome at Pontiac, Michigan, and the Hubert H. Humphrey Metrodome in Minneapolis.

Air-supported structures are perhaps the most cost-effective structure for very long spans.

6-73 *Silverdome at Pontiac, an example of an air-supported structure*

Chapter 7

Substructure

Introduction

Substructure refers to all the elements of a building from below ground level up to and including the damp-proof course. This includes the foundations, rising walls, filling (hardcore) and ground floors.

Once the substructure is complete, the building is out of the ground and the superstructure can be started. **Superstructure** refers to the parts of the building above damp-proof course level.

Clearing the site

Trees and vegetation

Trees planted near buildings can cause unequal settlement because the roots extract moisture from the soil. This causes soil around the tree roots to shrink.

Where trees occur on site, determine existing root growth. Check excavations carefully for root and fibrous material.

Tree roots can extend over long distances. It is important to note the type of trees, their location and their possible impact on foundations.

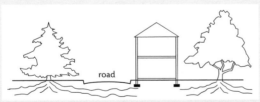

7-1 Tree roots may travel long distances in search of water. Roots absorb moisture and cause clay to shrink, with loss of ground support beneath foundations.

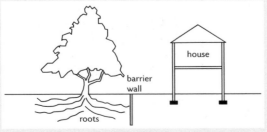

7-2 A barrier wall of 150 mm concrete will prevent root growth near a building.

7-3 Drain pipes should be encased in concrete if there is a danger of tree roots growing in the area.

Trees can add character to a site by enhancing its aesthetic value. Retain trees on site provided they do not present a risk to the fabric and services of the building.

Remove trees only as a last resort. Fully grown trees can now be transplanted with the aid of specialist machinery. This option should be considered in preference to cutting trees down.

The presence of trees maintains the water table at a lower level than if they were not present. This is due to the amount of moisture (water) trees need to survive. When trees are removed from a site the soil expands and flooding may occurs, depending on the number of trees removed.

Topsoil

Topsoil (also known as vegetable soil) refers to the top layer of soil in a site. It is usually no deeper than 300 mm. Topsoil is easily compressed, which makes it unsuitable as a base for a foundation.

Remove all topsoil from the entire area of the building prior to digging foundations. Stock-pile the topsoil for use in the gardens when the building work is complete.

Ruins and other site issues

Where ruins need to be removed, secure a demolition order if required. This is part of the planning process.

Ruins may yield a valuable source of building stone. Store this building stone carefully. It can be used for boundary walls and other features on the site at a later stage.

Before digging foundations, check with the relevant authorities that there are no underground service cables or pipes on the site. These include electricity, telephone, water mains and gas pipelines.

Common subsoils and bearing capabilities

When designing foundations it is essential to identify the rock or soil type on which the foundation will be built. Different soil types have different bearing capabilities.

Bearing capability (capacity) refers to the weight that the subsoil can support without movement occurring. Some initial movement is allowed during and immediately after the construction of a building. This is referred to as settlement.

Subsoil refers to the soil that remains after the topsoil is removed. There are four major subsoil classifications.

1. Rock

The hardest rocks are igneous such as granite and basalt. These may have 2–3 times the safe bearing capacity of hard sedimentary rocks such as sandstone and limestone, and up to 50 times the safe bearing capacity of clays or sands.

The bearing capacity of sedimentary rocks depends on the angle of stratification. Chalk is unreliable as it can soften and weaken in wet conditions.

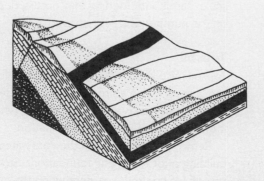

7-4 Angle of stratification refers to the angle the underlying layers of soil (strata) make with the earth's surface.

A bed of rock is an excellent base to build on. However, if it has to be levelled or excavated it can prove expensive.

2. Coarse-grained non-cohesive soils

This category consists of gravel and sands. Gravel and sands can fail under load by shear. Shear occurs when particles slide over each other.

However, when sand or gravel is confined and compacted it can form an excellent base on which to build. Sand can be vibrated. This will reduce its surface level and increase its load-bearing capacity.

Gravel has the ability to distribute uneven loading over a wide area.

The greater the load the more the frictional strength. Settlement occurs when these soils are loaded initially. After this initial settlement there will be little change and no 'recovery' if the load is removed.

Coarse sands and gravel are self-draining where the water table is low. This provides dry building sites and excellent conditions for buildings erected on them.

Gravel and sands are non-cohesive. Excavation of trenches requires timbering to prevent the sides of the trench from collapsing as the soil is removed.

3. Fine-grained cohesive soils

This category consists of clays and silts. Consisting of very fine microscopic particles, they become sticky when wet and hold together when dry.

Clays and silts absorb water by capillary action. This means that clay under a building may be damp.

Shrinkage and swelling occurs due to seasonal changes. Swelling is capable of exerting sufficient pressure to crack shallow foundations.

Foundations on clay should be placed at least 1 m below ground level. Clays are safe at this level from swelling and shrinkage due to frost or capillary action.

Clay will compress under load and expand when the load is removed. Cohesive soils cannot be easily compacted by vibration methods.

There are many types of clay, which results in considerable variation in bearing pressure ratings. Following are potential safe bearing capacities for a range of clay types:

Clay bearing capacities

Clay or sand type	Bearing capacity
Very stiff boulder clays and hard clays	420–650 kN/m²
Stiff clays and sandy clays	220–430 kN/m²
Firm clays and sandy clays	110–220 kN/m²
Soft clays and silt	55–110 kN/m²
Very soft clays and silts	0–55 kN/m²

Sulphates
any salt of sulphuric acid, such as sodium sulphate. A sulphate attack weakens concrete or mortar due to a chemical reaction between the cement and the soluble sulphates in clay.

Some clays cause deterioration of concrete and steel because they contain **sulphates**.

4. Peat and made-up ground

Peat is inadequate for any type of building load. Foundations should be carried down to a firmer strata below. Peat soils are very acidic.

Made-up ground is lands that may have been reclaimed from the sea, disused refuse tips or filled in ground.

The bearing capacity of made-up ground will depend on the fill materials, the method of filling and the degree of consolidation. The strength of the underlying soil must also be considered.

Inorganic
contains no living organisms.

Where it is necessary to build up a site using fill, it can be brought to a satisfactory load-bearing capacity by using good **inorganic** solid fill, natural or industrial waste. Lay this fill in layers not exceeding 300–450 mm. Compact it using heavy rolling equipment.

Piles
long columns of timber, concrete, or steel that are driven into the ground to provide foundations for a structure.

With made-up ground and peat it is safer to transfer the building loads to the underlying strata, using **piles**.

Typical subsoil bearing capacities

Type	Bearing capacity (kN/m²)
Rocks, granites and chalks	600–10,000
Non-cohesive soils Compact sands Loose uniform sands	100–600
Cohesive soils Hard clays Soft clays and silts	0–600
Peat and made-up ground	To be determined by investigation

Principles of foundation design

The engineer/designer analyses the soil and conducts a site investigation. On the basis of this information he/she designs the foundation for the building.

The engineer will understand the purpose of the foundation, be able to estimate the loads of the building structure and be aware of the range of foundation types available.

Foundations must be:
- able to safely sustain and transmit to the ground the combined **dead** and **live loads** so as not to cause any settlement in any part of the building.
- so constructed to avoid damage by swelling, shrinkage or freezing of the subsoil.
- strong enough to prevent downward vertical loads shearing through the foundation at the point of application.
- able to withstand attack from corrosive elements in the soil, e.g. sulphates.

In addition to these requirements, the foundations must comply with the Building Regulations (see Fig. 7-5).

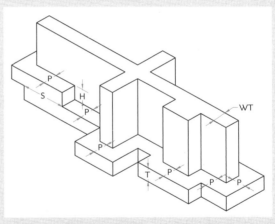

7-5 The Building Regulations as they apply to foundations:

T = minimum thickness of concrete foundation
WT = wall thickness
P = overall foundation width, less wall thickness WT divided by 2 gives projection P (P = foundation – WT/2)
S = minimum lap at change in level (see Fig. 7-7)
H = step height. Steps should course with walling material.

Settlement

Settlement results from:

- Consolidation of soil
- Cohesive soils bulging
- Removal of water from soil
- Plastic flow of soil from under the building
- Soil erosion by wind or water

Plastic flow
is the forming of a mass of solid (such as clay) into a desired shape through the application of forces.

Some settlement must be expected on all soil types, with the exception of solid rock. Settlement must be limited to an acceptable level. Foundation design must allow settlement to occur evenly to avoid straining or cracking.

Foundation types

Foundations are classified by their type such as strip, pad, raft or piles. The type of foundation to use involves an understanding of the bearing capacity of the soil, the type of soil and how foundations work.

The three fundamental principles of foundation design involve:

- the foundation bearing down on suitable subsoil. The strip foundation is the most common solution to this scenario.
- The foundation obtaining its strength from friction with the surrounding earth. Pile foundations are an example of this principle.
- The foundation floats on the surface of poor to good soil as exemplified in raft foundations.

Most types are suitable only for particular situations. Once all the variables are considered there is rarely a choice about which type to use.

Strip foundations

The majority of domestic buildings have strip foundations. These consist of a continuous strip of reinforced concrete resting on the soil. The depth and width of the foundation must be suitable for the soil type and the building load. Walls are placed centrally on the strip foundation.

Stepped strip foundations are used on sloping sites in order to reduce the amount of excavation required. The depth of each step is either 112 or 225 mm to suit block courses. The overlap of concrete at the step is not less than the depth of the concrete foundation, and never less than 300 mm.

Strip foundations are used on average to good bearing capacity soils. They are not suitable for very soft clay, silt or peat, or badly made-up ground.

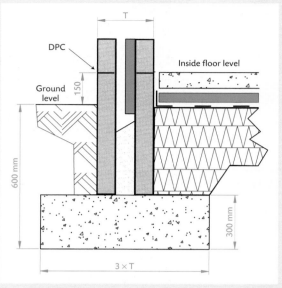

7-6 *A typical strip foundation showing dimensions required by the Building Regulations*
Note 1: Dimensions quoted are the minimum required.
Note 2: Cavity should be filled to a level between 150 and 225 mm below DPC.

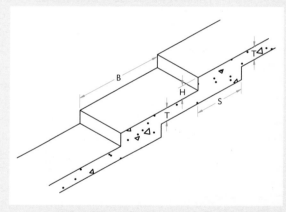

7-7 *Step foundation details*
Minimum overlap (S) = twice height of step, or thickness of foundation or 300 mm, whichever is greater.
H should not be greater than 2T
B = 1 metre minimum.

Wide-strip foundations

Wide-strip foundations are used where the load bearing capacity of the soil is low, e.g. soft clay, silt or made-up ground.

Transverse reinforcement is used to withstand the tensions that may arise. The depth of concrete for wide strip foundations should be the same as for ordinary strip foundations.

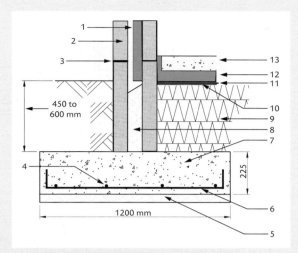

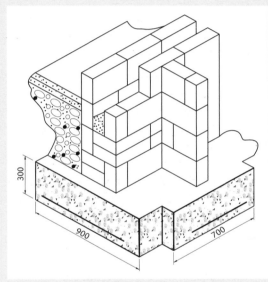

7-10 *Deep strip foundation*

7-8 **Wide strip foundation details**
  1 *Cavity wall insulation*
  2 *300 mm cavity wall*
  3 *DPC*
  4 *Longitudinal reinforcement for spread of loads*
  5 *50 mm blinding may be required*
  6 *Transverse reinforcing bars or fabric reinforcement*
  7 *Concrete foundation*
  8 *Cavity fill*
  9 *Compacted hardcore*
 10 *Sand blinding*
 11 *DPM*
 12 *Underfloor insulation*
 13 *Concrete floor slab*

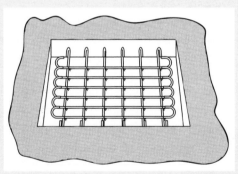

7-9 *Tranverse reinforcement turned up at end for extra support*

7-11 *Alternative to deep-strip foundation with solid-block rising wall*

Deep-strip foundations

A deep-strip foundation is a variation of the strip foundation. It is used where it is necessary to excavate to 900 mm or more in order to find a suitable strata to support the building.

The trench is filled to within 150 mm of ground level. Depending on the depth of concrete used it may be possible to reduce the width of the foundation. This would further reduce the amount of excavation, surplus soil and backfill required.

A recent development has been to use the traditional strip foundation and build a solid block wall to 150 mm below ground level. This wall must be equal in width to the standard cavity wall.

H Raft foundations

A raft foundation is a large concrete slab covering the whole building area and sometimes it includes the pavement.

All the loads from the building are transmitted through the raft to the soil. Rafts are used on low load bearing soils, such as soft natural ground or made-up ground. Rafts can also be used instead of strip foundations on average to good bearing capacity soils.

Rafts consist of a reinforced concrete slab up to 300 mm thick. The slab is thicker under load bearing walls.

Two layers of fabric reinforcement are used, one near the top and one near the bottom of the slab. An edge beam along the perimeter of the slab provides greater stiffness and also protects the ground.

7-12 *Raft foundation – Step 1: excavate soil to a suitable bearing.*

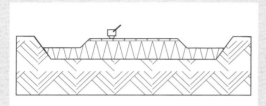

7-13 *Raft foundation – Step 2: fill and compact hardcore in 225 mm max. layers.*

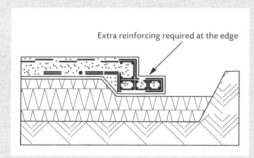

7-14 *Raft foundation – Step 3: position reinforcement, shutter, pour, vibrate and cure.*

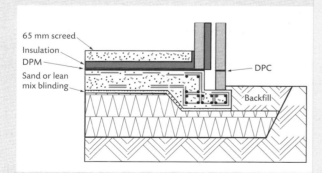

7-15 *Raft foundation – Step 4: Place DPM, insulation and 65 mm min. thick screed.*

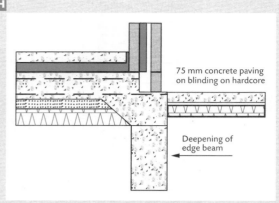

7-16 *Alternative arrangements for poor soils consist of deepening the edge beam and the provision of a path or pavement. In some cases the pavement may be cast with the main raft.*

Reinforcing of foundations

Concrete is strong in compression but weak in tension. The opposite is true for steel bars. This is why steel is used to improve the tensile strength of concrete.

Steel embedded in concrete is known as **reinforced concrete**.

The steel normally used for reinforcing bars is 'ordinary mild steel', which must have a failing stress of 450–500 N/mm^2.

In certain situations medium- and high-tensile bars are used for increased strength to compensate for weak foundations. They are also used for specialist detailing in raft foundations.

Deformed (twisted) bars and ribbed bars allow for a better bond with the concrete and give greater frictional resistance than round bars.

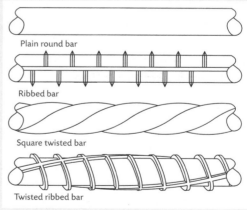

7-17 *Typical reinforcing bars*

Ensure that steel used for reinforcing is free from excessive rust. A thin film of rust or scale does not present a problem and may even increase the bond of steel with concrete.

Oil, grease, paint, dried mud and weak dried mortar must be removed from reinforcing steel.

Ensure that all steel reinforcement is firmly held in place before and during the pouring of the concrete. This is done using small concrete blocks, spacer bars or wires. Do not use rocks or wood supports because they might crack or decay over time and eventually allow moisture into the reinforcing steel.

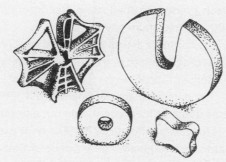

7-18 *A selection of spacers used to position the reinforcing bars and provide the necessary cover.*

The water table, capillary action and rising damp

Water table

Most ground water lies near the surface. Water seeps down through permeable rocks until it reaches an impermeable layer, where it accumulates. Spaces in the lower part of the permeable rock become filled with water. Scientists refer to this as the **zone of saturation**.

Permeable
A permeable material will allow or cause water to pass through it.

The top of the zone of saturation is called the **water table**. This rises and falls according to the amount of rain that falls on the surface.

The level below which the rocks are always saturated is called the **permanent water table**. Where the water table appears at ground level, for example in a depression, the water flows on to the surface, usually forming a lake.

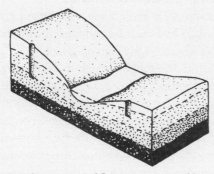

7-19 *Permanent and fluctuating water table*

Capillary action

Capillary action is related to the adhesive properties of water.

You can demonstrate capillary action by placing a straw into a glass of water. The water seems to 'climb' up the straw. This is because the water molecules are attracted to the straw molecules. When one water molecule moves closer to the straw molecules the other water molecules (which are cohesively attracted to that water molecule) also move up into the straw.

Capillary action is limited by gravity and, in this case, the diameter of the straw. The thinner the straw or tube, the higher capillary action will pull the water.

The absorption of water in a sponge and the rise of molten wax in a wick are familiar examples of capillary rise.

Water rises in soil partly by capillarity. It also rises through building materials that contain pores or very narrow spaces. Water enters these pores and, if the spaces are narrow enough, it will travel right through the material. The narrower the pores, the further the water will travel.

This rising of water (**rising damp**) will take place even against the force of gravity.

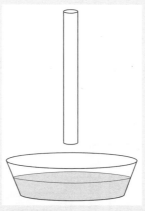

7-20 *Capillary action can easily be demonstrated with a straw and some water.*

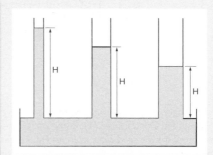

7-21 *The height **H** to which capillary action will lift water depends on the weight of water that the surface tension will lift.*

The **cavity wall** principle (used in the exterior walls of houses) prevents damp spreading horizontally to the inner leaf.

Damp-proof courses (DPCs) are used at the lower ends of walls to prevent damp rising vertically. Substances such as slate, lead and bituminous felt are impervious to water and are used as DPC materials.

Walls from foundations to DPC

Walls built from the foundations to the DPC level are referred to as **rising walls**.

The DPC level is a minimum of 150 mm above ground level.

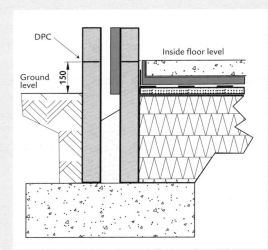

7-22 *Typical rising wall detail showing position for DPC and lean concrete cavity fill below ground level*

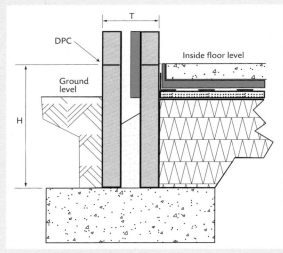

7-23 *The height of the rising wall (H) should not be greater than 3 times the wall thickness (T). Rising walls in excess of this height must use a solid block wall (see Fig. 7-11) with a maximum cavity of 450 mm high. Alternatively a reinforced concrete wall might be considered, or a raft foundation might be a cheaper option.*

The height of the rising wall should not be greater than three times the wall thickness.

Rising walls are usually of cavity wall construction. They must be filled with a weak concrete mix to within 150 mm below the ground level. This prevents undue pressure and prevents collapse.

Site fill

Site fill, otherwise known as **hardcore**, must be clean, graded, crushed stone, free from shale and 100 mm maximum size.

Lay hardcore in well-compacted layers not exceeding 225 mm in thickness. This prevents subsequent settlement.

The minimum depth of hardcore is 150 mm. The total depth of hardcore should not exceed 900 mm.

Use a suspended floor if 900 mm or more of hardcore is required. These can be of timber, in-situ reinforced concrete or precast concrete.

Place 20–50 mm of blinding on top of the compacted hardcore. This allows any remaining holes to be filled and provides a smooth surface for the damp-proof membrane.

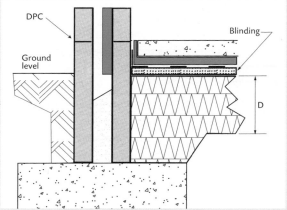

7-24 *The total depth of hardcore (D) should not exceed 900 mm except where a suspended floor is being used. A minimum thickness of blinding is required only to fill surface voids.*

Damp-proof membranes

A damp-proof membrane must be impermeable to moisture and must be continuous with the damp-proof course in the adjoining walls.

It must be tough enough to avoid being damaged during the laying of the finished screed. The DPM can be located below the floor screed (as in Fig. 7-25) or below the sub-floor as shown in Fig. 7-26. This is the ideal location because it keeps rising damp at a lower level than the detail employed in Fig. 7-25.

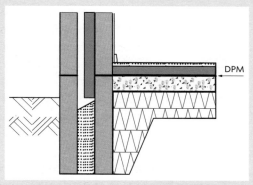

7-25 Damp-proof membrane placed above the concrete slab (sub-floor)

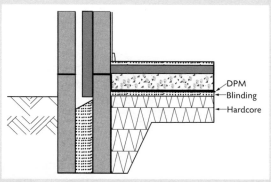

7-26 Damp-proof membrane placed underneath the concrete slab. Blinding is required on top of the hardcore to prevent the DPM from being punctured.

Polyethylene film is the most common material used for DPM. 1000 gauge is the recommended strength.

Other suitable materials include bitumen sheets with sealed joints, hot-applied pitch or three coats of cold applied bitumen.

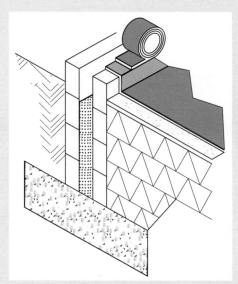

7-27 The DPM should lap under the DPC for full thickness of inner leaf.

Consider the following points in relation to the damp-proof membranes:

- Use only 1000 gauge polythene.
- Do not use recycled material.
- Avoid sharp edges that may damage the membrane.
- Take particular care at the junction of the DPM with the DPC, especially if a power float is used to finish the floor (see Fig. 7-27).
- Have the DPM in place before the walls are built above the DPC level. This ensures a positive connection between the two materials.

Damp-proof courses

The purpose of a damp-proof course is similar to that of a damp-proof membrane. It provides a barrier to the passage of moisture from an external source. DPCs may be either horizontal or vertical.

There are three broad areas where DPCs are used:

- below ground level, to prevent moisture rising from the soil;
- just above ground level, to prevent moisture rising up a wall by capillarity (rising damp);
- at openings, to prevent rainwater that falls directly onto the structure from entering the building.

Parapet
a low wall or railing along the edge of a balcony or roof. It is exposed to the elements on three of its four faces (see Fig. 8-17).

DPCs are also inserted in parapets and chimneys to resist the downward movement of moisture.

DPCs must be flexible enough to withstand fracture due to building movement and be easy to fit.

There are three categories of damp-proof courses:

- **Flexible:** used for most applications. They are the most suitable where stepped damp-proof courses are required and they can be dressed and shaped without fear of damage. Examples include lead, copper, bitumen, polyethylene and pitch/bitumen polymer.
- **Semi-rigid:** used in thick walls where they have to withstand high water pressure. Mastic asphalt is an example.
- **Rigid:** used where high bond strength is required. Examples include slate and dense bricks.

Ground-supported concrete floors (sub floors)

Ground-supported concrete floors are commonly referred to as **sub-floors**. The minimum depth of concrete for sub-floors is 100 mm. The norm is 150 mm. Do not build the edges of the concrete slab into the adjoining wall. This allows the two elements to move independently of each other in response to load variations.

The functions of ground floors are as follows:
- to withstand any imposed loads (live loads);
- to be of adequate depth to prevent the growth of vegetable matter within the building;
- to help prevent moisture or dampness from entering the building (a damp-proof membrane is inserted below the floor. Sometimes the DPM is placed above the floor, which results in moisture rising to the top of the sub-floor);
- to provide thermal insulation;
- to be durable (in order to minimise maintenance).

The majority of ground floors in domestic buildings consist of a concrete slab placed on a bed of hardcore. The advantages of this type of construction are:
- They are generally cheaper than suspended ground floors.
- There is no need for underfloor ventilation.
- No risk of dry rot (as in the case of suspended timber ground floors).
- A range of floor finishes is possible.

A cement and sand **screed** is usually placed on top of the concrete slab. Insulation can be placed at a number of locations.

A finished floor can be derived from a concrete slab using for example a power float. This eliminates the need for a screed and is faster and cheaper than using a screed. One disadvantage is the first-fixing of the service pipes must be in place at an earlier stage.

Floor screeds are advantageous for a number of reasons:
- They provide a smooth surface for the floor finish.
- They allow different floor thickness to be finished to the same level.
- Service pipes can be accommodated (provided the screed is thick enough).

The screed is placed after the concrete slab (sub-floor) has set. The top surface of the sub-floor is left in a rough state, which helps the screed to form a better bond with the sub-floor.

Sometimes a film of cement grout is applied to the sub-floor before the screed is poured. This further improves the bond between the screed and the sub-floor.

Reinforcement to concrete floors

Concrete floors are reinforced with a steel mesh. Reinforcement mesh is available in a range of standard formats.

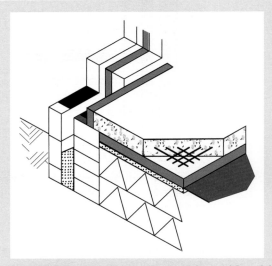

7-28 *Typical reinforced concrete suspended ground floor slab*

- Type A mesh has 10 mm diameter bars at 200 mm centres.
- Type B mesh has a 200 x 100 mm grid.
- Type C mesh has a 400 x 100 mm grid.

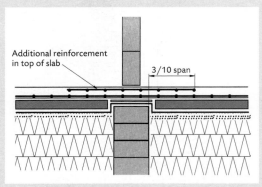

7-29 *Where a slab is continuous over a wall, additional reinforcement should be placed in the top of the slab to reduce the risk of cracking.*

Concrete floors are reinforced when they are suspended off thicker than normal rising walls.

Positions for piping in such slabs are shown in Fig. 7-30.

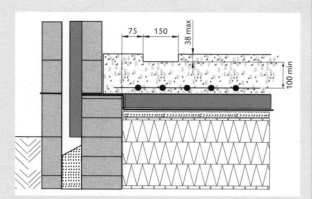

7-30 *Pipe recesses may only be formed in the perimeter of slabs.*

Timber ground floors

Timber ground floors are usually suspended, although timber floors placed on concrete screeds are becoming increasingly popular. These are known as floating floors.

Details of fixing timber floors to concrete are shown in Figs. 7-31 and 7-32.

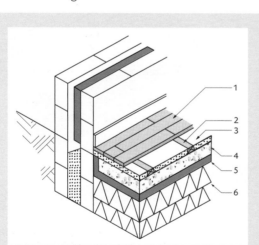

7-31 *Timber floorboard finish to concrete slab floor*

1   100 x 25 mm tongued and grooved flooring boards
2   75 x 38 mm dovetailed battens, treated with preservative at 400 mm centres
3   Cement and sand screed
4   150 mm concrete slab
5   DPM under insulation and not lower than sump level
6   Compacted hardcore

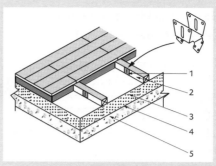

7-32 *Alternative method of fixing a timber floor to a concrete slab floor*

1   Galvanised steel clips set in screed to provide fixings for battens
2   50 x 38 mm battens at 400 mm centres
3   Sand/cement screed
4   Damp-proof membrane (DPM)
5   Concrete slab

Suspended timber floors consist of floorboards nailed to the floor joists. The floor joists are fixed to wall plates. The wall plates are placed on dwarf walls (also known as honey-combed and sleeper walls).

A damp-proof course separates the wall plates from the dwarf walls. The dwarf walls run at right angles to the joists (Fig. 7-33).

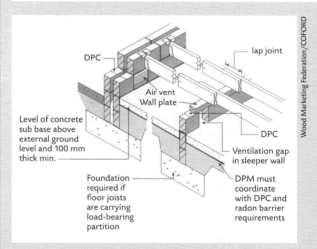

7-33 *Typical suspended ground floor details*

The Building Regulations specify certain requirements for the construction of suspended timber ground floors:

- A sub-floor must be laid to a minimum thickness of 100 mm.
- The top of the sub-floor must be above the highest level of the adjoining ground to avoid the sump effect.

- There must be a ventilated air space at least 75 mm from the top of the concrete to the bottom of the wall plate, and a minimum of 150 mm to the bottom of the floor joists.

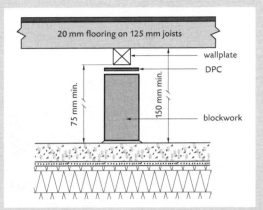

7-34 *Ventilation requirements for suspended timber floors*

- Ventilation openings must be placed in opposite external walls, so that ventilating air will have a free path. The area of opening must be equivalent to 1500 mm² for each metre run of wall.
- Pipes used to carry ventilating air across a cavity must be 150 mm min. in diameter. All openings must be fitted with grills to prevent rodents from entering.

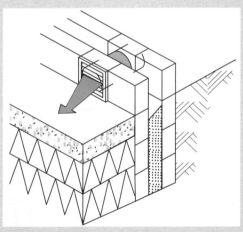

7-35 *Air vent sleeved across cavity*

Dwarf walls are built across each room up to a maximum of 2.0 m centres. The end walls should be positioned 50–100 mm from the room walls.

Airbricks are fitted at 3 m centres and should be located as high as possible.

Floor joists used are usually 125 x 44 mm, positioned at 400 mm centres. The ends of the joists are splayed and kept back approx. 20 mm from the surrounding wall. This prevents moisture being absorbed by the end grain of the joists.

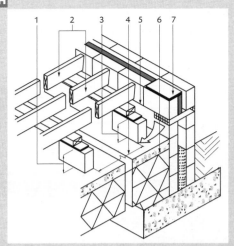

7-36 *Suspended timber floor with dwarf walls using standard floor joists at 400 mm centres, max. span 2.0 m*

1　150 mm to underside of joist
2　125 x 44 mm joists at 400 mm centres
3　75 mm min. to DPC
4　2.0 m maximum span
5　DPC
6　Concrete slab min. 100 mm thick
7　DPC tray above sleeved air vent

Suspended timber floors are insulated between the joists. Rolls of insulation are held in place by plastic netting that overlaps the joists.

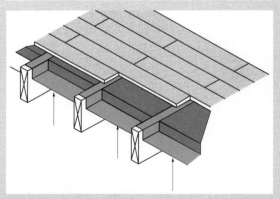

7-37 *Polypropylene netting used to support insulation quilts*

Rigid insulation boards are supported on battens fixed to the sides of the joists.

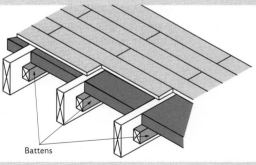

Battens

7-38 *Rigid insulation supported by battens fixed to joists*

H Where a hearth for a fireplace is required, specific arrangements must be complied with. See Figs. 7-39 and 7-40.

Ventilation must continue to be provided where a suspended timber ground floor meets a solid concrete floor. Ventilation pipes must be laid below

H the solid floor and connected to airbricks in the external wall. See Fig. 7-41.

The damp-proof membrane under the solid concrete floor must be connected to the damp-proof course in the dividing wall using a vertical damp-proof course.

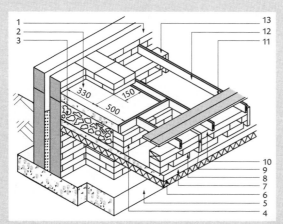

7-39 Joists at right angles to fireplace

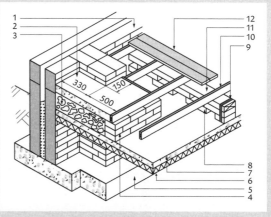

7-40 Joists parallel to fireplace

1 External wall	**1** External wall
2 Constructional hearth	**2** Constructional hearth
3 Rubble-filled void	**3** Rubble filled void
4 Fender wall	**4** Fender wall
5 Mass concrete strip foundation	**5** Mass concrete strip foundation
6 Compacted hardcore	**6** Compacted hardcore
7 Concrete sub-floor	**7** Concrete sub-floor
8 Dwarf walls @ 2.0 m centres	**8** Dwarf wall at 2.0 m centres
9 Holding down strap	**9** Holding down strap
10 100 x 75 mm wall plate on DPC	**10** 125 x 44 mm joist at 400 c/c
11 Flooring boards	**11** 100 x 75 mm wall plate on DPC
12 125 x 44 mm joists at 400 c/c	**12** Flooring boards nailed to joists
13 Dwarf wall	

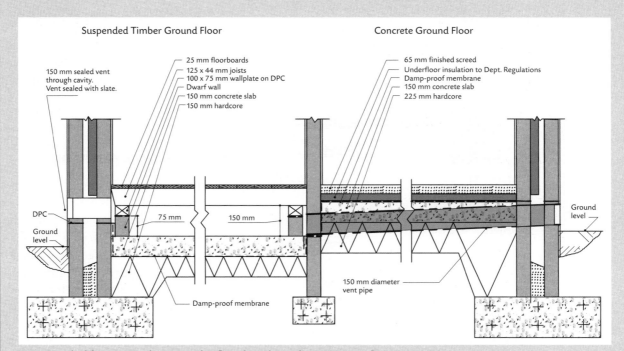

7-41 A method for cross ventilating a timber floor through an adjacent concrete floor

Precast concrete floors

There are a number of precast concrete floor systems suitable for use in suspended floor construction, at both ground floor and upper floor level. These are becoming an alternative to suspended timber floors, and even suspended in-situ concrete floors.

Precast concrete floors may be divided into three categories.

- **Hollow slab** (Fig. 7-42).
- **Precast plank** with in-situ concrete topping (Fig. 7-43).
- **Beam and block** (Fig. 7-44).

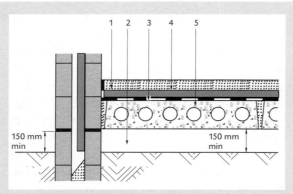

7-42 Typical hollow core slab detail

1   Screed thickness and reinforcement (where required) in accordance with manufacturer's recommendations
2   Ventilated underfloor void
3   500 gauge polythene vapour-control layer under insulation
4   Insulation
5   Proprietary hollow-core slab

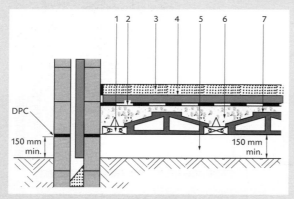

7-43 Typical precast plank and block floor

1   Proprietary reinforced plank
2   500 gauge polythene vapour-control layer
3   Screed thickness and reinforcement (where required) in accordance with manufacturer's recommendations
4   Insulation
5   Ventilated underfloor void
6   Concrete topping
7   Proprietary block

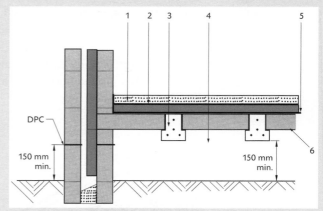

7-44 Typical beam and block floor

1   Screed thickness and reinforcement (where required) in accordance with manufacturer's recommendations
2   Insulation
3   Proprietary inverted T-beam
4   Ventilated underfloor void
5   500 gauge polythene vapour-control layer
6   Infill blocks between T-beams

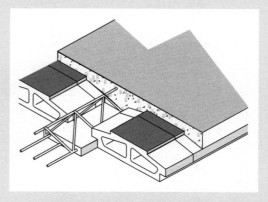

7-45 Pictorial view of precast plank and block floor

A ventilated air space measuring at least 150 mm is required from the ground to the bottom of the floor, or to the bottom of the insulation if used. This is the same as for suspended timber ground floors.

Pipe and duct positions

Pipes and ducts may run through a wall or a foundation. Where this is necessary create openings with at least 50 mm clearance all round the pipe and mask the opening with rigid sheet material.

Alternatively, build in a length of pipe as the wall or foundation is constructed. Ensure that the pipe is as short as possible, with its joints as close as possible to the wall faces (within 150 mm).

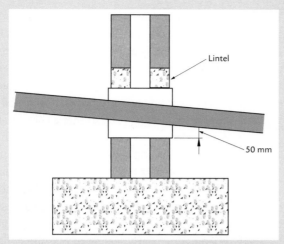

7-46 *Pipes penetrating buildings: arch or lintelled opening to give 50 mm space all round the pipe*

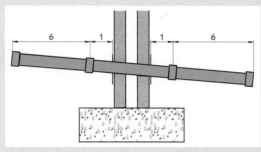

7-47 *Pipes penetrating buildings: short length of pipe bedded in wall*

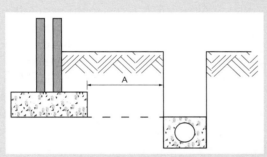

7-48 *Pipe runs near buildings: where A is less than 1 m, fill concrete trench to this level.*

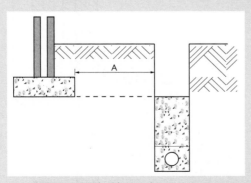

7-49 *Pipe runs near buildings: where A is 1 m or more, fill concrete trench to this level.*

Radon gas protection

Radon is a naturally occurring, colourless, odourless, radioactive gas. It enters buildings from the underlying soil and, in certain cases, can accumulate to such a concentration that it is considered a potential health hazard.

The Building Regulations require that measures are taken in the design and construction of buildings to prevent this from happening.

It is not possible to predict accurately the concentration of radon likely to occur in a proposed building on the basis of a pre-construction site investigation, but you establish if the site is in an area where high radon concentrations are common.

Some areas in Ireland are more prone to high radon levels than others. The Radiological Protection Institute of Ireland (RPII) measures radon levels in existing buildings. The RPII has produced 'radon maps' of each county showing the percentage of houses predicted to exceed the National Reference Level of radon for dwellings (200 becquerels per cubic metre, Bq/m³). Armed with this information, you can select the most suitable type of radon protection. See **www.rpii.ie**.

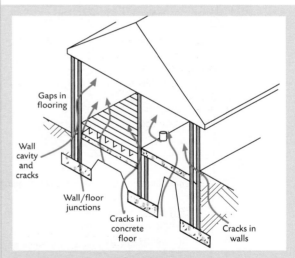

7-50 *Major entry routes for radon*

There are two main ways of achieving protection from radon in new houses:

THE PASSIVE SYSTEM This consists of an airtight and consequently radon-proof barrier. Use 1200 gauge polythene sheet across the whole of the building.

THE ACTIVE SYSTEM This consists of a powered radon extraction system consisting of a sump or sumps with ducts to the external walls. The system may need to be fan assisted.

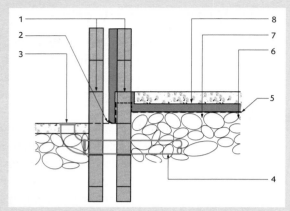

7-51 Radon details for a cavity wall/ground supported floor

1 DPC
2 Radon-resisting sealing tape
3 Pipe terminates outside dwelling and is capped.
4 100 mm diameter pipe to sump.
5 Continuous radon membrane with all joints lapped and sealed.
6 Hardcore
7 Sand blinding
8 Insulation underneath concrete slab

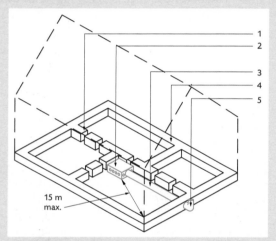

7-52 Typical radon sump location in a single dwelling

1 Gaps left in rising wall to allow radon to pass through
2 Radon sump located centrally
3 100 mm diameter pipe
4 Rising walls
5 Pipe terminates outside dwelling and is capped. Pipe can be extended and fan fitted should subsequent test readings require it.

Radon in existing dwellings

Tests have shown that the level of radon concentration and pressure of soil gas are the main factors contributing to indoor radon problems. The most common method of infiltration is through cracks and other openings in the ground floor and adjoining walls.

To control infiltration in an existing building it is necessary to make the floors and walls more effective barriers by sealing all the points of entry. This is not easily achieved and experience has shown that missing even minor openings in a sealing process will compromise the whole exercise.

For existing concrete floors, remove all coverings, skirtings etc. so that all cracks and leaks can be dealt with. Use sealing materials that are flexible, permanently elastic and capable of adhering to a variety of surfaces. High quality sealants, such as silicone, polysulphide and polyurethane, are most likely to be successful.

It is very difficult to seal timber floors in existing buildings. Similarly sealing of oversite concrete is not a practical proposition. Other options should be considered including the extraction of gas from the underfloor void.

Depressurisation of the underlying soil can be used to modify the pressure gradient between the soil and the building. This usually means providing a sump in the permeable hardcore layer under the concrete floor slab. Radon gas is drawn to the sump from which it is piped to the outside air. The sump may be located centrally or close to the external walls, depending on the likely area of influence.

A single sump has an influence over an area of at least 250 m^3 and for a distance of 15 m from the sump. A number of separate sumps may be required with pipework connected to a single rising pipe.

Alternatively access to the permeable hardcore layer may be gained from the exterior of the building. This would involve breaking through the rising wall, extracting fill to create a small void and inserting a pipe to reduce the underfloor pressure and draw off the soil gas out into the open air.

If a fan is required, consider locating it in the attic as durability and maintenance problems are likely to be greater when external pipework and fans are used.

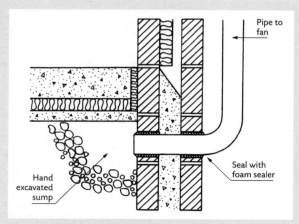

7-53 Externally excavated sump

The
External Envelope
& Superstructure

Concrete rooftiles are used extensively throughout the country, offering cost-effective and aesthetically pleasing solutions, which are particularly suitable for Irish weather conditions.

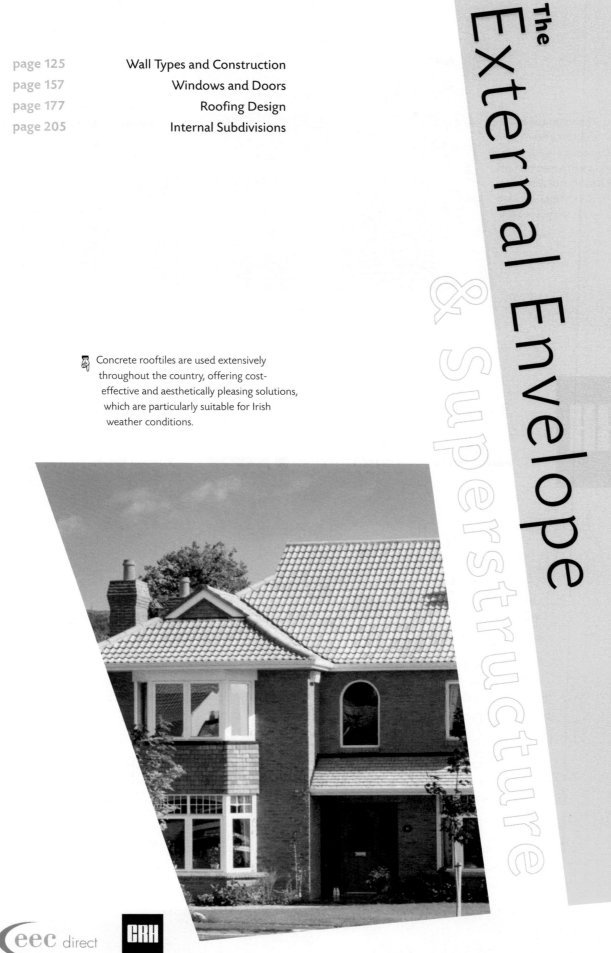

eec direct   CRH

The Schumann building, University of Limerick, which uses Ormonde's red clay facing bricks for its external walls. A standard brick of dimensions 215mm x 105 x 65mm was used for the this project.

Roadstone

Roadstone is a leading manufacturer of Rooftiles in the Republic of Ireland. Concrete roof tiles are an extensively used style of roofing throughout the country and are not only aesthetically pleasing but offer lasting protection against the vagaries of Irish weather. Concrete roof tiles offer a cost effective solution to a wide range of roofing requirements.

An effective roof covering performs many functions other than simply keeping a building weather tight. Among these are the need to provide adequate resistance to wind uplift forces and to ventilate the roof space beneath. The house displayed overleaf uses stack bonded Spanish Roll rooftiles, appropriate to its surroundings.

Ormonde Brick

Ormonde Brick is the leading producer of fired-clay facing bricks and special products of different colours and textures in the Rep. of Ireland. All bricks are manufactured from locally occurring shale and fireclay in Castlecomer, Co, Kilkenny.

Tyrone Brick

Tyrone Brick manufactures clay facing bricks in Dungannon, Co. Tyrone. Tyrone's main markets are Northern Ireland, the Republic of Ireland, England and Scotland. The raw materials for Tyrone's entire brick range are hewn from clay pits in the region.

Chapter 8

Wall types and construction

Principles of wall design

Walls are either **load-bearing** or **non-load-bearing**.

Load-bearing walls support the weight of floors and roofs. Non-load-bearing walls support at most their own weight. Each type may be further sub-divided into external and internal walls.

External non-load-bearing walls are referred to as panels, in-fill panels or cladding. The name used depends on how the walls are fixed to the framed structure.

Internal walls are also known as **dividing walls** or **partition walls**. The term 'partition' refers to either load-bearing or non-load-bearing walls that divide the space within a building.

The main functions of walls are to provide adequate:
- strength and stability
- weather resistance
- fire resistance
- thermal insulation
- sound insulation

Strength and stability

The **strength** of a wall is its measured resistance to stresses. Stresses on walls are set up by their own weight, superimposed loads and wind.

The **stability** of a wall is its resistance to overturning and buckling. Buckling results from wind pressure.

> **Superimposed**
> to place on or over something else.

Weather resistance

One of the main functions of walls is to prevent rain and wind penetration. Wind penetration is less of a problem than rain and dampness. Dampness may enter a building by a number of avenues.

Several tonnes of water are used in constructing a house by traditional means. It takes six to eight weeks for a typical house to dry out after construction.

Moisture can enter through roofs and chimneys, depending on how well they are sealed. Ensure that tiles and slates are laid to the correct pitch and are adequately fixed. It is difficult to seal flat roofs completely.

Most moisture penetration occurs through walls exposed to the prevailing wind and rain.

Properly detailed, well-constructed cavity walls will not allow penetration of rain. However, if construction standards are inadequate, the most likely area where penetration may occur in cavity walls is at openings. This is due to poor detailing. Dampness will also result from mortar droppings on wall ties.

Rising damp will not present a problem in new houses unless the damp-proof course is defective. The lack of damp-proof courses in older houses led to rising damp. Rising damp may result internally if a damp-proof membrane is absent or incorrectly lapped with the DPC.

> **Condensation**
> Water or other vapour in warm air turns to liquid when the air temperature drops below the dewpoint of the liquid. Ventilation removes water vapour. Dewpoint is the temperature at which water vapour in the air becomes saturated and dew begins to form.

Condensation is another means of dampness occuring inside a building.

Fire resistance

The Building Regulations require that walls are highly resistant fire barriers.

Walls divide buildings into smaller areas. These areas are required to contain a fire and minimise fire risks to the rest of the building. In this way walls provide a means of escape for the occupants in the event of a fire.

Party walls must be constructed up to roof level to prevent the spread of fire between buildings.

Wall and ceiling linings can contribute to the spread of fire and must be designed with this in mind. Plastered surfaces are acceptable.

Timber sheeting used as a lining is only permitted in small panels. The total area of timber panelling in a room should not exceed 20 m², or half the floor area of the room, whichever is less.

Timber sheeting fixed to the underside of floor joists will not meet the recommended levels of fire resistance. The ceiling must first be slabbed using plasterboard. The timber sheeting is then fixed to the plasterboard.

Traditional house construction techniques generally meet the requirements for fire resistance.

Thermal insulation

The external walls of a building, along with the roof, must prevent heat from inside escaping to the atmosphere. The reverse is also true, that they should prevent the interior heating up excessively during hot weather.

Thermal insulation helps to prevent condensation. It also reduces expansion and contraction of the building.

The thermal transmittance or **U-value** of a wall is a measure of its ability to conduct heat. The higher the U-value, the greater the rate of heat loss through the wall.

> U-values are expressed in $W/m^2\,K$ (watts per square metre for 1 kelvin difference between the internal and external temperatures).

Kelvin
The Kelvin temperature scale is the basic SI unit of thermodynamic temperature. It is denoted by either kelvin or K.

Sound insulation

Construction techniques ensure that noise is not a problem in most situations. Nevertheless, the number of openings in a wall is a weak point, because openings reduce the overall sound insulation value of the wall.

Materials used in wall construction

Bricks

There are three categories of clay brick available: common, facing and engineering bricks.

Engineering bricks are the strongest. Calcium silicate and concrete bricks are also available.

The standard brick measures 215 mm × 102.5 mm × 65 mm. The length of bricks is more than twice the width. This allows two bricks to be laid side by side with a 10 mm mortar joint between them.

Bricks and blocks are referred to by their designated size. This is the actual size of the brick or block plus a 10 mm joint width to each dimension.

Pressed bricks have a depression called a 'frog' on one or both faces. The frog reduces the weight of the brick and also forms a key for the bedding mortar.

Other bricks are perforated right through for the same purpose.

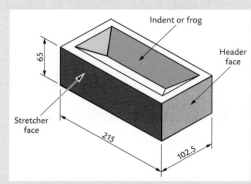

8-1 *Standard brick showing actual dimensions and different parts*

Concrete blocks

There are two main types of concrete block: solid and hollow. The normal size is 450 × 215 mm, with a range of thickness varying from 60 to 250 mm.

8-2 *Solid concrete block, 450 × 215 × 100 mm*

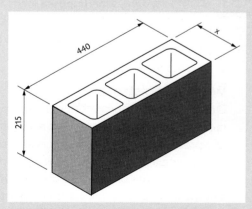

8-3 *Hollow blocks, also referred to as cavity blocks, are available in different thicknesses (x)*

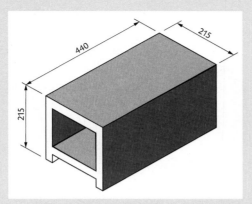

8-4 *The cavity in a hollow block can run horizontally as well as vertically.*

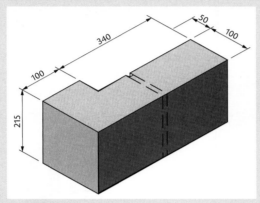

8-5 *Dual-purpose cavity closer*

Mortars

The mortar used in blockwork or brickwork transfers the stresses (tensile, compressive and shear) uniformly between adjacent bricks/blocks down to the foundation. To do this effectively mortar must:

- have adequate strength
- have good workability
- be plastic and flexible while the blocks/bricks are being laid
- be durable
- form a good bond
- be economical to produce

Shrinkage cracks will occur in the mortar if it is weaker than the blocks/bricks. If the mortar is stronger than the bricks/blocks, shrinkage cracks may be vertical, running through the bricks/blocks and thereby weakening the structure.

Mortar is a mixture of sand and cement, with or without the addition of lime. Lime makes the mix more workable. Plasticisers have the same effect and are now largely used instead of lime.

Damp-proof courses

Damp-proof courses are used in walls to prevent moisture penetration. They prevent the upward movement of moisture from the soil. The different types were dealt with in Chapter 7.

Lintels

Lintels are used to span openings and carry the loads from above to either side. The two most common types of lintel in use are:

- precast concrete lintels
- pressed metal lintels

Fig. 8-6 shows typical minimum bearing and DPC requirements.

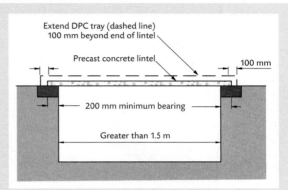

8-6 *Minimum bearing and DPC requirements for precast concrete lintels.*

Wall ties

Wall ties are available in a number of materials and types. Galvanised mild steel and stainless steel are the preferred materials. Plastic wall ties do not comply with the building regulations.

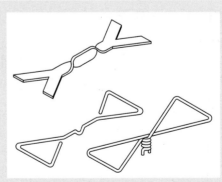

8-7 *Wall ties*

Wall ties must be long enough to ensure that 50 mm is embedded into the mortar bed of each leaf. A 200 mm long wall tie is used with a 100 mm cavity.

Wall ties must be installed with the drip downward. There must be no mortar droppings on the wall ties. The correct spacing and distribution of wall ties is shown in Fig 8-8.

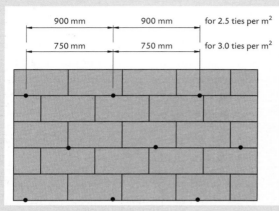

8-8 Spacing of wall ties: keep wall ties as near to openings as possible. Stagger vertical courses of wall ties.

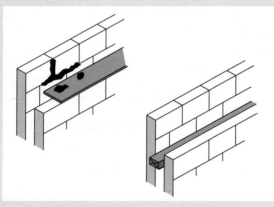

8-9 Two methods of preventing mortar droppings falling on to wall ties.

Cavity wall construction

A wall constructed of two leaves or skins with a space between them is called a cavity wall. This is the most common type of external wall construction used in domestic buildings.

Solid single-leaf walls are difficult to damp-proof. This led to the development of cavity walls. Cavity walls prevent the penetration of moisture to the inner leaf, provided the cavity is not bridged in any way.

The cavity is filled with lean concrete below DPC level. This gives the wall additional strength to resist the pressure of the soil and backfill pressing against it. If this were not done the two leaves would have a tendency to move towards each other.

Ensure that the cavity extends 150 mm below the DPC level.

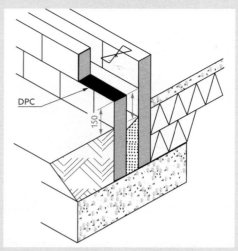

8-10 The DPC must be a minimum of 150 mm above ground level and the cavity should extend 150 mm below the DPC level.

A damp-proof course must be inserted over reinforced concrete lintels where openings occur, under windowsills and at jambs to openings.

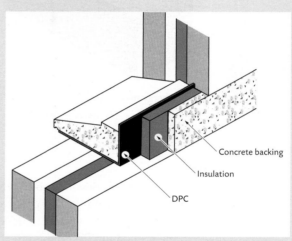

8-11 Provide DPC to bottom, back, and end of sills.

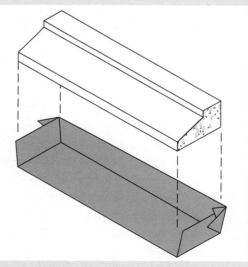

8-12 The DPC should be wrapped around the sill as shown.

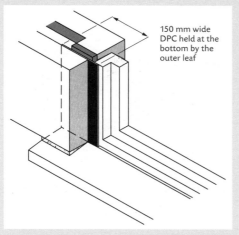

8-13 *Jamb detail: window frames should be installed behind the outer leaf.*

150 mm wide DPC held at the bottom by the outer leaf

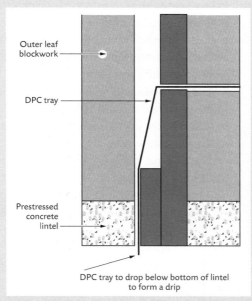

Outer leaf blockwork

DPC tray

Prestressed concrete lintel

DPC tray to drop below bottom of lintel to form a drip

8-14 *Prestressed concrete lintels: stepped DPCs or cavity tray DPCs must be used to all openings in cavity walls.*

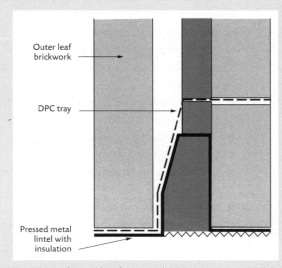

Outer leaf brickwork

DPC tray

Pressed metal lintel with insulation

8-15 *Pressed metal lintels: stepped DPCs or cavity tray DPCs must be used to all openings in cavity walls.*

A cavity wall should not be ventilated (except in the case of timber-frame construction). This will reduce its efficiency as a thermal insulator.

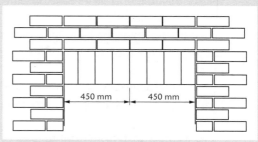

450 mm   450 mm

8-16 *Weepholes, at 450 mm max. centres, should be provided where the outer leaf is of brick construction.*

Parapet walls need careful design and consideration as they are exposed to the elements on three faces.

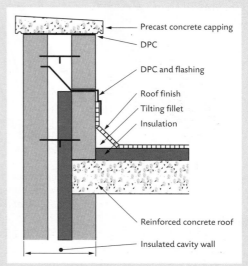

Precast concrete capping

DPC

DPC and flashing

Roof finish

Tilting fillet

Insulation

Reinforced concrete roof

Insulated cavity wall

8-17 *Parapet wall detail*

Advantages of cavity walls
- prevent moisture penetrating to the inner wall
- provide good thermal insulation
- inner leaf may be constructed of alternative materials such as timber or thermal blocks
- greater sound insulation than a solid single-leaf construction

Disadvantages of cavity walls
- greater care and accuracy required during construction
- damp-proof courses must be included to all openings
- more expensive than a solid single-leaf wall

Party wall construction

A party wall is the dividing wall between two houses, built as a pair of semi-detached houses. It is thicker than the normal internal dividing wall, min. 225 mm solid wall.

A party wall must be built right up to the top of the slope of the roof, to prevent fire spread and reduce sound transmission.

Joists should not be set into the party wall. Instead fix the joists using an appropriate joist hanger.

Joists must span from front to back of the house. This eliminates the need to secure them at the party wall.

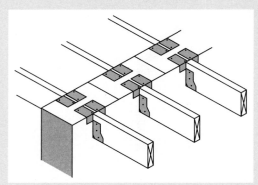

8-20 Joist hangers are used instead of setting the joists into the party wall.

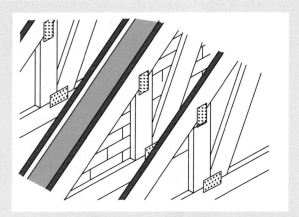

8-18 Party wall detail: leave a 25 mm gap between the top of the wall and the top of the rafter to allow for roof settlement. This gap will be packed with mineral fibre quilt at the roofing stage.

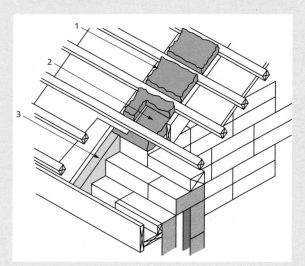

8-19 Typical party wall fire-stopping detail

1 Mineral fibre quilt suitable for cavity fire stopping to underside of roof covering
2 Mineral fibre quilt as fire stop along top of party wall to underside of felt
3 50 mm thick wire-reinforced mineral wool

Timber-frame construction

In most cases, the largest structural components in timber-framed houses – wall frames and roof trusses – are prefabricated. This reduces the amount of on-site labour required by limiting the work to erecting and fitting.

The principles and requirements of a timber-frame wall are the same as for a cavity or solid wall. It must still transmit all vertical and horizontal loads to the foundations.

The external leaf is usually 100 mm dense blockwork or brickwork. The external leaf is non-load-bearing. Its main function is to provide appropriate weatherproofing to the building.

The construction of two-storey timber-frame buildings involves erecting the first storey and fixing the floor decking. The floor deck is used as an erection platform for the second storey.

Timber-frame wall panels vary in size from 3.6 m in length (for manual handling), to full length panels (which are placed with a crane).

Vertical studs at 400 mm or 600 mm centres, nailed to top and bottom rails, form the construction for the wall panels.

Noggings are generally not required for structural purposes. Where they are used their function is to:

- provide support for partitions and/or the edges of plasterboard sheets
- provide support for fixings and fittings
- resist buckling of studs
- provide the required fire resistance, where necessary
- support joints in external plywood

Stress-graded timber must be used for timber-frame wall panels. The most common size is 89 × 38 mm. A wood-based sheet material nailed to the external face of the frame acts as wind bracing. This structural frame provides for high levels of insulation.

Fire resistance is achieved with the internal linings (usually plasterboard), the timber framing and the wall insulation. Using a double layer of plasterboard with staggered joints provides one-hour fire resistance.

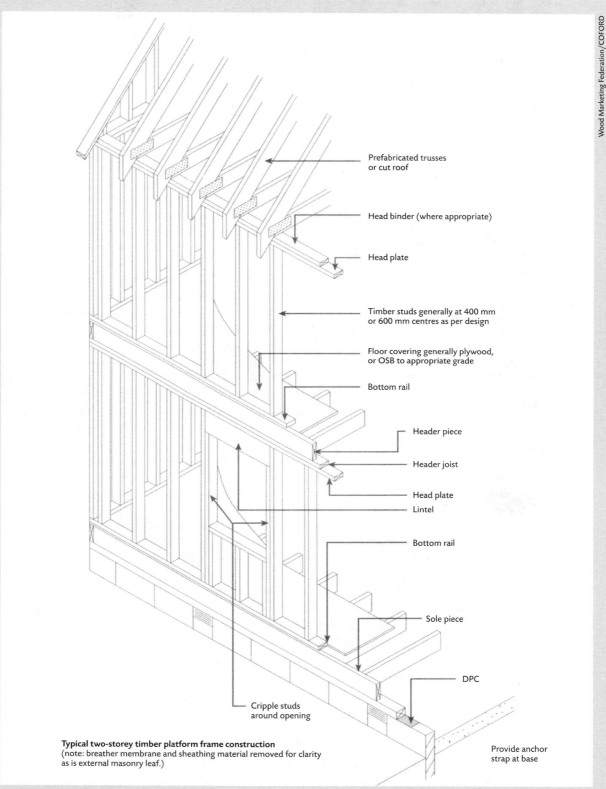

Wood Marketing Federation/COFORD

Prefabricated trusses or cut roof

Head binder (where appropriate)

Head plate

Timber studs generally at 400 mm or 600 mm centres as per design

Floor covering generally plywood, or OSB to appropriate grade

Bottom rail

Header piece

Header joist

Head plate

Lintel

Bottom rail

Sole piece

DPC

Cripple studs around opening

Provide anchor strap at base

Typical two-storey timber platform frame construction
(note: breather membrane and sheathing material removed for clarity as is external masonry leaf.)

8-21 Timber-frame component elements

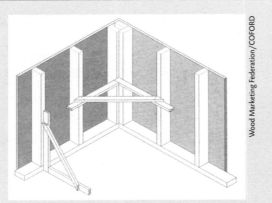

8-22 *Set out: accurate setting out of the sub-structure on which the timber frame sits is vital. Ensure the base is level and that all corners are set out square.*

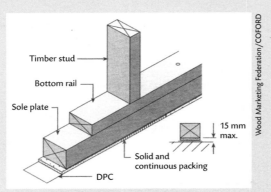

8-23 *Level sole plate: the sole plate is levelled before the wall frames are fixed.*

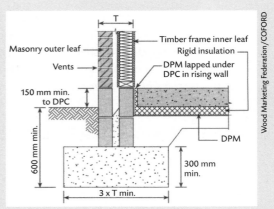

8-25 *Foundations: the continuous concrete strip foundation is the most common type used.*

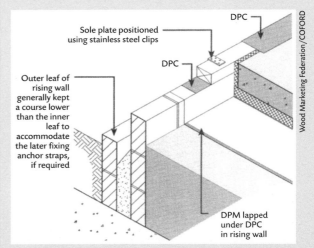

8-26 *Rising walls: the sole plate is fixed to the rising walls by means of stainless steel fixing clips located at 1200 mm centres. Sole plates should be pressure treated with preservatives.*

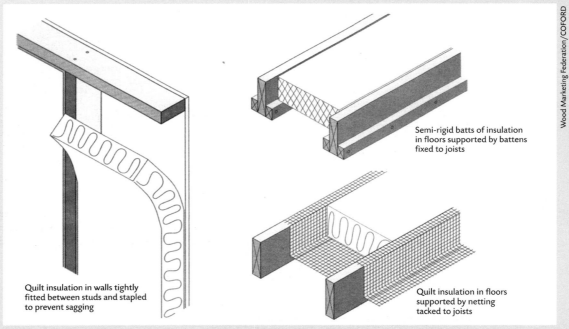

8-24 *Timber-frame insulation details. Mineral wool is the most common type of insulation used in timber-frame construction. It is available in rolled quilts or semi-rigid batts in a range of thicknesses, and is fitted into the void between studs. The area between the studs must be completely filled with insulation to avoid cold bridges.*

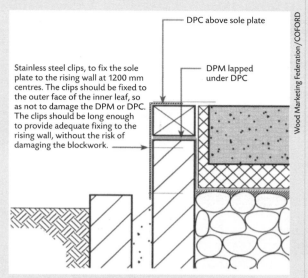

Stainless steel clips, to fix the sole plate to the rising wall at 1200 mm centres. The clips should be fixed to the outer face of the inner leaf, so as not to damage the DPM or DPC. The clips should be long enough to provide adequate fixing to the rising wall, without the risk of damaging the blockwork.

DPC above sole plate

DPM lapped under DPC

8-27 *Stainless steel clips to fix the sole plate in the cavity. The cavity void in timber-frame construction must be ventilated. This is achieved using proprietary ventilators at 1500 mm horizontal centres below DPC level in the external masonry leaf.*

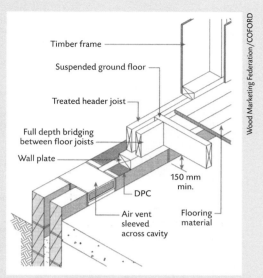

Timber frame

Suspended ground floor

Treated header joist

Full depth bridging between floor joists

Wall plate

150 mm min.

DPC

Air vent sleeved across cavity

Flooring material

8-29 *Floor types: timber-frame dwellings can be built with all the common types of ground floor.*

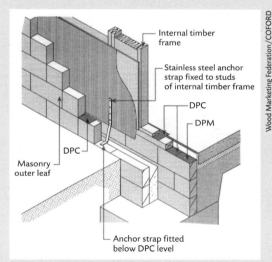

Internal timber frame

Stainless steel anchor strap fixed to studs of internal timber frame

DPC

DPM

DPC

Masonry outer leaf

Anchor strap fitted below DPC level

8-28 *In certain cases the timber frame may need to be anchored to the external masonry leaf, by means of stainless steel straps fixed to full height studs.*

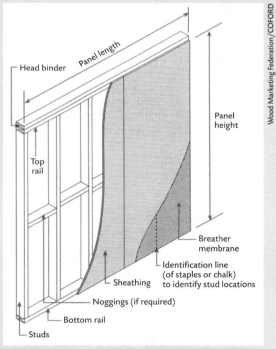

Head binder

Panel length

Top rail

Panel height

Breather membrane

Identification line (of staples or chalk) to identify stud locations

Sheathing

Noggings (if required)

Bottom rail

Studs

8-30 *Wall panel components: the external walls consists of three elements, the load-bearing timber-frame inner leaf, ventilated cavity and external non-load-bearing masonry leaf.*

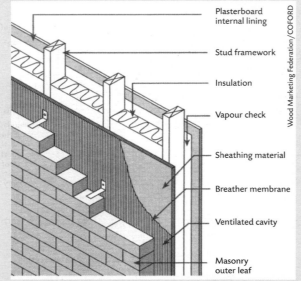

Plasterboard internal lining

Stud framework

Insulation

Vapour check

Sheathing material

Breather membrane

Ventilated cavity

Masonry outer leaf

Wood Marketing Federation /COFORD

8-31 Close-up of wall panel components: the function of the **stud framing** *is to act as the vertical load-bearing skeleton of the external wall and to resist lateral wind loads. Stud depths are generally 89 or 100 mm, but 150 mm is sometimes used to accommodate more insulation for improved wall 'U' values.*

The **sheathing material:**
– *provides the necessary stiffness to resist lateral loads*
– *reduces wind penetration of the structure*
– *provides rapid enclosure of the building during construction*
– *encloses and supports wall insulation*
– *provides a solid background onto which the breather membrane is fixed.*

Breather membrane: *the external face of the sheathing must be covered with a breather membrane. Its function is to protect the frame until the cladding is complete and to provide a second line of defence against wind-driven rain or moisture that may penetrate the cladding. The breather membrane must be waterproof, but permeable, to allow water vapour passing through the inner leaf to enter the ventilated cavity and thereby eliminate condensation within the wall panel itself.*

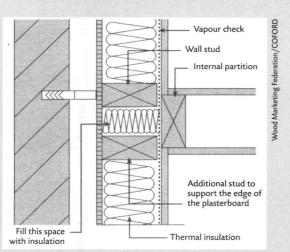

Vapour check

Wall stud

Internal partition

Additional stud to support the edge of the plasterboard

Fill this space with insulation

Thermal insulation

Wood Marketing Federation /COFORD

8-32 Plan view of typical wall junction.
Vapour check: *by fitting a vapour check between the internal wall and the warm side of the insulation the amount of water vapour passing through the wall and the likelihood of condensation occurring in the cavity due to different internal and external temperature levels will be reduced. 500-gauge polythene provides suitable vapour checks.*

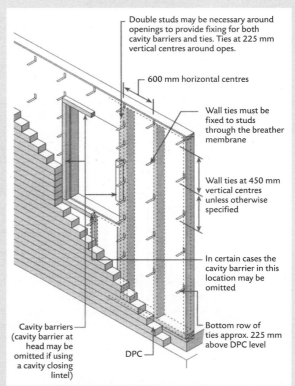

Double studs may be necessary around openings to provide fixing for both cavity barriers and ties. Ties at 225 mm vertical centres around opes.

600 mm horizontal centres

Wall ties must be fixed to studs through the breather membrane

Wall ties at 450 mm vertical centres unless otherwise specified

In certain cases the cavity barrier in this location may be omitted

Bottom row of ties approx. 225 mm above DPC level

Cavity barriers (cavity barrier at head may be omitted if using a cavity closing lintel)

DPC

Wood Marketing Federation /COFORD

8-33 Wall ties should be nailed to the timber frame at stud locations and should not be fixed to the sheathing material only.

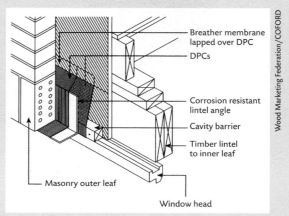

Breather membrane lapped over DPC

DPCs

Corrosion resistant lintel angle

Cavity barrier

Timber lintel to inner leaf

Masonry outer leaf

Window head

Wood Marketing Federation /COFORD

8-34 Head detail

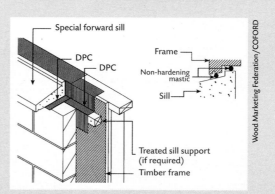

Special forward sill

DPC

DPC

Frame

Non-hardening mastic

Sill

Treated sill support (if required)

Timber frame

Wood Marketing Federation /COFORD

8-35 Sill detail

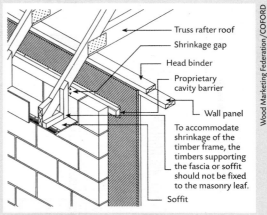

Timber frame

Vertical cavity barrier

Window frame

Vertical DPC

Masonry leaf

Non-hardening mastic pointing

8-36 Jamb detail

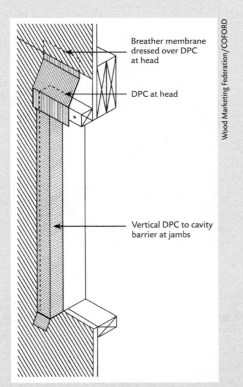

Breather membrane dressed over DPC at head

DPC at head

Vertical DPC to cavity barrier at jambs

8-37 Damp-proof courses should be provided at all external openings and to all timber cavity barriers.

Truss rafter roof

Shrinkage gap

Head binder

Proprietary cavity barrier

Wall panel

To accommodate shrinkage of the timber frame, the timbers supporting the fascia or soffit should not be fixed to the masonry leaf.

Soffit

8-38 Eaves detail: the soffit board should not be carried over the top of the masonry leaf. To accommodate natural shrinkage of the timber frame, a gap should be left between the roof timbers and the top of the masonry leaf.

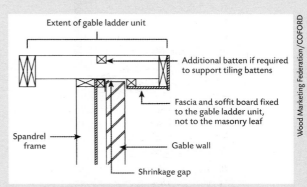

Extent of gable ladder unit

Additional batten if required to support tiling battens

Fascia and soffit board fixed to the gable ladder unit, not to the masonry leaf

Spandrel frame

Gable wall

Shrinkage gap

8-39 Gable verge detail formed with a gable ladder. Shrinkage requirements as for Fig. 8-38.

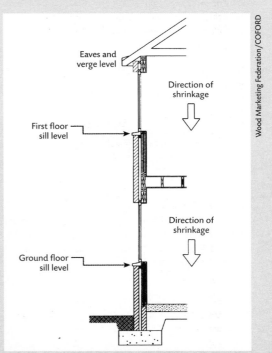

Eaves and verge level

Direction of shrinkage

First floor sill level

Direction of shrinkage

Ground floor sill level

8-40 Shrinkage gap locations: dimensional requirements for shrinkage gaps range from 3 mm to 12 mm.

Wood Marketing Federation/COFORD

Architectural Technology

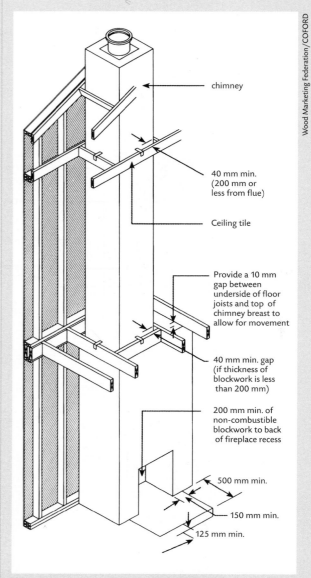

Proprietary perpend ventilators at eaves level

Cavity barrier at eaves level

DPC

Proprietary perpend ventilators below DPC level and 150 mm above ground level

8-41 Cavity ventilation

chimney

40 mm min. (200 mm or less from flue)

Ceiling tile

Provide a 10 mm gap between underside of floor joists and top of chimney breast to allow for movement

40 mm min. gap (if thickness of blockwork is less than 200 mm)

200 mm min. of non-combustible blockwork to back of fireplace recess

500 mm min.

150 mm min.

125 mm min.

8-43 Fireplaces and chimneys: Method 2 shows the fireplace and chimney stack built inside the room after the internal linings have been fixed. This type of construction requires that the floor and roof members be trimmed around the chimney stack.

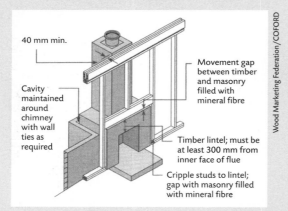

40 mm min.

Cavity maintained around chimney with wall ties as required

Movement gap between timber and masonry filled with mineral fibre

Timber lintel; must be at least 300 mm from inner face of flue

Cripple studs to lintel; gap with masonry filled with mineral fibre

8-42 Fireplaces and chimneys: there are two primary methods of constructing chimneys in external walls. Method 1, above, shows the fireplace and chimney stack located on the outside of the timber-frame external wall panel.

Wood Marketing Federation/COFORD

136

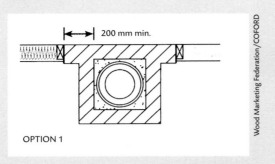

OPTION 1

Wood Marketing Federation/COFORD

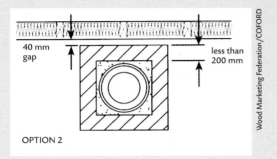

40 mm
gap

less than
200 mm

OPTION 2

Wood Marketing Federation/COFORD

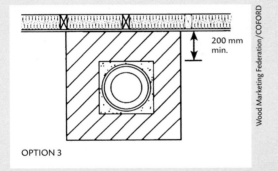

200 mm
min.

OPTION 3

Wood Marketing Federation/COFORD

8-44 *Dimensional requirements for chimneys in external walls*

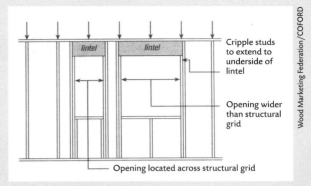

Cripple studs
to extend to
underside of
lintel

Opening wider
than structural
grid

Opening located across structural grid

Wood Marketing Federation/COFORD

8-45 *Lintel opening supports*

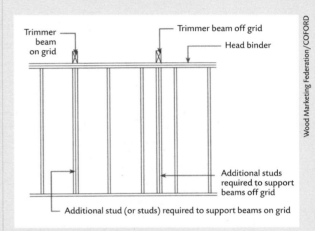

Trimmer
beam
on grid

Trimmer beam off grid

Head binder

Additional studs
required to support
beams off grid

Additional stud (or studs) required to support beams on grid

Wood Marketing Federation/COFORD

8-46 *Trimmer beam supports*

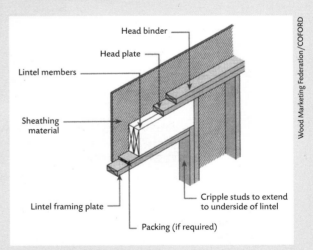

Head binder

Head plate

Lintel members

Sheathing
material

Lintel framing plate

Cripple studs to extend
to underside of lintel

Packing (if required)

Wood Marketing Federation/COFORD

8-47 *Load-bearing lintel*

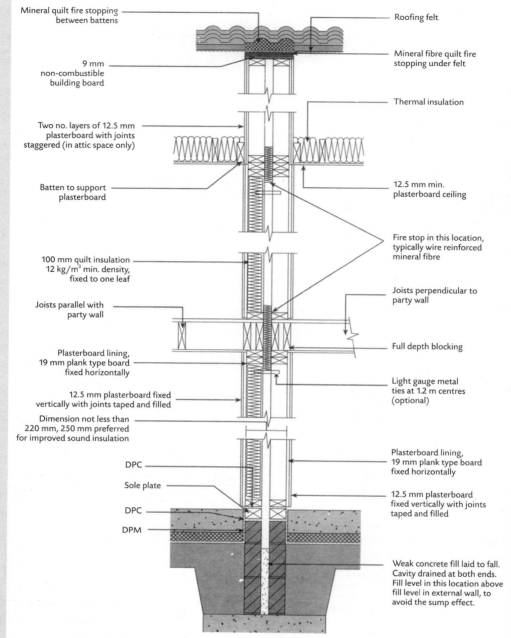

Mineral quilt fire stopping between battens

Roofing felt

9 mm non-combustible building board

Mineral fibre quilt fire stopping under felt

Thermal insulation

Two no. layers of 12.5 mm plasterboard with joints staggered (in attic space only)

12.5 mm min. plasterboard ceiling

Batten to support plasterboard

Fire stop in this location, typically wire reinforced mineral fibre

100 mm quilt insulation 12 kg/m³ min. density, fixed to one leaf

Joists perpendicular to party wall

Joists parallel with party wall

Full depth blocking

Plasterboard lining, 19 mm plank type board fixed horizontally

Light gauge metal ties at 1.2 m centres (optional)

12.5 mm plasterboard fixed vertically with joints taped and filled

Dimension not less than 220 mm, 250 mm preferred for improved sound insulation

DPC

Plasterboard lining, 19 mm plank type board fixed horizontally

Sole plate

DPC

12.5 mm plasterboard fixed vertically with joints taped and filled

DPM

Weak concrete fill laid to fall. Cavity drained at both ends. Fill level in this location above fill level in external wall, to avoid the sump effect.

Wood Marketing Federation/COFORD

8-48 Party walls are normally formed by two independent wall frames. Illustrated is a typical vertical section through a party wall in a two-storey semi-detached or terraced house. The function of the party wall is to provide an effective barrier against the spread of fire and sound transmission.

Note: 225 mm solid block party walls are used extensively in timber frame construction.

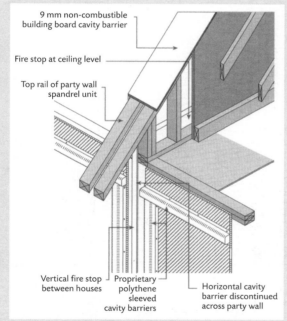

9 mm non-combustible building board cavity barrier carried down to abut the fascia board

Fascia board

Non-combustible building board or reinforced mineral fibre

Soffit board

Top rail of party wall spandrel panel

8-49 Fire stopping at eaves party wall: the void formed by the slope of the rafters and the horizontal soffit to the eaves must be adequately sealed against fire spread at each party wall position.

9 mm non-combustible building board cavity barrier

Fire stop at ceiling level

Top rail of party wall spandrel unit

Vertical fire stop between houses

Proprietary polythene sleeved cavity barriers

Horizontal cavity barrier discontinued across party wall

8-50 Fire stopping at party wall: the layout shown will maintain the integrity of the party wall against fire spread and sound transmission.

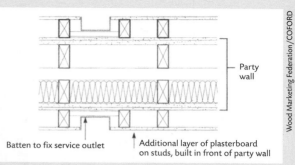

Party wall

Batten to fix service outlet

Additional layer of plasterboard on studs, built in front of party wall

8-51 Provision of services on the party wall: services must not be built into the thickness of the party wall proper.

Note: Cavity barriers can be combustible or non-combustible material, but fire-stops must be non-combustible.

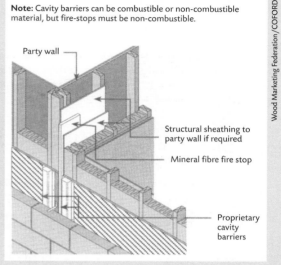

Party wall

Structural sheathing to party wall if required

Mineral fibre fire stop

Proprietary cavity barriers

8-52 Fire stopping: the cavity between the timber-frame party wall and the external masonry leaf must be closed with vertical barriers.

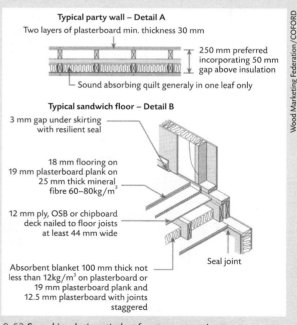

Typical party wall – Detail A
Two layers of plasterboard min. thickness 30 mm

250 mm preferred incorporating 50 mm gap above insulation

Sound absorbing quilt generaly in one leaf only

Typical sandwich floor – Detail B

3 mm gap under skirting with resilient seal

18 mm flooring on 19 mm plasterboard plank on 25 mm thick mineral fibre 60–80kg/m³

12 mm ply, OSB or chipboard deck nailed to floor joists at least 44 mm wide

Absorbent blanket 100 mm thick not less than 12kg/m³ on plasterboard or 19 mm plasterboard plank and 12.5 mm plasterboard with joints staggered

Seal joint

8-53 Sound insulation: timber-frame construction generally relies on structural separation and sound-absorbent quilt to achieve sound reduction. Sound insulation of party walls is achieved by the use of two separate timber-frame leaves, one of which contains a sound-absorbent quilt material.

Wood Marketing Federation / COFORD

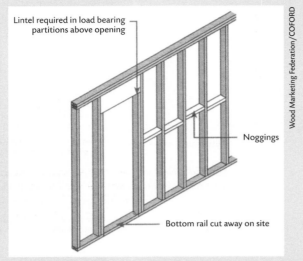

8-54 Internal wall construction is similar to external wall construction, with studs at either 400 mm or 600 mm centres, with noggings. The wall lining to internal partitions is generally 12.5 mm plasterboard.

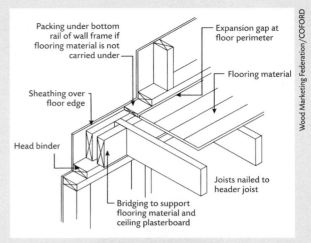

8-56 Floor supported on wall panel: the most common type of intermediate floor in domestic timber-frame construction is the platform floor, so called because it acts as a working platform on top of the ground floor wall panels, from which the first floor panels can be erected. The platform floor is generally factory made.

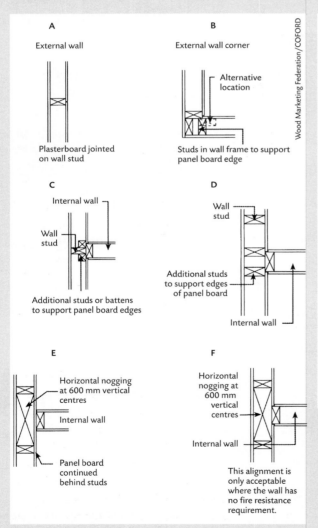

8-55 Internal wall junctions - plan views

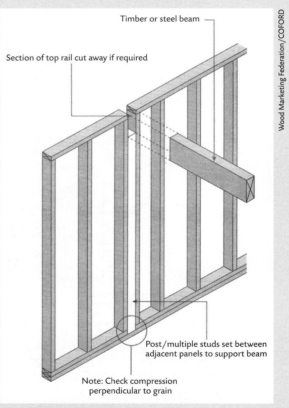

8-57 Floor beam support

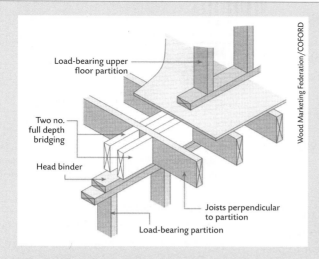

8-58 *Load bearing partitions: where load-bearing partitions occur above the floor, an additional joist (if partition is parallel to floor joists) or full-depth bridging (if partition is at right angles to floor joists) is required to transfer loads to the partition below.*

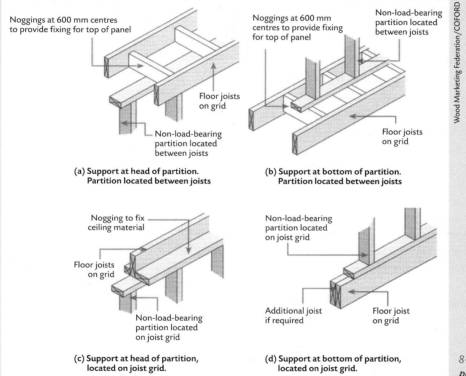

8-59 *Internal non-load-bearing partitions*

Insulation principles and requirements

The Building Regulations state that: 'A building shall be so designed and constructed as to secure, insofar as is reasonably practicable, the conservation of fuel and energy.'

The EU SAVE Directive requires all Member States to draw-up and implement programmes for the energy certification of buildings. The Heat Energy Rating is one of the measures taken to implement this Directive in Ireland.

The Heat Energy Rating of a dwelling is a measure of the annual energy output for appliance(s) that provide space and water heating for standardised room temperatures, levels of hot water use and conditions of operation. It provides the best single indicator of overall thermal performance.

The principle underlying this schedule in the Building Regulations is to ensure that occupants can achieve adequate levels of thermal comfort while minimising the use of scarce resources.

The Building Regulations require that buildings provide energy-efficient measures that:

- limit the heat loss and, where appropriate, maximise the heat gains through the fabric of the building;
- control the output of the space heating and hot water systems;
- limit the heat loss from hot water storage vessels and pipes.

Thermal conductivity

Thermal conductivity (i.e. λ-value) relates to a material or substance. It is a measure of the rate at which that material or substance allows heat to pass through it. It is expressed in units of Watts per metre per kelvin (W/mK).

U-values

Thermal transmittance (i.e. U-value) relates to a building component or structure. It is a measure of the rate at which heat passes through the component or structure when a difference in air temperature is maintained between one side and the other. It is expressed in units of Watts per square metre per kelvin of air temperature difference (W/m^{2}K).

U-values and λ-values are dependent on a number of factors, including the type of wall construction employed, the type of insulation used, the internal temperature, and the external temperature, which is also linked to the location of the dwelling.

Use certified test results for particular materials, products or components. In the absence of such data use values from reference tables.

Alternatively, U-values may be calculated. Calculate U-values to a minimum of two decimal places.

Disregard thermal bridging where the general thermal resistance does not exceed that in the bridged area by more than 0.1 m^{2}K/W.

For example, normal mortar joints need not be taken into account. A ventilation opening in a wall or a roof (other than a window, roof light, or door opening) and a meter cabinet recess may be considered as having the same U-value as the element in which it occurs. U-values are further dealt with in Chapter 12.

The new thermal performance and insulation standards for new dwellings is as follows:

Building element	Thermal performance	Insulation level*
	U-Value 2002	mm 2002
Roof	0.16	250–300
Wall	0.27	100–150
Floor	0.25	100

*Precise insulation levels will vary depending on manufacturers' individual products. This is acceptable as long as the products provide the recommended U-value for the building element.

Thermal bridging

Thermal bridges are areas of the building fabric where the heat flow is higher than through adjacent areas. For example, thermal bridges occur at openings in external walls when the cavities are closed with materials of poor insulating value.

Thermal bridges lead to increased energy demands because heat from within the building is lost through them. The higher heat flow through thermal bridges lowers the internal surface temperatures and is commonly associated with the occurrence of condensation and mould growth. Thermal bridging is sometimes referred to as **cold-bridging**.

Make provision to limit thermal bridging around windows, doors and other wall openings. This is necessary to avoid excessive heat loss and local condensation problems.

Lintel, jamb and sill designs similar to those shown in Fig. 8-60 are satisfactory. Heat loss due to thermal bridging can be ignored if these designs are used.

Take care to control the risk of thermal bridging at the edges of floors. Insulate the vertical edge of the slab. Extend the insulation at least 0.5 m vertically or 1.0 m horizontally. The U-value for floors is 0.25 W/m^2 K.

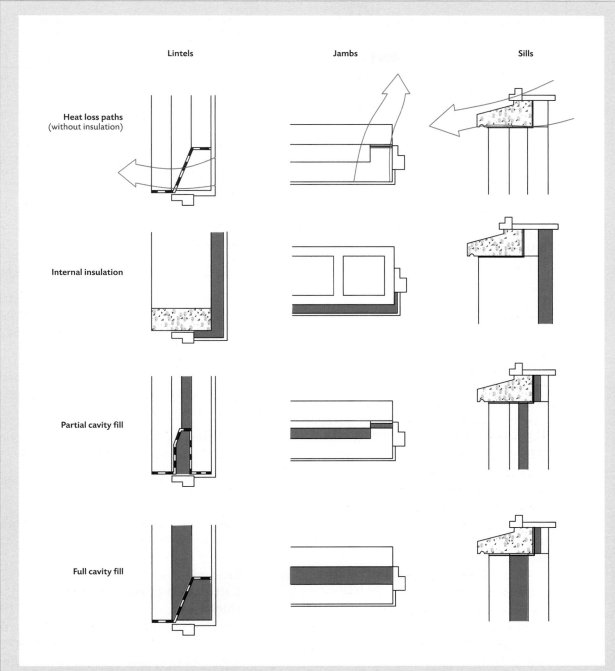

8-60 *Reducing thermal bridging around openings*

Calculation of U-values

Thermal conductivities of common building materials are given in Table 8-1, page 156.

Use the following standard values for thermal resistance of air spaces and surfaces in the calculation of U-values:

Exposed walls

Outside surface	0.06m²K/W
Inside surface	0.12m²K/W
Air space (cavity)	0.18m²K/W
Air space with aluminium foil surface	0.35m²K/W

Roofs

Outside surface	0.04m²K/W
Inside surface	0.10m²K/W
Roof space (pitched)	0.18m²K/W
Roof space (flat)	0.17m²K/W

Exposed floors

Outside surface	0.04m²K/W
Inside surface	0.14m²K/W

Thermal resistances of solid homogeneous materials (such as concrete) are calculated by dividing the thickness of the material (m) by its thermal conductivity (W/mK), or by multiplying the resitivity by the thickness. Resitivity (r = 1/K), i.e. r = 1 / conductivity (K).

The U-value of an element of construction is calculated by adding together the thermal resistance of the component parts of the construction, and then taking the reciprocal.

Example 1
Calculation of U-value of external cavity wall

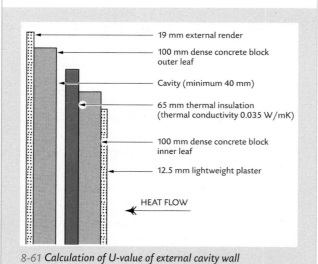

Component part of wall	Thickness of material (m)	Thermal conductivity (W/mK)	Thermal resistance of material (m²K/W)
Outside surface	–	–	0.06
External render	0.019	0.50	0.038
Concrete block	0.100	1.13	0.088
Cavity	–	–	0.18
Insulation	0.065	0.035	1.857
Concrete block	0.100	1.13	0.088
Plaster (lightweight)	0.0125	0.16	0.078
Inside surface	–	–	0.12
Total resistance	–	–	3.042

U-value of construction = 1/3.042 = 0.33 W/m²K

Where the thickness of insulation required to achieve a specific U-value is required and the conductivity of the insulation is known, the thickness is calculated as follows:

1. Add together the thermal resistances of the component parts of the construction (excluding the insulation).

2. Deduct the sum calculated from the reciprocal of the desired U-value.

3. Multiply the answer by the thermal conductivity of the insulation material.

This gives the insulation thickness required in metres.

Example 2
Calculation of required insulation thickness

Using the construction in Example 1, what thickness of insulation (thermal conductivity = 0.037 W/mK) is required to achieve a U-value of 0.27 W/m²K?

1. Sum of component resistance:
   (0.06 + 0.04 + 0.09 + 0.18 + 1.86 +
   0.09 + 0.08 + 0.12)
   = 2.52 m²K/W

2. Subtract from reciprocal of U-value:
   (1/0.27) – 2.52 = 1.18 m²K/W

3. Multiply by conductivity:
   1.18 × 0.037 = 0.044 m

Thickness required is 0.044 m or 44 mm.

8-61 Calculation of U-value of external cavity wall

The figure shows labels:
- 19 mm external render
- 100 mm dense concrete block outer leaf
- Cavity (minimum 40 mm)
- 65 mm thermal insulation (thermal conductivity 0.035 W/mK)
- 100 mm dense concrete block inner leaf
- 12.5 mm lightweight plaster
- HEAT FLOW

Finishes

External renderings

External rendering (plastering) must resist moisture penetration, weather uniformly, be durable and aesthetic.

External walls of block or brick do not provide resistance on their own to moisture penetration. Moisture may penetrate through the mortar joints, which makes some form of external treatment necessary.

Renderings consist of two coats. The undercoat is applied first and is 13 mm thick. The finished coat varies from 5 mm to 13 mm.

All renderings need a key to form a bond. This is provided in the form of an initial coat of 'scud'. This is a very wet mixture of sand and cement. It should be left approximately seven days before the undercoat is applied.

The main types of rendering are:

PEBBLEDASH (also known as dry-dash). A coat of mortar is first applied to the wall. Then small pebbles or crushed stone are thrown on to the mortar. A high degree of skill is required to obtain an even coat of pebbles over the wall surface.

8-62 Dry dash

ROUGHCAST (also known as wet-dash). This is a rough finish obtained by applying a wet mix that contains a proportion of coarse aggregate.

TEXTURED FINISH This involves creating a brick, block or stone effect finish on the final coat. A skilled craftsperson can make this finish very effective.

PLAIN FINISH (also known as napped finish). This is an even, smooth finish achieved with a timber float. Cork or felt-faced floats are also used.

MACHINE-APPLIED FINISHES Tyrolean is the main finish applied with the aid of a machine. Attempts have been made in the past to apply undercoats and final coats with the aid of a machine, so far with limited success.

8-63 Tyrolean machine

Pebbledash and roughcast are the most durable and stable finishes. Smooth finishes are prone to surface cracking, especially if they are rich in cement.

A number of techniques may be employed for special effects. These include the use of graded natural stone and glass.

Painting and maintenance of external renderings is expensive but necessary to reduce the impact of atmospheric pollution.

Renderings may fail due to inadequate bonding, or if the rendering is stronger than the previous coat. Conversely, the final coat may be too weak to prevent moisture penetration.

Each coat of render needs to be of slightly reduced strength from the previous coat applied. Cracks are evidence of failure. In extreme cases of failure the render becomes detached from the wall.

Materials for rendering

Renderings must be made of pure materials. Any dirt or contaminated materials will lead to defects and cause the render to deteriorate.

The materials used are: cements, limes, sands, aggregates and colour pigments.

Mix proportions depend on the type of wall type, the degree of exposure and the type of treatment.

Protection of renderings

The life of renderings will be prolonged if the following precautionary measures are included in the building of the structure:

■ Eave projections provide protection along the top edges of walls.
■ Parapets have projecting capping stones with an adequate weather drip.

- Sills are correctly installed with an effective drip to throw water clear of the render below.
- Effective and durable flashings are fitted.

Painting walls

Walls are painted to:

- improve their appearance
- waterproof them
- assist with cleaning and hygiene
- reflect or absorb light

Do not paint rendered surfaces until after the drying-out period. This is six to eight weeks. Salts and alkali, if present, will affect the paint.

Typical paints for use on external surfaces are:

CEMENT PAINT This contains white Portland cement with added pigments, an accelerator, water repellents and other additives mixed together with water. It is applied in two coats.

OIL PAINT Ensure that the rendered areas are completely dry before this paint is applied. It is applied in two or three coats. Any moisture present will eventually come to the surface and cause the paint to peel.

EXTERNAL GRADE EMULSION PAINT This is resin emulsion paint. It is easy to apply and gives a good covering. Any moisture present will evaporate through the surface without defects occurring.

STONE PAINT This is a resin emulsion paint containing fine grit aggregate particles. It is applied in one or two coats. Stone paint is durable and provides an imitation stone appearance suitable for external rendering.

Design principles of openings in buildings

Openings in walls are required for lighting, access or ventilation. Consider functional, structural and economical factors when determining the size and position of openings.

In windows, for example, the height and area of openings must relate to the size of the room that the window will light and ventilate.

Door openings must be wide enough for furniture, equipment and people. Fire doors must have minimum widths and comply with the specifications laid down by the Building Regulations.

Size of openings

The width of openings affects the structural design of buildings. The greater the width of the opening, the greater the weight that needs to be transferred to the foundation. The wall on either side of an opening must be strong enough to carry this increased load.

Special consideration needs to be given to a situation where a series of closely spaced openings occur. Narrow piers between such openings will affect their stability and bearing capacity, depending on their height.

In cavity wall construction, the inner leaf carries most of the loads over an opening, including floor loads. Buttressing or additional pillars are used as required.

Economical considerations refer to the width and position of openings. The dimensions of the brickwork, in particular, and blockwork between the openings should be based on the unit size of the brick or block where possible. This eliminates cutting and waste.

Terminology

Each part of the wall around the opening has a particular name.

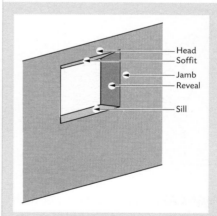

8-64 *Openings in walls*

Construction standards

Construction over openings and recesses must be properly supported. The ends of lintels and beams must have adequate bearing.

The minimum bearing length for all window and door lintels is 150 mm. The maximum length of an opening or thickness-reducing recess in any wall must not exceed 3 m.

It is recommended that openings should not exceed 2.4 m in height. The depth of chases for electrical provision should not exceed one-third of the thickness of the wall for a vertical chase, and one-sixth the thickness of the wall for a horizontal chase.

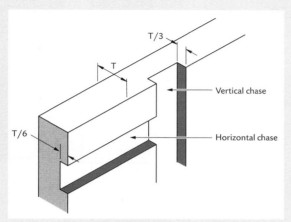

8-65 Dimensional details for chasing a wall

Carefully consider the layout of openings in walls to avoid problems of over-stressing of masonry. Guidelines are given in the Building Regulations and are illustrated in Figs. 8-66 and 8-67.

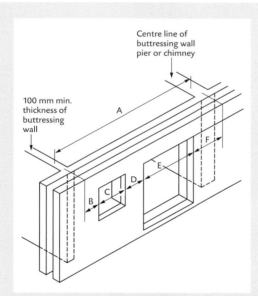

8-66 Typical external wall openings: the combined width of the openings should not exceed two-thirds the length of the wall, i.e. ope C + ope E should not be greater than 2A/3.

– No individual opening should exceed 3 m in width.

– A pier between an opening and a return wall should be at least one-sixth the ope width, i.e. pier B should be at least C/6, and pier F should be at least E/6.

– A pier between two openings should be not less than one-third the sum of the two openings, i.e. D should be not less than (C+E)/3.

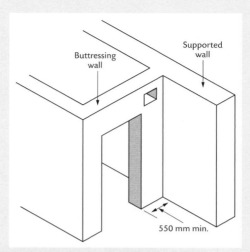

8-67 Openings in buttressing walls: any opening or recess greater than 0.6 m² should be at least 550 mm from the supported wall.

Lintels

The two most common types of lintels to bridge openings are pressed metal lintels and precast (prestressed) composite lintels..

A prestressed concrete lintel has no strength until it is combined with the block work built above it. This is why it is referred to as a 'composite' lintel. A prestressed concrete lintel depends on the joint action between itself and the surrounding block work to function properly. Construct the masonry so that lintels bear on whole solid blocks. Prop lintels at 1.2 m centres while the masonry is setting.

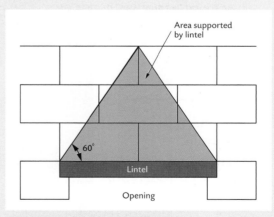

8-68 Portion of wall supported by lintel

A separate lintel is used under each leaf in cavity wall construction. This eliminates the cold bridge that would result from using a single lintel.

Insulation

Insulate around the perimeter of openings as well as in the general wall areas to prevent 'cold bridging'.

It is not necessary to close the cavity at door and window heads in domestic dwellings. It is common in conventional construction practice to partially close the cavity at the head with the aid of a 150 mm wide lintel.

The cavity must always be closed at wall-plate level and along the top of gables.

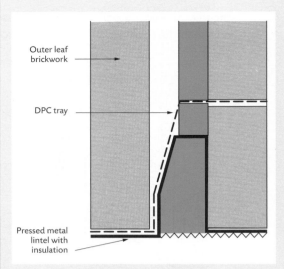

8-71 *Insulation details at head of opening for outer brick leaf and pressed metal lintels*

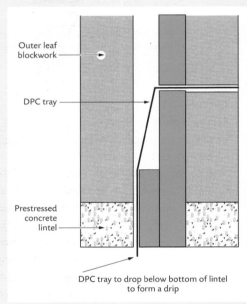

8-69 *Insulation details at head of opening for outer block leaf and prestressed concrete lintels*

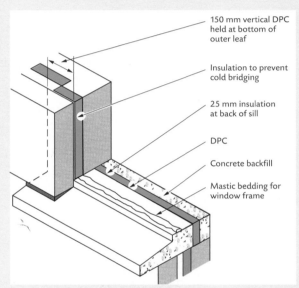

8-72 *Insulation details for sill area*

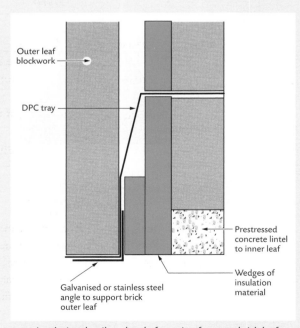

8-70 *Insulation details at head of opening for outer brick leaf supported on stainless steel or galvanised angle bracket*

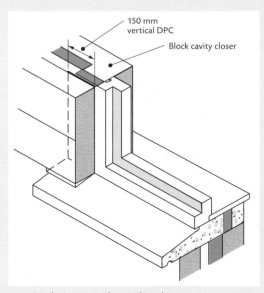

8-73 *Insulation around typical jamb*

Fireplaces and chimneys

The traditional means of providing heat in a domestic dwelling was the open fire or range, burning turf or coal. This source of heat is now declining due to its low efficiency compared to modern heating appliances.

All forms of heating, with the exception of storage heating, require some means of removing the products of combustion from the appliance or fireplace to the open air.

Terminology

The terminology associated with fireplaces and chimneys is as follows:

FIREPLACE the area where combustion of the fuel takes place.

CHIMNEY the building structure or fabric surrounding the flue. The chimney provides the flue with the necessary strength and protection.

FLUE the chamber or pathway through which the products of combustion pass. The modern flue is lined with **flue liners**. Flue liners can be made of clay; high alumina cement and kiln-burnt or pumice aggregates.

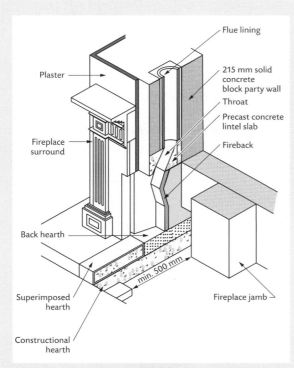

8-74 *Fire surround and hearth/chimney*

Flue construction

Flues were traditionally butt jointed but are now rebated or socket jointed. Fit the flue linings with the sockets or rebates pointing upwards. Use fireproof mortar for the joints.

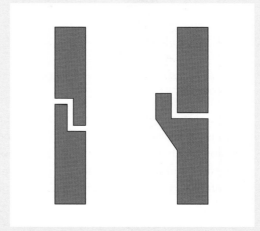

8-75 *Rebated and socketed flues: socketed flues are best. The socket should always be facing upwards, as shown.*

Fill the space between the flue liner and the chimney sides with a weak backfill mix (1 part cement to 20 parts (by volume) of lightweight aggregate beads, e.g. pumice, vermiculite).

Flue fires cause chimneys to crack. Cracking of chimneys by flue fires is the result of wrong backfill material, where ordinary aggregates or too strong a mortar mix was used. Filling should be carried out in lifts not exceeding 1 m.

All flues and chimney stacks should be tested for draught and smoke penetration using smoke pellets.

Function of fireplace and flue

The main functions of a fireplace and flue are:
- to secure maximum heat for the comfort of the occupants;
- to provide adequate protection against the spread of fire;
- to ensure that the products of combustion are removed;
- to prevent downdraught;
- to burn the fuel efficiently and safely.

Air is necessary for the efficient combustion of any fuel. The domestic open fire requires an upward movement of air. This is caused by cooler air flowing through and over the fire to replace the air that has been heated and moved up the flue.

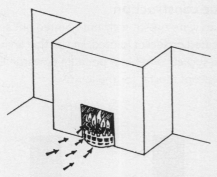

8-76 *The domestic open fire requires an upward movement of air.*

The air that is drawn into the flue from the room must be replaced. There must be some means to allow air changes to occur in the room. Possibilities include controlled vents or openings in windows. Ventilation will also assist in combating condensation.

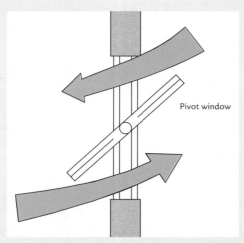

Pivot window

8-77 *Some form of ventilation is necessary to replace the air drawn into the flue.*

For a fireplace and a flue to operate efficiently the chimney must have adequate:

■ strength and stability
■ weather resistance
■ thermal insulation
■ fire resistance

Chimney strength and stability

A chimney's strength and stability is the same as that for a wall. As it will be higher and thicker than the wall in which it is situated, allowances must be made for this in the foundations.

The chimney must be self-supporting above the roof, where it will be subject to wind pressures. There are specific regulations controlling the height of chimneys to ensure that they will be stable enough to resist wind pressures.

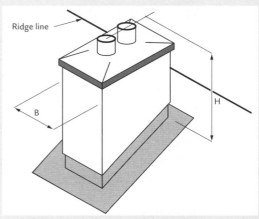

Ridge line

B

H

8-78 *Height and width of chimney: height (H) should not exceed 3.5 times least width (B).*

When calculating the height of a chimney, the chimney pot is disregarded. The chimney of a bungalow should extend at least 4.5m above the top of the fireplace to draw properly.

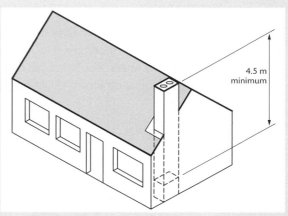

4.5 m minimum

8-79 *Chimney heights in bungalows*

Chimney pots are tapered to reduce the entry of rain. The taper improves the draught and flow of gases. Set chimney pots one quarter the length (150 mm) into the stack for adequate support.

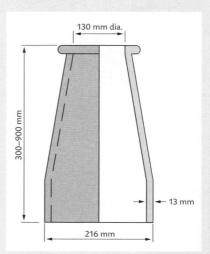

130 mm dia.

300–900 mm

13 mm

216 mm

8-80 *Tapered chimney pots*

Rafters and other roofing and flooring timbers, such as joists, are trimmed around the chimney. Keep all timbers a minimum of 40 mm away from the outside face of the chimneystack.

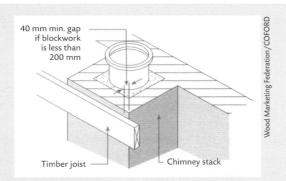

8-81 *Roof timbers must be a minimum of 40 mm away from the chimney stack.*

Weather resistance

The need to prevent the penetration of wind and rain is the same for chimneys as it is for external walls.

Take special care at the intersection of the roof with the chimney. Make the chimney watertight with the roof covering. This is achieved with the aid of a gutter and flashing at the top edge and an apron flashing at the bottom edge.

Soakers and stepped flashings are used at the sides. Lead is the main material used for flashing. Other materials such as copper and aluminium may be used.

The flashing arrangements for this area are shown in Fig. 8-83. The top of the stack must be detailed to throw off water and prevent any moisture entering the chimney at this point (Fig. 8-84).

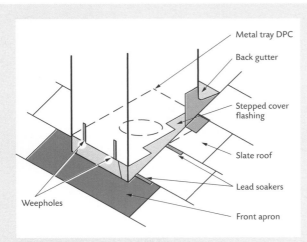

8-82 *Flashing details for a brick chimney*

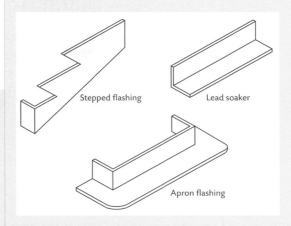

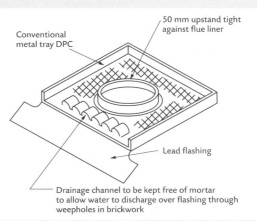

8-83 *Flashing components used in a brick chimney*

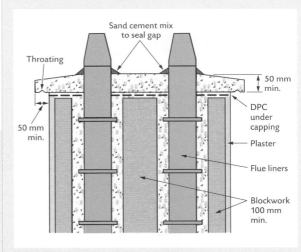

8-84 *In-situ concrete chimney capping: precast concrete chimney capping also available.*

Thermal insulation

Locate chimneys and flues on internal walls, where possible. This greatly improves the insulation provided to the flue. Insulation to the flue is necessary to prevent the flue gases cooling and the resultant slowing down of the airflow up the flue.

Poor insulation will lead to condensation on the walls of the flue. This can cause damage to the chimney, due to the sulphur compounds that are one of the by-products of combustion.

Fire resistance

Construction must be such that there are adequate distances between combustible materials and fireplaces, flues and chimneys. Details to satisfy these requirements in the Building Regulations are shown in Fig. 8-85.

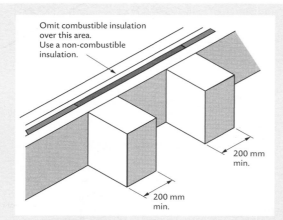

8-85 *Fireplace recess on external wall*

Fireplaces must have a non-combustible hearth as shown in Fig. 8-86. The walls of a flue should not get hotter than 65°C.

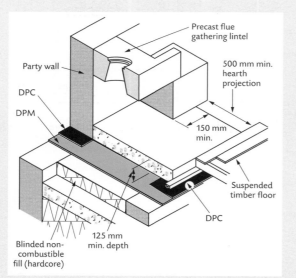

8-86 *Cut-away view of a typical fireplace showing non-combustible hearth and suspended timber floor*

Chimneys for use with solid fuel appliances should be capable of withstanding a temperature of 1100°C.

The flue outlet must be well above the roof to prevent downdraught and to carry the combustion by-products safely into the atmosphere. See Fig. 8-88 opposite.

Chimney wall thickness

The minimum thicknesses of walls of a brick or block chimney, excluding the thickness of any lining, are:

- 200 mm thick between one flue and another.
- 100 mm thick between a flue and the outside air.
- 200 mm thick between a flue and another compartment of the same building, another building or another dwelling.
- 200 mm thick between one flue and another where flues serve appliances located in separate compartments, buildings or dwellings.

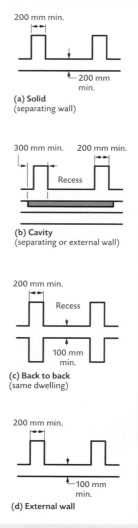

8-87 *Fireplace recesses*

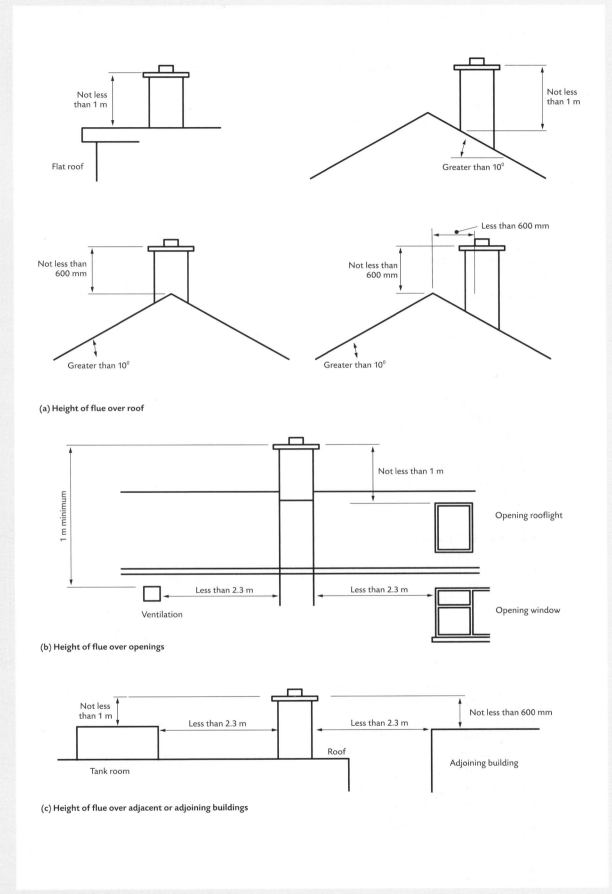

Not less than 1 m

Flat roof

Not less than 1 m

Greater than 10⁰

Not less than 600 mm

Greater than 10⁰

Less than 600 mm

Not less than 600 mm

Greater than 10⁰

(a) Height of flue over roof

1 m minimum

Not less than 1 m

Opening rooflight

Less than 2.3 m

Less than 2.3 m

Ventilation

Opening window

(b) Height of flue over openings

Not less than 1 m

Less than 2.3 m

Less than 2.3 m

Not less than 600 mm

Tank room

Roof

Adjoining building

(c) Height of flue over adjacent or adjoining buildings

8-88 Regulations governing outlets from flues

Constructional hearths

Constructional hearths should be of solid, non-combustible material at least 125 mm thick. Do not use combustible material under a constructional hearth unless: (i) it is to support the edges of the hearth, or (ii) there is an air space of at least 50 mm between the material and the underside of the hearth as shown in Fig. 8-89.

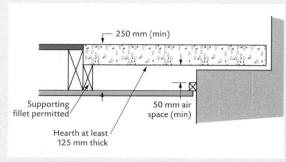

8-89 *Combustible material under hearth*

Fireplace design

The fireplace consists of a rectangular recess to suit the fireback or appliance to be fitted.

The walls that project into the room to form this recess are called the chimney breast.

A fireplace must have some means of reducing the width of the opening to that of the flue. This is achieved by using pre-cast flue gatherers as shown in Fig. 8-90.

The size and shape of the throat is important for the efficient removal of the by-products of combustion. The recommended size is 100 mm.

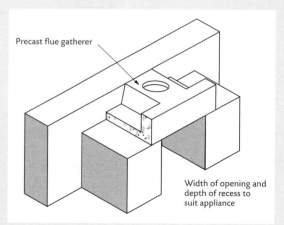

8-90 *Precast flue gatherer*

The fireback's function is to contain the burning fuel, prevent the heat damaging the wall behind it and to project the heat of the fire into the room by radiation.

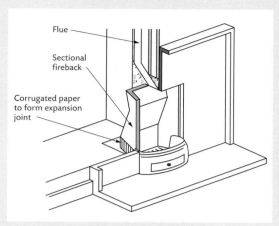

8-91 *Fireplace detail showing fireback in position*

Fill the space behind the fireback with a weak backfill mix, similar to that used for protecting the flue. Line the rear of the fireback with corrugated paper or some similar material. This will eventually smoulder away leaving an expansion gap.

A fireplace surround is fitted for aesthetic reasons. It also increases the effective depth of the fireplace.

Open fires with back boilers are relatively popular as they provide water heating as well as space heating. A boiler unit replaces the usual fireback.

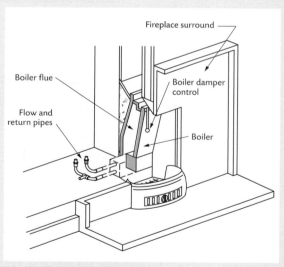

8-92 *Open fireplace with back boiler*

Deep ash pits

Ash containers for the normal fireplace are placed above the hearth. This means that the fire is raised off the floor.

For the fire to be at the level of the hearth, sink the ash pit below this level. Deep ash pits are designed to hold from three to seven day's ashes.

The air supply for this type of construction is below the floor level. A valve, usually at hearth level, controls it. Ducting from all of the external walls is fed into a balancing chamber in front of the fireplace as shown in Fig. 8-93. A cast iron pipe connects the balancing chamber to the ash pit.

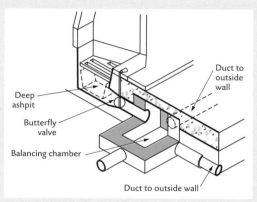

8-93 **Deep ash pits**

Faulty chimneys

If a chimney does not function properly smoke can be blown into the room through the fireplace opening. This can result from a number of factors, such as a blocked flue, inadequate air supply, throat not properly designed, flue not properly gathered, chimney not high enough to prevent downdraught, and the impact of trees or higher buildings in the area. A badly built offset would cause similar problems.

Build a chimney as straight as possible. This ensures the best draw. Where an offset is required it should not be less than 53° to the horizontal (127° to the vertical).

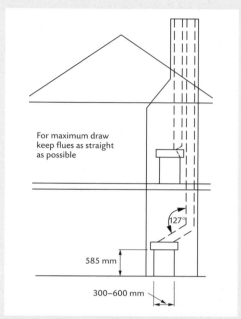

8-94 **Flue angle to the vertical should be approx. 127°.**

Thermal conductivity of some common building materials

Material	Density (kg/m³)	Thermal conductivity (W/mK)
General building materials		
Clay brickwork (outer leaf)	1700	0.77
Clay brickwork (inner leaf)	1700	0.56
Concrete block (heavyweight)	2000	1.33
Concrete block (medium weight)	1400	0.57
Concrete block (autoclaved aerated)	600	0.18
Cast concrete, high density	2400	2.00
Cast concrete, medium density	1800	1.15
Aerated concrete slab	500	0.16
Concrete screed	1200	0.41
Reinforced concrete (1% steel)	2300	2.30
Reinforced concrete (2% steel)	2400	2.40
Wall ties, stainless steel	7900	17.0
Wall ties, galvanised steel	7800	50.0
Mortar (protected)	1750	0.88
Mortar (exposed)	1750	0.94
External rendering (cement sand)	1800	1.00
Plaster (gypsum lightweight)	600	0.18
Plaster (gypsum)	1200	0.43
Plasterboard	900	0.25
Natural slate	2500	2.20
Concrete tiles	2100	1.50
Fibrous cement slates	1800	0.45
Ceramic tiles	2300	1.30
Plastic tiles	1000	0.20
Asphalt	1700	0.50
Felt bitumen layers	1100	0.23
Timber, softwood	500	0.13
Timber, hardwood	700	0.18
Wood wool slab	500	0.10
Wood-based panels	600	0.13
Insulation		
Expanded polystyrene (HD)	25	0.035
Extruded polystyrene	30	0.025
Glass fibre/ wool quilt	12	0.040
Glass fibre/ wool batt	25	0.035
Phenolic foam	30	0.025
Polyurethane board	30	0.025

Table 8-1 Thermal conductivity of some common building materials. Note: The values in this table are indicative only.

Chapter 9

Windows and doors

Principles of window design

The main function of a window is to admit air and light to the interior of a building. Windows also provide occupants with an outside view.

Windows are required to meet the ventilation requirements for the room that they serve. The ventilation requirements in the Building Regulations state that habitable rooms should have a ventilation opening with a minimum area of one twentieth of the floor area of the room, and some part of the opening to be at least 1.75 m above the floor level. This provides what is regarded as a reasonable ventilation standard of 3–4 air changes per hour.

A ventilation opening is any part of a window that opens directly to the outside air.

Window types

There are three different ways to classify windows:

1 The method of opening used.
   (a) Casements – either top-hung, side-hung, bottom-hung or tilt-and-turn
   (b) Pivot-hung – either horizontally or vertically
   (c) Sliding sash – horizontally or vertically (double-hung sash)
2 The materials used in their manufacture, such as wood, steel, aluminium and u-PVC.
3 The size of the window.

Window detailing

The detailing of a window is crucial to its performance and durability. The main areas, which require careful attention, are:
■ DPC and insulation
■ junction between window frame and structure
■ opening section

A 150 mm DPC lap is required at all joints. Do not fix the DPC to the frame. Carry the insulation down to meet the head of the window, so as to avoid any cold bridges. Weathering and insulation details are shown in Figs. 9-2 to 9-4 (overleaf).

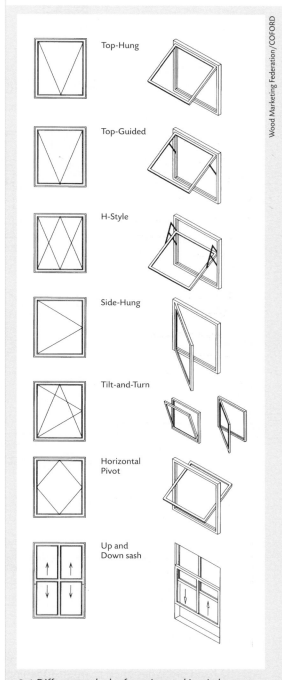

Top-Hung

Top-Guided

H-Style

Side-Hung

Tilt-and-Turn

Horizontal Pivot

Up and Down sash

Wood Marketing Federation / COFORD

9-1 Different methods of opening used in windows

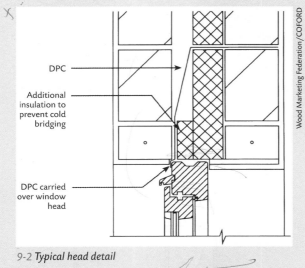

DPC

Additional insulation to prevent cold bridging

DPC carried over window head

Wood Marketing Federation/COFORD

9-2 Typical head detail

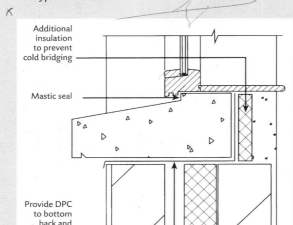

Additional insulation to prevent cold bridging

Mastic seal

Provide DPC to bottom back and sides of sill

Wood Marketing Federation/COFORD

9-3 Typical sill detail

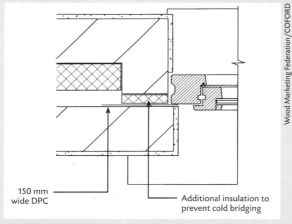

150 mm wide DPC

Additional insulation to prevent cold bridging

Wood Marketing Federation/COFORD

9-4 Typical jamb detail

Timber casement windows

Timber casement windows have sashes which may be fixed or be designed to open. Opening sashes may be hinged at the top, bottom, or side, to open inwards or outwards. The sashes, fixed or opening, are fitted to a solid frame.

Window frames and sashes are made from standard sections of softwood or hardwood timbers. Small top-hung sashes are used for basic ventilation requirements. The larger side-hung sashes provide greater ventilation in warm weather. Sashes are designed so that their edges are rebated over the external face of the frame. This forms a double barrier to the entry of wind and rain.

Variations in design are achieved by subdividing the frame. This can be done in any number of combinations. The vertical members used to subdivide a frame are called **mullions** and the horizontal members are called **transoms**.

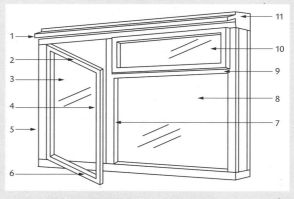

Wood Marketing Federation/COFORD

9-5 Standard casement window

1	Weatherboard (drip mould)	**7**	Mullion
2	Sash top rail	**8**	Deadlight
3	Side-hung casement	**9**	Transom
4	Stile	**10**	Vent light
5	Jamb	**11**	Head
6	Sash bottom rail		

Window frames are constructed using mortice and tenon joints. The sashes are generally constructed using bridle/comb joints.

Where sashes occur under each other, drip mouldings are housed, glued and pinned to the bottom rail of the top sash.

Anti-capillary grooves are machined in the outer edges of the sashes to correspond with similar grooves in the frames. These prevent moisture penetration by capillary action. Silicon or glazing beads secure the glass (Fig. 9-7). Putty was used before the arrival of silicon.

Design sills for frames and fixed sashes to provide good weathering.

Opening sashes are usually hinged using two-part alloy hinges. These allow the sash to be easily removed for glass cleaning or for maintenance. The sashes are closed with casement fasteners.

Casement fasteners allow the sash to be fixed open in a various positions (Figs. 9-8—9-12).

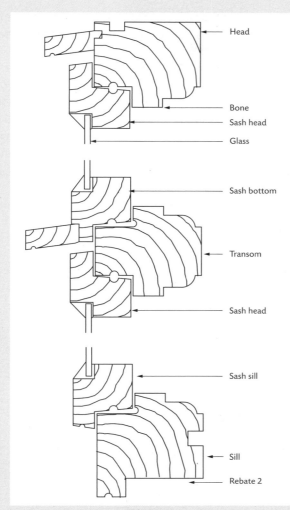

Head

Bone

Sash head

Glass

Sash bottom

Transom

Sash head

Sash sill

Sill

Rebate 2

9-6 *Typical sizes for the members of a casement window*

Sizes – head
Head 70 x 57
Rebate 25 x 12
Bone 20 x 5
Weather board 38 x 12
Sash 45 x 40
Sash rebate 25 x 12
Glass rebate 15 x 10
Glass 3 or 4

Sizes – transom/mullion
Transom 70 x 57
Rebate 25 x 12
Bone 20 x 5

Sizes – sill
Sill 70 x 70
Rebate 1 25 x 12
Rebate 2 50 x 12
Plough for window board 10 x 6

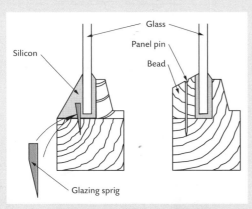

Glass

Silicon

Panel pin

Bead

Glazing sprig

9-7 *Glass may be secured with silicon and glazing sprigs, or wooden beads secured with panel pins*

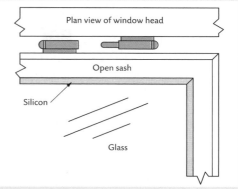

Plan view of window head

Open sash

Silicon

Glass

9-8 *Two-part alloy hinges*

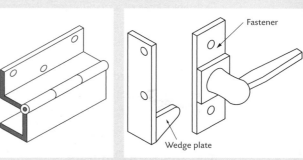

Fastener

Wedge plate

9-9 *A storm-proof hinge is used in exposed locations.*

9-10 *Casement fastener: wedge plate fixed to frame, fastener fixed to sash*

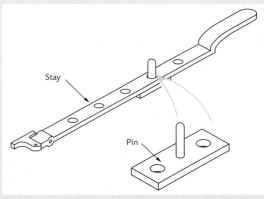

Stay

Pin

9-11 *Casement stay: stay fixed to sash, pin fixed to frame*

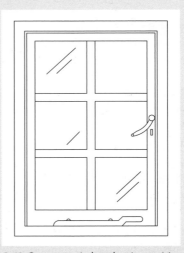

9-12 *Casement window showing position for casement stay and casement fastener*

Advantages of wooden frame windows include:

- Made from a renewable resource.
- Aesthetic.
- Easily painted to a variety of colours.
- Generally cheaper than other window materials such as aluminium and u-PVC.
- Good insulators.
- Available in both hardwood and softwood. Hardwood windows are generally varnished but can also be stained and varnished to achieve a particular colour. Softwood windows are generally painted for weather protection.

Disadvantages of wooden frame windows include:

- Regular painting or varnishing is required.
- Softwood windows in particular are prone to rotting over a 10–20 year life cycle.
- Hardwood windows have a tendency to warp if the wood is not seasoned correctly.
- Difficult to seal wooden window sash openings. This may lead to draughts.

Tilt-and-turn windows

Tilt-and-turn windows originated in Germany. They open inwards with a double action sash. This means that when bottom-hung the inward opening is called a tilt, and when side-hung the opening is called a turn. The opening handle controls the hinge mechanism. The position of the opening handle determines whether the sash will tilt or turn.

Tilt-and turn-windows make cleaning easy but can be awkward with curtains. They are popular in offices and are gaining in popularity as a fire escape exit for domestic buildings. This is because the casement is hinged from the side of the frame only and therefore opens inwards like a door. The casements are usually the full length of the window. They are available in wood, aluminium and u-PVC.

Pivot-hung casements

Centre pivot-hung windows are popular for areas that are difficult to access, such as positions high up from the floor and roof windows. These windows have a solid frame with no rebate. The pivots are fixed off-centre nearer the top to allow for self-closing.

Beads are fixed at certain locations to act as a stop for the sash. Sashes can be fully reversed and fixed in that position for cleaning. Sashes can also be pivoted vertically if the design requires it.

Horizontal sliding casements

Casements can be fitted to slide horizontally, similar to a patio door. Rollers attached to the bottom rail run on a brass track fixed to the sill of the frame. The top rail slides in a channel fitted to the frame.

French casements

French casement windows function like doors because they are the same height as a standard door. They provide access to gardens, patios and balconies. They are usually designed in pairs and can open either inwards or outwards. Toughened safety glass should be used to reduce the risk of accident, and the glass should be made visible.

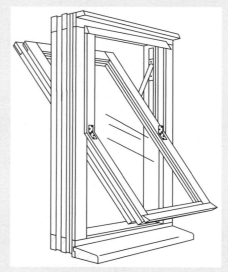

9-13
Centre-pivot hung casement window

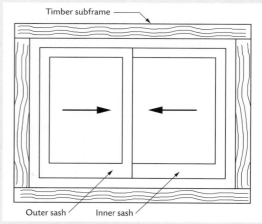

9-14 *Horizontal sliding casements*

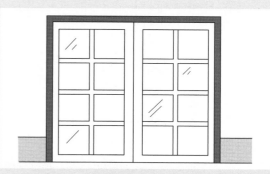

9-15 *French casement windows could also be described as doors*

Double-hung sash windows

These windows are sometimes called vertical sliding sash windows or 'box' windows. They consist of two sashes sliding vertically over one another. In timber construction the sashes may be suspended by weight balances or by spring balances. Spring balance mechanisms have generally replaced weight balances in modern construction.

For weight balances, the frame (box) used to conceal the weights consists of an inner and outer lining, pulley stile and back lining. The parting bead, which separates the two sashes, is housed into the pulley stile. Cords fixed to the sashes pass over pulleys in the frame and are then attached to the weights. A pocket in the pulley stile provides access to the weights.

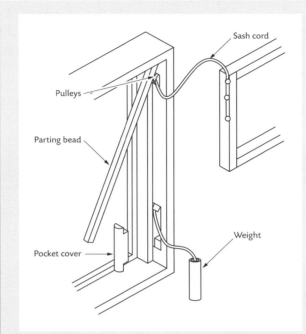

9-16 *Components of a sash window: the sash cord is nailed to the edge of the sash and tied to a weight.*

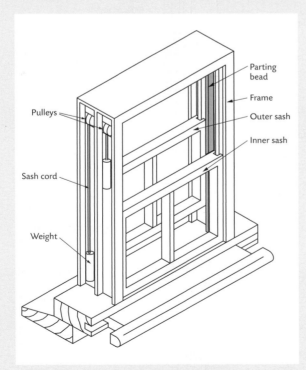

9-17 *In double-hung sash windows the inner sash is always at the bottom.*

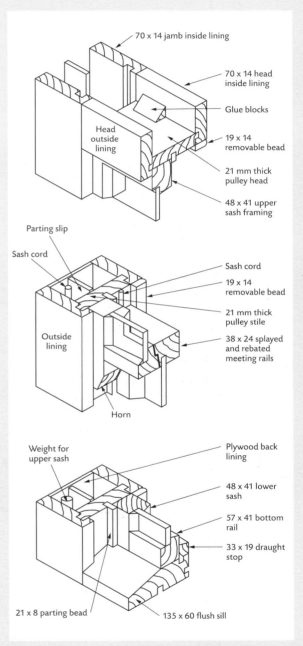

9-18 *Details of double-hung weight-balanced sash windows*

Spring balances are available in various sizes to suit different sashes. The barrel of the balance is housed in either the sash or the frame. Windows fitted with spring balances therefore take up less space and allow more light than the box construction.

Dowelled mortice and tenon joint

114 x 33 solid head

19 x 14 removable bead

21 x 8 parting bead

48 x 41 upper sash framing

21 x 28 parting bead

114 x 33 solid stile

19 x 14 removable bead

Spring balance

38 x 24 splayed end rebated meeting stiles

48 x 14 lower sash framing

57 x 41 bottom rail

33 x 19 draught stop

48 x 21 outside lining

135 x 60 flush sill

9-19 Details of double-hung spring-balanced sash windows

Hole for fixing screw

Aluminium tube with spiral spring fitted inside

Twisted rod

Sash attachment for fixing to bottom of sash

9-20 Unique sash balance for vertically sliding sash windows

Steel windows

Steel windows are made from hot-rolled steel sections. The sections are mitred and welded at the corners. To resist corrosion steel windows are hot-dip galvanised.

Handles and stays for steel windows are usually made from brass, zinc-based or aluminium alloys. Silicon mastic and spring wire glazing clips are used for glazing.

Steel windows can be fixed directly to block or brick walls using metal lugs. The practice of fitting steel windows to timber frames greatly improves their appearance as they have a very narrow cross-section.

The joints between the timber frame and the wall, as well as the joints between the window and the timber, must be adequately sealed.

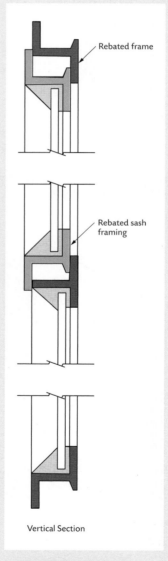

Rebated frame

Rebated sash framing

Vertical Section

9-21 Typical steel window

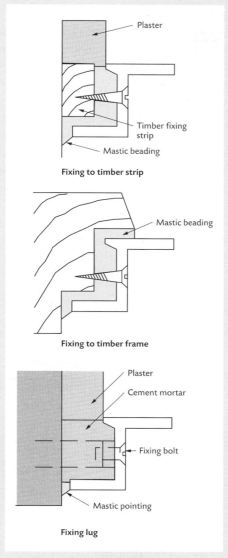

Fixing to timber strip

Fixing to timber frame

Fixing lug

9-22 Steel windows - fixing details

Fitting steel windows to timber frames reduces condensation. Steel windows allow in more light for the same opening size compared with other materials. This is due to their narrow cross-section.

Other advantages of steel windows include:
- Minimum maintenance.
- They will not rot, once they have been adequately protected.
- They are not subject to insect attack.
- They will not warp.

Disadvantages of steel windows include:
- They are poor insulators.
- Prone to condensation.
- Not very aesthetic.
- Difficult to replace broken glass.
- Not suitable for double glazing units.

Aluminium windows

Aluminium frames are poor insulators, which means they are good conductors of heat. To overcome this problem aluminium frames need to incorporate a 'thermal break'. This is a plastic insert to reduce the amount of heat that is transmitted to the outside of the building. Thermal breaks help prevent condensation on the frames in cold weather.

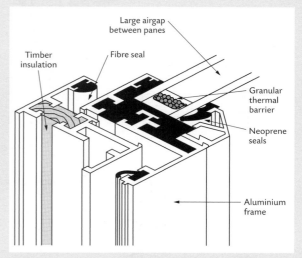

9-23 Air gaps and various insulating materials form thermal barriers.

Aluminium frames are made from aluminium alloy extrusions, normally finished with a white polyester powder coating. This is a durable finish and needs no maintenance other than the occasional washing. Other finishes are also available, such as bronze and stainless steel clad. The frames are assembled using mechanical joints, cleats or welds.

Glass is held in place in the frames with the aid of glazing gaskets and glazing beads. The frames need to be handled with care during installation as they are easily scratched.

Aluminium windows are more expensive than similar wood or steel windows and they require regular cleaning.

The sashes are usually fitted with frictionless hinges and closed using a concealed multi-point espangolette lock (see Fig. 9-25 overleaf). These window systems provide improved sound and thermal insulation, excellent air-tightness and weather resistance.

> ***Espangolette locks*** *allow the sash to be locked at a number of points by one movement of the handle.*

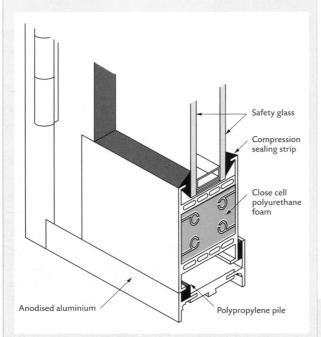

9-24 *This aluminium frame uses rigid polyurethane foam within the inner frame as a heat insulator.*

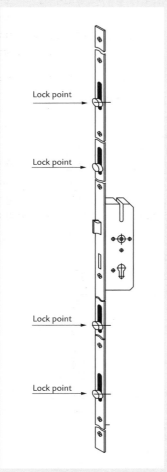

9-25 *Espangolette hinge locks the unit/sash at 3 or 4 points (multi-locking).*

u-PVC windows

u-PVC window frames are made from extruded profiles of u-PVC compound. Corner joints are heat welded. Other joints may also be heat welded or jointed mechanically. Virtually all window types are now available in this material.

u-PVC stands for unplasticised polyvinyl chloride. Basic formulations of u-PVC are rather brittle, especially when cold. u-PVC for windows is specially formulated for improved toughness. Other additives are used to limit the deterioration caused by ultraviolet sunlight.

u-PVC is not as stiff as wood or metal, so profiles are made with a fairly large cross-section. Galvanised metal reinforcement is usually placed within the profile to stiffen it.

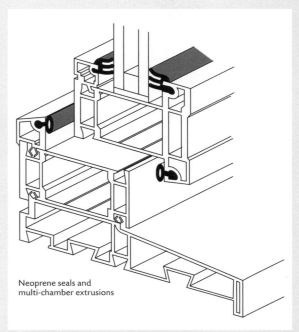

9-26 *Typical cross-section for a u-PVC window*

The dark colour of some windows causes them to become quite hot during summer sunshine. u-PVC expands considerably when heated, so it is important to make allowances for this expansion and to ensure that opening sashes do not jam. Temperatures can approach levels at which u-PVC begins to soften and distort.

u-PVC windows have a life expectancy of 30-40 years and they need regular cleaning. Colours available include white, brown, mahogany, light and dark oak wood grain effect.

Glazing

Glazing refers to the process of securing glass in prepared openings in windows, doors and partitions.

Glazing without beads, sometimes referred to as wet glazing, is suitable for domestic window and door panes. The glass is bedded in a compound, such as silicon, and secured with sprigs or clips and fronted with silicon. The glass pane should be cut to allow a minimum clearance of 2 mm all round. Sufficient silicon should be applied to give at least 2 mm of back silicon when the pane is pressed into the rebate.

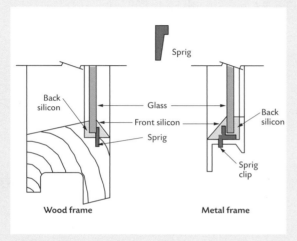

9-27 Glazing without beads

Glazing with beads is generally applied to high-class joinery. The beads are secured with either panel pins or screws. The glass is bedded in a compound, as for glazing without beads. Beads are usually mitred at the corners to allow continuity of the moulding.

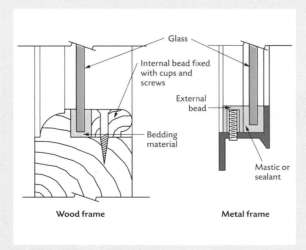

9-28 Glazing with beads

Glazing materials

Annealed glass is the most common glazing material, even though it is vulnerable to breakage.

SAFETY GLASS

Safety glasses are being specified more often nowadays because they are safer in the event of a breakage. The following three types are the main safety glasses in use.

- **Laminated** glass is no stronger than annealed glass of similar thickness, but after a breakage the broken pieces are held together by the interlayer. Laminated glass for domestic use is made with two sheets of glass laminated together under heat and pressure with a Polyvinylbutyral (PVB) interlayer.

> **Annealed** means to temper or toughen by heat treatment. Annealing removes internal stresses, crystal defects and dislocations.

- **Wired glass** is weaker than non-wired annealed glass, but the advantage is that after a breakage the pieces are held together.
- **Thermally toughened glass** is stronger than annealed, both in terms of impact resistance and of thermal stress. It does, however, shatter when broken, though the pieces are quite small.

The ideal situation can be obtained with sheets of laminated toughened glass.

Double-glazing

Double-glazing has a lower heat transmittance (U-value) than single glazing, and can improve the comfort of building occupants in areas of rooms near to windows. Double-glazing makes a significant improvement to noise insulation.

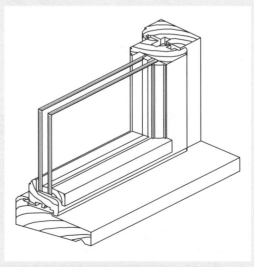

9-29 Double glazing consists of two parallel panes of glass with a sealed air space between them.

A double-glazed unit normally consists of two panes of glass held a fixed distance apart by a continuous spacer bar located around the perimeter of the glass, which is then sealed.

Most types of glass can be used for double glazing. The spacer is normally manufactured from mill-finished aluminium, although plastics are also used. Typical sealants used include polysulfide, polyurethane, silicone, hot-melt butyl and polymercaptan.

In all double-glazing units a desiccant is held within the hollow spacer bar.

A 20 mm air space gives the best result, while widths down to 12 mm are almost as effective. An air space in the range of 12–20 mm will halve the thermal transmittance of single glazing.

For effective sound insulation a minimum air space of 150 mm is required, but 200–300 mm is recommended.

> A **desiccant** absorbs water vapour sealed in the double glazed unit at the time of manufacture and absorbs moisture that permeates through the edge seal. The desiccant is intended to prevent misting within the air space during the service life of the units. Typical desiccants used are molecular sieves, silica gel, or mixtures of both.

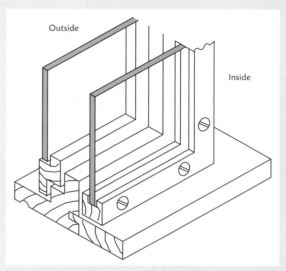

9-31 *One of many techniques of securing secondary glazing to existing frames*

space between the cavities cannot be expected to remain airtight.

Secondary glazing is usually fitted to draughty windows where the original material in the windows does not warrant replacement. Double sashes sliding on metal sliders are fitted to the original frame. Access to the original sashes and window is still possible.

9-30 *For effective sound-proofing of windows the air gap between the panes of glass should be between 150 and 300 mm.*

Some reduction in light transmission results from using double-glazing, 70 per cent compared with 85 to 90 per cent for single glazing.

Secondary glazing

Secondary glazing consists of fixing a second line of glazing usually to existing frames. It is not a substitute for proper double-glazing, as the air

9-32 *With secondary glazing, access to the main windows can be achieved using horizontal sliding sashes or opening sashes.*

Glazing techniques

The two principal glazing systems for both single- and double-glazing are known as drained-and-ventilated and fully bedded systems. The drained-and-ventilated is the preferred system, particularly for installing double-glazed units of all types into frames.

In the drained and ventilated system weather-proofing is provided by gaskets or by foam strips with a sealant capping making intimate contact with the glass. Any moisture that breaches these seals is drained away via a sloping rebate and drainage holes. Pay particular attention to the type and position of setting blocks, to ensure that they do not inhibit either drainage or ventilation.

Drained-and-ventilated glazing systems can be designed for all types of window frame, including those made of aluminium, steel, u-PVC and timber.

The alternative method, the fully bedded method, means just that. In order to function properly the bedding must be perfect. These systems should only be used where drained-and-ventilated systems are impractical or are unavailable.

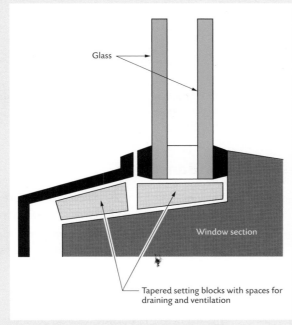

Glass

Window section

Tapered setting blocks with spaces for draining and ventilation

9-33 The drained and ventilated glazing method

Weather tightness

If a window is not weather tight, the surrounding materials and finishes may become damp and deteriorate. Some typical problems are:

- Windows may leak air and water around the backs of frames if they are positioned too close to the face of the building.
- Damaged or cracked sills or sills projecting incorrectly can result in water penetration under the window.
- Cavity wall construction without a vertical DPC or cavity tray can lead to a risk of penetration at the head and sides.
- Excessive shrinkage of glazing beads may allow water penetration around the glass.

Ventilation

Old draughty windows ensure a high rate of natural 'trickle' ventilation. A change to multi-locking weather-stripped units will improve comfort and reduce energy requirements, but may promote internal condensation and higher levels of pollutants in internal air.

Windows make a contribution to the balance of heating and ventilation and therefore the control of condensation in buildings. Opening windows minimise draughts by providing ventilation to the upper levels of a room, preferably 1.75 m above the finished floor.

Ventilation of new buildings is covered by the Building Regulations. Guidance is given for opening areas for rapid ventilation according to whether an opening window is present in rooms, such as bathrooms, and according to the floor areas of habitable rooms.

Background ventilation consists of a wall or window ventilator with a controllable ventilation grill, located to reduce drafts.

Rapid ventilation refers to large adjustable ventilation openings which allow the movement of a substantial volume of air in a short time e.g. an opening window or door, with some part of the ventilation opening at least 1.75 m above the floor level.

A **habitable room** is a room used for living or sleeping purposes but does not include a kitchen having a floor area of less than 6.5 m^2.

In a habitable room, provision should be made for:
1 background ventilation having a total area of not less than 6500 mm², and
2 rapid ventilation having a total area of at least 1/20th of the floor area of the room.

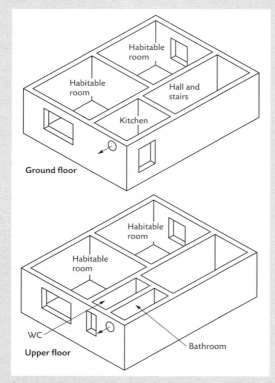

Ground floor

Upper floor

9-34 Ventilation details of a typical dwelling:

Habitable rooms: 1/20th floor area and 6500 mm²

Kitchen: 1/10th floor area or 60 l/s intermittent and 6500 mm²

WC: 1/20th floor area

Bathroom: 1/20th floor area or 15 l/s intermittent

Daylighting requirements

Daylighting requirements of windows provide for an open space outside windows of habitable rooms. It is in effect a shaft of open space free from obstructions.

The minimum size of the open space is related to the height of the wall containing the window under consideration. The height is measured from the lower window level, provided it is a minimum of 1.2 m above the floor, to the top of the wall. The top of the wall may be defined as either:

■ the underside of a flat roof
■ the lowest part of the eaves of a pitched roof
■ the top of a parapet

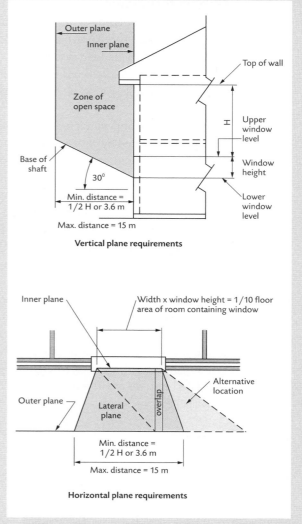

Vertical plane requirements

Horizontal plane requirements

9-35 Regulations governing zones of open-spaces outside windows in habitable rooms

Condensation

Condensation from windows occurs more during cold weather on single glazing and metal parts of windows without thermal breaks (see 9-23). The extent to which condensation occurs depends on heating, ventilation and the amount of moisture generated by those living in the building.

Condensation on glass, provided it is drained effectively to the outside, can be beneficial; the glazing acts as a dehumidifier, tending to reduce the moisture content of the internal atmosphere and the risk of condensation on other parts of the building fabric.

External doors

Doors are used to open and close an opening into a building or between rooms. Doors can be made of timber, glass, metal, u-PVC or any combination of these. The way doors open and function can be designed so that they swing, slide, roll, fold or revolve. This section concentrates on external doors only.

The main function of external doors is to close the access to a building and to provide security.

Secondary functions include aesthetics and appearance. Doors need to be weather resistant since they are exposed to the elements.

All doors providing access to a building should be robust and capable of withstanding rough treatment. Solid protection is provided in domestic construction with 44 mm thick doors.

Front doors are the main entry and exit routes from a house and are normally the main escape route in an emergency. Such doors should be provided with:

- a mortice deadlock operated from either side only by a key

- a rim automatic deadlock
- a door chain or limiter
- a door viewer
- a letter plate

Additional bolts should not be fitted to the main entrance door since they may delay escape of the occupants in an emergency.

Other external doors do not need to perform as escape doors and can generally be secured from the inside before occupants leave the building.

Sliding patio doors are a common point of entry for intruders. Unless precautions are taken during fitting, it is comparatively easy to lever them out of their tracks.

Following are general requirements for external entrance doors:

- Wooden doors should be solid and a minimum thickness of 44 mm.
- Wooden doors should be securely fixed to the frame by one and a half pairs (3) of steel/brass butt hinges, and be fitted with appropriate locks.

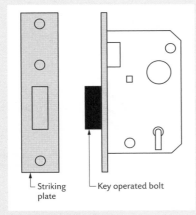

Striking plate   *Key operated bolt*

9-36 *Mortice deadlock*

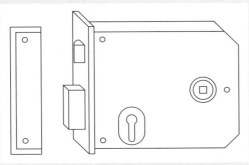

9-37 *Rim lock is surface mounted on the internal face of the door*

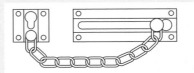

9-38 *Security door chain*

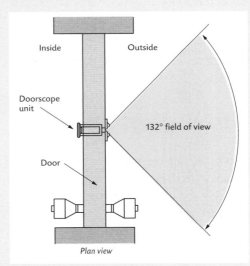

Inside   Outside

Doorscope unit

132° field of view

Door

Plan view

9-39 *Door viewer/doorscope unit*

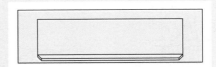

9-40 *Typical letter plate*

- The frames should be securely fixed to the surroundings, using a minimum of two fixing points per metre run.
- A glass panel fitted to a door or adjacent to a door should be of a size, position or glass type to prevent it being smashed to allow access for an intruder.
- Additional hinge bolts should be fitted where external hinges are fitted and the hinge pins are accessible from the outside.

The external walls of a building are designed to meet certain thermal and sound insulation regulations. Doors in such walls should be constructed, where possible, to maintain the insulation properties of the building fabric. A solid, unglazed timber door has an average thermal insulation value (U-value) of 3.0 W/m^2K.

For noise and sound insulation, it is very difficult to improve the performance of external doors to more than around 30 dB(A). Where this figure needs to be improved upon, consideration should be given to including a lobby.

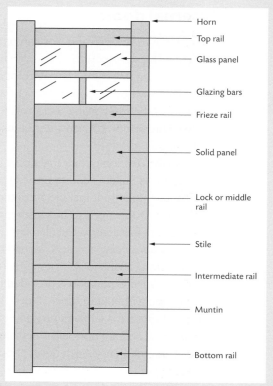

9-41 Door parts

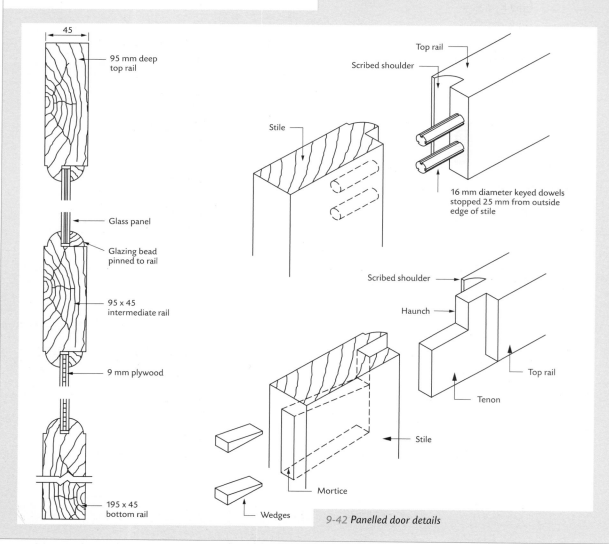

9-42 Panelled door details

Door construction

There are four door categories based upon their method of construction. These categories mainly apply to timber doors, although other materials can easily adopt the aesthetic features. The categories are:

1. PANELLED AND GLAZED DOORS.

The number of panels can vary from one up to twenty-one or more. The panels can be of plywood, glass or solid wood.

The joints used in framing the doors are usually mortice and tenon, but dowelled joints are also used. Through tenons are secured using wedges and glue is applied to the faces of all tenons before they are inserted in the mortices.

The main parts of a door are shown in Fig. 9-41 Timber or plywood panels are usually framed into tight fitting grooves. To allow for expansion the panels should be 2 mm smaller all round from the groove dimensions. Panels, other than plywood, are generally moulded and raised where the centre portion of the panel is thicker than the edges (Fig. 9-42).

In purpose-made doors mouldings may be planted on to the frame as shown in Fig 9-43. These are more expensive to produce and are more difficult to finish.

Openings for glazing are usually rebated and moulded out of the solid. The glass is held in place using mitred glazing beads. The same rules apply to glazing doors as applies to windows.

2. FLUSH DOORS

External flush doors are normally of the solid core type. The core consists of block or lamin board, and as with all flush doors they are faced with plywood and edge lipped with a corresponding timber, usually hardwood.

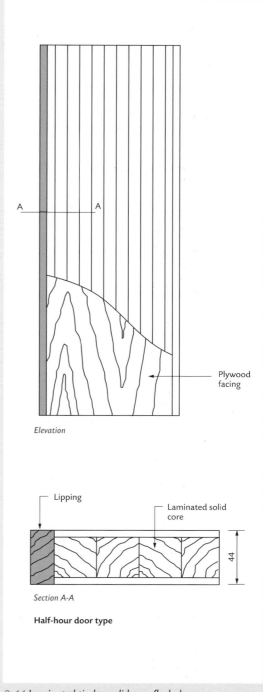

9-43 Bolection moulding refers to a moulding that projects outwards from the door stile or rail.

9-44 Laminated timber solid-core flush door

3. MATCHBOARDED DOORS

These doors are mainly used as external doors to outhouses and garages. Some types are suitable for use as a rear entrance door. In some instances they are used as internal doors to create a cultural or heritage type atmosphere. There are two types of matchboarded doors: a ledged and braced door, and a framed, ledged and braced door.

The face of the door is made from tongued, grooved and v-jointed boards held together with ledges. A brace is fitted between the ledges to keep the door square. The braces slope downwards towards the hanging side. A cheaper less satisfactory version of this door does not include the braces.

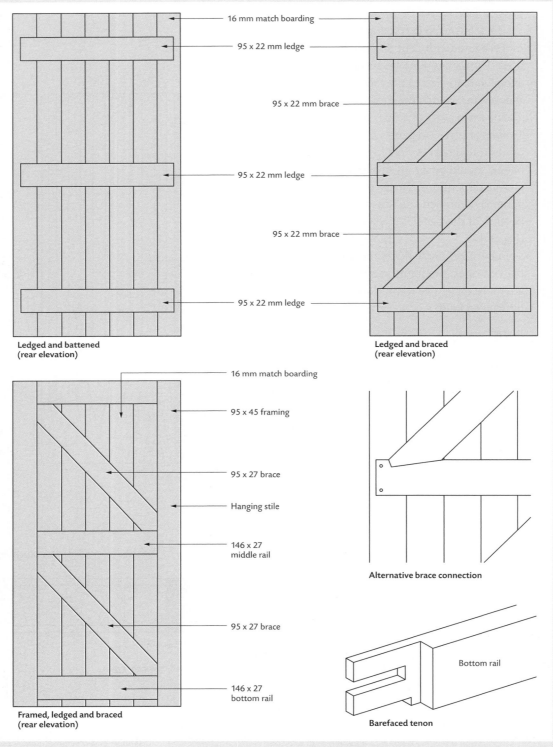

9-45 *Matchboarded door details*

The second type of matchboard door includes a mortice and tenon frame. The frame surrounds the tongue and grooved boards and provides extra strength and rigidity. This type is suitable for rear entrance doors to dwellings. Braces are also incorporated as shown in Fig. 9-45.

4. FIRE-CHECK FLUSH DOORS

Fire-check doors are designed to provide an effective barrier to the spread of fire for the time designated by their type. To be effective fire doors must be fitted to the correct frame.

The two main types of fire door are the half-hour and the one-hour resistance. The resistance is obtained by the thickness of the door and the materials used in its construction (see Fig. 9-48 overleaf).

The door furniture should consist of at least one pair of metal hinges, non-combustible with a melting point of not less than 800°C. Rim locks should be mounted on the non-risk side of the door.

Fire doors can greatly limit fire damage by keeping smoke and flames from spreading. However, they cannot function if they are left open. Fire doors should be fitted with self-closing devices.

Intumescent strips swell on heating (140°C–300°C) and close the gap between the door and the frame.

To achieve the full thirty minutes protection for fire resistance, an **intumescent strip** should be fitted to either the door or the frame.

The effectiveness of a fire door depends on the performance of the whole assembly of door, frame and door furniture. In the fire test the assembly is judged on its ability to:

- remain in position in the opening
- prevent the passage of flame through cracks or gaps
- restrict excessive transmission of heat

Door frames

Door frames are made from rectangular section timber, usually 100 × 75 mm. Frames are used for most external doors. A timber frame consists of the head, two vertical members, called jambs, and in some instances a sill or threshold.

*A **draw-dowel joint** means the holes for the dowel in the head and stile are slightly off-centre so that when the dowel is inserted it pulls the stile against the head to keep the joint closed.*

The members are scribed and framed together using either a mortice and tenon joint or a combed joint. A 'draw-dowel' joint is sometimes used instead of wedging the mortice and tenon.

Door frames that do not have a sill can have a steel dowel inserted into the base of the jambs. This is cast into the floor slab to provide extra rigidity. Door frames are usually fixed with three metal fixing lugs, screwed to the back of each jamb. The lugs are then fixed to the face of the wall using special fixing bolts.

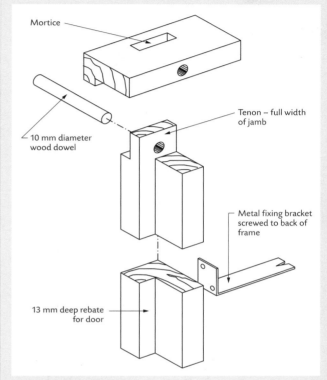

9-46 *Door frames*

Thresholds

The external door threshold has always been one of the problem areas in the external envelope so far as danger of tripping, rain penetration and thermal bridging are concerned.

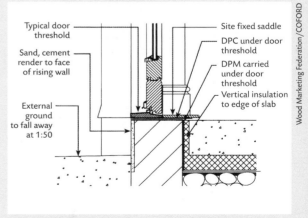

9-47 *Typical threshold detail for inward opening door on a concrete floor*

173

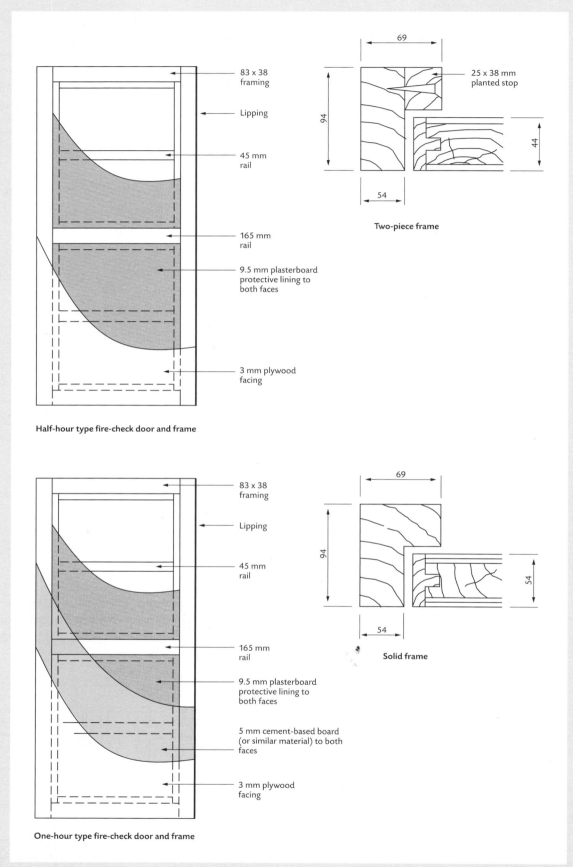

83 × 38
framing

Lipping

45 mm
rail

165 mm
rail

9.5 mm plasterboard
protective lining to
both faces

3 mm plywood
facing

Half-hour type fire-check door and frame

69

25 × 38 mm
planted stop

94

44

54

Two-piece frame

83 × 38
framing

Lipping

45 mm
rail

165 mm
rail

9.5 mm plasterboard
protective lining to
both faces

5 mm cement-based board
(or similar material) to both
faces

3 mm plywood
facing

One-hour type fire-check door and frame

69

94

54

54

Solid frame

9-48 Fire-check doors and frames

Flat thresholds at entrances are now required to provide access for disabled people. Details of a flat threshold are shown in Fig. 9-49.

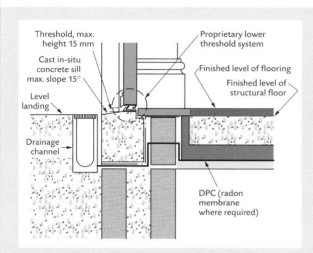

9-49 New regulations governing threshold to one entrance

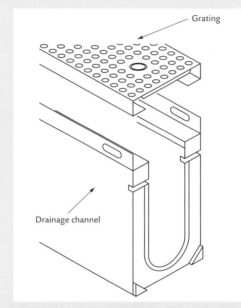

9-50 Typical proprietrary drainage channel assembly

Traditionally upstands of around 15 mm have been used. If condensation is to be avoided, adequate thermal insulation must be provided to link with the insulation in the remainder of the external wall. The higher the upstand, the better the detail will be in resisting water being driven over it. A minimum fall of 1 in 40 should be applied to paved areas outside entrance doors.

u-PVC doors

u-PVC doors are available in a range of different types. u-PVC sliding or patio doors have become very popular. These doors are waterproof, draught-proof, attractive and safe. u-PVC doors can also be used for front and rear entrance doors. It is important that both the frames and the door stiles are fully reinforced.

Metal doors

Aluminium patio doors and garage doors are the main uses of metal doors. 'Up and over' or 'roller' garage doors are often made from steel or aluminium to a variety of designs. Most steel doors are hot-dip galvanised, but must still be painted. Aluminium doors can be left unpainted but must be cleaned regularly.

Chapter 10
Roof design

Introduction

The most important function of roofs is to provide protection from the weather. This chapter will deal with the two broad categories of roof, flat and pitched.

The main functional requirements of all roofs include the following:

■ **Weather resistance.**

■ **Strength and stability.** The roof must be able to support both dead and live loads. The effect of wind pressure requires special consideration. Wind speeds vary depending on the location of the site, its altitude and the season of the year. Secure fixing is necessary because uplift in high wind pressure areas may exceed the dead weight of the roof.

■ **Durability.** The quality of the original work and the quality of materials used are important factors in durability. Other factors that affect durability include industrial and natural pollutants and organisms that may attack the roofing materials.

■ **Thermal insulation.** The provision of thermal insulation in roofs is essential to reduce heat loss from the interior of the building and to prevent excessive heat gain from the exterior in hot weather.

■ **Ventilation.** The roof space must be adequately ventilated to prevent condensation.

■ **Fire resistance.** This is necessary to give protection against the spread of fire to and from adjacent buildings, to prevent early roof collapse and to protect means of escape where they occur through the roof.

■ **Sound insulation.** When considering sound insulation the roof is as important as the walls. Most roofs offer adequate levels of sound insulation.

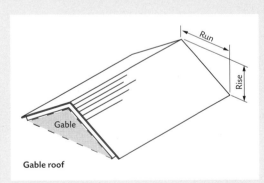

Gable roof

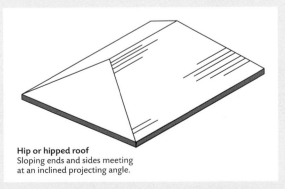

Hip or hipped roof
Sloping ends and sides meeting at an inclined projecting angle.

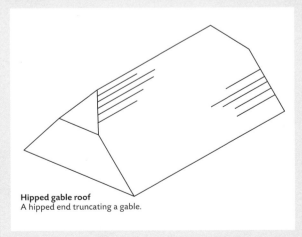

Hipped gable roof
A hipped end truncating a gable.

10-1a Roof types (continued overleaf)

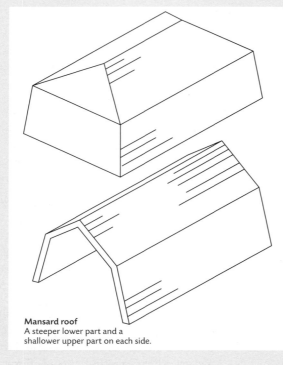

Mansard roof
A steeper lower part and a
shallower upper part on each side.

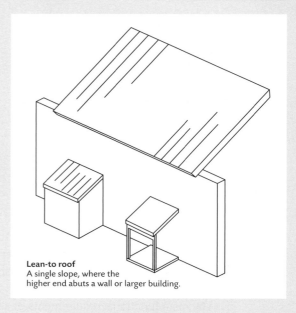

Lean-to roof
A single slope, where the
higher end abuts a wall or larger building.

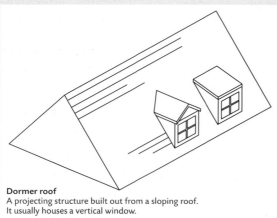

Dormer roof
A projecting structure built out from a sloping roof.
It usually houses a vertical window.

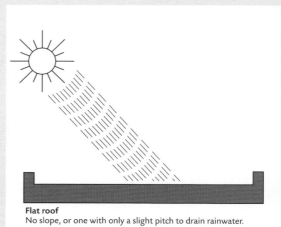

Flat roof
No slope, or one with only a slight pitch to drain rainwater.

10-1b Roof types (continued)

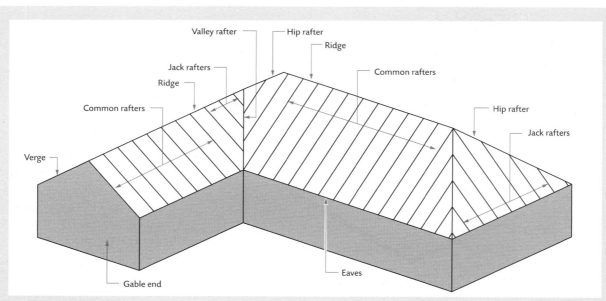

10-2 Roofing terminology

Valley rafter — Hip rafter
Ridge
Jack rafters
Ridge
Common rafters
Common rafters
Hip rafter
Jack rafters
Verge
Gable end
Eaves

Pitched roofs

A pitched roof may be defined as any roof surface that makes an angle of between 10° and 70° to the horizontal. Surfaces below 10° are categorised as flat roofs and surfaces greater than 70° are regarded as walls. Fig. 10-2 gives roof terminology.

Roof members

COMMON RAFTERS These are the main load-bearing elements of the roof. They span between the wall plate and the ridge. They are notched and nailed to a wall plate, which is in turn secured to a load bearing wall, usually the external cavity wall. The notch is referred to as the 'bird's mouth' and its depth should not exceed one-third the depth of the rafter.

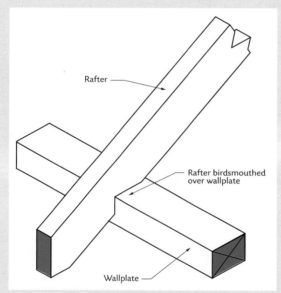

Rafter

Rafter birdsmouthed over wallplate

Wallplate

10-3 Support at wall plates. The rafters are birdsmouthed over and skew-nailed to the wall plate.

RIDGE Every pair of common rafters is nailed to a ridge board at the apex of the roof.

HIP RAFTERS These are longer and heavier than common rafters and are located at the intersection of external angles.

VALLEY RAFTERS Similar to hip rafters except that they are located at the intersection of internal angles.

JACK RAFTERS These are used to fill in the area from ridge to valley rafter or from the hip rafter to the wall plate. Consecutive jack rafters decrease in length by a set amount. The longest jack rafter will be shorter than the common rafter.

WALL PLATES These are fixed to load-bearing walls using galvanised steel straps. The roof members are fixed to the wall plate. Wall plates distribute the loads evenly over the load bearing walls.

PURLINS These act as beams and provide support to the rafters. They are usually built-in to the wall in a gable roof. Purlins are supported by struts which bear onto a load-bearing wall. In a hipped roof they are mitred at the corners and supported by struts.

STRUTS These transfer the loads from the purlin to roof members below. Struts are always in compression.

COLLARS Usually referred to as collar ties, these connect the common rafters and prevent them from spreading outwards. They are usually positioned from one-third to one-half the height of the rise. Collar ties are in tension.

CEILING JOISTS These tie the roof at the base, on top of the wall plate. They are connected to the rafters and to the wall plate. The spacing of the ceiling joists is important because the plasterboards, which form the ceiling, are fixed to the bottom of the ceiling joists.

RUNNERS Also called binders, they stiffen and give support to the ceiling joists.

HANGERS These vertical members connect either the rafter or purlin to the runners.

EAVES The part of the roof that overhangs the walls.

VERGE The part of the roof covering that overhangs the gable wall.

Pitched roof categories

Single roofs

LEAN-TO ROOFS
The lean-to is the best example of this type of roof, where one wall is built to a higher level than the other and the rafters span the space between. The ridge board for lean-to roofs is normally rag-bolted to the wall.

This type of roof is common in garages but it can also be incorporated into a dwelling house design. Its main limitation is that it is only suitable for spans of approximately 2.5 m. See Fig. 10-4 overleaf.

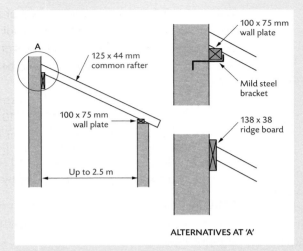

10-4 *Lean-to roof details*

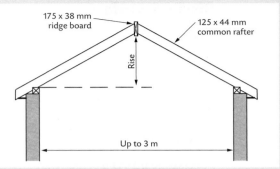

10-5 *Couple roof*

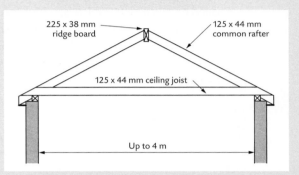

10-6 *Close couple roof*

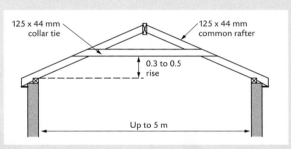

10-7 *Collar roof*

COUPLE ROOFS consist of rafters fixed to a ridge board and wall plates. As can be seen from Fig. 10-5 there is no tie, so the weight of the roof tends to put an outward push on the walls. This principle makes couple roofs practical only for very small spans (up to 3 m).

THE CLOSE COUPLE ROOF is an improvement on the couple roof because it contains a ceiling joist, which acts as a tie (Fig. 10-6). As a result spans may be increased to 4 m.

COLLAR ROOFS are used where increased headroom is required (Fig. 10-7). They do not contain a ceiling joist and the collar should be placed from one-third to one-half the rise. Collar roofs are suitable for spans up to 5 m.

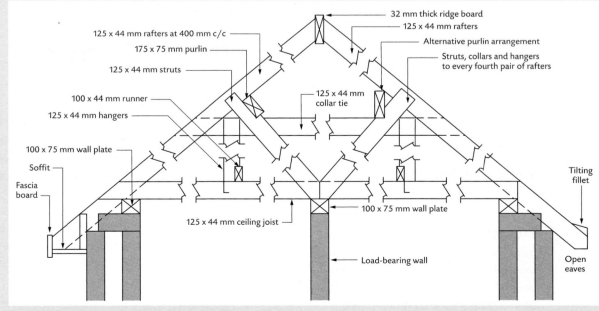

10-8 *Double roof (purlin roof) details for spans up to 7.2 m*

Double or purlin roofs

Single roofs become uneconomical for spans in excess of 5 m. Instead, a double roof is used (see Fig. 10-8).

The purlins give intermediate support to the rafters, and they are in turn supported by struts. The struts transfer the loads to load-bearing walls or to beams spread across a number of ceiling joists (a minimum of five ceiling joists).

Collar ties are fitted at every fourth pair of rafters for additional strength and stiffness. If additional bracing is required (for larger roofs) hangers are fitted from the purlin to the runner. The runner is secured to the top of the ceiling joists.

Double or purlin roofs are usually constructed on site, i.e. they are 'cut roofs'. Figs. 10-9 to 10-12 show the various constructional details for a well-designed cut-roof. Refer also back to Fig. 10-3.

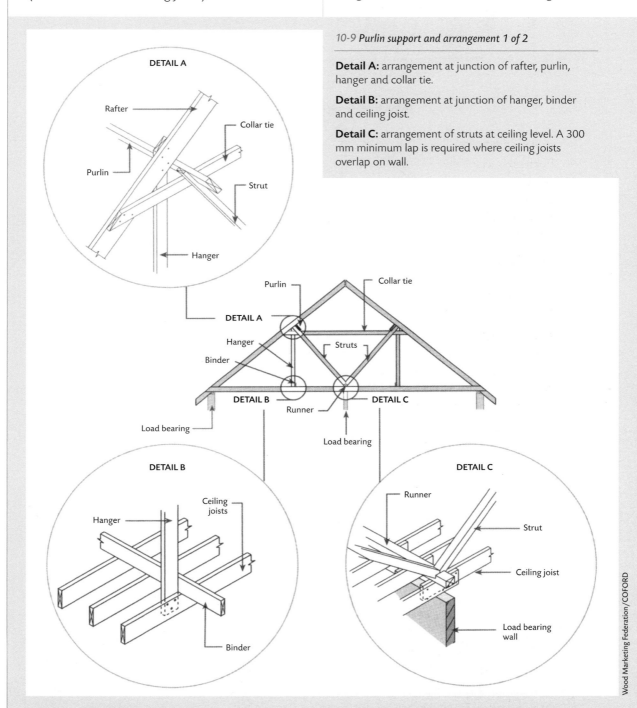

10-9 Purlin support and arrangement 1 of 2

Detail A: arrangement at junction of rafter, purlin, hanger and collar tie.

Detail B: arrangement at junction of hanger, binder and ceiling joist.

Detail C: arrangement of struts at ceiling level. A 300 mm minimum lap is required where ceiling joists overlap on wall.

Wood Marketing Federation/COFORD

DETAIL E

150 mm
min. lap

Purlin

Strut

Detail D: strutting of purlin on to a load-bearing wall.

Alternative detail D: where a purlin cannot be propped onto a load-bearing wall it may be propped on a specially designed joist(s) or beam. The load is transferred to a load-bearing wall or the frame arrangement.

Detail E: splice joint detail for connecting purlins.

DETAIL E

DETAIL D

DETAIL D

Strut

Restraining
piece

Ceiling
joists

Load
bearing wall

DETAIL D (alternative)

Strut

Specially
designed
joist or beam

25 mm
min. clearance

Binder

Wood Marketing Federation/COFORD

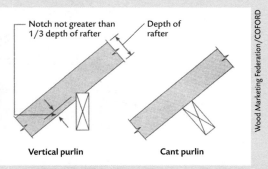

Notch not greater than
1/3 depth of rafter

Depth of
rafter

Vertical purlin

Cant purlin

Wood Marketing Federation/COFORD

10-11 Support at purlins. The 'cant' purlin arrangement is the more common. The rafter is skew nailed to the purlin.

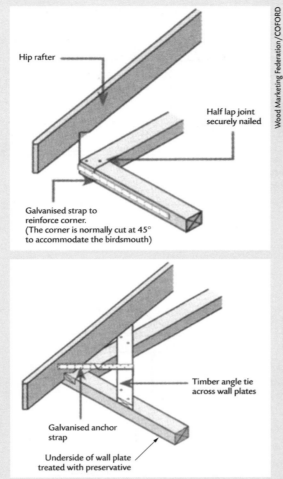

Hip rafter

Half lap joint securely nailed

Galvanised strap to reinforce corner.
(The corner is normally cut at 45°
to accommodate the birdsmouth)

Timber angle tie across wall plates

Galvanised anchor strap

Underside of wall plate treated with preservative

10-12 Support at hipped ends. Reinforce wall plates using a galvanized strap (top). For heavily loaded hips use a galvanized anchor strap fixed to a timber angle (bottom).

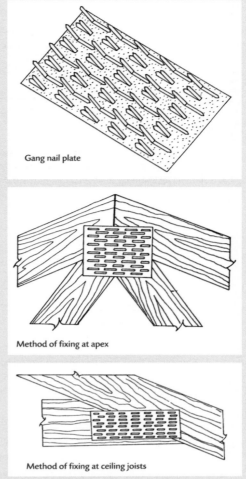

Gang nail plate

Method of fixing at apex

Method of fixing at ceiling joists

10-13 Metal plate fixing, also known as a gang nail plate. Used at all joint locations in a trussed rafter.

Prefabricated trussed rafters

The majority of modern dwelling roofs are built using prefabricated trussed rafters. They are suitable for large spans, often in excess of 7.5 m.

Trussed rafters are usually placed at 600 mm centres, but they can be placed at 400 mm centres to reduce the amount of bracing required and to provide greater strength and stiffness to the roof.

Trusses must be:
- designed and made specifically for the structure they will roof;
- joined using galvanised punched metal plate fixings (Fig. 10-13);
- adequately braced;
- securely fixed to the wall plate;
- protected from the distribution of point loads such as water tanks;
- made from stress-graded, kiln-dried timber.

One of the main advantages of using trussed rafters is the clear span made possible by the absence of the need for intermediate supports (Figs. 10-14 to 10-18).

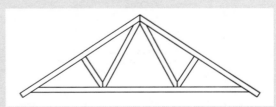

10-14 W or Fink truss (up to 8 m span). This is the most common type of truss.

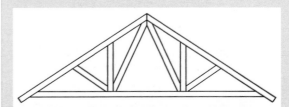

10-15 The fan truss is designed for spans from 8–11 m.

Wood Marketing Federation/COFORD

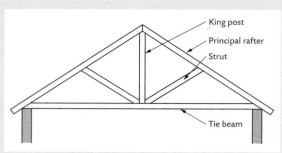

10-16 King post truss. *A traditional timber roof truss with a vertical post from the apex to the centre of the bottom tie beam. It is suitable for spans up to about 11 m. Rarely if ever used in new work.*

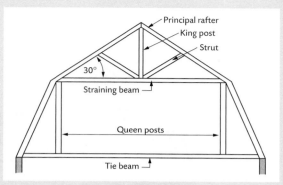

10-18 Mansard truss. *This is used for a pitched roof with a shallow top part and a steeper lower part. Generally used with dormers in the attic space.*

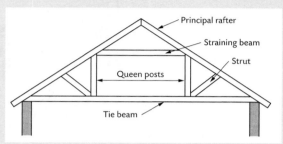

10-17 Queen post truss. *This truss has no central post, unlike the king-post truss. Like the king-post truss it is not now used in new work.*

Bracing is essential for a prefabricated trussed roof to ensure that the whole roof structure acts as a single unit. The following details show good design and bracing details that should be observed when using trussed rafters (Figs. 10-19 to 10-48).

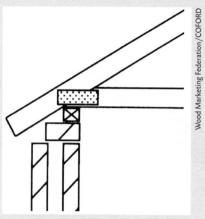

10-19 Truss support – standard heel

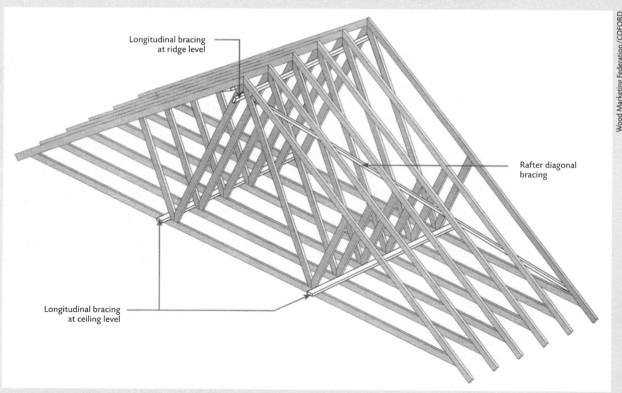

10-20 Prefabricated roof truss – minimum bracing so that roof structure acts as a unit

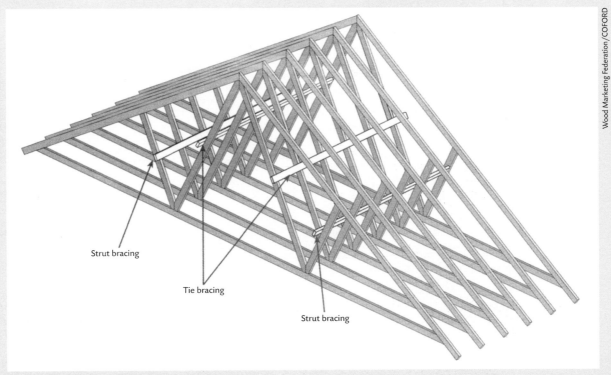

Wood Marketing Federation/COFORD

Strut bracing

Tie bracing

Strut bracing

10-21 Prefabricated roof truss – additional bracing

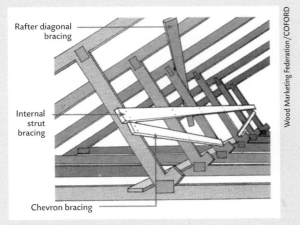

Rafter diagonal bracing

Internal strut bracing

Chevron bracing

Wood Marketing Federation/COFORD

10-22 Internal bracing – 1 of 2

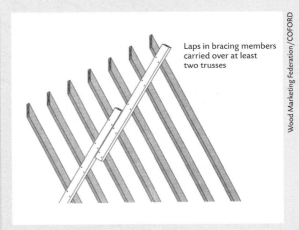

Laps in bracing members carried over at least two trusses

Wood Marketing Federation/COFORD

10-24 Fixing bracing

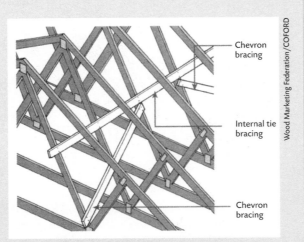

Chevron bracing

Internal tie bracing

Chevron bracing

Wood Marketing Federation/COFORD

10-23 Internal bracing – 2 of 2

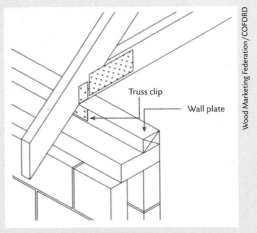

Truss clip

Wall plate

Wood Marketing Federation/COFORD

10-25 Truss fixing to wall plate

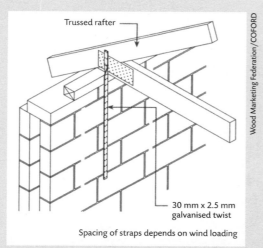

10-26 *Truss fixing. An alternative to truss clips is to use galvanized twist straps, 1000 mm long min.*

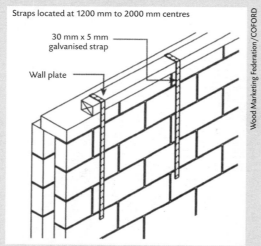

10-27 *Wall plate fixing*

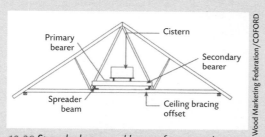

10-28 *Spreader beams and bearers for supporting water tank*

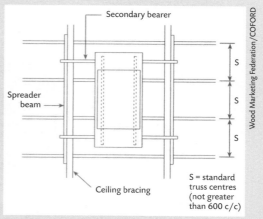

10-29 *Water tanks with a nominal capacity of up to 270 litres should be spread over four trusses*

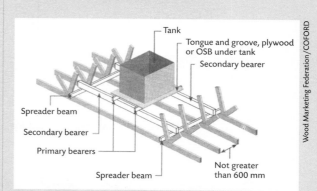

10-30 *Pictorial view of supports for water tank*

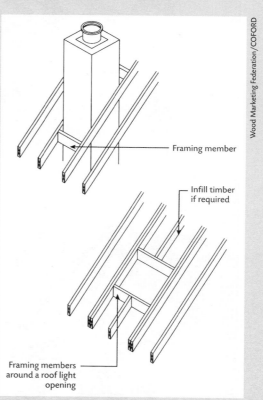

10-31 *Chimney and roof lights. Where possible accommodate chimney, roof windows, etc., in the standard spacing between trusses. Provide appropriate framing members as required.*

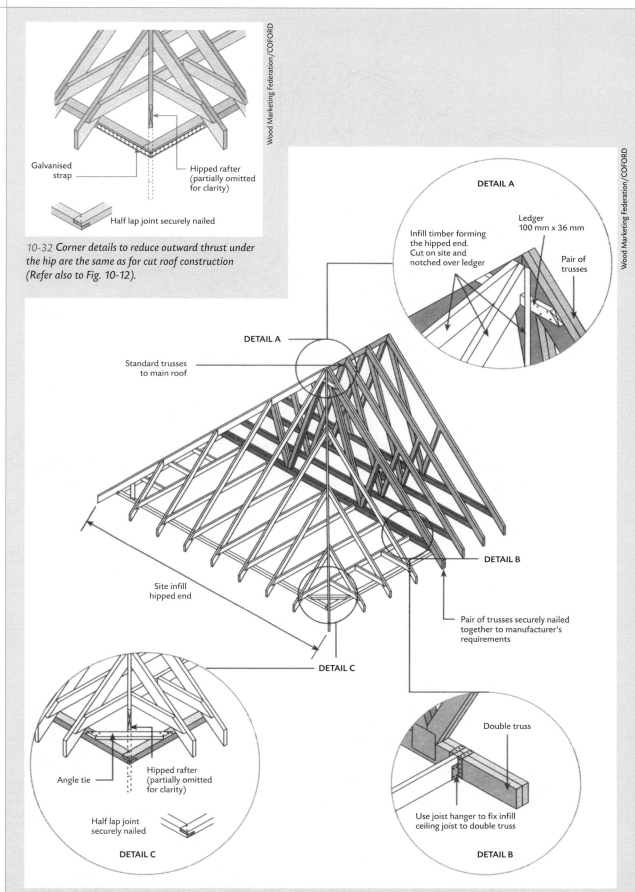

Galvanised strap

Hipped rafter (partially omitted for clarity)

Half lap joint securely nailed

10-32 Corner details to reduce outward thrust under the hip are the same as for cut roof construction (Refer also to Fig. 10-12).

Wood Marketing Federation/COFORD

DETAIL A

Infill timber forming the hipped end. Cut on site and notched over ledger

Ledger 100 mm x 36 mm

Pair of trusses

DETAIL A

Standard trusses to main roof

Site infill hipped end

DETAIL B

Pair of trusses securely nailed together to manufacturer's requirements

DETAIL C

Angle tie

Hipped rafter (partially omitted for clarity)

Half lap joint securely nailed

DETAIL C

Double truss

Use joist hanger to fix infill ceiling joist to double truss

DETAIL B

10-33 Trussed rafter roofs – hipped ends. Site infill timbers are used to form the hipped ends where the span does not exceed 6 m.

DETAIL A

Infill rafter

DETAIL C

Regular

DETAIL B

DETAIL D

Infill ceiling joist

10-34 *Truss spacing to accommodate openings for rooflights, dormer windows and chimneys may require infill support*

Wood Marketing Federation/COFORD

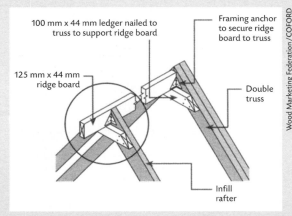

100 mm x 44 mm ledger nailed to truss to support ridge board

Framing anchor to secure ridge board to truss

125 mm x 44 mm ridge board

Double truss

Infill rafter

10-35 *Detail A: ridge level infill*

Wood Marketing Federation/COFORD

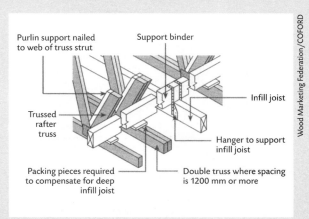

Purlin support nailed to web of truss strut

Support binder

Infill joist

Trussed rafter truss

Hanger to support infill joist

Packing pieces required to compensate for deep infill joist

Double truss where spacing is 1200 mm or more

10-36 *Detail B: support of infill joist*

Wood Marketing Federation/COFORD

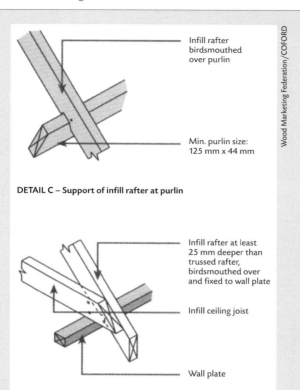

DETAIL C – Support of infill rafter at purlin

- Infill rafter birdsmouthed over purlin
- Min. purlin size: 125 mm x 44 mm

- Infill rafter at least 25 mm deeper than trussed rafter, birdsmouthed over and fixed to wall plate
- Infill ceiling joist
- Wall plate

DETAIL D – Support of infill rafter at wall plate

10-37 Support of infill rafter

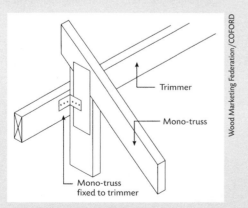

'Bobtail' truss

DETAIL 10-39

Mono-truss

DETAIL 10-40

10-38 Specially designed mono-trusses are an alternative to site-cut infill timber around an opening.

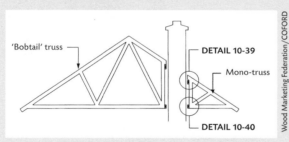

- Trimmer
- Mono-truss
- Mono-truss fixed to trimmer

10-39 Mono-truss support – 1 of 2

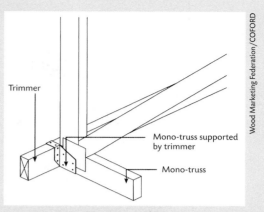

- Trimmer
- Mono-truss supported by trimmer
- Mono-truss

10-40 Mono-truss support – 2 of 2

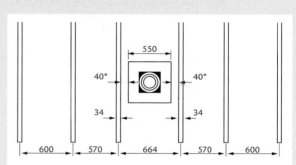

550

40*   40*

34   34

600 | 570 | 664 | 570 | 600

*All timbers must be 40 mm clear of chimney for fire safety reasons. This applies where blockwork or brickwork is 100 mm.

All dimensions are in millimetres

10-41 Dimensions for hatch and chimney openings for a standard block chimney with a single flue serving one house

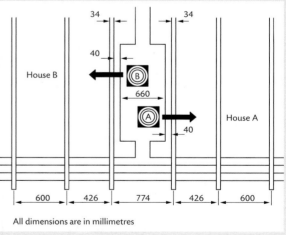

House B

34   34

40

B

660

A

40

House A

600 | 426 | 774 | 426 | 600

All dimensions are in millimetres

10-42 Truss spacing dimensions for standard block chimney on party wall

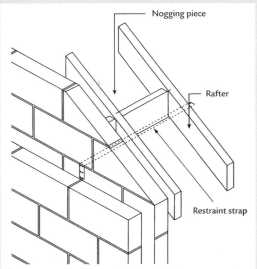

10-43 *Truss spacing dimensions for a standard block chimney with two flues within the same house*

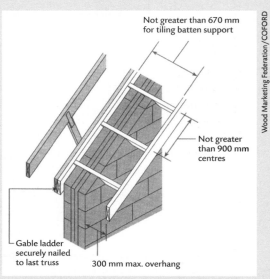

10-46 *Solid packing and noggins, fixed horizontally, prevents twisting of restraint strap.*

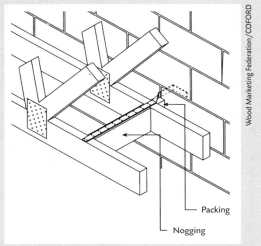

10-44 *Prefabricated trusses should be adequately fixed to the external wall to which they are parallel to provide the necessary lateral support to the wall at roof level.*

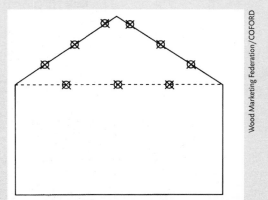

10-47 *Gable ladders are used where a roof overhang is required at a gable end. The overhang should not be greater than 300 mm.*

10-45 *Recommended strap positions. Straps should be provided at rafter and ceiling level. They should be 30 x 5 mm in cross-section, galvanized and carried over a minimum of two trusses.*

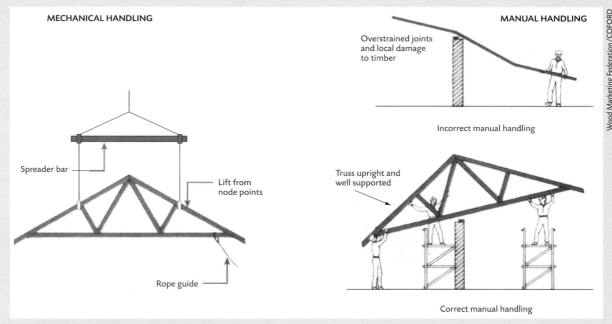

Wood Marketing Federation/COFORD

MECHANICAL HANDLING

Spreader bar

Lift from node points

Rope guide

MANUAL HANDLING

Overstrained joints and local damage to timber

Incorrect manual handling

Truss upright and well supported

Correct manual handling

10-48 *Mechanical handling technique of trusses to prevent damage to the truss members and gang nail plates.*

H Dormer roof construction

It is common practice to include accommodation within the roof space. Such a roof is referred to as a dormer roof. A dormer bungalow means simply a bungalow with accommodation in the roof.

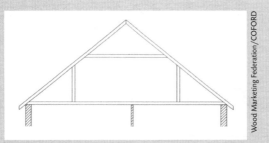

Wood Marketing Federation/COFORD

10-49 *A typical 'attic truss' designed for accommodation within the roof space*

Particular attention must be paid to the construction of a dormer roof in comparison to a non-dormer roof. For example, joists must be heavier, in order to accommodate the increased loads in the attic (Fig. 10-50a).

In some cases it may be necessary to use structural steel members such as RSJs (rolled steel joists) as part of the roof structure (Fig. 10-50b).

The principle of triangulation, used in the design of all roofs, must also be incorporated in dormer roofs.

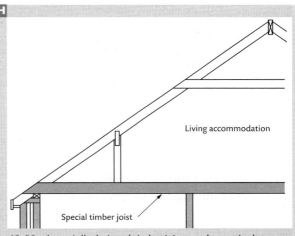

Living accommodation

Special timber joist

10-50a *A specially designed timber joist may be required to support the extra load.*

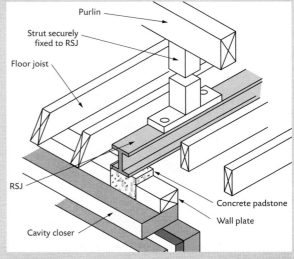

Purlin

Strut securely fixed to RSJ

Floor joist

RSJ

Cavity closer

Concrete padstone

Wall plate

10-50b *Alternatively, an RSJ may be used to provide under-purlin support.*

Dormer roofs may be of the traditional 'cut-roof' design or they may be designed using prefabricated dormer trusses. The minimum ceiling height for any habitable room is 2.4 m. In an attic the minimum ceiling height of 2.4 m should be equal to or not less than half of the area of the room measured on a plane 1.5 m above finished floor level, i.e. area ABCD to be at least half the area of WXYZ in Fig. 10-51.

Dormer windows or roof lights are used to provide daylight to rooms in dormer roofs. Rooflights may be either an opening light or a fixed light. They are set into the roof in line with the pitch of the roof (Fig. 10-52).

Dormer window frames should not carry roof loads, therefore the roof framing around the window must be independent of the window frame (Figs. 10-53 to 10-57).

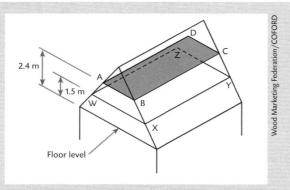

10-51 *Minimum ceiling height in dormer construction. The minimum ceiling height for any habitable room is 2.4 m. In an attic truss the minimum ceiling height of 2.4 m should be equal to or not less than half of the area of the room measured on a plane 1.5 m above finished floor level, i.e. area ABCD to be at least half the area of WXYZ.*

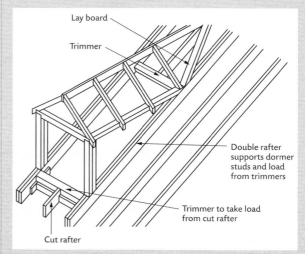

10-53 *Dormer window construction*

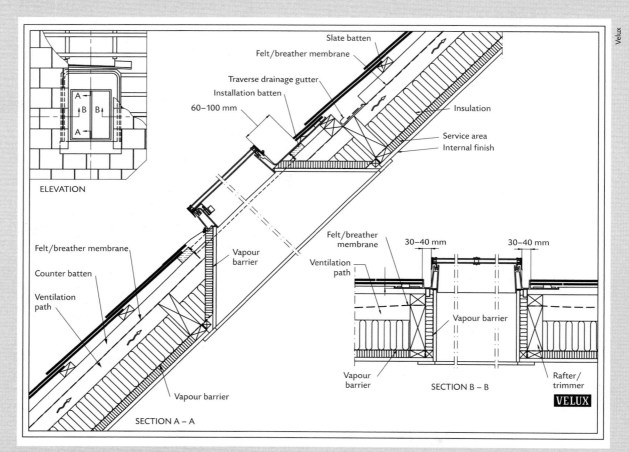

10-52 *Typical rooflight details*

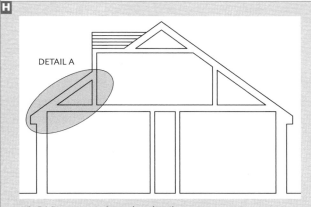

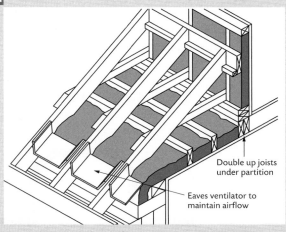

DETAIL A

10-54 *Dormer window – key detail*

Double up joists
under partition

Eaves ventilator to
maintain airflow

10-56 *Typical detail under dormer window where floor joists run parallel with wall plate*

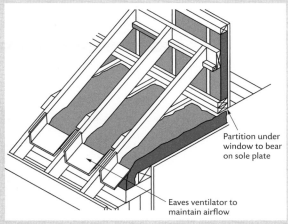

Partition under
window to bear
on sole plate

Eaves ventilator to
maintain airflow

10-55 *Typical detail under dormer window where floor joists are perpendicular to the wall plate*

10-57 *Alternative locations for water tanks in dormer roof construction*

A valley intersection is formed by a series of specially fabricated diminishing trusses collectively called a valley set. The valley set transfers the rafter loads down to the underlying trusses in a uniform manner. Each truss in the set must be secured to each rafter it crosses (Fig. 10-58).

Wood Marketing Federation/COFORD

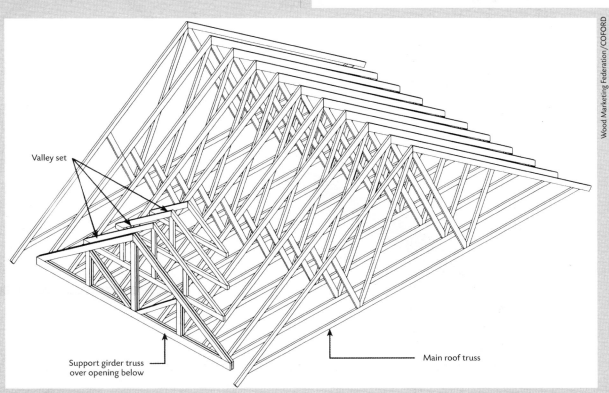

Valley set

Support girder truss
over opening below

Main roof truss

10-58 *Valleys in trussed rafter roofs*

Dormer roofs must be adequately ventilated to prevent condensation. A vapour barrier must be fitted on the warm side of the insulation.

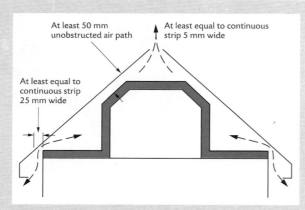

10-59 *Dormer roof ventilation requirements*

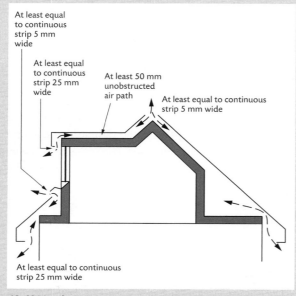

10-60 *Ventilation requirements to a dormer roof with a flat roof dormer window*

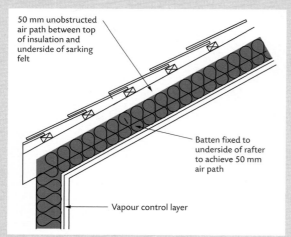

10-61 *Special detailing may be required to achieve the 50 mm unobstructed air path. Deeper rafters are an alternative to the detail shown in the diagram.*

Roof ventilation

Ventilation for roofs serves the same purpose as for all other locations, i.e. to remove water vapour and prevent condensation. Ventilation has become more important as a result of increased standards of insulation, coupled with household activities that generate water vapour within buildings.

The following diagrams show the requirements for ventilation openings for the various roof types to comply with the Building Regulations.

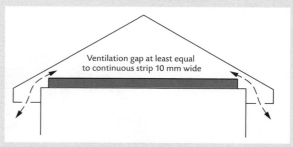

10-62 *Ventilation requirements to a pitched roof with a pitch greater than 15°*

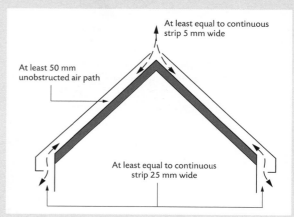

10-63 *Ventilation requirements when the ceiling follows the pitch of the roof*

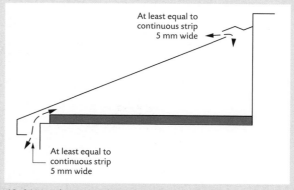

10-64 *Ventilation to a lean-to roof*

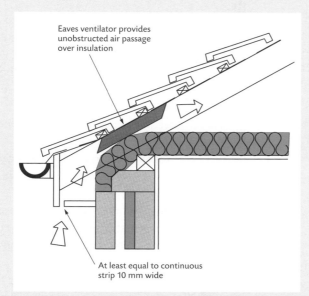

10-65 The conventional method of ventilation at eaves. Provide mesh to obstruct insects etc.

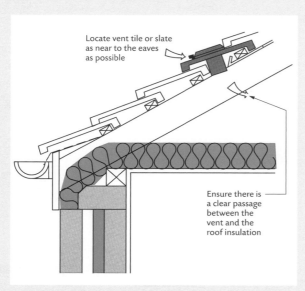

10-66 Ventilation at eaves using a vent tile

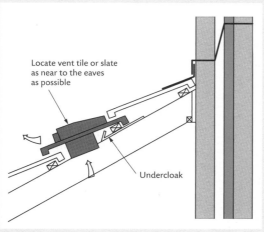

10-67 Ventilation of lean-to roof at abutment

Openings should be provided on opposite sides of the roof at least equal to a continuous ventilation strip running the full length of the eaves. The width of the strip depends on the roof type.

Vapour barriers reduce the amount of moisture reaching the roof, but are not an alternative to ventilation. Vapour barriers are fixed on the warm side of the insulation. Use 500 gauge polythene with sealed laps.

Party wall fire protection

To prevent the spread of fire between dwellings, the party wall is completed along the line of the slope of the roof and adequately fire-stopped with a suitable material.

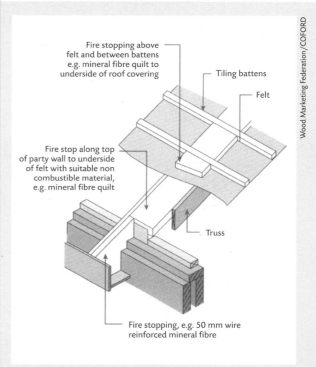

10-68 Fire stopping details at party wall

Flat roofs

Roof surfaces pitched at 10° or less are classified as flat roofs. This type of construction should be avoided, where possible, due to maintenance costs and the high risk of leaking. Good detailing is required to prevent condensation occurring.

The disadvantages of flat roofs are:
- They are poor insulators.
- Their life expectancy is low due to the materials used and construction details employed.
- They are not aesthetic and look unfinished.

Construction

Timber flat roofs consist of joists, 44 mm thick, spaced at 400 mm centres. The fall is achieved by using firring pieces. The roof joists generally bridge the shortest span and the boarding (decking) is fixed in the direction of the fall.

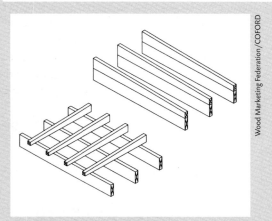

10-69 *Firring pieces used to achieve the required fall in flat roofs. Firring pieces can either be fixed in line with the joists (top) or alternatively be laid across the joists.*

Exterior grade plywood, OSB or tongued and grooved boarding is generally used. Treat the timber with preservative other than creosote. Creosote is harmful to bitumen and gives off an offensive odour.

Three layers of felt are used to weatherproof the roof. These are laid so that the joints are broken in each layer. They are bonded using hot bitumen adhesive. Overlaps should be a minimum of 50 mm.

Continuous coverings on flat roofs are more prone to movement than tiles or slate used on pitched roofs.

Timber flat roofs are subject to moisture movement and concrete flat roofs are subject to drying shrinkage.

Asphalt is not recommended on timber flat roofs because it is unable to accept movement.

The recommended fall for flat roofs is 1 in 40. This ensures that water is effectively removed and that ponding doesn't occur.

Ensure that insulation used is dry because it becomes ineffective and may deteriorate when wet.

To prolong the life of the roof, white stone chippings are sometimes placed on the covering. This protects the covering from extremes of expansion and contraction.

Condensation is a particular problem for flat roofs. It is necessary to cross ventilate the spaces between joists in timber flat roofs. The following flat roof designs highlight the ventilation requirements.

COLD DECK ROOF

In this type of construction the insulation is placed between the ceiling joists at ceiling level. Heat loss through the ceiling is therefore restricted and this keeps the cavity, roof deck and covering at a low temperature, especially during winter.

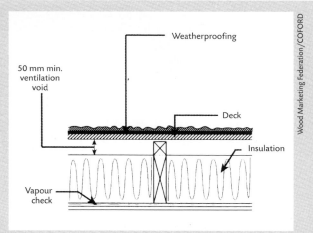

10-70 *Cold deck construction*

Ventilation of this roof design is very important if condensation is to be avoided (Fig. 10-71). Use foil-backed plasterboard for the ceiling and fix a vapour barrier (500 gauge polythene) to the bottom of the joists to control moisture build-up in the insulation (Fig. 10-72).

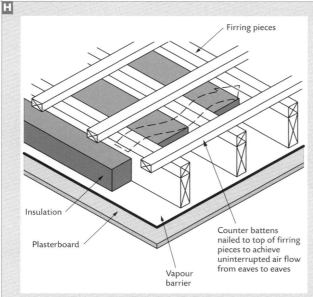

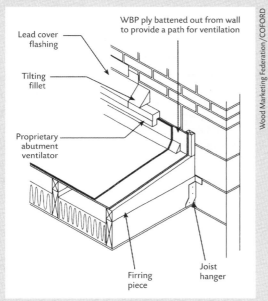

10-71 *Cold deck roof showing counter battens nailed to the top of firring pieces to achieve uninterrupted air flow*

10-72 *Flat roof abutment detail – cold deck*

WARM DECK ROOF

In this type of construction the insulation is placed below the waterproof covering and on top of the roof deck and vapour barrier. This means that the deck is maintained at warm temperatures during the winter.

Bonding or mechanical fixings are used to secure the insulation to the decking. The waterproof covering is bonded to the top of the insulation (Fig. 10-73). This is the preferred design for flat roofs as higher levels of thermal insulation are achievable and condensation is less of a problem.

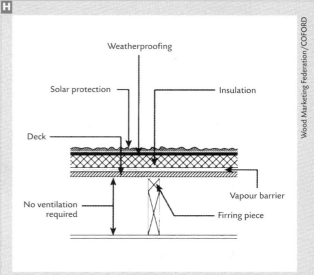

10-73 *Warm deck roof*

INVERTED WARM DECK ROOF

In this design the insulation is placed on top of the weatherproofing material. This allows for the complete roof construction to be kept at warm temperatures during the winter.

A further advantage is that the roof covering will be kept at moderate temperatures during the summer. The insulation used must have low moisture absorption properties.

Vapour barriers are not required with this type of roof (Figs. 10-74–10-76).

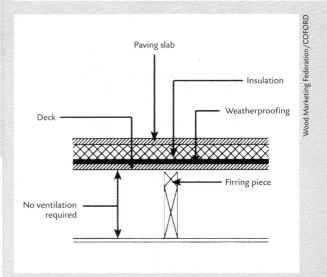

10-74 *Inverted warm deck roof*

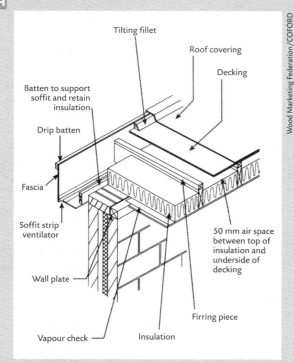

10-75 *Flat roof verge detail – cold deck*

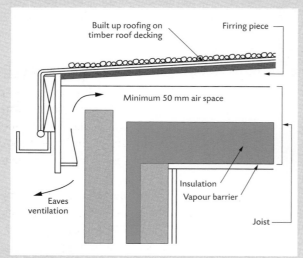

10-76 *Flat roof eaves detail*

Securing flat roofs

Holding down straps (30 × 5 mm in cross section) at least 1 m long are placed at between 1.2 m and 2 m centres. Fix the straps to the masonry using masonry nails or wood screws into plugs.

Use a minimum number of three fixings on each strap, one of which should be at least 150 mm from the bottom of the strap.

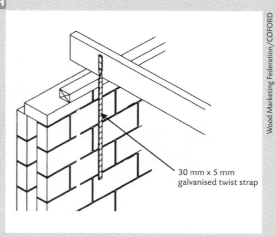

10-77 *Holding down joists using galvanized twist strap*

Flat roof coverings

■ **Built-up bitumen felt** (see page 196).
■ **Polymeric single-ply membranes**. These are made from synthetic polymers or rubbers and are thermoplastic. Joints are formed either by gluing or welding.

Asphalt is any of several black semi-solid substances composed of bitumen and inert mineral matter. These substances occur naturally in parts of America and as a residue from petroleum distillation: used as a waterproofing material and in paints and fungicides. Asphalt mixed with gravel is used in road-surfacing and roofing materials.

■ **Asphalt**. Common for use with concrete roofs. Because it is prone to movement, a layer of felt should separate it from the concrete. Asphalt should always be applied in two layers with the finished thickness not less than 20 mm.
■ **Lead, zinc, copper and aluminium** may also be used but require specialised detailing.

Pitched roof coverings

The most widely used pitched roof coverings for dwellings are tiles and slates. Factors such as cost, location, and appearance (aesthetics), will influence which is to be used. Before dealing with slates and tiles in detail, we will look at felt and battens.

Sarking felt

Sarking felt prevents any water that may get through the outer covering from penetrating the roof (Fig. 10-78).

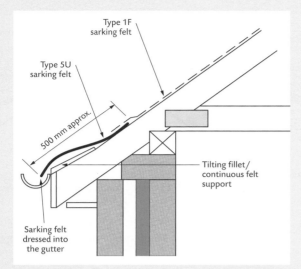

10-78 *Sarking felt at eaves level. Type 5U sarking felt is more durable than type 1F and is therefore more suitable for use in the vicinity of the eaves.*

Great care is therefore required for the fixing of felt. Ensure that vertical laps are at least 100 mm and occur over a rafter. Horizontal laps should be between 100 mm and 225 mm and occur as illustrated in the sketches.

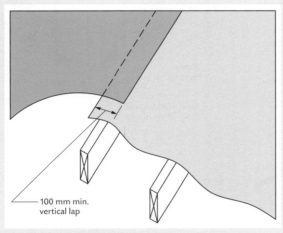

10-79 *Vertical/side laps in felt should occur over a rafter*

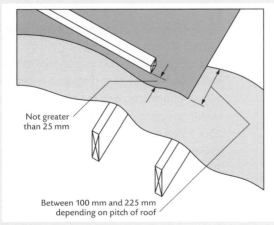

10-80 *Horizontal laps in sarking felt*

The felt is carried over the ridge, ensuring that a lap of 150 mm is maintained.

At the eaves sarking felt is dressed 50 mm into the gutter. A tilting fillet should be provided to avoid a water trap behind the fascia board.

An extra layer of felt is provided at the hips, at least 600 mm wide.

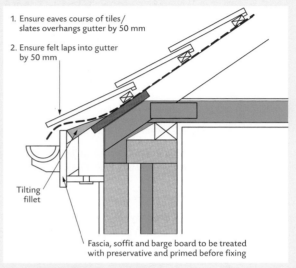

10-81 *Detail of tiled roof at eaves*

Battens

Battens must be long enough to be nailed to at least three rafters. They must be equally spaced to suit the recommendations of the tile/slate manufacturer for the tile/slate being used. The length of the nails used to fix battens should be between 32 and 45 mm longer than the thickness of the batten.

If extra grip is required, use circular ring shank nails. These nails thread into the rafters as they are driven. Not more than one batten in four should be joined over any truss or rafter.

Tiles

Tiles can be made from clay or concrete in a variety of colours. Plain tiles measure 400 × 300 × 12 mm. They are usually cambered in their length and across their width to ensure that they sit tightly on each other and also to prevent water entering by capillary action (Fig. 10-82 overleaf).

Each tile has two nibs for correct positioning over the battens and there are two nail holes close to the head for securing it to the battens. Aluminium alloy, copper, silicon bronze or stainless steel nails are used on every third or fourth course, while the eaves, verges, top and bottom courses are always nailed.

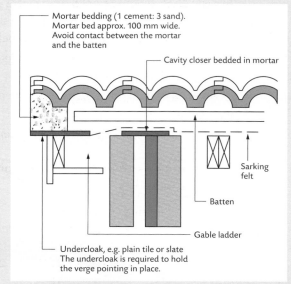

10-82 *Typical bedded verge detail for pantiles. The principle of this detail also applies to plain tiles.*

Sarking felt is used as standard under the tiling battens. A variety of ventilating tiles is available which are watertight and provide ventilation of the roof space.

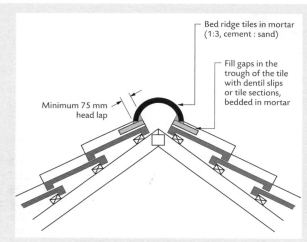

10-83 *Typical bedded ridge detail for tiles*

ROOFING TERMS AND FORMULAS

The 'gauge' is the distance between centres of battens and is calculated by using the formula:

Gauge = length of tile minus the lap

For plain tiles with a lap of 100 mm the gauge would be:

400 – 100 = 300 (Fig. 10-84)

The 'margin' is the exposed area of each tile on the roof and is equal to the gauge.

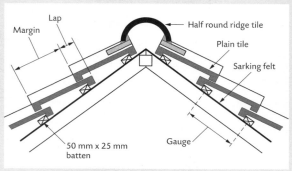

10-84 *Details of 'gauge', 'margin' and 'lap' as applied to tiles*

The tiles should overhang the wall by a minimum of 50 mm to give adequate protection against the weather.

Hips and ridges are covered with half-round tiles bedded in mortar. A typical valley arrangement for tiles is shown in Fig. 10-85.

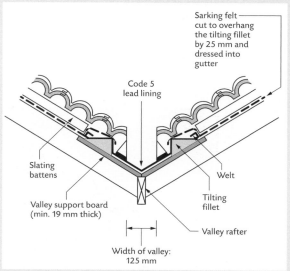

10-85 *Typical valley detail for tiles*

Single lap tiles are the most common, where the tile overlaps the head of the tile in the course below. The lap should not be less than 65 mm. These tiles also have a side lap, which is usually interlocking. The standard size for single lap tiles is 418 × 330 mm.

Single lap tiles result in a lighter roof covering and allow a lower roof pitch than plain tiles.

The minimum pitch for tiles is 25° and the maximum pitch is 55°. Suitable batten sizes are 35 × 35 mm or 50 × 25 mm for rafters up to 450 mm centres. For rafters up to 600 mm centres 50 × 35 mm battens are recommended.

Slates

Slate is a natural material, but it is seldom used in its natural form for roof coverings. Slates of asbestos cement were the most popular until recently when concerns were raised about the health hazards posed by asbestos.

Fibre-reinforced cement slates are now the recommended choice, even though their life expectancy is less than the former.

The minimum pitch for slates is 25°. Batten sizes of 50 × 25 mm are suitable for rafters up to 450 mm centres and 50 × 35 mm for rafters up to 600 mm.

The typical slate size is 600 × 300 mm. Each slate is fixed using two nails either at the head or the centre of the slate. The lap for slates is the amount by which the tails of slates in one course overlap the heads of slates in the next course.

Centre nailing is common practice for all but the smallest slates. Head-nailed slates have a tendency to lift in strong winds.

THE GAUGE FOR SLATES The gauge is the distance between the nail holes in one slate and those in the adjoining slate, above or below. It varies depending on whether the slate is head nailed or centre nailed.

- For centre-nailed slates:
  gauge = (length − lap) ÷ 2
  For example, taking 600 mm long centre-nailed slates,
  the gauge = (600 − 100) ÷ 2 = 250 mm.

- For head-nailed slates:
  gauge = [length − (lap + 25)] ÷ 2
  For example, taking 600 mm long head-nailed slates,
  the gauge = [600 − (75 + 25)] ÷ 2 = 250 mm.

Slates should be laid so that side joints in one course are over the centre of slates in the course below. The short slates at the eaves are head nailed and should overhang the fascia board by 50 mm. Slating details for various locations follow.

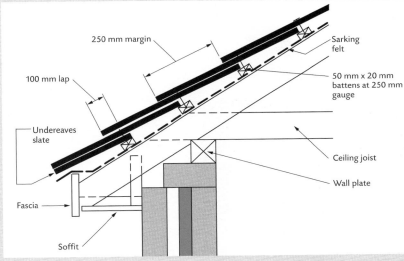

10-86 Centre-nailed slating using 600 x 300 mm slates. The undereaves slate is 375 mm long. This is calculated using the formula 'G + L + 25 mm', where G = the gauge and L = the lap.

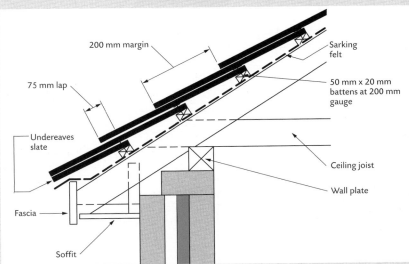

10-87 Head-nailed slating using 500 x 250 mm slates. The undereaves slate is 300 mm long. This is calculated using the formula 'G + L + 25 mm', where G = the gauge and L = the lap.

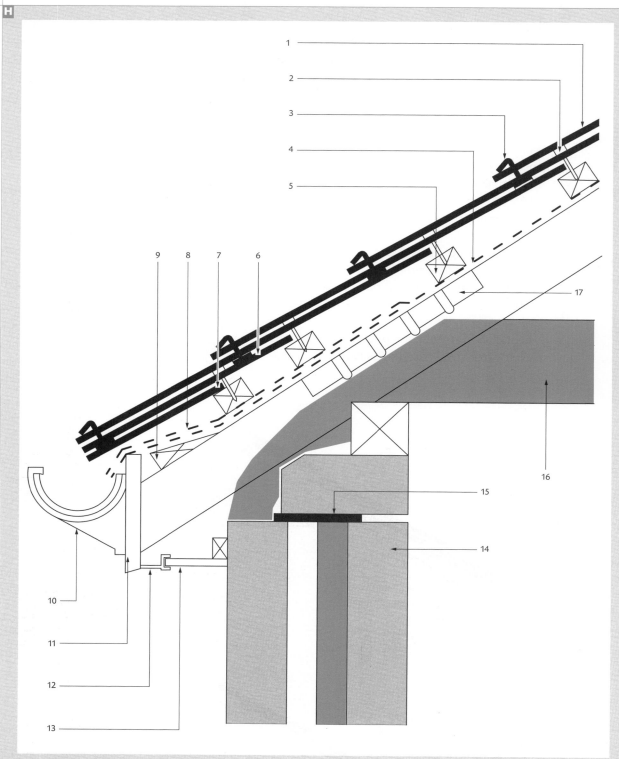

10-88 *Standard eaves slating detail (centre-nailed)*

1	Slate	**10**	Gutter
2	30 mm x 2.65 mm copper nails	**11**	Fascia board
3	Copper crampion	**12**	Continuous soffit vent for flat soffit, screwed to fascia board
4	Sarking felt		
5	Slating batten	**13**	Soffit board between 4–10 mm thick
6	Second undereaves slate course	**14**	External cavity wall
7	First undereaves slate course	**15**	Cavity closer
8	500 mm wide strip of durable felt	**16**	Insulation at ceiling level
9	Continuous timber tilting fillet	**17**	Eaves ventilator

H

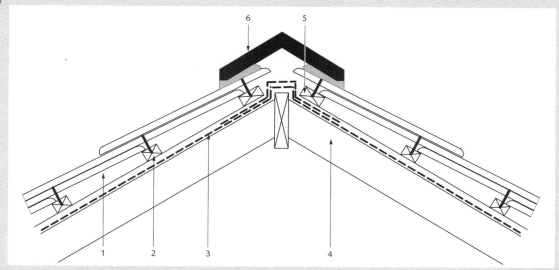

10-89 Standard bedded ridge slating detail

1 Natural slate
2 Slating batten
3 Sarking felt
4 Truss/rafter
5 Extra wide batten at ridge
6 Ridge cap bedded in mortar

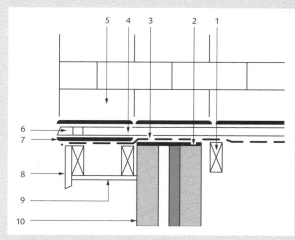

10-90 Standard pointed verge slating detail

1 Truss/rafter
2 Cavity closer
3 Sarking felt to carry out over barge board
4 Slating batten
5 Natural slate
6 Mortar pointing angled back
7 Undercloaking slate laid face down
8 Fascia board
9 Barge soffit
10 Cavity gable wall

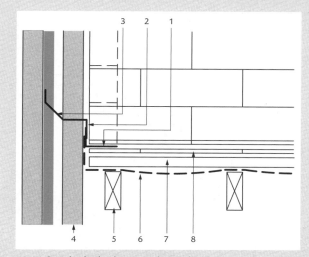

10-91 Standard side abutment slating detail

1 Metal soaker interleaved with slates
2 Metal cover flashing
3 Stepped cavity tray
4 Cavity wall
5 Truss/rafter
6 Sarking felt carried up ends of battens
7 Slating battens
8 Slates

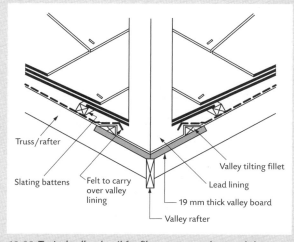

Truss/rafter

Slating battens

Felt to carry over valley lining

Valley tilting fillet

Lead lining

19 mm thick valley board

Valley rafter

10-92 Typical valley detail for fibre cement and natural slates

Roof drainage

Roof drainage is provided by a system of gutters and downpipes. The system should be capable of carrying the equivalent of 75 mm of rainfall per hour. The flow into gutters depends on the area to be drained and whether it is a flat or pitched roof. The pitch of the roof also affects the flow.

In order to slow the rate of flow in high-pitched roofs bellcasts are sometimes included. These may also be included for aesthetic reasons. Gutters must be fixed with a slight fall towards the nearest downpipe. Downpipes discharge into a drain, gulley, soakpit or another downpipe.

Gutters are available in a variety of materials – seamless aluminium is very popular, but they are also available in PVC-U and cast iron.

Seamless gutters are fabricated on site. The name is a bit misleading as there are seams in the system. These occur only at the corners, however, and instead of slip fittings, these joints are riveted and sealed for stability and leak resistance. This system might be more correctly named 'continuous gutters'.

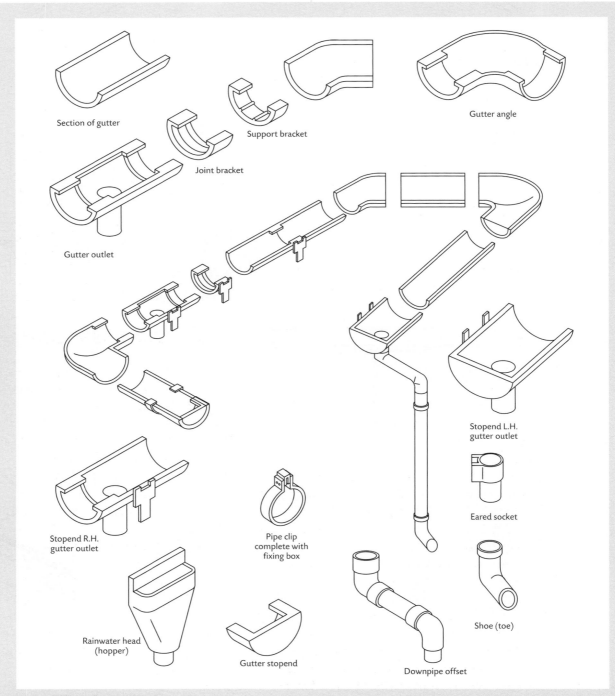

Section of gutter

Support bracket

Joint bracket

Gutter angle

Gutter outlet

Stopend R.H. gutter outlet

Pipe clip complete with fixing box

Rainwater head (hopper)

Gutter stopend

Downpipe offset

Stopend L.H. gutter outlet

Eared socket

Shoe (toe)

10-93 Traditional guttering system

Chapter 11

Internal subdivisions

Internal walls and partitions

Walls that divide the interior of a building into accommodation and circulation areas are called partitions or internal walls. They may be further classified as load bearing or non-load bearing, depending on whether they support roofs and/or floors. Internal walls and partitions may be constructed from a wide variety of materials.

Load-bearing walls usually are constructed from blocks and bricks, and are bonded to the external walls. Load-bearing walls have good fire resistance and sound insulation properties. The main disadvantage with this type of wall is its permanence; it allows no flexibility in changing internal layout.

Openings for doors are made in the same manner as for external walls, by the use of lintels.

Non-load bearing partitions are usually constructed in timber, although all the other materials can also be used (block/brick/metal). Their main function is to support their own weight. In timber-frame construction the timber frame is a load-bearing structure.

Construction details

When made of timber or metal, internal walls in traditional construction are referred to as 'stud' partitions.

Stud partitions are very common in the upstairs areas of two-storey buildings. Timber or metal stud partitions are lighter than block or brick partitions, but they do not provide the same degree of sound or fire insulation.

A typical non-load bearing timber stud partition consists of a layer of plasterboard fixed to each side of a timber framework. The timber used should be straight and dried to at least 20% moisture content so as to prevent warping.

The standard size for the studs is 44 mm × 75 mm and they should be spaced at 400 mm centres. It is possible to construct a load-bearing timber stud partition by using studs of 44 mm × 100 mm

with a minimum spacing of 400 mm centres. Such partitions should have a double header and double sole pieces.

It is recommended that all stud partitions have two rows of staggered noggings as in Fig. 11-1.

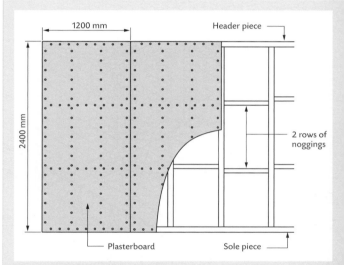

11-1 Typical stud partition (non-loadbearing)

Double-nail each end of the nogging. Nail the plasterboard slabs at least 12.7 mm in from the edges and ensure that the nails are driven straight.

Non-load bearing stud partitions are built off double joists to avoid the risk of ceiling deflection or cracking (Fig. 11-2 overleaf). Alternatively, if the partition does not line up with an existing joist, an additional joist is added (Fig. 11-3).

A double sole piece is used where partitions run at right angles to the joists. The first sole piece is securely fixed to the joists to provide an effective means of spreading the load (Fig. 11-4).

The heads of partitions are fixed to the ceiling joists when the partition is at right angles to the joists (Fig. 11-5).

If the partition is running parallel to the joists, nogging pieces are fitted at 400 mm centres between the joists and the partition fixed to the noggings (Fig. 11-6).

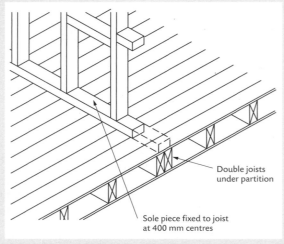

11-2 *Support for non-loadbearing stud partition, built off timber floor, with double joists beneath*

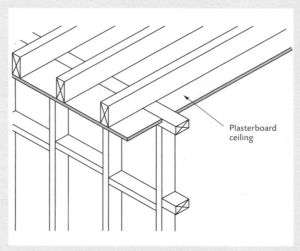

11-5 *Details at head of partition when the partition is at right angles to the joist*

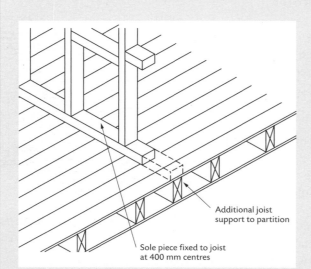

11-3 *Additional joist used when the partition does not line up with existing joist*

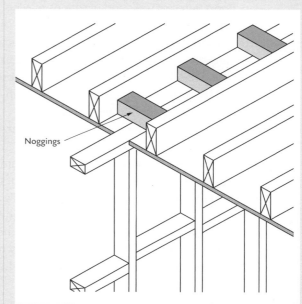

11-6 *Details at head of partition when partition is parallel to joist*

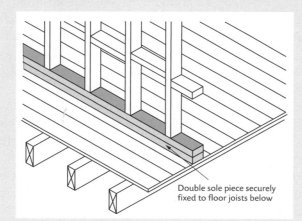

11-4 *Double sole piece used when partition is at right angles to joist*

Typical details of construction techniques are shown in Figs. 11-7 to 11-11.

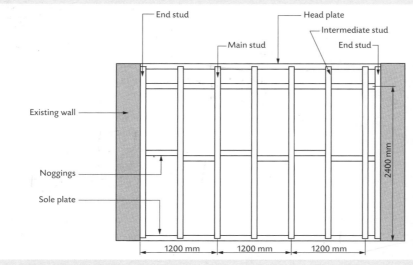

11-7a *Typical timber stud partition details*

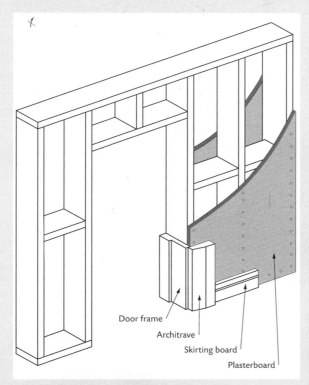

11-7b *Typical timber stud partition details*

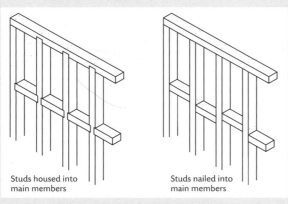

11-8 *Studs can either be housed or nailed into the head and sole plate.*

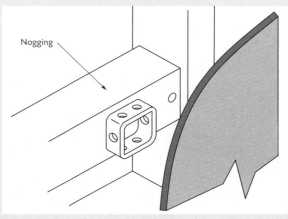

11-9 *For electrical fittings an extra nogging has to be fixed to the studs.*

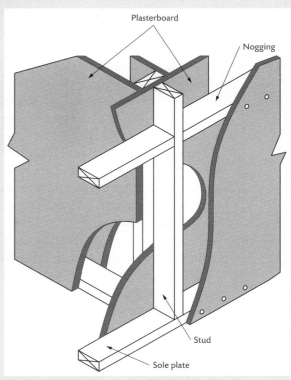

11-10 *Position of studs at junction*

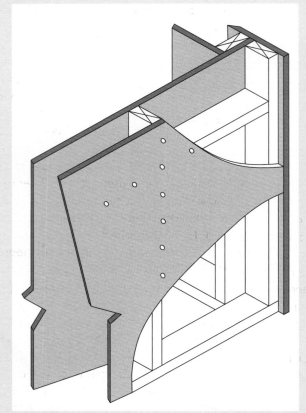

11-11 Position of studs at corner

H Principles of sound insulation

Buildings are required to protect their occupants from noise and vibration from a wide variety of fixed and mobile sources. Sometimes buildings will be required to protect areas inside the building. The outside environment may also need protection from noisy activities taking place within the building. Where the building has to protect the occupants from external noise, the building envelope will have to encompass the required amount of sound insulation.

Sound insulation may be defined as the reduction of sound transmission from one space to another. In buildings the sound that passes through a wall decreases as the wall's mass increases. This is known as the **mass law**.

Block or brick walls used as partitions or as cavity walls readily meet sound insulation requirements.

Discontinuous construction greatly increases sound insulation performance. Examples of this include cavity walls and double-glazing.

Sound insulation is greatly reduced by small gaps in walls and floors and also by the number of windows and doors incorporated into the fabric of the building.

Sound measurement

Sounds differ in their level (loudness), frequency range (pitch), and they may vary with time.

Noise level is described on a logarithmic scale in terms of decibels (dB). If the power of a noise source is doubled (e.g. two compressors instead of one) the level will increase by 3 dB. While this increase is noticeable it is not large.

Frequency content

The human ear can respond to sounds over a wide frequency range (approximately 20 Hz to 20 kHz for perfect hearing). Most environmental noises lie between 20 Hz and 5 kHz.

The ear is more sensitive to sounds of some frequencies than others, and is particularly sensitive to sounds between about 500 Hz and 5 kHz.

The 'A weighting' is an electronic circuit built into a sound level meter to make its sensitivity approximate to that of the ear. Measurements made under the weighting are expressed as dB(A). An increase of 10 dB(A) doubles the perceived loudness of the sound.

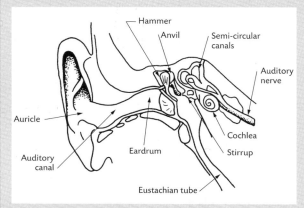

11-12 A cross-section of the human ear

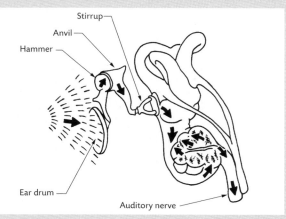

11-13 Arrows show path of sound through the inner ear. The ear is particularly sensitive to sounds in the 500 Hz to 5 KHz range.

H

Airborne sound insulation

Airborne sound insulation of walls depends largely on the type of material used. Approximate values are as follows:

- External walls
  with opening windows   20–28 dB
- External walls
  without opening windows   45–50 dB
- Partitions   30–35 dB
- Party walls   50–55 dB

Direct transmission of sound

Direct transmission means the transmission of sound directly through a wall or floor from one of its sides to the other (Fig. 11-14).

The reduction in the level of airborne sound transmitted through a solid masonry wall depends on the mass of the wall. A heavy wall is not easily set into vibration by sound, whereas a light wall may vibrate and hence transmit sound easily.

Walls with two or more leaves depend partly on their mass and partly on structural isolation between the leaves (cavity) to prevent sound passing through.

With masonry walls, mass is the main factor but stiffness and damping (which turns sound energy into heat) are also important. Cavity walls need at least as much mass as solid walls because their lower degree of stiffness offsets the benefit of isolation.

Floors should reduce airborne sound, and if they are above a dwelling, reduce impact sound.

> **Impact sound** is structure-borne sound generated by physical impact such as footsteps or the moving of furniture.

A heavy solid floor depends on its mass to reduce airborne sound and on a soft covering to reduce impact sound at source.

A floating floor uses a resilient layer to isolate the walking surface from the base and this isolation contributes to both airborne and impact sound insulation. The resilient layer is only effective if it is not too stiff, so it is important to choose a suitable material and to make sure it is not bypassed with rigid bridges such as fixings and pipes. See Figs. 11-15 to 11-18.

Air paths must be avoided – porous materials and gaps at joints in the structure must be sealed.

Resonances must also be avoided. These may occur if some part of the structure (such as a dry lining) vibrates strongly at a particular sound frequency (pitch) and transmits more energy at this pitch.

> **Resonance** is sound produced by a body vibrating in sympathy with a neighbouring source of sound.

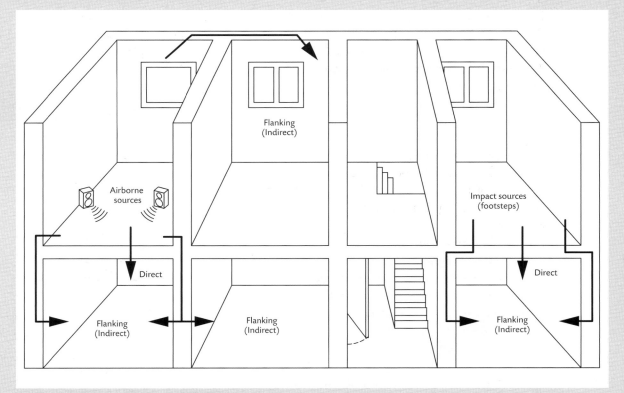

11-14 Sound transmission (direct and indirect)

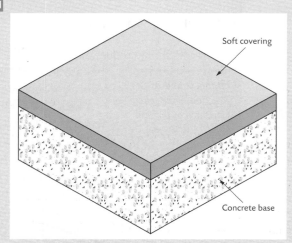

11-15 *Type 1 floor – concrete base with soft covering. The resistance to airborne sound depends on the mass of the concrete base. The soft covering reduces the impact sound at source.*

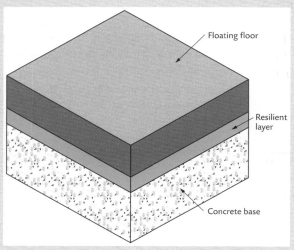

11-16 *Type 2 floor – concrete base with a floating layer. The floating layer reduces the transmission of impact sound to the base and to the surrounding construction.*

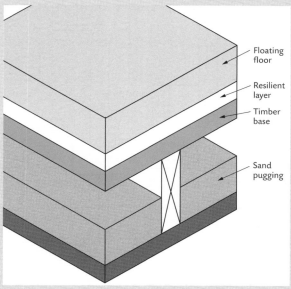

11-17 *Type 3 floor – timber base with a floating layer. A timber floor needs less mass than a concrete floor because the material is softer and radiates sound less efficiently.*

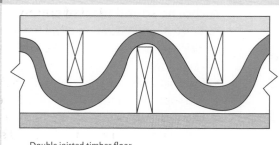

Double joisted timber floor with acoustic insulation

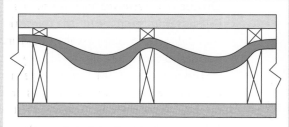

Batten and joist timber floor with acoustic insulation

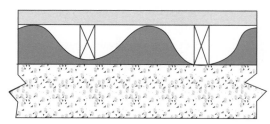

Batten and boarded floor on acoustic insulation on reinforced concrete slab

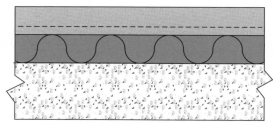

Reinforced sand/cement screed on expanded polystyrene on reinforced concrete slab

11-18 *Floating floors – timber and concrete slabs*

H

Flanking transmission of sound

Flanking transmission means the indirect transmission of sound from one side of a wall or floor to the other side (see Fig. 11-14).

Flanking transmission happens when there is a path along which sound can travel between elements on opposite sides of a wall or a floor. This path may be through a continuous solid structure or through an air space (such as the cavity of an external wall).

Usually, paths through structures are more important with solid masonry elements, while paths through an air space are more important with thin panels (such as studwork and ceilings), in which structural waves do not travel as freely.

The junction of a sound-resisting element and a flanking element provides some resistance to structural waves. However, this may not be sufficient to block sound transmission unless the flanking element is heavy or is divided by windows or similar openings into small sections that do not vibrate freely.

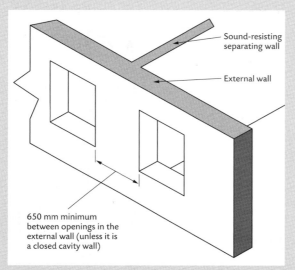

11-19 Key junctions in construction. Separating walls act as a sound-resisting element.

A minimum mass is required for thin panels connected by paths through air spaces (such as ceilings connected by air in roof spaces and over the ridge of the separating wall). The mass, which is required, may be less if the path is blocked by non-porous material.

Internal doors and screens

In the simplest domestic construction, the strap-hinged, ledged and braced match boarded door in softwood was unrivalled until after the 1939–45 war, when the flush door took over. In more expensive domestic buildings, the butt-hinged, framed and panelled door, in softwood or in hardwood was the norm.

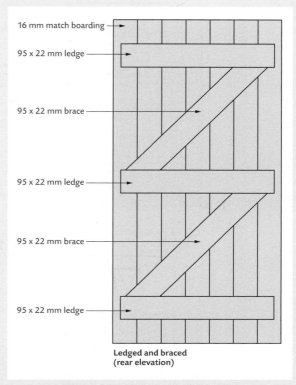

11-20 Strap-hinged, ledged and braced matchboarded door

Flush doors are available in many forms, with cores that may range from rolled paper to solid timber, and veneers from thin cellulose fibreboards to plywood faced with exotic timber species. All need to be provided with sections of sufficient size to accommodate hinges and furniture. See Fig. 11-21 overleaf.

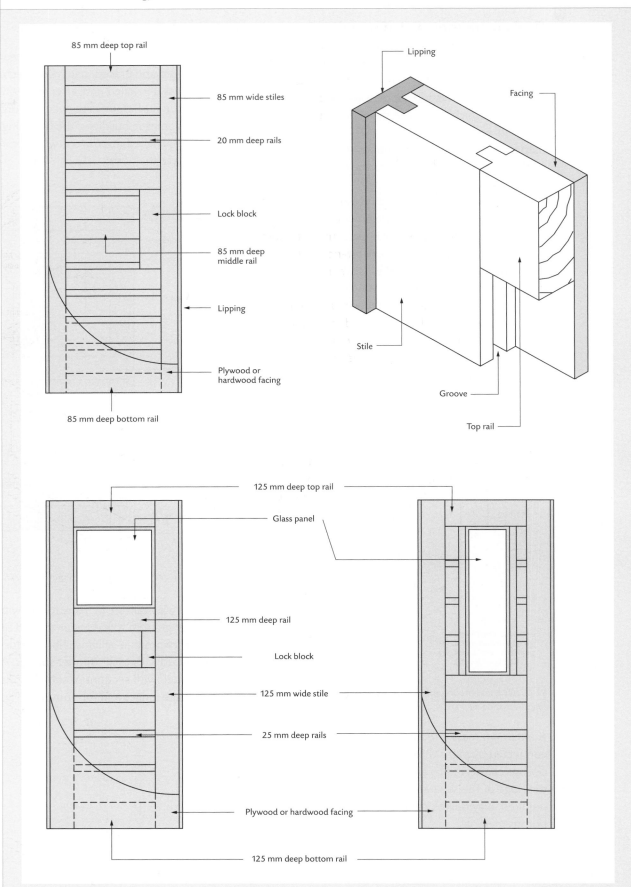

85 mm deep top rail

85 mm wide stiles

20 mm deep rails

Lock block

85 mm deep middle rail

Lipping

Plywood or hardwood facing

85 mm deep bottom rail

Lipping

Facing

Stile

Groove

Top rail

125 mm deep top rail

Glass panel

125 mm deep rail

Lock block

125 mm wide stile

25 mm deep rails

Plywood or hardwood facing

125 mm deep bottom rail

11-21 *Flush door details*

Glazing for internal doors

Glazing of internal doors ranges from the provision of one or more vision panels to half or fully glazed doors where light transmission is required. Fully glazed internal doors may be frameless, and supported by pivots at the head and foot rather than by hinges.

Glass used internally should:

- break safely
- be robust or in small panes, or
- be permanently protected.

If a door is glazed to the floor people may walk into it accidentally, and in these circumstances clear glazing should not be placed lower than 900 mm above the finished floor level.

Obscured glass or a guardrail at 900–1000 mm will improve the visibility of a glass door. Glass in doors has to be strong enough to withstand everyday use and slamming. Toughened or laminated glass is recommended.

For new buildings, hinged door sets are increasingly being specified complete with frame. This is important in relation to sound and fire performance.

Internal doors depend on the strength and fixing of the frame or lining for their support. Stops may be planted on to the face of the lining or rebated from the frame. Internal doorframes do not usually have a sill, as an external doorframe does. With the increase of factory-made building components, such as complete door sets, thresholds to internal doors may become more common.

The banging of internal doors is one of the noises most easily transmitted to adjoining dwellings. The best remedy is to fit a suitable door closer.

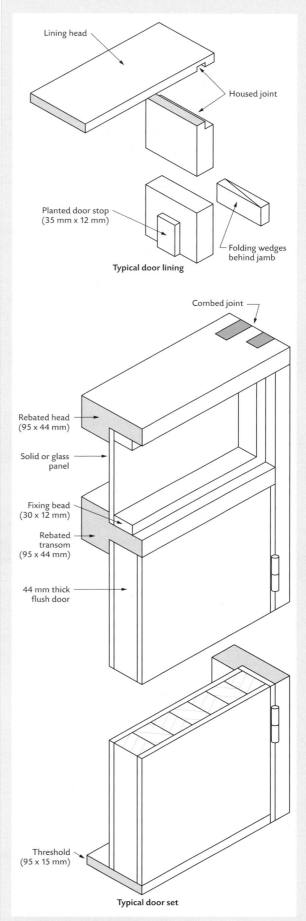

11-22 Door linings and door sets

Timber first floors

The main functions of timber first floors (or timber upper floors) are to provide:

■ a level surface with adequate strength to support the expected dead and live loads.

■ adequate thermal and sound insulation.

■ the necessary level of fire protection as specified in the Building Regulations.

Timber has been the main material used for constructing first floors in domestic buildings. It is now facing a challenge from hollow-core concrete beams. Timber construction consists of timber floorboards fixed to timber joists, which are supported by load-bearing walls.

Joists used to support first floors usually span greater distances than joists used in suspended ground floors. This necessitates the use of deeper joists.

A typical formula for calculating the depth of joists is 1/25th span in mm + 50 = depth in mm, assuming a thickness of 50 mm and spacing at 400 mm centres.

For example, if the span for joists is 4.2 m, then their depth = 4200/25 + 50 = 218 mm. In this instance the nearest standard size joist available on the larger size (225 mm) would be used. The most common size joist used for supporting first floors is 225 × 44 mm.

Holes for services should be bored through the centre of the joist only, because holes in any other position have the effect of reducing the strength of the joist.

The centre of a joist, as for all structural members, is a neutral zone for stress. For the same reason, notches removed from the top or bottom of joists must comply with the specified regulations.

The ends of joists can be supported by a variety of means. Usually they rest on the inner leaves of external cavity walls or load-bearing internal walls. The ends going in to the walls are treated with preservative and a space is left all around.

Ensure that joists do not penetrate into the cavity. This may lead to contact with moisture and eventual decay of the joists. The ends of joists are usually tapered to provide a runoff for any moisture that may accumulate.

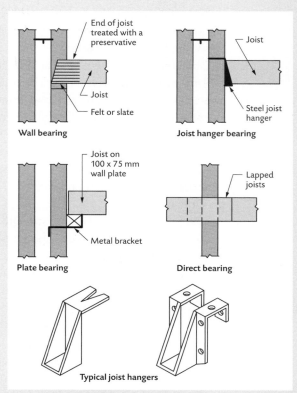

11-24 *Typical joist support details*

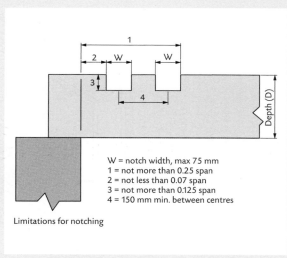

11-23 *Notching and drilling joists*

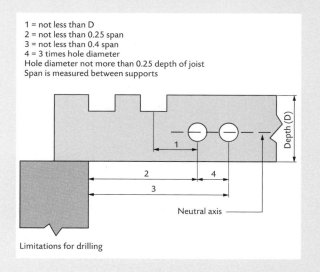

Fix joists supported on an internal wall to a wall plate. Other methods of supporting joists include joist hangers, and galvanised mild steel bearings built into the external wall. Joists are overlapped and nailed to each other where they meet on an internal load-bearing wall.

Strutting

Strutting is used to prevent the joists twisting and to strengthen the floor. Strutting is necessary where spans exceed 2.5 m. The distance between rows of strutting should be approximately 2 m. There are two types of strutting, solid and herringbone.

Solid strutting may be in-line or staggered. Staggered strutting is easier to nail, as skew nailing is not required.

Herringbone strutting is the most effective type, because when shrinkage occurs in the joists the strutting tightens against the joists, unlike solid strutting. It consists of 40 × 40 mm or 40 × 50 mm section timber cut at an angle to fit between the

joists as shown in Fig. 11-25. As well as being nailed to the joists they should be nailed to each other where they overlap. Metal struts, which are nailed to the top of one joist and the bottom of the next joist, are also used.

Trimming

Trimming is the term used to describe the arrangement of the joists around an opening for a stairwell, hearth for a fireplace, or around the ope for a chimney in a roof.

There are three types of joists associated with trimming around an opening. They are:

TRIMMING JOIST has the same span as for a common joist but it is usually 25 mm thicker because it supports the trimmer joist (Fig. 11-26).

TRIMMER JOIST is at right angles to the main span. It fits between two trimming joists and supports the trimmed joist. It is also 25 mm thicker than the common joist.

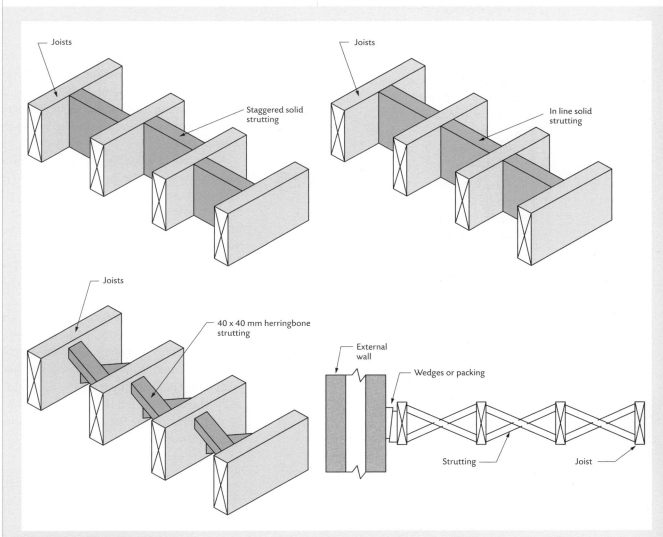

11-25 Solid and herringbone strutting

TRIMMED JOIST has the same thickness as the common joist but is shorter because it has been cut to allow for the opening.

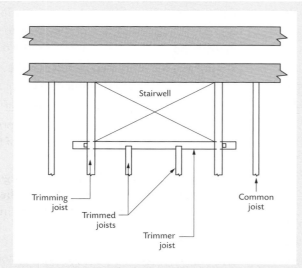

11-26 Trimming to stairwell (or any opening in joists)

The joints used between this arrangement of joists need to be well constructed. The tusk tenon joint is the traditional joint used between the trimming and trimmer joist (Fig. 11-27).

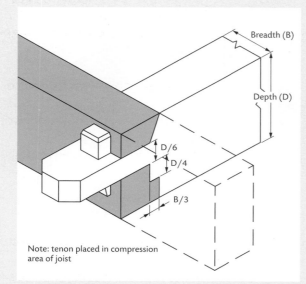

Note: tenon placed in compression area of joist

11-27 Tusk tenon joint

Stopped dovetail or stopped housing joints can be used between the trimmer and trimmed joists. Alternatively, galvanised steel hangers can be used to connect the joists to each other (Fig. 11-28).

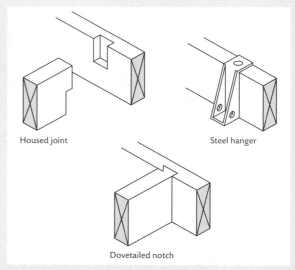

Housed joint   Steel hanger

Dovetailed notch

11-28 Other joints used in trimming arrangements

Sound insulation

Poor sound insulation is one of the main disadvantages of the standard method of constructing timber first floors. A method of improving the sound insulation value of timber first floors is to use expanded metal lath on the ceiling and apply three coats of plaster.

Alternatively, a double layer of plasterboard may be fitted with the joints from the previous layer overlapped with the second layer. In addition, 50 mm of dry sand (pugging) may be placed between the joists. This improves the stiffness of the overall construction.

A properly detailed floating floor will ensure discontinuous construction and prevent sound travelling through the structure.

The floating floor consists of plywood or some other suitable board material nailed to battens. The battens rest on a resilient quilt, which overlaps the joists. This construction should not be nailed to the joists and should be free from the surrounding walls. The battens used should be approximately 50 × 50 mm and the flooring should be approximately 20 mm thick.

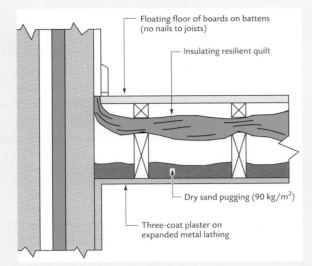

11-29 Insulated timber floor with heavy pugging

Labels on figure:
- Floating floor of boards on battens (no nails to joists)
- Insulating resilient quilt
- Dry sand pugging (90 kg/m²)
- Three-coat plaster on expanded metal lathing

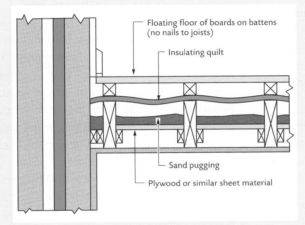

11-30 Alternative floating floor construction

Labels on figure:
- Floating floor of boards on battens (no nails to joists)
- Insulating quilt
- Sand pugging
- Plywood or similar sheet material

Precast concrete first floors

Precast concrete first floors are used as an alternative to timber first floors or suspended in-situ concrete floors. There are three categories of precast concrete floors:

1. **Hollow slab** (see Fig. 7-42)
2. **Precast plank** (or plate) with in-situ concrete topping (see Fig. 7-43)
3. **Beam and block** (see Fig. 7-44)

The following general points should be noted during installation along with any specific recommendations from the manufacturers:

- Spans and supports (propping may be required in some instances).
- Arrangements for screeding and/or grouting.
- Design details for point loads such as partitions.

- Position of damp proof course.
- The bearing of precast concrete floor units on a concrete block wall must be a minimum of 90 mm in all cases.
- Position for insulation and method for fixing. Type and size of insulation to be used to satisfy the Building Regulations and to ensure that cold bridging does not occur.

Provide thermal insulation to the edges of suspended concrete first floors. Cavity wall insulation is not interrupted because the precast concrete floor units sit on the inner leaf of the cavity.

To eliminate the possibility of cold bridging, place insulation along the perimeter and below the structural floor for a distance of 800 mm from the inner wall.

Advantages of pre-cast concrete first floors

- Airborne sound transmission is approximately one-sixth of the airborne sound transmitted through a standard suspended timber floor.
- No sound is generated as a result of movement on a concrete floor.
- The overall structure is more stable as a result of using this type of floor.
- Concrete floors have excellent fire-resisting properties.

Disadvantages of pre-cast concrete first floors

- Floor must be propped and supported while setting.
- Specialist machinery is required to lift the components into position.

Finishes for floors

Consider the following factors when selecting a floor finish.

- **Durability** and resistance to wear. This refers to the expected life span of the material.
- **Cost**. The initial purchase cost and any subsequent maintenance costs.
- **Resistance to moisture**, oil, chemicals and grease. Important for kitchen and bathroom floors.
- **Warmth**. Timber finishes, for instance, are warmer than ceramic tiles.
- **Sound absorption**. Important in libraries and study areas.

- **Resilience**. Some degree of movement or flexibility is important for human comfort, especially in kitchens.
- **Non-slip properties** are important in kitchens and bathrooms.

Types of floor finish

TERRAZZO is a decorative concrete made from white cement and crushed marble aggregate. It may be cast in-situ, but terrazzo tiles have become very popular.

CORK TILES provide a warm and resilient floor and are economical. They are made from granulated cork in a variety of sizes, 300 × 300 mm being the most popular.

CARPET is widely used in domestic buildings. It must be laid in dry conditions on an underlay, usually felt or latex, and held in place with adhesives. Recent concerns on the connection of asthma to carpet have led to a reduction in its use. Unless vacuumed regularly with a powerful cleaner, the dust mite is claimed to thrive in carpet.

LINOLEUM Lino, as it is more commonly referred to, is manufactured from linseed oil, cork, resin gums, fibres, wood flour and pigments applied to a canvas or glass fibre backing. Waterproof adhesive is used to bond it to the floor. A variety of colours and patterns are available. It forms a resilient and easily cleaned floor.

RUBBER TILES are usually made from synthetic rubber, but natural rubber may also be used. Epoxy adhesive is used to bond rubber tiles to the floor. Tiles are available in a variety of colours, patterns and textures. Rubber floor tiles are resistant to moisture and are non-slip. They are also quiet and resilient.

CLAY TILES There are two categories of clay tiles:
1. Quarry tiles, 20–32 mm thick, made from unrefined clays and
2. Ceramic tiles, 9.5–19 mm thick, made from refined clays.

Quarry tiles are laid on a bed of cement, sand and lime. An expansion joint is provided along the perimeter of a tiled floor.

CONCRETE TILES Coloured cement and hardwearing aggregate are used to make concrete tiles. Thickness ranges from 15 to 40 mm. They are hard and durable and resistant to moisture.

WOOD BLOCK floors are made of interlocking wood blocks which measure 150 to 400 mm in length, with widths up to 90 mm. Thickness varies from 18 to 38 mm. Wood block floors are expensive but are also warm, hard wearing and resilient. There are various other timber floor systems available, defined by their method of construction. They can be veneered, laminated or solid wood.

Plaster finishes

Traditional lime-based wall plasters, consisting of slaked lime and sand mixes, with perhaps a little grit added, have been used for thousands of years. They took longer to harden than the modern gypsum-based plasters. Animal hair was sometimes added to the mix to provide a crack-free surface.

The traditional specification for plastering on laths was a three-coat render, float and set. The coarse mix for the render was commonly 1:2 or 3 lime to sand with a pound (0.5 kg) of ox hair to two cubic feet of plaster. The surface was scratched to provide a key for the floating coat of 1:3 or 4 with less hair. This was levelled with a straight edge rule between screeds and brushed to provide a key for the setting coat of lime plaster.

Vermiculite belongs to a group of minerals consisting mainly of hydrated silicate of magnesium, aluminium, and iron. On heating they expand and exfoliate and in this form are used in heat and sound insulation, and fireproofing.

Perlite, also referred to as pearlite, is a variety of obsidian consisting of masses of small pearly globules. It is used as a filler and insulator.

Obsidian is a dark glassy volcanic rock formed by very rapid solidification of lava.

Most wall plasters used since the demise of lime plasters are retarded beta hemi-hydrates of gypsum. Some may be suitable for gauging with sand; some are available premixed with vermiculite or perlite for additional thermal insulation properties.

Gypsum is a crystalline combination of calcium sulphate and water. The raw material is crushed, screened and heated to dehydrate the gypsum. The amount of water remaining at the end of this process determines the type of plaster.

Powdered gypsum heated to 170°C loses approx. three quarters of its combined water and is known as hemi-hydrate gypsum (plaster of Paris).

Powdered gypsum heated to 260°C loses nearly all its combined water and is known as anhydrous plaster.

It is normal for the undercoat to have a thickness of 8–16 mm. The undercoat is normally thicker than the final coat, to avoid cracking and loss of adhesion.

Render coats are used where there is a risk of penetrating damp. Mixes of around 1:5 cement to sand has been found to be satisfactory for most applications.

All plasters should be stored in dry conditions. The strength of plaster is considerably reduced if it absorbs moisture before mixing. Gypsum plasters should not be applied to frozen backgrounds and they are not suitable for temperatures in excess of 43°C.

The selection of the type of plaster and the number of coats to be applied will depend on the background surface. The two main properties for consideration are roughness and suction. The roughness provides a key for the plaster to bond to. If the surface is smooth it should be roughened prior to applying the plaster. Alternatively, bonding agents may be used.

The drying rate of the plaster can be affected by the suction properties of the background. The background absorbs the moisture of the mix. If too much is absorbed the plaster may not set properly and thereby lose its adhesion with the background. If the suction is not adequate the plaster will retain excess water, which will result in drying shrinkage cracks.

Dry lining techniques

Internal walls and partitions are usually covered with a wet finish (either plaster or rendering) or with a dry lining using plasterboard, insulated plasterboard, insulated fibreboard, timber or plywood.

A permanent finish can be applied to all of these surfaces or they can be finished direct with paint or wallpaper.

The most common material used for dry lining walls is plasterboard. This is a rigid board made from a core of gypsum, surfaced with a strong durable paper. The standard sheet size measures 2.4 m × 1.2 m and it is available in thickness of 9.5 mm and 12.7 mm. It can be specified with an aluminium foil back or rigid insulation attached for increased thermal insulation.

There are a number of methods used to fix the board material to the wall.

■ **Timber battens.** The plasterboards are nailed to the timber battens. The battens are spaced to suit the boards. This is an expensive method but

is suitable to counteracting damp penetration in old buildings. Increased thermal insulation is achieved by fitting polystyrene sheets between the battens. The thickness of the battens will then be governed by the thickness of the insulation used.

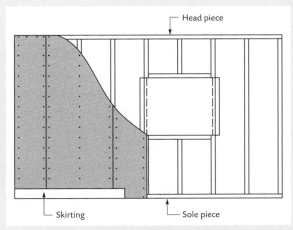

11-31 A typical arrangement for timber battens for dry-lining. This takes into consideration full board widths and the presence of a window.

■ **Plaster 'dabs' or 'dots'.** Pieces of bitumen-impregnated fibreboard are stuck to the wall with board finish plaster. The dots measure approximately 75 mm × 50 mm, and they are positioned at the top, bottom and middle of each joint along with intermediate rows. They are levelled in all directions over the whole wall surface. Once they have set, thick dabs of board finish are applied between the dots. The dabs are applied heavier than the dots so that they stand proud of the dots.

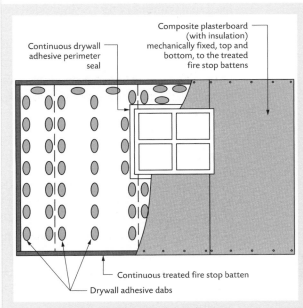

11-32 Dry-lining using plaster 'dabs' or 'dots'

The plasterboards are then positioned and firmly tapped into place until they make contact with the dots. As the boards are tapped into position the dabs spread giving an increased surface area of contact with the board. Finally the boards are nailed to the fibre packs. On occasions double-headed nails are used to give temporary security while the bonds are setting.

Plasterboard ceilings

Gypsum plasterboard is the most common material used to finish ceilings. It is available with aluminium foil on one face, which is fitted against the joists. This greatly improves thermal insulation. The boards are fixed in place with 40 mm clout headed nails. Joints should be staggered beside parallel boards. Joints between boards are filled with gypsum plaster or joint-filler compound and are usually taped.

The intersection of the ceiling with the wall is usually reinforced with a 'scrim' layer. This is a canvas type material (jute) that helps prevent cracking at this vulnerable position. Finally, the ceiling is finished with a layer of gypsum plaster finish (board finish), which may be up to 5 mm thick.

Ceilings may be finished by other means such as sprayed plaster, which gives a coarse texture, or it may be trowelled smooth if desired. Patterned ceiling papers may be applied direct to the plaster-board. Some such papers need no further decoration, similar to wallpaper, while others require one or more coats of paint.

Suspended ceilings are used in buildings with higher than normal wall heights. These ceilings are fixed to a framework that is suspended from and supported by the main structure. A void exists between the ceiling and the structure. This void accommodates the services such as electrical, heating and ventilation. Ceiling tiles in a variety of materials and finishes are available for suspended ceilings.

Stairs

A stairs is a number of steps, which provides access, by foot, from one floor level to another. The total rise of a stairs is the distance from the finished floor level on the ground floor to the finished floor level on the first floor.

For safety reasons, door openings should be kept a minimum of 400 mm from the top and bottom of a stairway.

A single-flight stairs is the most common layout, but there are alternative designs to suit particular situations. These include the dog-leg, open-well and quarter-turn.

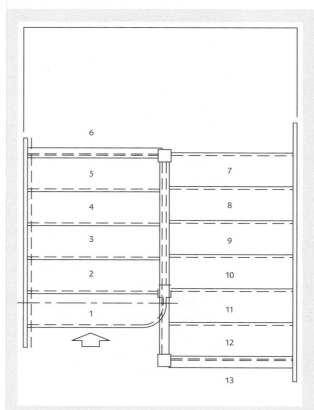

11-33 Dog-leg stairs

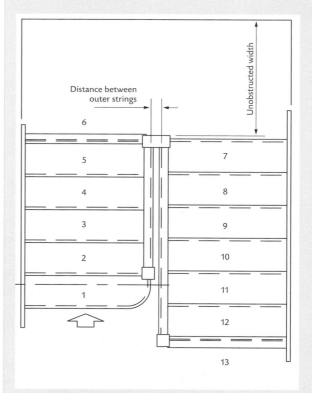

11-34 Half-landing stairs (showing open well or open newel)

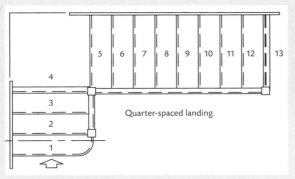

5 6 7 8 9 10 11 12 13

4

3

2

1

Quarter-spaced landing

11-35 Quarter-turn stairs

Stair terminology

Some of the main terms associated with stair construction and design are:

- **Stairs**: the number of steps and landings leading from one floor level to another.
- **Stairwell**: the space occupied by the stairs.
- **Tread**: the upper surface of a step (where the foot is placed).
- **Riser**: the vertical member connecting two treads (see Fig. 11-37).

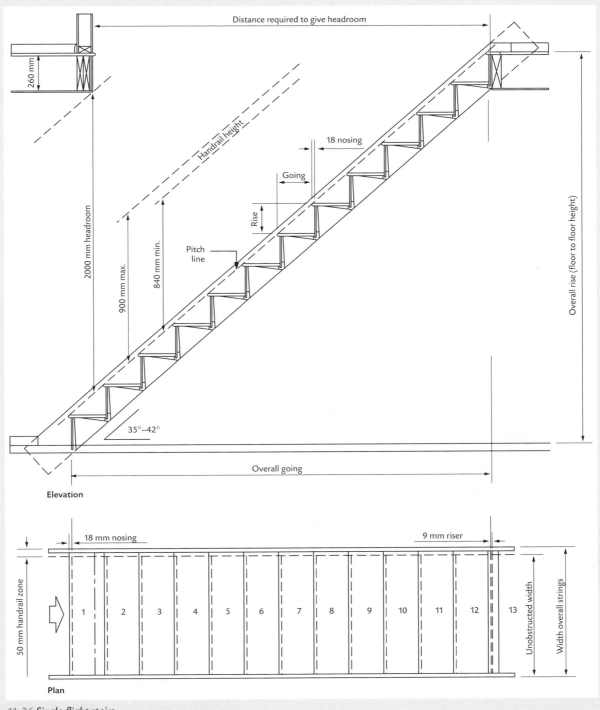

260 mm

Distance required to give headroom

2000 mm headroom

900 mm max.

840 mm min.

Handrail height

18 nosing

Going

Rise

Pitch line

35°–42°

Overall going

Overall rise (floor to floor height)

Elevation

18 mm nosing

9 mm riser

50 mm handrail zone

1 2 3 4 5 6 7 8 9 10 11 12 13

Unobstructed width

Width overall strings

Plan

11-36 Single-flight stairs

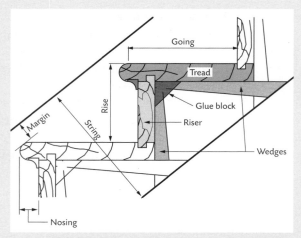

11-37 *Components of a step showing tread, riser, nosing, glue blocks and wedges*

- **Nosing**: the projecting edge of a tread. It is usually rounded or splayed.
- **Step**: consists of the riser plus the tread.
- **Flight**: the part of the stairway between landings.
- **Going**: the horizontal distance between the nosing of a tread and the nosing of the tread above or below it. It may also be calculated from the face of two consecutive risers. The going for a stairs is the horizontal distance between the top and bottom risers.
- **Rise**: the vertical distance between the top of a tread and the top of the tread above or below it. The rise of a flight is the overall height from the finished level of one floor or landing to the finished level of the adjoining floor or landing.
- **Tapered step**: a step, the nosing of which is not parallel to the nosing of the step or landing above or below it.

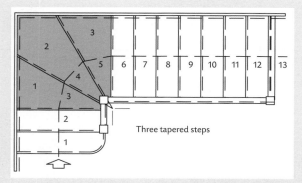

11-38 *Tapered steps are used where either the going or the rise is restricted. For tapered treads the going must conform with the regulations when measured as follows:*
– If the flight is narrower than 900 mm, measure in the middle.
– If the flight is 900 mm or wider, measure 270 mm from each side.

- **Strings**: an inclined member that receives the ends of the steps. The ends of the steps are usually housed into the strings.

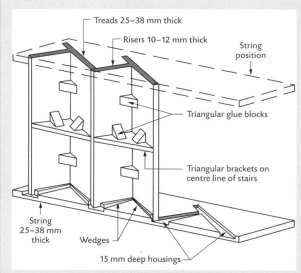

11-39 *Stair construction details. The ends of the steps are usually housed into the strings.*

- **Newel**: the post connecting flights of stairs with landings or fixing the lower ends of strings to floors.

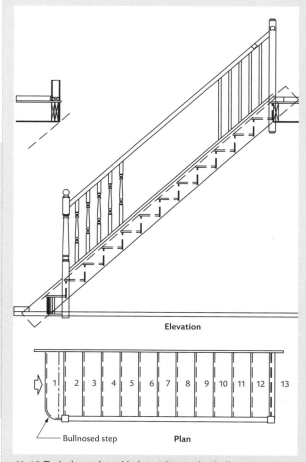

11-40 *Typical newels and balustrading with a bullnosed step*

- **Handrail**: a member parallel to the string. It may be fixed between two newel posts or to a wall.
- **Balustrade**: infill between the handrail and the string. Provides protection on the open side of the stairs.
- **Baluster**: a single vertical member that forms part of the balustrade.
- **Pitch**: the angle between the line of nosings and the floor.
- **Pitch line**: a line connecting all the nosings in a single flight.
- **Headroom**: the vertical distance between the pitch line and any obstacle over the stairs.

Rise, going and pitch

Steps in a stairs must be of appropriate dimensions to comply with the Building Regulations. All steps in a flight must have the same rise. Likewise all parallel steps must have the same going.

To check that the rise and going dimensions comply with the Building Regulations the following formula is used:

The sum of twice the rise plus the going (2R+G) should be between 550 mm and 700 mm with an optimum (ideal) of 600 mm.

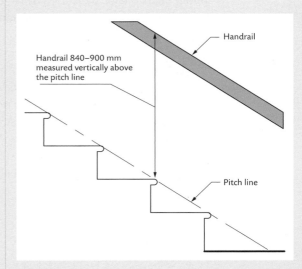

Handrail 840–900 mm measured vertically above the pitch line

Handrail

Pitch line

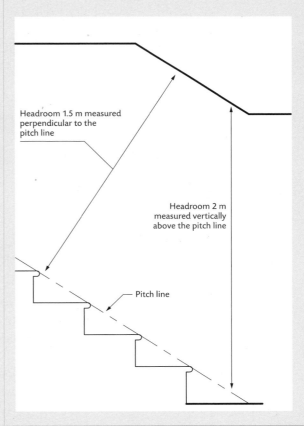

Headroom 1.5 m measured perpendicular to the pitch line

Headroom 2 m measured vertically above the pitch line

Pitch line

Ensure that a 100 mm diameter sphere cannot pass through any opening in the balustrade or guarding

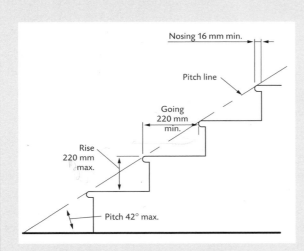

Nosing 16 mm min.

Pitch line

Going 220 mm min.

Rise 220 mm max.

Pitch 42° max.

11-41 *Building regulations governing stairs construction*

Stairs	Rise (mm)		Going (mm)		Pitch (degrees)	
	Optimum	Maximum	Optimum	Minimum	Optimum	Maximum
Private	175	220	250	220	35	42
Public	150	180	300	280	27	33

Table 11-1

Table 11-1 gives recommendations on maximum rise, minimum going and maximum pitch, and optimum values for private and public stairs.

A **private stairs** means stairs used by a limited number of people who are generally very familiar with the stairs, such as the internal stairs in a dwelling.

A **public stairs** means stairs used by large numbers of people at one time, as in schools or hospitals.

Construction techniques

Steps must have level treads. Steps may have open risers but in such cases the nosing of any tread should overlap the tread below by at least 16 mm.

A stairway with open treads should be constructed so that a 100 mm diameter sphere cannot pass through the opening between adjacent treads.

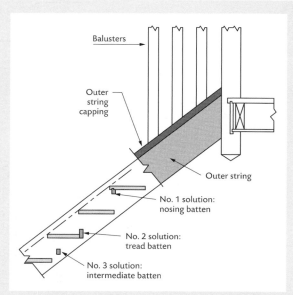

11-42 *Open riser stairs must be designed so that the gap between treads is restricted to 100 mm. The diagram shows three possible solutions to this problem.*

Headroom over the whole width of any stairs, measured as shown in Fig. 11-41, must not be less than 2 m. This may be lower for loft and attic conversions.

Private stairs should have a width of not less than 800 mm. A handrail should be fitted between 840 mm and 900 mm vertically above the pitch line. A handrail must be fixed on each side of a stairs if it is 1 metre wide or more.

There should not be more than sixteen risers in any one flight. This is the maximum number of steps that the average person can climb safely without requiring a rest. A flight containing one or two risers should be situated at the bottom of the stairs.

A level landing should be provided at the top and bottom of every flight. The width and going of the landing should be at least as great as the smallest width of the flight.

The dimensions of the treads and risers must be constant for all steps in a flight of stairs, otherwise accidents may occur due to the change in the rhythm of movement.

The rise for the step is calculated by dividing the overall rise by the chosen number of risers. The going for the step is selected to suit the available floor area while ensuring that, together with the rise the Building Regulations are complied with. The number of steps in any one flight will be one less than the number of risers. This is because the last riser connects with the landing.

Steps are housed, glued and wedged into the strings to form a rigid construction. Glue blocks are positioned between the tread and the riser to provide extra support and to prevent creaking.

Stairs usually have one string fixed to a wall while the other string is supported at both ends by a newel post.

The newel post is notched over the trimmer. The part tread used with the top riser is nailed to the trimmer. The stairs is supported by the trimmer rather than fixed to it. The bottom newel is sometime left longer at the base and is set into the concrete floor.

Ramps

The slope for a ramp should not exceed 1:20 in general and must never exceed 1:12.

Ramps and their landings should have clear headroom of at least 2 m. There should be no obstructions in the ramp area. For example a door should not swing across the sloping part of any ramp.

Private ramps must have a clear width of not less than 800 mm. A ramp less than 1 m wide should have a handrail on at least one side. If wider than 1 m it should have a handrail on both sides. Handrail heights are the same as for stairs, i.e. between 840 mm and 900 mm above the slope.

A landing should be provided at the top and bottom of every ramp. Ramps and their landings should be guarded at the sides in the same way as stairs.

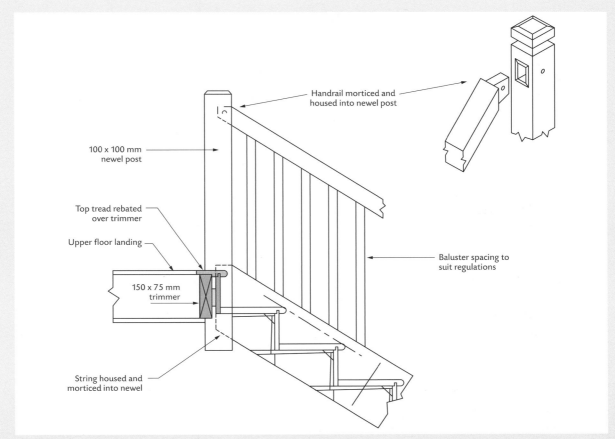

Handrail morticed and housed into newel post

100 x 100 mm newel post

Top tread rebated over trimmer

Upper floor landing

150 x 75 mm trimmer

Baluster spacing to suit regulations

String housed and morticed into newel

11-43 **Landing details**

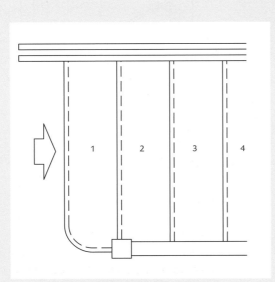

11-44a **Single-end bullnose step**

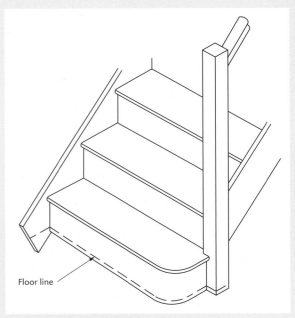

Floor line

11-44b **Single-end bullnose step**

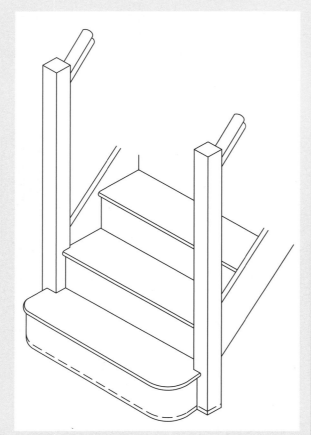

11-44c *Double end bullnose step*

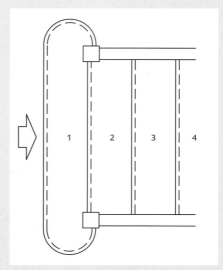

11-45b *Double-end curtail step*

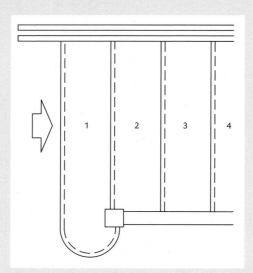

11-45a *Single-end curtail step. Curtail steps at the foot of a flight of stairs are widened at one or both ends and terminated with a scroll on the handrail.*

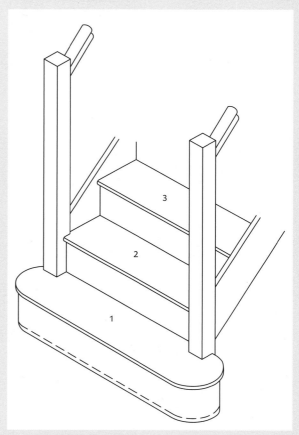

11-45c *Double-end curtail step*

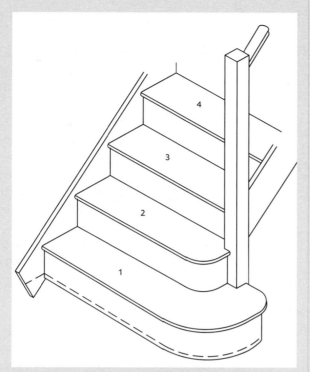

11-45d Single-end curtail step with a single-end bullnose step

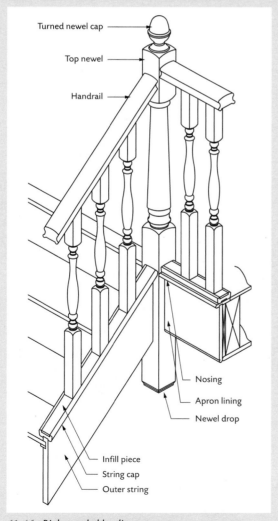

Turned newel cap

Top newel

Handrail

Nosing

Apron lining

Newel drop

Infill piece

String cap

Outer string

11-46a Right-angled landing return

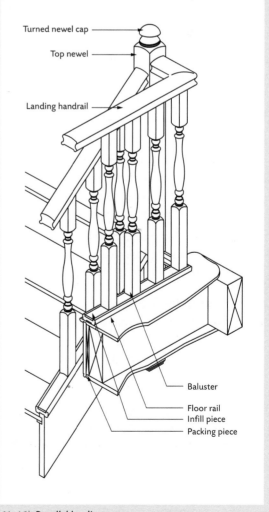

Turned newel cap

Top newel

Landing handrail

Baluster

Floor rail

Infill piece

Packing piece

11-46b Parallel landing return

Fire regulations

Part B of the Second Schedule to the Building Regulations, 2000, provides as follows:

Means of escape in case of fire

- **B1.** A building shall be so designed and constructed that there are adequate means of escape in case of fire from the building to a place of safety outside the building, capable of being safely and effectively used.

Internal fire spread (linings)

- **B2.** For the purposes of inhibiting the spread of fire within a building, the internal linings:

  (a) shall offer adequate resistance to the spread of flame over their surfaces; and

  (b) shall have, if ignited, a rate of heat release which is reasonable in the circumstances.

Internal fire spread (structure)

- **B3. (i)** A building shall be so designed and constructed that, in the event of fire; its stability will be maintained for a reasonable period.

  (ii) (a) A wall common to two or more buildings shall be so designed and constructed that it offers adequate resistance to the spread of fire between those buildings (party wall).

  (b) A building shall be subdivided with fire resisting construction where this is necessary to inhibit the spread of fire within the building.

  (iii) A building shall be so designed and constructed that the unseen spread of fire and smoke within concealed spaces in its structure or fabric is inhibited where necessary.

  (iv) For the purposes of sub-paragraph (ii) (a), a house in a terrace and a semi-detached house are each to be treated as being a separate building.

External fire spread

- **B4.** The external walls and roof of a building shall be so designed and constructed that they afford adequate resistance to the spread of fire to and from neighbouring buildings.

Access and facilities for the fire service

- **B5.** A building shall be so designed and constructed that there is adequate provision for access for fire appliances and for such other facilities as may be reasonably required to assist the fire service in the protection of life and property.

Typical means of escape situations were detailed in Chapter 5, beginning at page 75.

Wall and ceiling linings can contribute to the spread of fire and must therefore be controlled. Plastered surfaces give adequate protection but other materials are not suitable.

Doors forming direct connections between garages and areas within houses should be the self-closing type and should open over a 100 mm step down from the house to the garage (see Fig. 5-17). All walls, floors or ceilings connecting a garage to a house must provide a half-hour fire resistance.

All bedrooms in all houses should be provided with windows of a type and size that can be deemed escape windows.

Party walls

A party wall separates adjoining buildings and is found in both semi-detached and terraced houses. Certain regulations apply to the construction of party walls to avoid excessive sound transmission and avoid the risk of the spread of fire. The specific regulations are:

1. Party walls must have a minimum thickness of 225 mm.
2. Joists should not be built into party walls. Joists at right angles to party walls should be fixed with joist hangers. Ideally, joists should span from front to back of the house.
3. Party walls must continue into the attic and up to the slope of the roof. This is necessary for the prevention of fire spread.
4. There must be no holes or opes in party walls.
5. Fire-stopping material must be placed along the top of the party wall to the underside of the roof covering (mineral wool or any suitable non-combustible material may be used as fire stopping). Refer to Fig. 5-19.

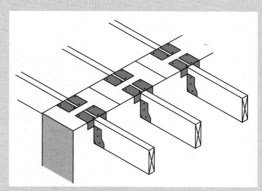

11-47 Joist hangers used to fix joists at right angles to party walls

Services & Environmental Technologies

The Ringsend Sewage Treatment Plant was commissioned in 2003. This wastewater treatment plant in Dublin Bay processes the capital's sewage, using a variety of treatments including ultraviolet light, so that only decontaminated water is discharged into the bay, meeting the highest international environmental standards. Approximately 100,000 m³ of readymixed concrete was used in its construction, most of which was supplied from a mobile plant on the construction site.

There are various after-uses for land where aggregate extraction has taken place. Worked-out Hard Rock Quarries are typically made safe and secure and are restored to a form that allows them to be reintegrated into the surrounding landscape. Worked-out Sand and Gravel Pits are more easily restored to beneficial after-use such as agricultural and recreational use or as a wildlife habitat such as the sand and aggregate facility at a John A. Wood location in Co. Cork (above).

Aerobord

Aerobord is Ireland's premier supplier of expanded polystyrene insulation and packaging products. Its products are widely used in the construction industry, mainly as thermal insulation, where technical standards continue to increase for improved comfort and to reduce energy consumption in buildings. The Company through its environmental policy is committed to a cleaner, healthier environment for its customers, employees and the local community.

Clogrennane Lime

Down through the ages, lime has been used successfully in the making of concrete, mortar and plaster. Clogrennane Lime operates a state of the art facility in Co. Carlow for the production of high quality burnt and hydrated lime for the building, chemical and environmental protection industries.

Chapter 12

Services for domestic construction

Conditions affecting human comfort

A major trend in dwelling construction has been improvement in the degree of control exercised over the interior environment of buildings – increasingly precise regulation of air temperature, light and sound levels, humidity, odours, air speed, and other factors that affect human comfort is now possible.

Air

The four main atmospheric conditions that affect human comfort are:

- temperature
- humidity, or moisture content
- air purity
- air movement

Temperature

Thermal comfort is governed by the physiological mechanisms of the body and is subjective. In any given environment it is difficult to get 50 per cent or more of people to agree that the conditions are comfortable.

Heat is transferred from the body by convection, radiation and evaporation. The amount of heat produced by a person depends on their size, age, sex, activities engaged in and their clothing.

Clothing has a considerable effect on the air temperature that is required for comfort because clothes act as thermal insulators for the body.

Room temperatures and temperatures of the surrounding air combine to affect the thermal comfort of people. This is noticeable when sitting near the cold surface of a window because the heat radiated from the body increases, leading to discomfort.

Humidity

Humidity is a measure of the amount of moisture in the air. This affects condensation in buildings and also affects human comfort. Outside, humidity depends on local weather conditions; inside a building the thermal properties and function of the building affects humidity.

The following definitions relate to humidity:

- **Moisture content**: the amount of water in air expressed as a percentage of the 'dry' weight of air.
- **Dew point**: the temperature at which air becomes saturated.
- **Relative humidity**: the weight of water vapour in air compared with saturated air at the same temperature, usually expressed as a percentage. Relative humidity changes as air temperature changes, thereby affecting human comfort.

   The comfort zone for relative humidity is between 40 and 70 per cent. High humidity and high temperature feels uncomfortable and natural cooling of the body by perspiration has little effect. High humidity and low temperatures result in the air feeling chilly.

CONDENSATION is linked to humidity. Condensation occurs whenever warm moist air meets surfaces that are at or below the dew point of the air. Condensation becomes a problem when it results in unhealthy conditions and is of general concern to the inhabitants.

Condensation may be divided into two types:

- **Surface condensation** occurs on the surfaces of walls, windows, doors, ceilings and floors.
- **Interstitial condensation** occurs within the fabric of a building component. Moist air (water vapour) is capable of passing through most building materials. As it passes through the building fabric the air may cool. If it reaches the dew point temperature, condensation will begin to occur inside the material. Interstitial condensation can cause damage to important structural components and reduce the effectiveness of insulation.

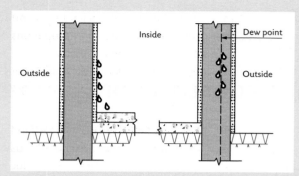

12-1 Surface condensation (left); interstitial condensation (right)

Condensation can be overcome by **ventilation**, **heating** and **insulation**.

Air purity

Research has shown that air quality in Ireland is substantially better than air quality in the United Kingdom. The level of air pollution in Ireland has been gradually reducing.

The World Health Organisation refers to air pollution as 'limited to situations in which the outdoor ambient atmosphere contains materials in concentrations which are harmful to humans'.

In terms of volume, the main emissions to the atmosphere resulting from human activity are carbon dioxide, carbon monoxide, dust, smoke and other particles. The atmosphere may convert many of these substances to other substances in its cleansing process. The danger arises when some of the newly formed substances become greater sources of air pollution than the original emissions.

However, human activity is not responsible for all the elements and compounds in the atmosphere.

Nature adds gases and solids through sea-spray, dust, storms, forest fires, volcanoes etc.

Though polluted water can often go unnoticed for some time, this is seldom the case with air. Dust levels become a nuisance long before they pose a danger to health. This has the advantage of bringing instances of air pollution to the attention of the relevant authorities and to the public at an early stage.

There are five kinds of smoke that give offence and thereby affect human comfort: smoke from chimneys, from diesel-powered vehicles, smoke from burning rubbish, smoke from stubble burning, and cigarette smoke. Legislation now exists to control smoke emissions from diesel engines, chimneys and cigarette smoke.

Air movement

Air movement in a room leads to draughts and increases the amount of heat lost from the body. Higher temperatures are required to combat the effect of air movement.

In 1806 Admiral Beaufort devised a scale to classify wind speeds at sea. This scale has proved to be so useful that it is used to cover land conditions and conditions of human comfort. Table 12-1 shows the Beaufort scale and the associated conditions for comfort.

Wind speeds in excess of 10 mph for considerable periods are considered uncomfortable for humans, while speeds in excess of 25 mph are considered unpleasant. Speeds over 47 mph are considered dangerous as people can be blown over or injured by pieces falling from buildings.

Beaufort Number	Wind speed (mph)	Description	Comfort
0	0–1	Calm	Smoke rises vertically
1	1–3	Light air	Smoke rises slowly
2	4–7	Light breeze	Wind felt on face, leaves rustle
3	8–12	Gentle breeze	Hair disturbed, leaves and twigs in constant motion
4	13–18	Moderate breeze	Hair disarranged, small branches are moved
5	19–24	Fresh breeze	Force of wind felt on body, small trees sway
6	25–31	Strong breeze	Difficult to walk steadily, large branches in motion
7	32–38	Near gale	Difficult to walk, whole trees in motion
8	39–46	Gale	Balance difficult in gusts, twigs break off trees
9	47–54	Strong gale	People blown over in gusts, slight structural damage
10	55–63	Storm	Structural damage, trees uprooted
11	64–72	Violent storm	Widespread damage
12	73–83	Hurricane	Extreme destruction

*Table 12-1 **The Beaufort Scale***

Illumination of rooms

Humans learnt to use fire for illumination at least 500,000 years ago. Since then lighting has become increasingly sophisticated, and in the modern age whole streets and buildings can be lit at the flick of a switch.

The sun is the main source of natural lighting and is therefore important in building design. The shape, size and spacing of rooms and buildings is controlled to a large extent by illumination (daylighting) requirements.

Buildings with large glazing areas can lead to severe discomfort due to glare. Overheating can also occur unless preventative measures are taken.

Following are some definitions for lighting and illumination:

- **Luminous intensity** refers to the luminous power of a source in one direction. It is measured in **candelas** (cd), and one candela emits 4π lumen.
- **Luminous flux** refers to the flow of luminous energy emitted by any source or received by any surface. It is measured in **lumens** (lm).
- **Illumination** is the process of lighting an object and it is the luminous flux incident per unit area on a surface. It is measured in **lux** (lx), which equals 1 lm/m².
- **Luminance** refers to the intensity of the light emitted by the unit area of a surface in a given direction. The units are 1 cd/m².
- **Inverse square law of illumination**. The illuminance produced by a point source of light decreases in inverse proportion to the square of the distance from the source.

Glare
light that is too bright, causing discomfort and eyestrain. It can be prevented by shading or solar-control glazing.

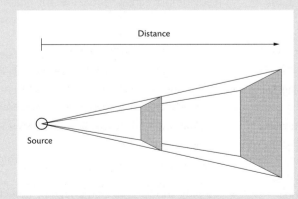

12-2 The inverse square law

In the past people had a greater awareness of the sun's behaviour and how it influenced their lives. Nowadays people are less conscious of the sun's movement due to artificial lighting, central heating, improved infrastructure and occupations based indoors, such as teleworking etc.

Consider two scenarios when discussing illumination: light from the overcast sky and direct rays from the sun.

LIGHT FROM THE OVERCAST SKY In Ireland and many other areas of the world, critical daylighting conditions occur when the sky is clouded. The movement of clouds has a significant effect on illumination.

For daylighting analysis a heavy overcast sky is assumed, giving a total unobstructed illumination of 5000 lux. This is known as the Standard Overcast Sky. Tests and research show that between 8.00 am and 5.00 pm in Ireland the illumination from the sky is, on average, 5000 lux for 85 per cent of the time.

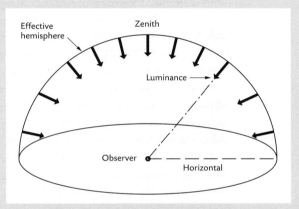

12-3 The CIE sky is a standard overcast sky in which the luminance steadily increases above the horizon. The luminance of the CIE sky at the zenith is three times brighter than at the horizon.

Outdoor illumination varies, which makes it unrealistic to use specific values for the design of room interiors. This problem is overcome by using a ratio called the **Daylight Factor**.

The Daylight Factor expresses the daylighting received at a point indoors as a percentage of the daylighting received at the same time out of doors by an unobstructed point.

There are three components in the daylight factor:

- the direct light from the sky that falls on the specified point (known as the sky component);
- the reflected light from external surfaces (the externally reflected component); and
- the light received by reflection from the internal surfaces of the room (the internally reflected component).

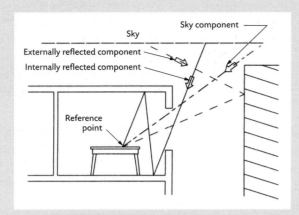

12-4 *Components of the daylight factor*

In rooms that are illuminated by windows, most of the light penetrates almost horizontally. This results in the walls being well lit, giving an overall pleasant interior.

DIRECT RAYS FROM THE SUN Sun penetration into buildings is a strong psychological need of many people. It is generally recommended that residential buildings with a southern orientation should have at least one hour of sunshine on the 1st March.

However, there are disadvantages with sun penetration because the sun's rays can cause human discomfort due to glare. Sunshine entry into rooms is not taken into account until the horizontal angle between the sun's rays and the plane of the window is more than 22.5° and more than 5° above the horizon. (Refer to Figs. 5-10 and 5-11.)

Electrical services – safe use

Electricity is so much part of modern living that we can often take it for granted. It is a powerful and versatile energy source but can be dangerous if it is not used properly.

In Ireland serious accidents with electricity in the home are rare, but each year there are a small number of serious injuries. Most of the accidents that occur are due to either carelessness or a lack of awareness of some basic rules.

The safety of the electrical wiring installation on the customer's side of the ESB meter is the responsibility of the householder. So also is the way in which electric appliances are used and maintained.

An ETCI (Electro Technical Council of Ireland) Completion Certificate should be obtained from the electrical contractor for the wiring of new or existing dwellings. This certificate verifies that the installation complies with the National Wiring

Rules. This certificate will also be required by ESB before a new supply can be connected.

Using electrical appliances safely

Always read the manufacturer's instructions carefully before you use a new appliance. The most vulnerable part of most appliances is the connecting flex and its plug. Most accidents associated with electric appliances are caused either by damaged or badly repaired flexes, or through incorrectly wired plugs.

Helpful dos and don'ts

FLEXES
- Do check flexes regularly for signs of wear, particularly on electric irons, kettles, vacuum cleaners and portable tools.
- Do treat flexes with care; they are vulnerable to damage.
- Do make sure you have a long enough flex to work comfortably without straining the flex.
- Don't make joints in a flex, replace it with one of adequate length.
- Don't repair a defective or damaged flex; replace it.
- Don't use 'bell-wire' or telephone/alarm wire for any mains-voltage appliances or connections.

HANDLING AND USING APPLIANCES
- Don't drag an appliance by the flex nor pull on the flex to remove a plug from the socket.
- Don't plug any appliance into a light bulb holder.
- Do note the maximum load allowed for a coiled extension lead – its rating is much lower with the cable fully wound than fully unwound. Many leads cannot safely handle electric heaters; they are only suitable for smaller appliances such as light portable tools.
- Avoid using multiple outlet adaptors; use fused multi-socket boards instead. Better still, have additional sockets fitted.
- Try to avoid 'spaghetti-junction' type cable connections behind music systems or computer equipment.
- Try to keep power cables separate from other connecting cables.
- If a plug shows signs of damage or defective operation – cracked or broken casing, signs of excessive heating, marked pitting of the metal contact – replace it without delay.

Kitchen safety

Special care should be taken when using appliances in the kitchen, where the combination of electricity, water, trailing flexes and hot surfaces makes it potentially more dangerous.

FIRE RISK WHEN DEEP-FRYING WITH OIL

Carelessness when using an old style 'chip pan' for deep-fat frying is the cause of many kitchen fires. Hot oil can ignite suddenly and the fire can quickly get out of control.

Most fire authorities recommend that householders get rid of these chip pans and switch to a safer method of deep-fat frying, such as an electric deep fat fryer.

The main safety features of an electric deep-fat fryer are the thermostatic control that prevents the oil from overheating and the absence of a source of ignition. Keep the air filter clean to ensure that the thermostat continues to operate properly,

Bedroom safety

Electric heaters and electric blankets/duvets are the appliances most usually used in the bedroom.

Take great care with electric blankets and electric duvets, especially where elderly or infirm people are concerned. A wide range of extra-safe electric blankets is now available for all-night use. It is very important to carefully read and follow the manufacturer's instructions for the individual blanket you use.

Wall-mounted panel radiators, portable fan heaters, convectors and oil-filled radiators are the safest heaters to use in bedrooms. Whatever heater is used keep it away from bedclothes, clothing and curtains to avoid any risk of fire.

Never drape clothes over heaters.

Bathroom safety

Special precautions are necessary regarding wiring and the use of appliances in the bathroom. The wet surroundings pose a greater risk of electric shock than anywhere else in the house.

SOCKET OUTLETS AND PORTABLE

APPLIANCES No socket outlets, other than specially designed shaver outlets, are allowed in bathrooms and this rule also applies to en-suite bathrooms.

Under no circumstances should portable appliances, such as a hair-dryer, electric fire, or even a mains-operated radio be brought into a bathroom, even if it is plugged into a socket outside the room.

ELECTRIC HEATERS AND TOWEL RAILS

Wall-mounted fan-heaters, small storage heaters and heated towel rails are typically used in bathrooms. All electric heaters and water heaters in a bathroom must be fixed and permanently wired. They must not be used through a plug and socket. In addition, a room heater must be fixed out of reach of a person in the bath, i.e. greater than 0.8 metres from the nearest edge of the bath. It must only be controlled by a pull-cord switch or by a switch located outside the bathroom.

ELECTRIC SHOWERS An instantaneous electric shower must always be wired back through its own circuit to the customer's distribution board and the circuit must be protected by an RCD.

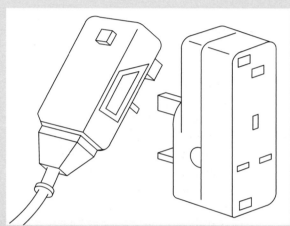

12-5 Residual current device (RCD), also called earth leakage circuit breaker, or residual current circuit breaker (RCCD) – an automatic protective device that detects any leakage of electricity to earth from the circuit and quickly cuts off the supply

EN-SUITE SHOWERS/BATHROOMS

The same requirements regarding wiring and the use of appliances apply in en-suite units.

⊞ Electrical installation

The electricity supply into your home comes through the ESB main fuse and the ESB meter. Both of these items are sealed by the ESB and must never be interfered with.

Newer installations have an isolating switch between the ESB meter and the customer's distribution board, older installations have direct connections between the meter and the distribution board. The customer is responsible for the electrical installation on his or her side of the ESB meter.

Repair work on the fixed electrical installation or to electrical appliances should only be carried out by a competent and qualified person and should not be attempted by the layperson.

Fuses and MCBs (miniature circuit breakers)

The customer's distribution board (or fuse board) contains the MCBs or fuses which protect individual circuits that carry electricity to your sockets, cooker, lights etc.

These circuits have different size wires (large for a cooker, small for the lights) and, for this reason, have different strengths of MCBs or fuses protecting them. The strength is measured in amps and will be clearly marked on the MCB or fuse.

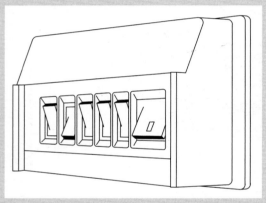

12-6 Consumer unit, containing the main switch and circuit breakers

An MCB or fuse is a safety device that cuts off the flow of electricity to a circuit if a fault in the circuit or in an appliance causes an overload.

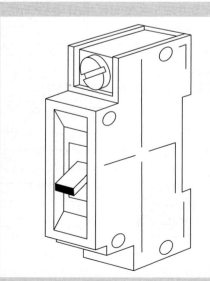

12-7 Circuit breaker (MCB) – a small switch that automatically disconnects a circuit when a fault occurs that causes excess current to flow in the circuit

An MCB can be reset when the fault is identified and repaired. A blown fuse must be replaced with one of similar strength. It is most important when a fuse fails that one of the same strength replaces it and never by a stronger one.

A fuse has a small coloured disc in the base and the colour identifies the strength. The colours are:

Disc colour	Strength	Circuit
Green	6 Amp	Lights
Red	10 Amp	Lights
Brown	16 Amp	Socket outlets – radial
Blue	20 Amp	Water heater, storage heaters
Black	35 Amp	Socket outlets – ring Cooker Electric shower

MCBs

Most modern installations will have MCBs fitted instead of fuses. They are more convenient to use. When the fault or overload that caused the MCB to switch off is located and remedied the MCB is reset to the upward 'on' position.

RCDs

Residual Current Devices (RCDs) installed in the fuse board protect the sockets, immersion group and bathroom water heater (or shower). These provide a high degree of safety on these circuits. Press the 'test' button at least every 3 months to ensure they are operating properly.

Homes are supplied with electricity at 230 volts, 50 Hz. The main consumer unit or fuse board is at the electricity supply intake position. The main switch is also located here and it will switch off all electricity to the installation.

A chart labelling the circuits will be found at the fuse board position. The final circuits are protected by miniature circuit breakers (MCB).

If an RCD trips, like an MCB it will not reset until the fault has been remedied. This can sometimes be difficult, particularly on socket circuits feeding electrical appliances.

To trace a fault on the socket circuit, first unplug all plugged in appliances, switch on the RCD and then plug in the appliances one after the other until the faulty appliance is found. If this procedure does not rectify the problem it is advisable to have the circuit examined by a RECI contractor.

RECI
Register of Electrical Contractors of Ireland

Transformers

A transformer is a very simple device. An alternating current is fed through a primary coil of wire, which produces an alternating magnetic field in the ring-shaped core of soft iron. This in turn creates a voltage in a secondary coil, from which the output current can be drawn.

If the secondary coil has more turns than the primary, the output voltage is higher than the input voltage. This is a 'step-up' transformer. A 'step-down' transformer has more turns in the primary coil than in the secondary coil to reduce the voltage.

Electricity supply

In conventional power stations, fuel is converted to steam at high temperature and pressure and used to drive turbines, which generate electricity at 25 kV alternating current.

In hydro-electric power stations, moving water is used to drive turbines.

The high current produced enables the voltage to be transformed up to 132, 275 or 400 kV for national transmission.

In Ireland, a 'supergrid' of 400 kV has been introduced gradually to provide the carrying capacity needed to match demand.

Fig. 12-10 (overleaf) shows how electricity is conveyed and transformed through substations from source to consumer.

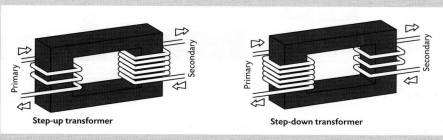

12-8 Step-up and step-down transformers

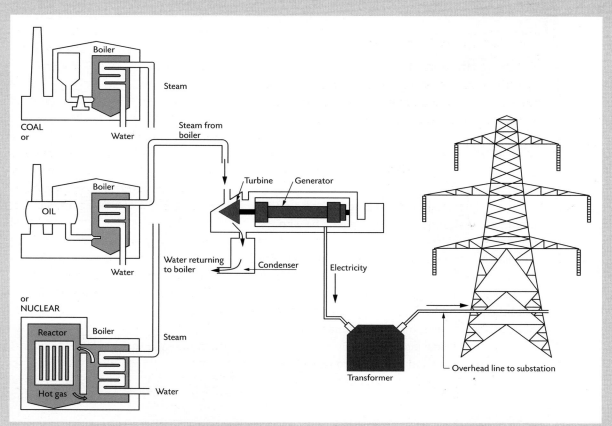

12-9 Position of transformer in the production of electricity

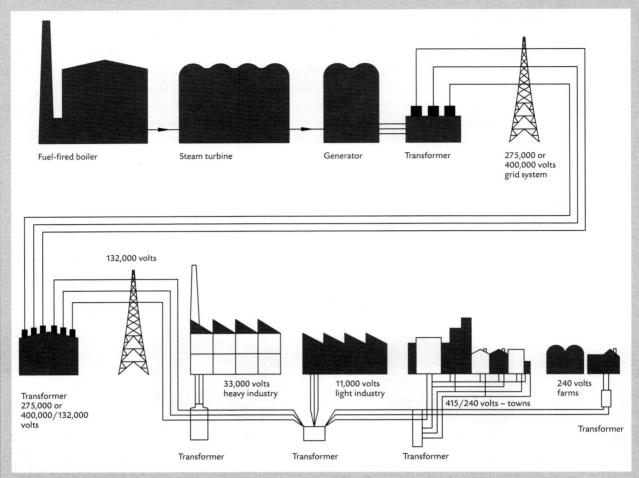

Fuel-fired boiler

Steam turbine

Generator

Transformer

275,000 or
400,000 volts
grid system

132,000 volts

Transformer
275,000 or
400,000/132,000
volts

33,000 volts
heavy industry

11,000 volts
light industry

415/240 volts – towns

240 volts
farms

Transformer

Transformer

Transformer

Transformer

12-10 *Electricity production and distribution*

Earthing the system

Safety regulations require an earth continuity bond to be connected to water and gas pipes to prevent them becoming live in the event of an electrical fault.

To install an earth bond there must be an earthing point near the meter. This is the main earth terminal.

To bond the metal services around the house run an earth wire to the mains water pipe. The wire should be at least 10 mm^2. Make the connection to the pipe using a purpose-made earth tag. Wrap the earth wire around the screw terminal and tighten it to make a secure connection. Clamp the earth wire onto the pipe below the stopcock, or in the event of a polythene mains, make the connection to the first section of metal pipe.

Both metal sinks and baths should be earthed. Modern stainless steel sinks should have a tag already fitted, ready to secure an earth cable using a nut and bolt.

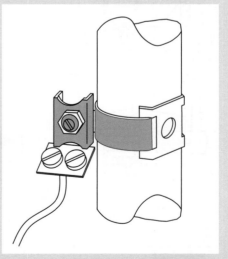

12-11 *An earth clamp. Ensure that painted pipes are scratched before fitting.*

Central heating pipes must also be earthed in this way in case a fault develops in the electrical controls.

It is important to note that electricity will always find the easiest route to the ground. Bonding all metal parts ensures that the easiest route is provided through the earth conductor and not through a person's body.

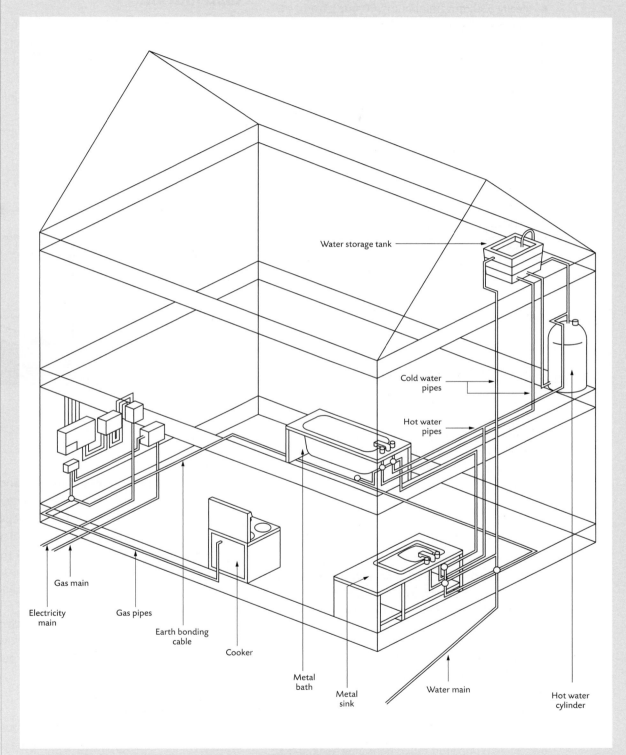

Water storage tank

Cold water pipes

Hot water pipes

Gas main

Electricity main

Gas pipes

Earth bonding cable

Cooker

Metal bath

Metal sink

Water main

Hot water cylinder

12-12 Bond all metal services and fittings, including central heating pipes for maximum safety.

Positioning of electrical outlets and controls

The locations of electrical outlets and lighting and other control switches must be:

- within the reach of a wheelchair user: 400–1200 mm over floor level;
- ideally 500 mm (minimum 300 mm), from internal corners;
- of contrasting colour with their surroundings;
- easy to operate, with rocker type switches where possible.

Twin socket outlets are easier to operate when the switches are sited to the outside of the plate rather than between the two plug tops.

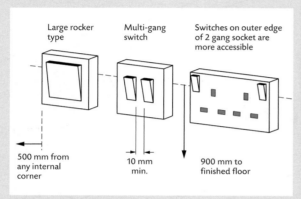

Large rocker type

Multi-gang switch

Switches on outer edge of 2 gang socket are more accessible

500 mm from any internal corner

10 mm min.

900 mm to finished floor

12-13 Switches and sockets

Locate light fittings to avoid glare and give uniform light spread. Lighting controls should be easy to operate. Wall-mounted switches should be fixed 1000 mm over floor level, minimum 300 mm from internal corners.

In accessible bedroom accommodation, it is essential that users can control lights from the bed. This can be done by additional two or three way switching reachable from the bed, remote control operation, or press cable control switches.

Locate door intercoms at an appropriate level of 1000–1200 mm over finished ground or floor level. A large, easily operated 'bell-push' helps those with poor hand function. The most suitable doorbell is one which gives a visual indication of its operation, e.g. a light flashes when the button is pressed.

Hot water safety

People with poor heat register may be unable to detect temperatures that might cause injury, while people with impaired movement may be unable to react quickly when scalding water issues from a tap or shower head.

These types of hazards can be greatly reduced by restricting the hot water temperature to 43°C (particularly in public buildings).

Water supply, storage and distribution

Precipitation is the main source of water for drinking purposes. A percentage of rainfall evaporates soon after it falls, a percentage runs off the ground to join streams and rivers and a percentage seeps through the ground to join underground supplies.

Sources of water supply consist of surface water and underground water.

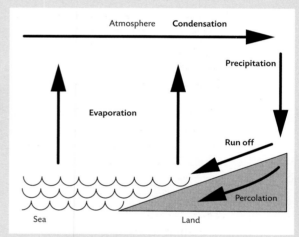

Atmosphere   **Condensation**

Precipitation

Evaporation

Run off

Percolation

Sea   Land

12-14 The water cycle

Surface water

This includes water collected from roofs and paved areas as well as streams, rivers, lakes and reservoirs. This water is liable to contamination by vegetation and farm pollutants. Sewage and industrial waste are sometimes fed into rivers without any purification treatment. These same rivers are usually expected to supply fresh water for towns and villages.

Rivers have the ability to purify themselves, especially if they are fast flowing and shallow. Despite this, water taken from a river for public use should be treated before consumption.

Underground water

Rain that seeps through the ground may eventually reach an impervious layer, where it may be held as in a reservoir or it may flow like an underground stream on top of the impervious layer. Layers of 'water' are called aquifers.

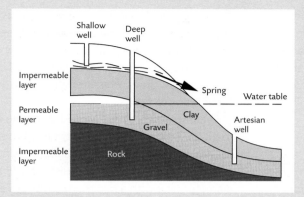

12-15 *Underground water supply*

SPRINGS. There are two types of springs. A main spring, which is usually deep and connects to the aquifer layer; and a shallow or simple spring, which connects to underground surface water. The latter is likely to be intermittent.

Spring water is usually pure, because of the natural purification that occurs as the water permeates through the ground.

WELLS. Wells are different to springs, as the ground has to be bored to reach the water. Springs occur naturally. The upper part of a well must be lined to prevent possibly polluted surface water entering.

Water treatment

Water to be used in a public water supply is required to be fit for drinking. This implies that it poses no danger to health. It should be colourless, clear, odourless, sparkling and pleasant to taste.

There are four main techniques used for the treatment of water. They are:

- storage
- filtration
- sterilisation
- softening

Storage

Water is stored in reservoirs where contaminants/impurities settle to the bottom (sedimentation). Pathogenic bacteria (disease-producing) find it difficult to survive in reservoirs due to the lack of food, low temperatures and the effect of sunlight.

If water is stored for long periods, algae tend to grow. The growth of algae can be controlled with chemicals such as copper sulphate.

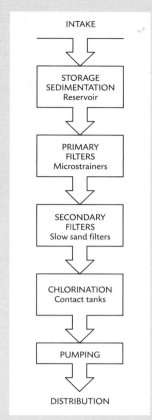

12-16 *Water treatment scheme*

Filtration

Water is passed through sand or a fine wire mesh to remove particles. Rapid sand filters act as a physical filter, leaving the water in need of chemical treatment. Slow sand filters provide physical and chemical action.

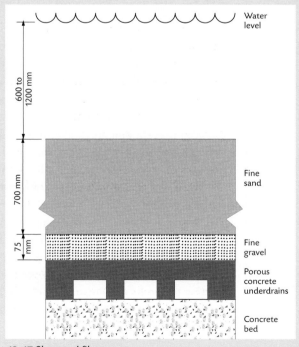

12-17 *Slow sand filter*

In a slow sand filter, water slowly percolates down through the sand. Fine particles, micro-organisms, and microscopic plant life are retained in the sand bed. The bed must be emptied for cleaning after a number of weeks. The slow sand filter produces high-quality water that needs little further processing.

Sterilisation

Water must be sterilised before humans can consume it. Chlorine is added to the water for public supply, but this isn't always feasible for small installations.

Chlorine kills bacteria, which makes the water safe to drink. Ammonia is sometimes added to the water after sterilisation to reduce the offensive taste left by the chlorine.

For smaller installations, water is passed through a very fine filter capable of removing bacteria.

Softening

Hard water is recommended for drinking but it has disadvantages. Scale may be deposited in hot water pipes and boilers, and soap does not lather in hard water. There are a number of ways to soften water.

- **Base exchange** methods change hardness compounds into compounds that do not cause hardness.
- **Demineralisation** is a process to remove all chemicals dissolved in the water.
- **Lime-soda treatment** depends on chemical reactions to make the calcium and magnesium in the hard water insoluble and they are then removed.

Mains water supply

Most dwellings and buildings, including those in rural areas, are supplied with water from a public water supply, otherwise known as the mains supply.

The design of a mains water supply needs to consider present demand and anticipated future demand, the size of the water mains, and the pressure of water in the mains – this is known as the 'head' – the height to which the water would rise in a vertical pipe.

The standard size for water mains is 75 mm diameter if it is supplied from both ends and 100 mm if it is supplied from one end only. The minimum head of water recommended for fire-fighting purposes is 30 m, and a head of 70 m is recommended to minimise waste and reduce noise in pipes.

The head is achieved by locating reservoirs at appropriate heights above the buildings being served. Full pressure (head) from the reservoir is seldom available, as flow in the mains will be taking place at most times. Pressure is further reduced by friction due to flow.

Water mains are usually sited along the edge of a roadway. Permission must be obtained to connect to the mains and to cut the road if this is necessary.

A domestic connection consists of a 15 mm diameter pipe with a minimum cover of 750 mm below ground as protection from frost. This is usually a black plastic, heavy-duty pipe. The walls are thicker than the normal plastic pipe (6 mm) to protect against perforations due to soil movement and frost damage.

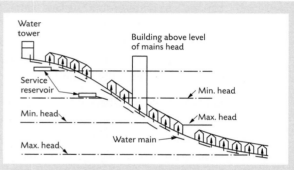

12-18 Principles of distribution of water from service reservoirs

Cold water storage and distribution

The connection to the mains water supply is usually taken to the boundary of the site and finished with a stop valve or stop cock, housed in a suitable box or purpose-built chamber. This chamber may be fitted with a hinged cast iron cover.

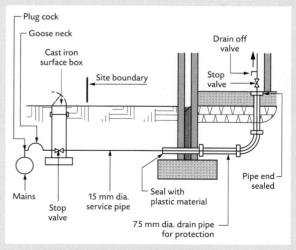

12-19 Connection to the mains water supply

The cold water supply for the dwelling is taken from the stop valve to the building, 750 mm below ground level. A second stop valve should be fitted on the service pipe where it enters the building. Where possible this should be at the kitchen sink, although the location is not critical.

Inside the house a drain cock should be fitted above the stop valve to allow the cold water system to be drained down.

There are two main types of cold water supply systems within the house. These are known as **direct** and **indirect**.

Direct cold water supply system

Water from the cold water service pipe feeds all the cold water outlets including the sanitary appliances. This system may be found in old houses, but otherwise it is not recommended for the following reasons:

- In the event of mains failure there is no reserve.
- Mains supply exerts increased pressure on fittings.
- During peak demand the pressure may be reduced.

Advantages of this system include:

- Economical on pipe work
- Only a small cold water storage cistern required to feed the hot water tank.
- Drinking water available from all the cold water outlets.

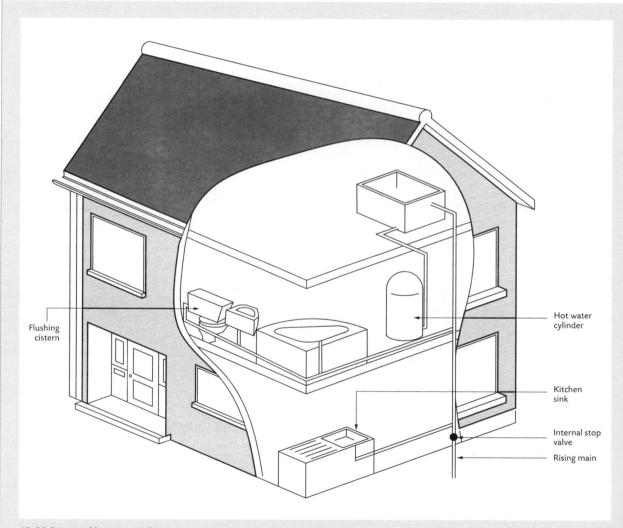

12-20 Direct cold water supply

Flushing cistern

Hot water cylinder

Kitchen sink

Internal stop valve

Rising main

Indirect cold water supply system

All cold water outlets with the exception of one drinking water outlet are supplied indirectly from a cold water storage cistern, usually located in the roof space. 'Indirect' means the water is not coming directly from the mains to the outlets, it is piped to and stored in the cistern in the attic. This is the most common system in use.

The advantages of this system are:
- A reserve supply in case of mains failure.
- Less pressure on the taps and valves resulting in less wear.

Disadvantages of this system include:
- More pipe work required.
- Provision and installation of a storage cistern in the attic.

Hot water supply

Hot water for domestic purposes is usually taken from a hot water tank or cylinder. The heat source is usually in the form of a solid fuel, oil or gas boiler. Other water heating alternatives include a back boiler to an open fire, and an electric immersion heater fitted to the hot water cylinder.

A hot water supply system must be capable of producing sufficient hot water to meet all demands by the household, should be economical to run and easy to install and maintain.

There are two main systems of hot water supply: **direct** and **indirect** systems.

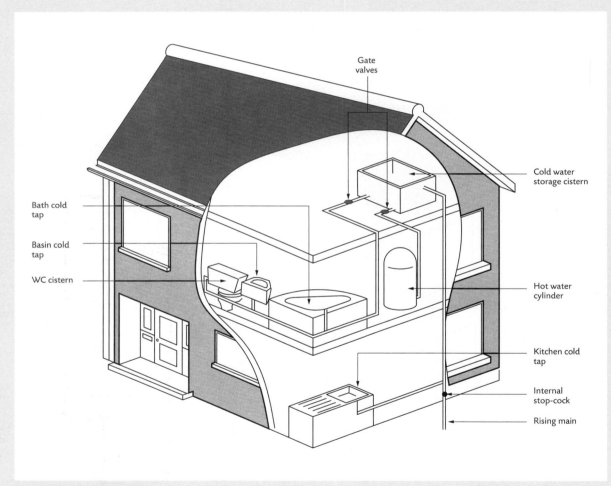

12-21 Indirect cold water supply

Direct hot water system

Cold water is heated in the water jacket in the boiler. The heated water rises through convection currents and is replaced by cold water coming from the bottom of the hot water cylinder. A circulation is thereby set-up.

Hot water is drawn off as required for domestic use and is in turn replaced by cold water from the cold water storage tank in the attic. The hot water draw-off is taken from the top of the hot water cylinder where the hottest water is stored. An expansion pipe connects to a horizontal pipe at the top of the hot water cylinder and runs vertically from the hot water distribution pipe to the cold water storage tank.

In the direct hot water system the water that is heated in the boiler and subsequently stored in the cylinder is the same water that is drawn-off for domestic use. This makes this system unsuitable for supplying a central heating circuit.

The direct hot water system is also not suitable for hard water areas due to lime scale deposits, which may eventually block the pipe work. Lime scale deposits occur when water is heated to temperatures ranging from 50° to 70°C and this is the typical temperature range for domestic hot water.

This system is seldom used due to the disadvantages described.

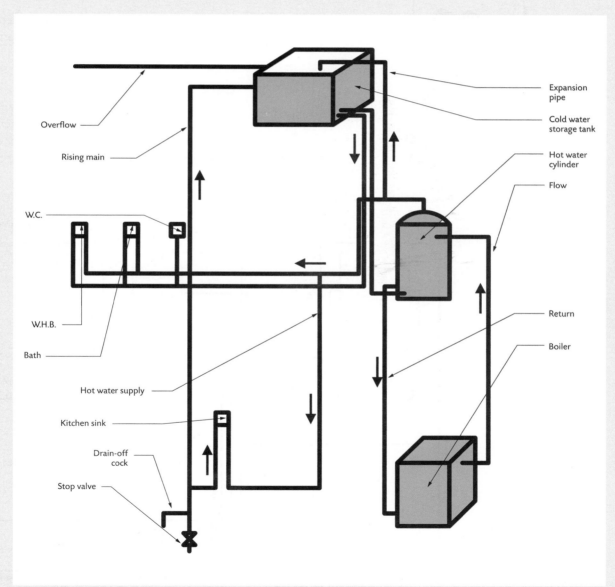

12-22 Direct hot water system

Indirect hot water system

Hot water circulates between the boiler and the hot water cylinder. The cylinder is an indirect cylinder that contains a coil. This means that the water that is circulating between the boiler and the indirect cylinder is travelling in a closed circuit and it does not mix with the stored water in the cylinder. Its sole purpose of travelling through the cylinder, in the coil, is to raise the temperature of the stored water.

The water that is heated in the boiler and travels through the cylinder is referred to as the 'primary' circuit. The 'secondary' circuit refers to the stored water in the hot water indirect cylinder, which is used for domestic draw-off and replaced with water from the cold water storage tank in the attic.

In the primary circuit it is the same water that is circulating continuously, apart from any water that needs to be replaced due to expansion and evaporation.

The advantages of the primary circuit are:
- No lime scale build-up (furring) as fresh cold water is not constantly being introduced.
- A central heating loop can be connected to the primary circuit; this is not possible with the direct hot water system.

A disadvantage of this system is that extra piping is required and a second (smaller) feed cistern is required for the primary circuit.

Cisterns

Cold water storage cisterns are usually made of plastic, although galvanised mild steel cisterns were common in the past. The standard size for cold water cisterns is 228 litres. This is deemed adequate

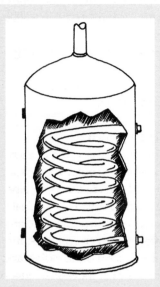

12-23 *Indirect cylinder*

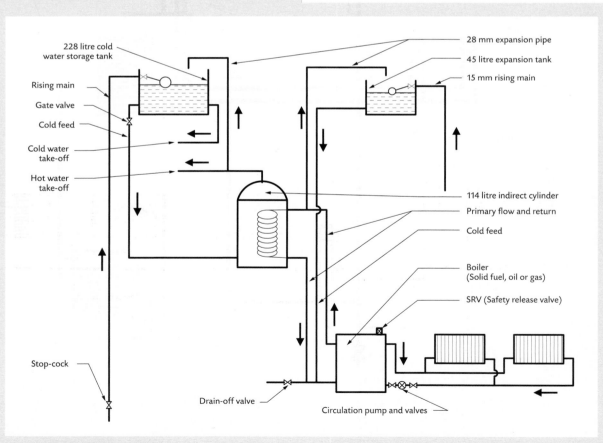

12-24 *Indirect hot water system*

to serve both the cold and hot water supplies and provide a reserve in the event of mains failure.

The standard size for the hot water storage cylinder is 114 litres. This is normally situated in the 'hot press' (airing cupboard) and is made from copper. New installations must have factory-applied insulation to conserve energy.

Pipe work is usually copper, although plastic pipes are gaining in popularity. The service pipe from the mains is usually polythene.

Ball valves are fitted on all cold water storage cisterns to prevent overflow. A ball valve floats in the cistern and automatically closes when the water reaches a certain level.

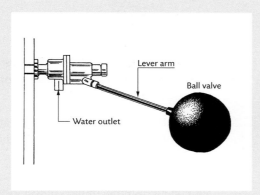

12-25 *Ball valve*

Heating systems and layout

The pipe work supplying water to radiators may be small-bore (12, 15 or 22 mm diameter) or microbore (6, 8 or 10 mm diameter). It is important that the correct size of pipe is used to supply radiators of various sizes with the correct amount of heat.

When determining the correct size of radiator to use, consider the amount of heat/energy required to combat heat losses in a specific room and the temperature at which the radiator will be required to operate.

The two main methods of supplying hot water to radiators are:

■ the one-pipe or single-pipe system
■ the two-pipe system.

The one-pipe system
Hot water from the boiler is fed to each radiator consecutively with the cooler water from each radiator being fed back to the same pipe. As a result the temperature of the water is gradually getting lower as it enters each successive radiator. This makes the control of the heat distribution difficult.

The one pipe system is the easiest and cheapest to install, but control of individual radiators is virtually ineffective.

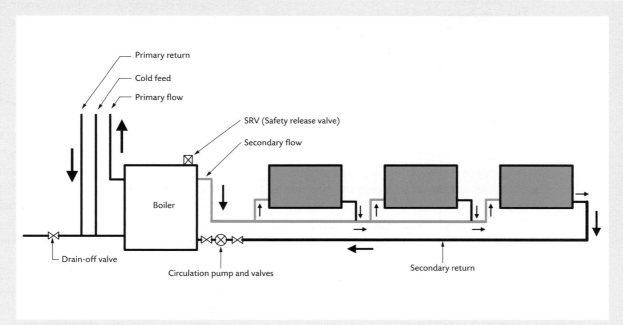

12-26 *The one-pipe system*

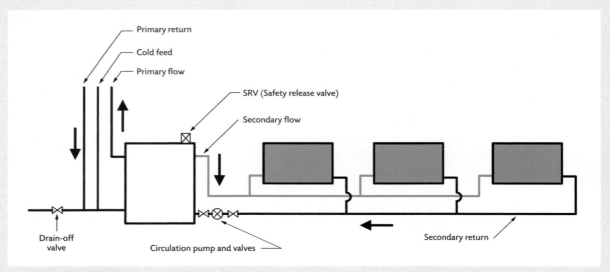

12-27 **The two-pipe system**

The two-pipe system

Hot water from the boiler is fed to each radiator by one pipe and the cooler water coming from each radiator is fed to a second pipe and returned to the boiler for heating. This is the more common heating system used.

Depending on the length of the circuit, each radiator receives water at approximately the same temperature. This allows greater control of individual radiators, and also provides for a faster warm-up time.

The majority of small-bore heating systems used in dwellings use the indirect hot water supply system. Connections can be made to the primary flow and return circuits or separate connections can be made to the boiler unit.

Controls

Some degree of control is essential in order to achieve a comfortable level of heating within a building. Space and water heating systems should be effectively controlled to ensure the effective use of energy.

The main types of control are concerned with adjusting the flow of water through the radiator as the temperature of the radiator is directly linked to the flow. The following minimum level of control is recommended:

- Automatic control of space heating on the basis of room temperature.
- Automatic control of heat input to stored hot water on the basis of stored water temperature.
- Separate and independent automatic time control of space heating and hot water.

- Shutdown of boiler or other heat source when there is no demand for either space or water heating from that source.

Provision should be made to control heat input on the basis of room temperature, e.g. by the use of room thermostats, thermostatic radiator valves or other equivalent form of sensing device.

Independent temperature control should generally be provided for separate zones that normally operate at different temperatures, e.g. living and sleeping zones. The maximum floor area for single zone control should not exceed 100 m².

Typical controls in use are:
- **Circulating pump**. This is positioned on the return pipe beside the boiler. It pumps the hot water in the circuit to all radiators.
- **Radiator valves**. Each radiator has two valves: a wheel valve, which can be adjusted by hand to open or close the supply of hot water to the radiator, and a lock shield valve, which is fitted on the return side of the radiator to balance the amount of heat in each radiator.
- **Thermostatic valves** allow control of individual room temperature.
- **Air bleed valve**. This is located at the top of the radiator to allow trapped air to be vented. Trapped air prevents water from entering the radiator, meaning that it doesn't heat.
- **Gate valves** allow a section of the system to be shut off, without the need to drain the complete system. Gate valves should be placed at each side of the pump to allow the pump to be removed without draining the system.

H

- **Boiler thermostat**: controls the temperature of the water in the boiler.
- **Room thermostats** are set to the desired room temperature and electronically control the circulating pump.
- **Time switch**. Usually located near the boiler, it controls when the whole system comes on and for how long.

Hot water storage vessels should be fitted with thermostatic control that shuts off the supply of heat when the desired storage temperature is reached.

H

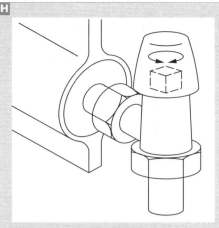

12-31 *A lockshield/balancing valve*

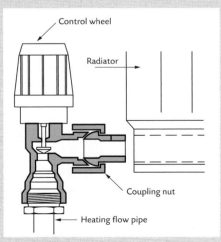

12-28 *Circulating pump*

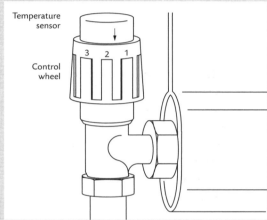

12-32 *Thermostatic valve*

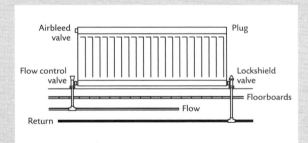

12-29 *Position of radiator valves*

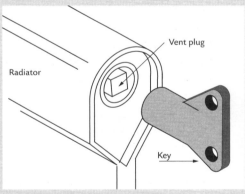

12-33 *Air cock/vent valve*

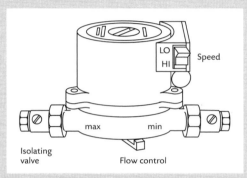

12-30 *A wheel valve*

12-34 *Gate valve*

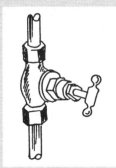

12-35 *A stop cock allows water to flow in one direction only.*

Insulation of hot water storage vessels, pipes and ducts

All hot water storage vessels, pipes and ducts associated with the provision of heating and hot water in a dwelling should be insulated to prevent heat loss, except for hot water pipes and ducts within the normally heated area of the dwelling that contribute to the heat requirement of the building.

Adequate insulation of hot water storage vessels can be achieved by the use of a storage vessel with factory-applied insulation. A 35 mm coating of PU-foam of zero ozone depletion potential and a minimum density of 30 kg/m^3 satisfy the regulations.

Use an insulating jacket in older houses. The jacket must be installed with the segments tied together so as to provide unbroken insulation cover for the hot water cistern. This option no longer meets Building Regulation requirements for new houses.

All pipes, other than those that do not contribute to the useful heat requirements of a room or space, should be provided with 40 mm insulation. The insulation material should have a thermal conductivity of 0.045 W/mK.

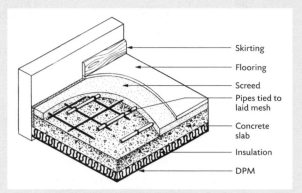

12-37 *underfloor heating contained within a screed on an insulated slab*

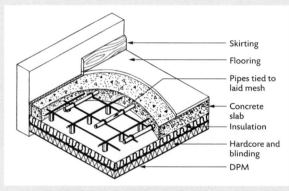

12-38 *underfloor heating contained within a single-pour slab*

UFH provides many advantages over traditional radiator based systems. In large warm surfaces, such as a floor, it is possible to achieve comfortable conditions with a cooler air temperature. For the same comfort level the room air temperatures can be 2°C lower because radiant heat warms the surfaces rather than the air around the surfaces.

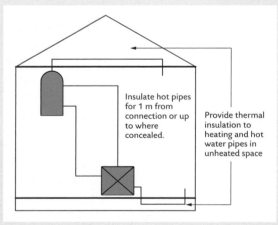

12-36 *Insulation of hot water storage vessels and pipes*

Underfloor heating

Underfloor heating (UFH) is gaining in popularity for heating domestic and commercial properties. Low temperature water (50°C) circulates through a series of continuous pipe loops laid under the floor, turning it into one large radiant surface. The pipe loops for each room (or zone) run from and back to the system manifold. The underfloor heating pipework is within the concrete screed (or slab) with a variety of floor finishes available.

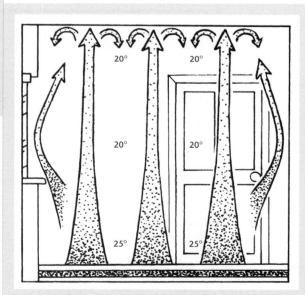

12-39 *underfloor heating systems work at lower temperatures than standard radiator heating systems. Warmth is generated where it is required, not at ceiling height.*

This makes underfloor heating more energy efficient and comfortable than traditional radiator systems.

It is more comfortable to have a constant evenly distributed temperature of 20–24 degrees, than it is to have a single high temperature heat source, such as a radiator, in one location of the room. The radiant heat from UFH reduces the constant air circulation, resulting cold drafts and dust.

Other advantages of underfloor heating include:
- The heating effect is concentrated in the occupied area, not in the ceiling area.
- A major component of the heating effect is radiant, which feels more comfortable than the convectional heat from radiators.
- The warm, dry floor inhibits the growth of house dust mites.
- It allows greater freedom in the design and layout of the room.

Noise control principles and design details

Noise is frequently referred to as unwanted sound (see also section on *Principles of sound insulation* beginning on page 208, Chapter 11).

What is sound? Sound is a pressure wave travelling in air or water, or a solid element of construction, such as a wall or a floor. A sound wave resembles the surface wave made when you throw a stone into a calm pool of water, except that:
- a sound wave consists of tiny fluctuations in air pressure rather than fluctuations in water height
- a sound wave can travel in three dimensions rather than two
- the wave speed is much faster (340 metres per second in air).

Sound is usually generated by vibration of an object or surface such as a speaker cone, a violin body, or human vocal cords. The vibrating surface 'radiates' pressure waves into the adjoining air or water as sound. (Sound can also be generated by turbulent airflow, by bubbles collapsing, or by many other phenomena.)

The frequency (number of wave crests per unit time that pass a fixed location) measures the tone or pitch of a sound. For example, a bass guitar plays lower frequencies than a violin.

The wavelength, or distance between wave crests, is related to frequency. Lower frequencies have longer wavelengths. In air, all frequencies of sound travel at the same speed.

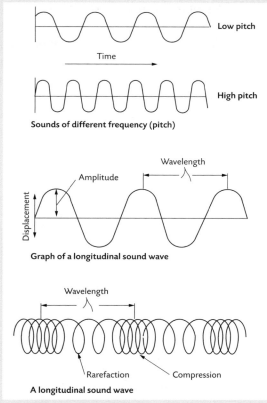

12-40 *Sound wave details*

Noise control

There are many types of noises that can annoy people within a building. How noise is transferred within a building depends on the type of sound involved. There are two main types of sound: airborne and impact sound.
- **Airborne sound** may be defined as sound that travels through the air, such as human voices, music, traffic and aircraft noise etc. Airborne sound produces vibrations in walls and floors.
- **Impact sound** is caused due to direct impact on a building component, such as footsteps, moving furniture, banging on a door, etc.

Some noise sources may generate both types of sound.

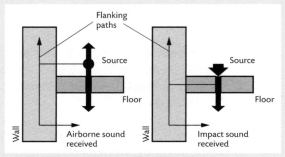

12-41 *Airborne sound transmission (left); impact sound transmission (right)*

External noise

The way sound travels can be described by an inverse square law (i.e. doubling the distance from the source reduces the intensity by four times). Sources of noise should therefore be kept as far away from people as possible.

Placing an obstruction in its path can stop most noise. The heavier and more solid the obstruction the greater the sound reduction achieved.

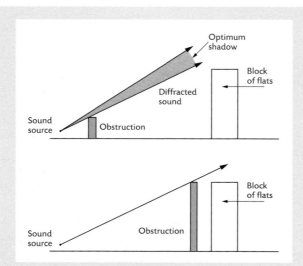

12-42 *Two positions for placing obstructions to reduce the impact of external noise*

Heavy structures transmit less sound than light structures because the sound waves in dense materials have low amplitude vibrations. This means that the sound that is re-transmitted into the air is also of low amplitude.
This relates to the **mass law**, which states that the sound insulation of a partition is dependent on its mass per unit area.

Trees may be used as a sound insulation shield and are often planted beside motorways for this purpose. This type of insulation is ineffective in reducing aircraft noise.

For sound insulation to be effective the following points must be observed:

- To conform to the **mass law** the material used in the building must have as large a mass per unit area as possible.

- The **overall insulation** of a wall is only as good as its weakest point. The 'completeness' of a wall or structure depends on air tightness and uniformity.
  - **Air-tightness**. Air gaps are often found around ceilings, windows, doors etc. Doors and window systems should be airtight when closed. 'Sound leaks' should be treated as seriously as water leaks.

  - **Uniformity**. In a composite structure, the component with the lowest insulation value should be improved first, as the overall structure acts as a complete whole. The overall sound insulation value of a composite component is usually closer to the insulation value of the poorest component.

- The **stiffness** of a partition or wall depends on the elasticity of its materials and on how it is fixed. Very stiff components can result in loss of insulation at certain frequencies if there are resonance and coincidence effects.
  - **Resonance**. Sound produced by an object vibrating when it is subjected to sound waves that have the same frequency as the natural frequency of the object itself.
  - **Coincidence**. Sometimes sound waves impact on an object at angles other than 90°. This may result in sound bending wave frequency, due to the object becoming flexible. Coincidence occurs when the sound wave frequency and the bending wave frequency coincide.

- **Isolation** can be a very effective means of sound insulation. Otherwise known as 'discontinuous construction'. It works on the basis of sound being converted to different wave motions where it meets different materials. This results in energy being lost from the sound. Isolation is a common technique used for noise insulation and it is the principle employed in floating floors, carpets, and air cavities in windows. Great care is needed as flanking transmission can result from the use of a single nail. (Refer to Figs. 11-29 to 11-31, pages 216–217.)

Internal noise

The same rules apply to the control of noise inside a building as to the control of noise from outside.

Noise transmitted from one room to another may be divided into two different types: directly transmitted noise and indirectly transmitted noise (or flanking transmission). These terms should not be considered in isolation as they are connected with sound types covered earlier. Both types of sound can be transmitted either directly or indirectly.

DIRECTLY TRANSMITTED NOISE. This refers to the direct transmission of sound through a wall or floor from one of its sides to the other.

The reduction in the level of airborne sound transmitted through a solid masonry wall depends on the mass of the wall. Heavy walls are not easily set into vibration. Walls with two or three leaves depend partly on their mass and partly on structural isolation between the leaves.

Floors should reduce airborne sound and, if they are above a dwelling, impact sound. A heavy solid floor depends on its mass to reduce airborne sound and on a soft covering to reduce impact sound at source.

A floating floor uses a resilient layer to isolate the walking surface from the base. This isolation contributes to both airborne and impact sound insulation. The resilient layer is only effective if it is not too stiff, so it is important to choose a suitable material and to make sure that it is not bypassed with rigid bridges such as fixings and pipes.

Air paths must be avoided, and porous materials and gaps at joints in the structure must be sealed.

Resonances must also be avoided. These may occur if some part of the structure (such as a dry lining) vibrates strongly at a particular sound frequency (pitch) and transmits more energy at this pitch.

FLANKING TRANSMISSION OF SOUND

Flanking transmission means the indirect transmission of sound from one side of a wall or floor to the other side. (Refer to Figs. 11-11 and 12-41). Because a solid element may vibrate when exposed to sound waves in the air, it may cause sound waves in the air on both sides. Flanking transmission happens when there is a path along which sound can travel between elements on opposite sides of a wall or floor. This path may be through a continuous solid structure or through an air space.

Dwellings should be designed so that quiet areas or rooms are grouped together and located as far away as possible from noisy areas.

Air infiltration

Infiltration of cold outside air should be limited by reducing unintentional air paths where possible.

Take the following precautions:
- Seal the gap between dry-lining and masonry walls at the edge of openings and at the junctions with walls, floors and ceilings.
- Seal vapour control membranes in timber-frame constructions.
- Fit draught-proof stripping in the frames of opening components of windows, doors and roof lights.
- Seal around loft openings.
- Seal around ducting for concealed services.

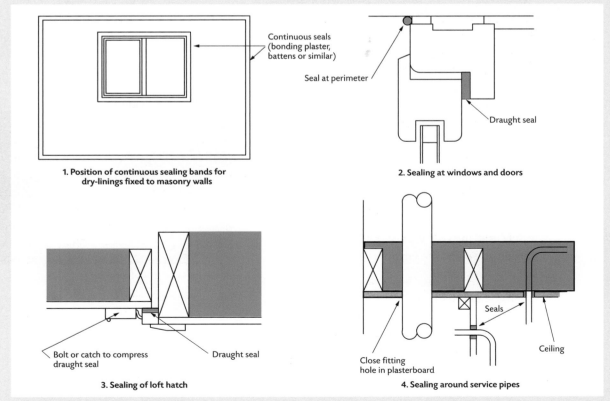

1. **Position of continuous sealing bands for dry-linings fixed to masonry walls**

Continuous seals (bonding plaster, battens or similar)

Seal at perimeter

2. **Sealing at windows and doors**

Draught seal

Bolt or catch to compress draught seal

Draught seal

3. **Sealing of loft hatch**

Close fitting hole in plasterboard

Seals

Ceiling

4. **Sealing around service pipes**

12-43 *Limiting air infiltration in dwellings*

Energy sources and environmental considerations

Energy for warmth and light is obtained from coal, oil, gas, wood, peat, wind, water, sun and nuclear power.

Many of these sources are used to produce electricity, which in turn is used in the manufacture of all our physical needs, such as clothes, medicines, heat and light. Some fuel sources are used for transport.

There are costs involved in producing energy sources, both financial and environmental. Environmental considerations should always be considered against the financial and comfort costs.

Coal, oil, natural gas and peat have taken many thousand of years to form in the earth. They are being used up very rapidly at present and cannot be replaced. They are non-renewable and are referred to as fossil fuels. Wood is renewable but takes many years to replace.

Nuclear fusion is the energy-producing process that takes place continuously in the sun and stars. At the core of the sun, at temperatures of 10–15 million degrees Celsius, hydrogen is converted to helium, providing enough energy to sustain life on Earth.

Nuclear fission can be used to produce energy, but has well-known safety concerns. Nuclear fusion could be an everlasting source of energy in the future if it can be developed successfully.

The sun, wind and water can also be used as sources of energy and these can be used indefinitely. They, along with nuclear fusion, are said to be renewable sources of energy. At present, fossil fuels are the most used sources of energy and they are exploited mainly by the western world.

Environmental damage is inevitable from all fuels and has to be accepted to some degree if we are to maintain energy use at present levels.

The economic cost of meeting environmental needs is being funded by the introduction of techniques such as flue gas desulfurisation in the case of coal, in an attempt to reduce the amount of gases emitted to the air. Unleaded petrol is now widely used in cars. Ways of reducing carbon dioxide emissions the environment are being actively investigated.

Renewable energy

Renewable sources of energy offer sustainable alternatives to our dependency on fossil fuels, a means of reducing greenhouse emissions and opportunities to reduce our reliance on imported fuels.

Renewable energy from sources such as the wind, the sun, wood, waste and water are abundantly available in Ireland. Several renewable energy technologies are now commercially viable and capable of supplying clean, economical heat and power.

Wind energy

Wind energy can be harnessed to provide a clean competitive reliable and predictable electricity source to power Ireland in the 21st century.

Wind-generated electricity respects the environment. This results in ancillary costs normally associated with other energy sources being saved; for instance there are no greenhouse gas emissions, no waste to be recycled, no resulting public health problems, etc. It is the ultimate clean energy.

12-44 *Part of a typical wind farm*

The development of wind farms can also contribute to the community within which they are situated, through the generation of both jobs and income.

Solar energy

Solar energy is the ultimate renewable energy source. The sun powers natural cycles on earth like the wind, water flow and plant growth. Humans have learned to use those natural cycles for their energy needs e.g. by making fire for cooking and heating, sailing across oceans, generating electricity with hydropower.

But the sun is also such a reliable source of heat and light that we sometimes take it for granted. Generations have used glass and other materials and structures to capture and magnify the sun's energy and these systems have gradually evolved to form the basis of mature techniques that are used today to harness solar energy.

Three approaches are used to gain maximum benefit of solar energy in buildings:

1. **Passive solar architecture**, a design approach which seeks to:
   - maximise solar gains in the building (through good orientation, layout, and glazing);
   - avoid heat losses through ensuring a high level of insulation and air-tightness of the building;
   - ensure a high degree of comfort by using controlled ventilation and daylighting.
2. **Active solar heating**, a technology that uses solar collectors to transform sunlight into heat to provide space and/or, more commonly, water heating. A correctly sized solar water heating system will cover between 50% and 60% of hot water heating requiremenst with free solar energy.
3. **Solar photovoltaic systems**, which use semiconductor materials to convert solar energy into electricity. This technology is widely used in consumer products such as solar calculators, watches or garden lights, and is increasingly used as a cost-effective solution in Ireland for stand-alone applications where a grid connection is too expensive (e.g. parking meters, caravans or remote holiday homes).

Sustainability and ecology

'Green design', 'energy-conscious design', passive solar design', 'ecological design' and 'sustainable architecture' are all terms that have been used in recent years in relation to the issue of sustainability.

The basic principles of sustainable design are to:
- minimise artificial lighting, heating and mechanical ventilation
- avoid air-conditioning
- conserve water
- use site and materials wisely
- recycle where possible

Sustainable design can produce buildings that are more economic, more comfortable, more humane and more beautiful than conventional designs. Building services make a large contribution to the pollution of air, water and the physical environment. The construction of buildings makes considerable demands on natural resources, and using them makes even more demands.

Buildings generate 'greenhouse gases', which are thought to contribute to global warming. Carbon dioxide (CO_2) emissions account for 50 per cent of greenhouse gases released by human activity.

In Western Europe half of these emissions are produced from the heating, lighting and cooling of buildings.

In Ireland, housing services alone produce more CO_2 than either the transport or industrial sectors.

Carbon dioxide is also produced during electricity generation, which is required for the manufacture of building materials and for the construction of buildings.

The production of timber for the building industry contributes to deforestation, which in turn reduces the Earth's capacity to convert carbon dioxide into oxygen.

The quantity of CFCs (chlorofluorocarbons) in the atmosphere is relatively small, but weight for weight they are ten to twenty times more damaging than carbon dioxide. In Western Europe 10 per cent of CFC use is related to refrigerants, insulation and solvents used in buildings.

Electricity used for building services accounts for a significant proportion of sulphur dioxide (SO_2) and nitrous oxide (NO_X) emissions. Dissolved to form acid rain, these chemicals are killing forests, threatening animal life and damaging buildings across Europe.

At a more local level these chemicals in the air cause health problems, particularly to children, pregnant women, the elderly and people with respiratory problems.

The EU is monitoring CO_2 emissions and the use of CFCs.

Sustainable architecture

Traditional building practices were intelligent responses to familiar circumstances. The need to site buildings so as to maximise shelter, or to create it through planting, was taken for granted. The movement of water was controlled, ground water was directed through stone drains, and materials that allowed the building to breathe resisted the penetration of water.

An awareness of daily and seasonal cycles was reflected in the arrangement of spaces and the placing of openings. Simple vernacular buildings demonstrated intelligent decision-making. This arose from an appreciation to work with, rather than against, the characteristics of site and nature, and from a thorough understanding of techniques and materials.

The context within which building occurs is complex and ever changing. The informed design response to site and climate, and the willingness to exploit environment-friendly materials and technologies must meet the demands of today.

How sustainable can you get?

No building can be completely green. There are degrees of sustainability, and the client along with the design team must decide what is appropriate, what is feasible, and what is affordable.

General principles of sustainable design:
- An integrated approach will produce better results than a piecemeal one.

    For example, there is little point in reducing the glazing ratio on the north-facing facades to control heat loss, if it means that artificial lighting has to be switched on all day.
- Simple solutions are preferred to complex ones and over-design.

    For example, it is better to provide just enough conventional glazing than to specify larger or smaller areas of high technology windows, which may need daylighting devices.
- The energy used during the life of a building is always much greater than the energy embodied in its fabric.

- Saving energy is usually more cost effective than producing or reclaiming it.
- The smaller a building's energy requirements, the greater the chance that renewable energy will suffice.
- Primary energy consumption, rather than consumption at point of use, is what matters.

    For example, about two-thirds of the energy used to generate electricity goes to waste. This means that a unit of electricity results in nearly three times as much CO_2 emissions as a unit of gas or oil used in an efficient boiler.
- Many sustainable design decisions have a multiplier effect.

    For example, specifying water-conserving bathroom taps reduces the demand on water supplies, reduces the load on sewage treatment plants, and saves on the energy used in both processes.
- Design for durability is superior to design for recycling. And recycling is superior to waste.

Insulation standards for new houses

New standards introduced in 2003 have reduced energy requirements for space and water heating by 23% to 33%, depending on the type and size of dwelling. This will give a reduction in CO_2 emissions of more than 300,000 tonnes per year for 2012.

Approximately 40% of CO_2 emissions are attributable to energy used in the heating, cooling, and lighting of buildings. Since energy use in buildings is a major part of the greenhouse gas problem, energy conservation in buildings must be an integral part of the solution.

Thermal performance and insulation standards for new dwellings (2003) are as follows:

Building element	Thermal performance U-value w/m²K	Insulation level millimetres (mm)
Roof	0.16	250–300
Wall	0.27	100–150
Floor	0.25	100

Note: It is not possible to specify insulation thickness required for any particular building element because of the variety of insulation materials of varying characteristics available in the market place, and because of the flexibility allowed to designers as to how compliance is to be achieved. Lower thicknesses of insulation are possible if materials with better thermal conductivity, are used. For example, for walls, 60 mm urethane boards achieve the required U-value of 0.27 w/m²K. This means no design change is required in relation to cavity wall details.

Limitation of heat loss through the building fabric

Thermal conductivity (λ-value) relates to a material or substance, and is a measure of the rate at which heat passes through that material or substance. It is expressed. It is expressed in units of Watts per metre per Kelvin (W/mK).

Thermal transmittance (U-value) relates to a building component or structure, and is a measure of the rate at which heat passes through that component or structure when unit temperature difference is maintained between the ambient air temperatures on each side. It is expressed in units of Watts per square metre per Kelvin of air temperature difference (W/m²K).

Average U-values used or calculated relate to elements exposed directly or indirectly to the outside air. This includes floors directly in contact with the ground, suspended ground floors and elements exposed indirectly through unheated spaces.

U-values and λ-values are dependent on a number of factors. For particular materials, products and components, measured values should be used, where available.

In the absence of certified measured values, values of thermal conductivity given in Table 12-2 may be used. This table contains λ-values for some common building materials. In the absence of certified measured values, U-values may be derived by calculation.

Note: the values in this table are indicative only. Certified values should be used, if available. This applies particularly to insulation materials.

Material	Density (kg/m³)	Thermal conductivity (W/mK)	Material	Density (kg/m³)	Thermal conductivity (W/mK)
Clay brickwork (outer leaf)	1700	0.77	Natural slate	2500	2.20
Clay brickwork (inner leaf)	1700	0.56	Concrete tiles	2100	1.50
Concrete block (heavyweight)	2000	1.33	Fibrous cement slates	1800	0.45
Concrete block (medium weight)	1400	0.57	Ceramic tiles	2300	1.30
Concrete block (autoclaved aerated)	600	0.18	Plastic tiles	1000	0.20
Cast concrete (high density)	2400	2.00	Asphalt	1700	0.50
Cast concrete (medium density)	1800	1.15	Felt bitumen layers	1100	0.23
Aerated concrete slab	500	0.16	Timber, softwood	500	0.13
Concrete screed	1200	0.41	Timber, hardwood	700	0.18
Reinforced concrete (1% steel)	2300	2.30	Wood wool slab	500	0.10
Reinforced concrete (2% steel)	2400	2.40	Wood-based panels		
Wall ties, stainless steel	7900	17.00	(plywood, chipboard etc.)	600	0.13
Wall ties, galvanised steel	7800	50.00	Expanded polystyrene (HD)	25	0.035
Mortar (protected)	1750	0.88	Expanded polystyrene (SD)	15	0.037
Mortar (exposed)	1750	0.94	Extruded polystyrene	30	0.025
External rendering (cement, sand)	1800	1.00	Glass fibre/wool quilt	12	0.040
Plaster (gypsum lightweight)	600	0.18	Glass fibre/wool batt	25	0.035
Plaster (gypsum)	1200	1.43	Phenol foam	30	0.025
Plasterboard	900	0.25	Polyurethane board	30	0.025

Table 12-2 Thermal conductivity of some common building materials

Calculation of U-values

To calculate the U-value of a building element (wall or roof), the thermal resistance of each component is calculated, and these thermal resistances, together with surface resistances are combined to yield the total thermal resistance and U-value. Following are three typical construction details which highlight the procedure for calculating U-values.

EXAMPLE 1 Masonry cavity wall

See Fig. 12-39 and Table 12-3.

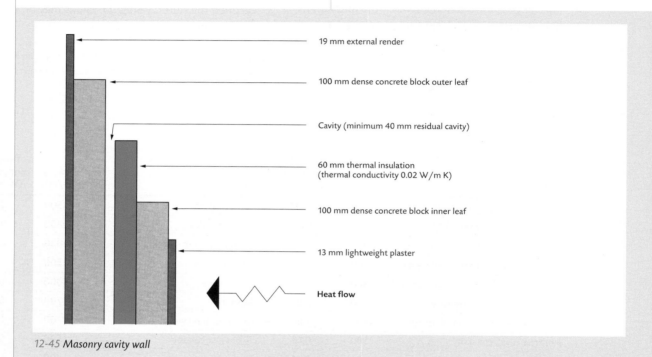

19 mm external render

100 mm dense concrete block outer leaf

Cavity (minimum 40 mm residual cavity)

60 mm thermal insulation
(thermal conductivity 0.02 W/m K)

100 mm dense concrete block inner leaf

13 mm lightweight plaster

Heat flow

12-45 Masonry cavity wall

Surface	Thickness (m)	Conductivity (W/mK)	Resistance (m²K/W)
External surface			0.04
External render	0.019	0.57	0.03
Concrete block	0.100	1.13	0.09
Air cavity			0.18
Insulation	0.060	0.020	3.00
Concrete block	0.100	1.13	0.09
Plaster (lightweight)	0.013	0.18	0.07
Internal surface			0.13
Total resistance			3.63

U-value of construction = 1/3.63 = 0.27 W/m²K

Table 12-3 Example 1, masonry cavity wall

EXAMPLE 2 Timber-frame wall
See Fig. 12-40 and Table 12-4.

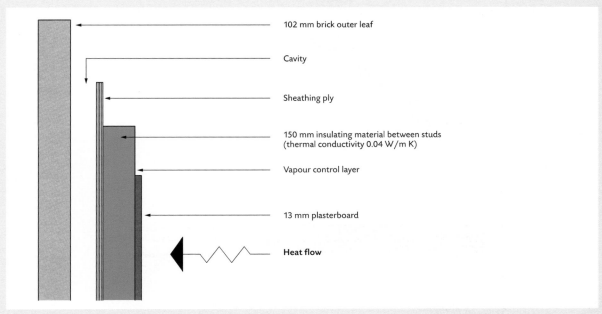

102 mm brick outer leaf

Cavity

Sheathing ply

150 mm insulating material between studs
(thermal conductivity 0.04 W/m K)

Vapour control layer

13 mm plasterboard

Heat flow

12-46 Timber-frame wall

Surface	Thickness (m)	Conductivity (W/mK)	Resistance (m²K/W)
External surface			0.04
Brick outer leaf	0.102	0.77	0.132
Air cavity			0.18
Sheathing ply	0.012	0.13	0.92
Mineral wool insulation	0.150	0.04	3.75
Timber studs	0.150	0.13	1.154
Plasterboard	0.013	0.25	0.052
Internal surface			0.13
Total resistance			5.53

U-value of construction = $1/5.53$ = 0.18 W/m²K

Table 12-4 Example 2, timber frame wall

NOTE Timber frame construction using the 89 mm
stud can still be retained, provided it is filled with
quilt and insulated on the room side using a 50.5
mm insulated plasterslab.

**EXAMPLE 3 Domestic pitched roof
with insulation at ceiling level
(between and over joists)**

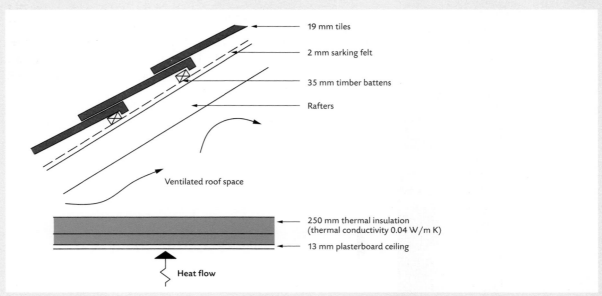

19 mm tiles

2 mm sarking felt

35 mm timber battens

Rafters

Ventilated roof space

250 mm thermal insulation
(thermal conductivity 0.04 W/m K)

13 mm plasterboard ceiling

Heat flow

12-47 Domestic pitched roof

Surface	Thickness (m)	Conductivity (W/mK)	Resistance (m²K/W)
External surface			0.04
Roof space (including sloping construction and roof cavity)			0.20
Mineral wool (continuous layer)	0.150	0.04	3.75
Mineral wool (between joists)	0.100	0.04	2.50
Timber joists	0.100	0.13	1.154
Plasterboard	0.013	0.25	0.052
Internal surface			0.100
Total resistance			7.796

U-value of construction = $1/7.796 = 0.13$ W/m²K

Table 12-5 Example 3, domestic pitched roof

NOTE The Health and Safety Authority have expressed concerns regarding the use of a 250–300 mm quilt in the attic, as the joists are no longer visible. The electrical services will be concealed under the quilt, increasing the possibility of overheating.

As an alternative, consider using a 150 mm quilt with an insulated plasterslab fixed to the underneath of the joists.

Calculation of u-values for common constructions from tables

For many typical roof, wall and floor constructions, the thickness of insulation required to achieve a particular U-value can be calculated approximately by the use of the appropriate table. The tables can also be used to estimate the U-value achieved by a particular thickness of insulating material. Intermediate U-values and values of required thickness of insulation can be obtained from the tables by linear interpolation.

EXAMPLE 4
Partially filled cavity
Determine the U-value of the construction shown.

Table 12-6 gives U-values of 0.29 W/m²K and 0.25 W/m²K for 100 mm insulation of thermal conductivity of 0.035 W/mK and 0.030 W/mK respectively. By linear interpolation, the U-value of this construction, with 100 mm of insulation of thermal conductivity of 0.032 W/mK, is 0.27 W/m²K.

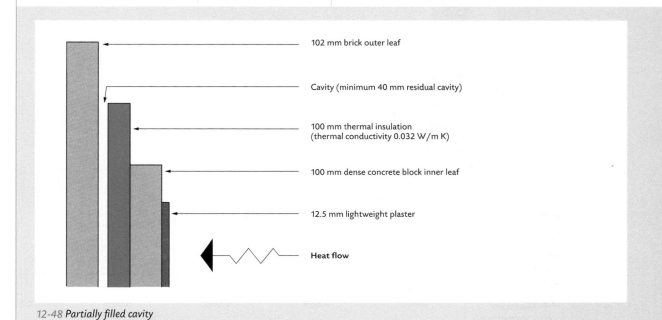

102 mm brick outer leaf

Cavity (minimum 40 mm residual cavity)

100 mm thermal insulation
(thermal conductivity 0.032 W/m K)

100 mm dense concrete block inner leaf

12.5 mm lightweight plaster

Heat flow

12-48 Partially filled cavity

Thickness of insulation (mm)	Thermal conductivity of insulation [W/mK]				
	0.040	0.035	0.030	0.025	0.020
	U-value of construction [W/m²K]				
60	0.48	0.43	0.39	0.33	0.28
80	0.39	0.35	0.31	0.26	0.22
100	0.32	0.29	0.25	0.22	0.18

Table 12-6 U-values for brick (or rendered dense concrete block) external leaf, partial fill insulation, dense concrete block inner leaf, plaster (or plasterboard) internal finish

EXAMPLE 5
Timber frame wall
Determine the U-value of this construction.

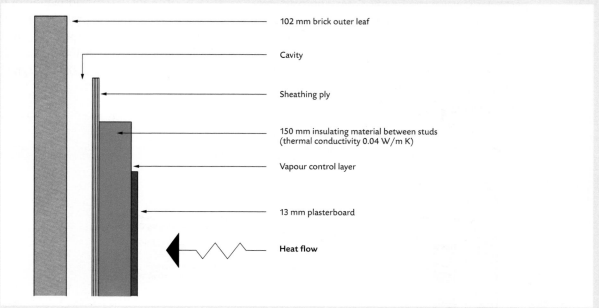

102 mm brick outer leaf

Cavity

Sheathing ply

150 mm insulating material between studs
(thermal conductivity 0.04 W/m K)

Vapour control layer

13 mm plasterboard

Heat flow

12-49 Timber-frame wall

Table 12-7 gives the U-value for 150 mm of insulation of thermal conductivity of 0.04 W/mK as 0.27 W/m²K.

Thickness of insulation (mm)	Thermal conductivity of insulation [W/mK]				
	0.040	0.035	0.030	0.025	0.020
	U-value of construction [W/m²K]				
100	0.38	0.35	0.32	0.29	0.26
120	0.32	0.29	0.27	0.24	0.22
150	0.27	0.25	0.23	0.21	0.18
175	0.24	0.22	0.20	0.18	0.16

Table 12-7 U-values for brick (or rendered dense concrete block) external leaf, timber frame inner leaf, insulation between timber studs, plasterboard internal finish

EXAMPLE 6
Pitched roof
Determine the U-value of this construction.

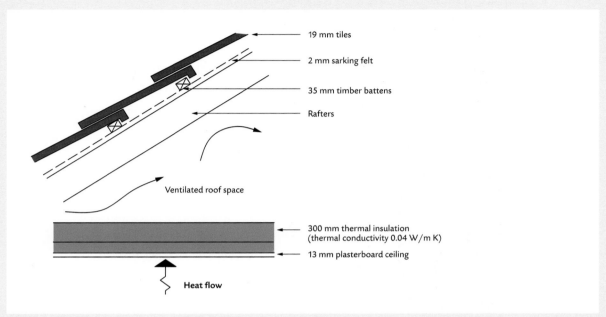

19 mm tiles

2 mm sarking felt

35 mm timber battens

Rafters

Ventilated roof space

300 mm thermal insulation
(thermal conductivity 0.04 W/m K)

13 mm plasterboard ceiling

Heat flow

12-50 Pitched roof

Table 12-8 gives the U-value for 300 mm of insulation of thermal conductivity of 0.04 W/mK as 0.13 W/m²K.

Thickness of insulation (mm)	Thermal conductivity of insulation [W/mK]				
	0.040	0.035	0.030	0.025	0.020
	U-value of construction [W/m²K]				
150	0.26	0.24	0.21	0.18	0.15
175	0.23	0.20	0.18	0.15	0.13
200	0.20	0.18	0.15	0.13	0.11
225	0.18	0.16	0.14	0.12	0.10
250	0.16	0.14	0.12	0.10	0.09
275	0.14	0.13	0.11	0.09	0.08
300	0.13	0.12	0.10	0.09	0.07

Table 12-8 U-values for tiled or slated pitched roof, ventilated roof space, insulation placed between and over joists at ceiling level

Many other tables exist for variations in common constructions. It would be outside the scope of this text to deal with all possible variations. Additional information may be obtained from the Department of the Environment website (www.environ.ie).

Chapter 13

Drainage and waste disposal

Clean water and air

Clean water

The management of the world's water supplies will be one of the major challenges of the 21st century. More than 97 per cent of the world's water supply is in the oceans, with another 2 per cent frozen in ice sheets and glaciers. Groundwater accounts for about 0.6 per cent, rivers and lakes 0.02 per cent and water vapour in the atmosphere about 0.001 per cent.

THE WATER CYCLE Groundwater is constantly moving downwards towards the oceans (because of gravity), and therefore plays an important part in the water (hydrological) cycle. The water cycle consists of the continuous exchange of water between the oceans and the land through the atmosphere.

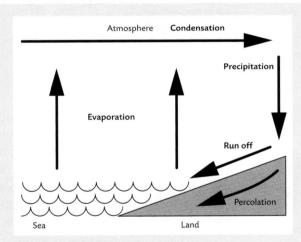

13-1 The water cycle

The stages in the water cycle are:

- **Evaporation.** Through the heat of the sun, water evaporates from the liquid state to water vapour. This warm moisture-laden air rises into the atmosphere where it is circulated.
- **Condensation.** This occurs when the water vapour cools below its dew point and liquid water appears as clouds.
- **Precipitation.** This is a further step in the condensation process. The water droplets in the clouds become too large to remain suspended in the air and fall as rain, snow or hail.
- **Run-off.** Most of the water that falls on the land flows towards the sea by two main routes:
  - as **surface water** in streams and rivers, and
  - as **groundwater**, which permeates through the soil.

WATER CONSUMPTION has increased considerably due to a variety of factors, including an increase in the number of household appliances such as dishwashers and washing machines. The average daily consumption in the home amounts to about 180 litres per person, which is the equivalent of about two baths.

WATER QUALITY The quality of water is affected by its physical properties, including colour, temperature and taste; its biological properties, including bacteria content and the amount of dissolved oxygen; and its chemical properties, including hardness and dissolved solids.

Pollution occurs when agricultural or industrial waste, or untreated sewage, enters the water cycle. Warm water entering a river reduces the oxygen content of the river water, which affects the fish population. Most developed countries now have laws that prohibit water pollution.

In order to provide clean, fresh water for drinking, cooking and washing, the water supply is treated to make it safe to drink. Different types of treatments are used to remove natural impurities and human pollutants.

Typically, water from a river is first passed through a coarse mesh to remove large particles of debris, fish and plants. It is then pumped into a reservoir where it is stored for a number of weeks. This period allows impurities to settle to the bottom, and bacteria numbers decline because there is less material present on which they can feed.

Chlorine and/or other chemicals may be added to kill off any remaining bacteria.

The water is then passed through a very fine mesh to remove any remaining tiny particles and plants. Finally the water is passed through filters to remove any dead bacteria or extremely fine particles. At this stage water may be aerated to increase the amount of oxygen it contains and give it a fresher taste.

Clean air

Air pollution has been a problem since the Industrial Revolution. Burning coal and petroleum produces sulfur oxides. Fluorides result from smelting and glass and ceramics manufacture. Levels of ammonia, chlorine, ethylene, mercaptans, carbon monoxide, and nitrogen oxides in the air are rising. Motor vehicles and the growing needs of rising human population produce photochemical air pollution.

Photochemistry is the branch of chemistry concerned with the chemical effects of light and other electro-magnetic radiations.

The mixture of pollutants from all sources, including agriculture, has released a host of contaminants into the air. The effect of these pollutants on food, fibre, forage, and forest crops is variable, depending on concentration, geography, and weather conditions. Damage to crops by air pollution results in economic loss.

Pollutants that enter the air from sources other than agriculture are classified as: acid gases; products of combustion; products of reactions in the air; and miscellaneous effluents.

It is the immediate effect of air pollution on urban atmospheres that is most noticeable and causes the strongest public reaction.

The task of cleaning up air pollution is not insurmountable. Methods of controlling air pollution include:

- use of fuels that are low in pollutants, such as low-sulfur forms of petroleum
- more complete burning of fossil fuels, at best to carbon dioxide and water
- 'scrubbing' of industrial smokestacks or precipitation of pollutants from them, often in combination with a recycling of the pollutants
- the shift to less-polluting forms of power generation, such as solar or wind energy in place of fossil fuels

Major improvements in air quality are achievable, as Dublin's switch to 'smokeless' coal, has shown.

Climatic effects of polluted air

The climatic effects of air pollutants are less obvious than local concentrations of pollution, but potentially more important. As a result of the growing worldwide consumption of fossil fuels, atmospheric carbon dioxide levels have increased steadily since 1900, and the rate of increase is accelerating.

The output of carbon dioxide is believed by some to have reached a point such that it may exceed the capacity of plant life both to remove it from the atmosphere and the rate at which it goes into solution in the oceans. (The ocean is a large potential repository for carbon dioxide. Eventually the ocean absorbs over 85% of the carbon dioxide released to the atmosphere.)

GLOBAL WARMING Carbon dioxide and other gases create a 'greenhouse effect' in the atmosphere. Like glass in a greenhouse, this allows light rays from the sun to pass through, but it does not allow the heat generated when sunlight is absorbed by the surface of the earth to escape.

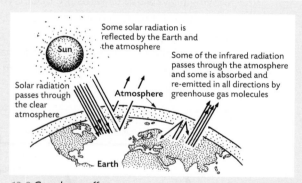

Some solar radiation is reflected by the Earth and the atmosphere

Some of the infrared radiation passes through the atmosphere and some is absorbed and re-emitted in all directions by greenhouse gas molecules

Solar radiation passes through the clear atmosphere

Atmosphere

Earth

13-2 Greenhouse effect

An increase in the amount of carbon dioxide in the atmosphere can cause an increase in the temperature of the lower atmosphere. If allowed to continue, this could cause melting of the polar ice caps, a rise in sea levels, and flooding of coastal areas of the world. There is every reason to fear that such a climatic change may take place.

OZONE DEPLETION Scientists fear that the ozone layer of the atmosphere is being depleted by the chemical action of chlorofluorocarbons emitted from aerosol cans and refrigerators and by pollutants from rockets and supersonic aircraft. Depletion of the ozone layer, which absorbs ultraviolet radiation from the Sun, would have serious effects on living organisms on the Earth's surface, including increasing frequency of skin cancer among humans.

ACID RAIN is another climatic effect of pollution. It is caused when sulfur dioxide and nitrogen oxides from the burning of fossil fuels combine with water vapour in the atmosphere. The resulting precipitation is damaging to water, forest, and soil resources.

13-3 Acid rain formation

Acid rain is blamed for the disappearance of fish from many lakes, for the widespread death of forests in Europe, and for damaging tree growth in the United States and Canada. Reports also indicate that it can corrode buildings and be hazardous to human health. Because the contaminants are carried long distances, the sources of acid rain are difficult to pinpoint and therefore difficult to control.

To reduce the impact of acid rain use 'green' fuels where possible and ensure that boilers are operating efficiently by having them serviced regularly. Proper industrial monitoring procedures will help reduce and eventually prevent current toxic emission levels.

Surface water drainage

The surface water discharge from roofs, paved areas and yards must be conveyed to a suitable drainage system. Roofs are designed with suitable falls towards the gutters. The gutters are in turn connected to vertical down-pipes, which carry the water to the drainage system.

The drainage system can consist of:
- drains connected to a soak-way
- drains connected to the sewer
- drains connected to a surface water sewer, or a surface water drain

If the drain is connected to a combined sewer, then an indirect connection to the drain must be fitted.

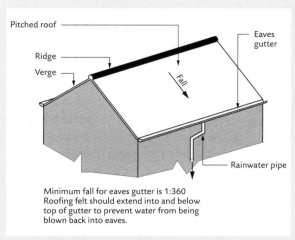

Minimum fall for eaves gutter is 1:360
Roofing felt should extend into and below top of gutter to prevent water from being blown back into eaves.

13-4 Surface water removal from roofs

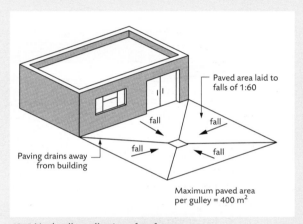

13-5 Yard gulley collection of surface water

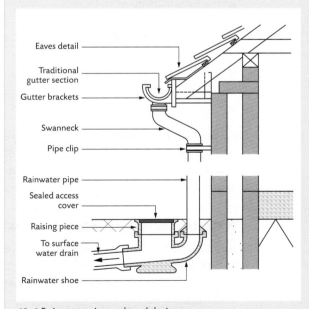

13-6 Rainwater pipework and drainage

Soakaways

For soakaways to be successful, permeable soil and a water table some way below the surface are required.

The construction of a soakaway consists of digging a pit (hole), filling it with rubble and directing the drain into the rubble. The pit is then filled over. This is usually unsatisfactory as silting occurs and cleaning is not possible. Over time the soakaway becomes ineffective.

An improvement is to build a chamber over the soak-pit to allow for cleaning. A series of percolating drains can also be directed from this chamber, using land drainage pipes.

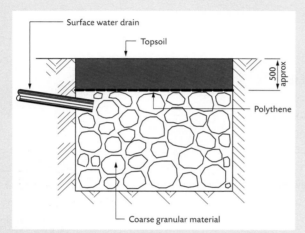

13-7 *Filled soakaways are the most common in this country*

For a soakaway to function effectively the following factors should be taken into account:

- the permeability of the soil
- the area to be drained
- the capacity required to deal with run-off from storms, etc.
- Building Regulations and local authority requirements
- depth of the water table

Following an analysis of these factors more than one soakaway may be required. The size of a soakaway depends on the volume of water discharging to it and the geology of the site.

Kitchen and sanitary hardware

Sanitary appliances can be divided into two sections:

- **Soil appliances:** those used to remove soil water and human excreta, such as water closets and urinals.
- **Waste water appliances:** those used to remove the waste water from the kitchen sink, washbasins, baths and showers.

General requirements for all sanitary appliances:

- made from an impervious material
- quiet when used
- easy to clean
- well-designed shape, fixed at a suitable height

The materials used for sanitary appliances include:

- **Vitreous china.** This is white impervious clay, which is very strong and possesses a high resistance to crazing and staining. Appliances made from vitreous china are non-corrosive, hygienic and easily cleaned.
- **Glazed fire clay.** This is a semi-permeable material, which is very strong and resistant to impact damage.
- **Vitreous enamel.** This is a type of opaque glass used to give a protective coating to a steel or cast-iron base. It is used on baths, sinks and draining boards.
- **Plastic materials.** Perspex, nylon, polypropylene, and glass fibre reinforced plastics require no protective coatings. Appliances made from this range of plastics are very strong, light and do not chip easily. They are easily scratched, however, and they are more expensive than ceramic or vitreous enamel products.
- **Stainless steel.** Stainless steel contains 18% chromium and 8% nickel and this combination gives it a natural resistance to corrosion. Appliances made from stainless steel are light and very durable. Appliances generally consist of sinks and draining boards.

Consider the following factors when selecting sanitary appliances:

- cost
- hygiene
- appearance
- function
- weight, especially if the appliance is supported from the wall

A range of sanitary appliances is shown in Figs. 13-8 to 13-13.

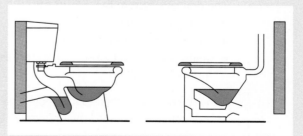

13-8 *Siphonic water closet pans: double trap (left); single trap (right)*

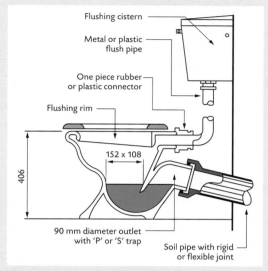

13-9 *Ceramic washdown WC pan*

Flushing cistern

Metal or plastic flush pipe

One piece rubber or plastic connector

Flushing rim

152 x 108

406

90 mm diameter outlet with 'P' or 'S' trap

Soil pipe with rigid or flexible joint

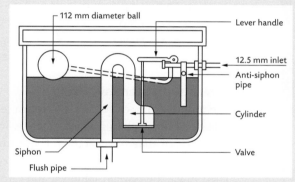

13-10 *WC flushing cistern with anti-siphon pipe*

112 mm diameter ball

Lever handle

12.5 mm inlet

Anti-siphon pipe

Cylinder

Siphon

Valve

Flush pipe

457 x 635 mm

Overflow slot

790

165

32 mm waste

Support bracket

38 mm seal 'P' trap

'S' traps also available

Cleaning eye

Pedestal

838 mm

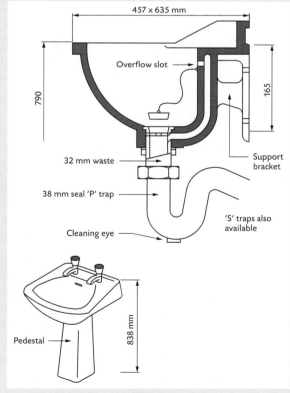

13-11 *Typical wash basin details*

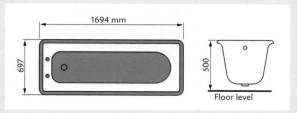

1694 mm

697

500

Floor level

13-12 *Bath details*

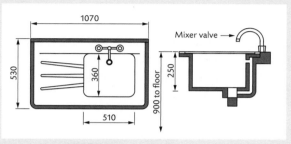

1070

530

360

Mixer valve

250

510

900 to floor

13-13 *Typical sink details*

Effluent/sewage disposal

Domestic sewage consists of human wastes, paper and vegetable matter. This is organic waste because it consists of compounds of carbon and can be broken down by microorganisms into simpler compounds.

Sewerage, as distinct from sewage, is a system of pipes used to collect and carry sewage from domestic premises.

Public sewers, where they exist, are the simplest and best method for disposing of effluent. Where there is no access to a public sewer, a private treatment plant, usually a septic tank and percolation area, must be provided.

The principle of sewage disposal is to pipe it to treatment works where solids are separated and the water is made pure enough to return safely to rivers.

Most towns and cities treat their sewage before disposal to destroy its offensive and unhealthy content. Unfortunately, some coastal towns still discharge raw, untreated sewage directly into the sea. In ideal conditions, seawater rapidly dilutes the sewage, allowing organisms in the sea to digest the waste and render it harmless. Unusual winds or tides, however, may prevent dispersal and sewage may sometimes be swept towards the shore.

Discharging large amounts of untreated sewage directly into the sea would lead to an unacceptable level of coastal pollution. This is the reason local authorities treat sewage.

Sewage treatment processes

In modern treatment works sewage goes through several stages of treatment.

Preliminary treatment deals with large solids which are removed by screening. The sewage then moves on to primary treatment. Here the sewage is allowed into sedimentation tanks where solids settle in the form of sludge.

Secondary treatment is the next stage, also called biological treatment. In secondary treatment the microorganisms are used to take organic matter out of solution so as to form a sludge. The sludge is settled out in a final settling tank.

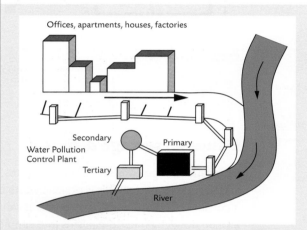

13-14 *Collection and primary, secondary and tertiary treatment of local authority sewage*

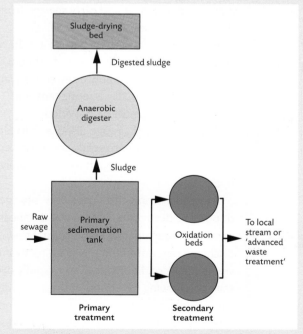

13-15 *Schematic diagram of sewage treatment plant*

Tertiary treatment, if necessary, can reduce the organic matter content further. Several forms of tertiary treatment are available, including:

- passing the effluent over grass plots
- retaining the effluent in lagoons
- filtering through sand beds
- using a bed of pebbles or wedge wire in the final settling tanks

A number of treatment plants in Ireland have tertiary treatment (using the grass plot or pebble bed/wedge wire system).

Septic tanks

Septic tanks are used in rural areas that do not have access to a public sewer. A septic tank is a private sewage treatment plant, which liquifies and partially purifies sewage. Septic tanks need very little maintenance or servicing, and should remain fully functional for a number of years.

Water containing disinfectants or detergents should be prevented from entering the septic tank. Such water will prevent the tank operating properly by killing the bacteria that break down the solids.

How a septic tank works

The purpose of a septic tank is to retain sewage for at least 24 hours, during which time it is liquified by the action of anaerobic bacteria. These are micro-organisms that thrive in the absence of oxygen. They attack the sewage, liquefy it and cause it to form three distinct layers.

At the surface a thick scum forms, in which the bacteria breed. Beneath this scum is a layer of liquid from which the solids are disposed. The solids settle at the bottom and are digested or liquified, until their volume is significantly reduced. The liquid in the middle is drained off without disturbing the scum above or the sludge beneath. Periodically the remaining solids will have to be removed.

The function of the septic tank is not to purify the sewage but to break it down. In order to function properly, the inlet pipe must not disturb the scum level. It normally consists of a dip pipe, which discharges below the surface of the scum. For the same reason, a variety of baffles prevent the scum from being swept from inlet to outlet.

The liquid that flows from the outlet is far from pure but can be made harmless by being percolated through a filter bed. A filter bed of pebbles or clinker aerates the liquid effluent so that a different type of bacteria, aerobic bacteria, gets to work.

Aerobic means the process depends on oxygen (or air).
***Anaerobic** means the process is not dependent on oxygen.*

Due to the limitations of septic tank treatment, the bacteria in the liquid is still anaerobic when it enters the soak-pit and the change to aerobic takes place gradually.

Septic tank capacity

Septic tanks are available in pre-cast concrete units or they can be built on site. The minimum size is 2725 litres for the tank itself. The size needed will depend on the number of people using it. Each person normally uses 180 litres of water per day and this must be stored for a minimum of 24 hours for the bacterial process to take place.

The total tank capacity is arrived at by making allowances for sludge storage (0.16 m³ per person per year) and additional settlement space according to the average flow over two days (0.36 m³ per person).

The capacity of the septic tank is based on the following formula:

$$C = (180P + 2000) \text{ litres}$$

where C = tank capacity and P = number of persons served, provided that a minimum size for 4 persons is allowed

The tank must be located a minimum distance of 7 m from the dwelling it serves, and must not be

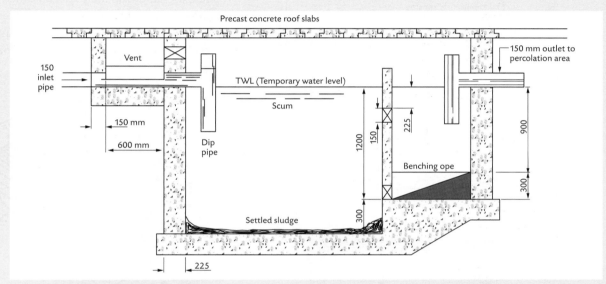

13-16 Section through a septic tank

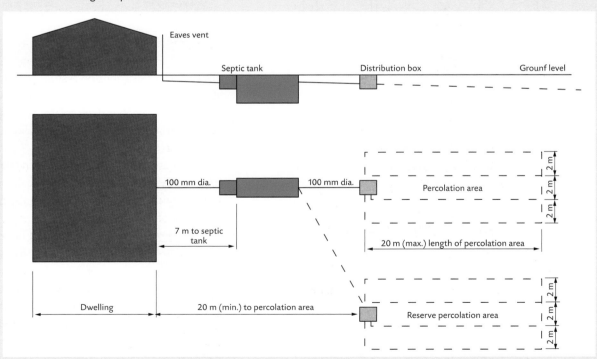

13-17 Typical plan and section of septic tank, distribution box and percolation areas

nearer than 20 m from the nearest point of any other dwelling. The percolation area must be a minimum distance of 20 m from the dwelling served. The percolation area must be a minimum of 10 m from the nearest boundary, stream or ditch and a minimum of 3 m from the boundary of an adjoining site.

The tank length should be three times the tank width with a minimum of 1.5 m below water level. The inlet drain of 100 mm is usually of u-PVC and the pipe from the septic tank outlet should be at least 100 mm in diameter.

No. of bedrooms in the house	Minimum capacity (litres)	Dimensions (metres)		
		L a* d*	W b*	D c*
3	3000	2.0 1.0	1.0	1.0
4	3500	2.2 1.0	1.0	1.1
5	4000	2.4 1.0	1.0	1.2

Minimum capacity of septic tank (litres)

Plan

Section A-A

Section B-B

13-18 *Diagrammatic layout of septic tank*

Liquid effluent treatment systems

A number of effluent treatment systems now exist that can be integrated with new and existing septic tanks or as stand-alone units to meet Building Regulations requirements.

The Puraflo liquid effluent treatment system is one example (Developed by Bord na Mona). It is an aerobic system used in addition to a septic tank. It is fitted with an outlet filter system. The Puraflo system can be used where septic tanks and their percolation areas are not acceptable or where sites fail the percolation tests.

The system consists of:
- a peat filter system fitted to the outlet of the septic tank
- an effluent collecting chamber (sump)
- a pump
- a number of biofibrous media containing modules

The modules are made from polyethylene. Each module uses approximately 2.5 cubic metres of biofibrous media (peat).

Most peat filter systems incorporate a sump after the septic tank. The tank effluent is pumped from

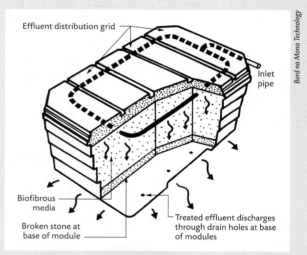

13-19 *Cutaway view of the Puraflo module*

this sump to a distribution system above the peat filter. The effluent is evenly distributed over the surface of the peat and percolates through the media before emerging as a treated liquid at the base of the unit.

The treatment of the waste within the system is achieved by a combination of physical, chemical and biological interactions between the pollutants and the biofibrous media.

Biochemical Oxygen Demand (BOD) *is a measure of the organic pollution of water; the amount of oxygen, in mg per litre of water, absorbed by a sample kept at 20°C for five days.*

Peat-based filters can achieve BOD, SS (suspended solids) and Coliform removal rates in excess of 95%. Based on current information, peat filters should operate satisfactorily for many years before replacement is necessary.

Because of the modular nature of the Puraflo system, it can be expanded to meet large population equivalent requirements. The disposal rate for the treated effluent will depend on local conditions.

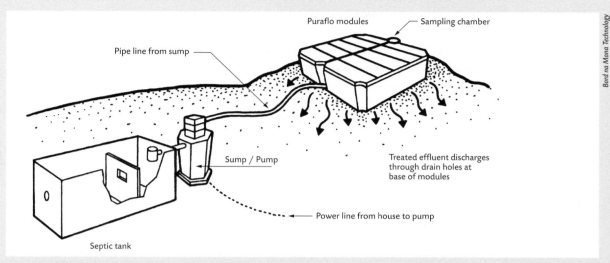

13-20 Single house Puraflo installation with standard concrete sump

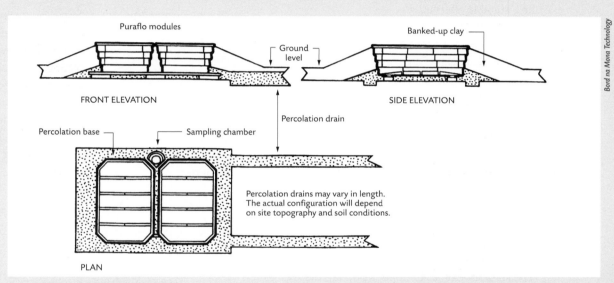

13-21 Typical sub-surface disposal field

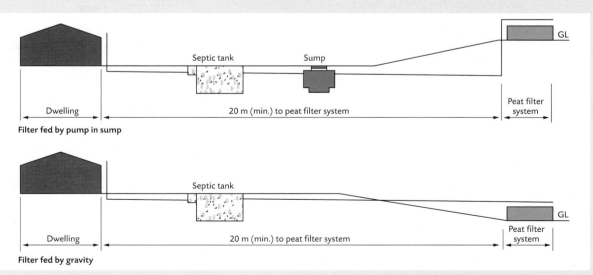

13-22 Layout of peat filter system

Other systems for treating domestic effluent include biological filtration and activated sludge. For these to work properly it is important that the manufacturer's instructions are adhered to and that regular maintenance is carried out.

One of the key features of the alternative treatment plants is the effluent is fed directly to the plant without the need for a septic tank. Depending on the type used little or no percolation may be required as the effluent produced is capable of entering the watercourse.

Trial holes and percolation testing

In many areas in Ireland the soil and subsoil are unsuitable for the treatment and disposal of septic tank effluent. As a result, dwellings with septic tank systems are not recommended in these areas. An effluent treatment system, as described above, may be a suitable alternative.

A percolation area is considered the most effective means of treating the effluent from the septic tank. Soakpits are no longer an acceptable means of treating effluent.

Some definitions related to this topic:

■ **Distribution box:** a chamber between the septic tank and the percolation area, designed to distribute the effluent in equal quantities through the distribution pipes.

■ **Percolation area:** the area of the site where the tank effluent seeps through the soil into the water table. A system of distribution pipes is used.

Site suitability assessment

The suitability of a site depends on factors such as soil type, subsoil and the characteristics of the groundwater. The primary function of the soil and subsoil is to treat and dispose of the effluent in an environmentally safe manner.

The subsoil percolation rate must be high enough to allow the effluent to pass through it without ponding, and low enough to allow purification of the effluent by filtration of harmful microorganisms.

Assessment of the site to determine suitability is based on:

■ a trial hole test to determine groundwater level

■ a second trial hole test to determine percolation

■ a visual inspection of the site and trial hole.

TRIAL HOLE TEST A trial hole measuring 1 m × 1 m × 2 m deep is dug below the invert level of the lowest percolation pipe. The hole is then covered

and left for a minimum of 48 hours. The depth of water (if any) in the hole is then measured.

The site fails if the water in the trial hole is more than 1 m deep. In some instances local information might need to be considered in determining the result.

PERCOLATION TEST This test is to determine the percolating property of the soil and from that the size of the percolating area required. Table 13-1 is used for this purpose.

Subsoil type	Expected percolation rate or value of 'T'
Clean sand and gravel, jointed rock	Less than 5
Fine sand, clayey sand	5–15
Sandy clay, sandy boulder clay	15–30
Clayey boulder clay, silty clay, clay	More than 30

Table 13-1 *Relationship between subsoil types and 'T' values*

The **test procedure** is: test holes measuring 0.3 m × 0.3 m × 0.4 m deep are dug below the invert level of the percolating pipe.

Invert level: the lowest inner surface of a drain.

Approximately 50 litres of water are required for this test. The clear water is poured into the holes to a depth of 300 mm. Water should be added as required to maintain a depth of water of at least 300 mm until the subsoil has swollen and become saturated.

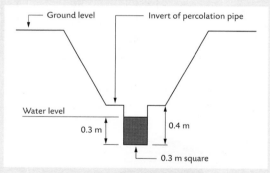

13-23 *Percolation test hole*

Once saturation is reached, the time required for the water to drop 100 mm is recorded. This time expressed in minutes divided by 4 is the time for the water to drop 25 mm and is the percolation value 'T'.

Two percolation tests should be made in the percolation area. A further two tests may be required in the case of sites having an area of 4000 m² or greater, or sites having a slope greater than 1 in 20 or where ground conditions are unfavourable.

The time for the 25 mm water drop ('T') for each of the test results shall be averaged to give the value 'T'. The relationship between the value 'T' and the length of distribution piping required for the percolation area are given in Table 13-2.

Value of 'T' distribution	Length of piping in m
From 5 up to 10	30
Above 10 up to 15	36
Above 15 up to 30	48
Above 30 up to 60	96

Table 13-2 Percolation areas

Notes on 12T-2:
'T' values less than 5 may indicate a percolation rate that is too fast.

'T' values greater than 30 may indicate a percolation rate that is too slow.

'T' values greater than 60 fail the test.

The size of the percolation area may be calculated from the information in this table and by adhering to the following criteria:

1 No distribution pipes should be longer than 20 m.
2 There should be a minimum distance of 2 m between distribution pipes.
3 No part of the percolation area should be within 10 m of the nearest road, boundary, stream or ditch or within 3 m of the boundary of the adjoining site.
4 Site conditions may permit improvement of the above dimensions.
5 No water mains or service pipes should be located within the percolation area.
6 No access roads, driveways or paved areas should be located within the percolation area.

Drainage systems

Above-ground drainage

There are two main types of above-ground drainage. These are the single-stack system and the two-pipe system.

THE SINGLE-STACK SYSTEM This is the most commonly used system (Fig. 13-27 overleaf). The soil and waste water discharges into a single pipe or stack. The efficient working of a single-stack system is dependent on all the branches being as short and as closely grouped on the stack as possible.

Regulations and specific guidelines exist for correct installations of branches and appliances.

For effective operation of the single-stack system the following points must be adhered to:
- each appliance should be connected separately to the stack
- the stack should be vertical to avoid plug formations
- observe the regulations for the diameter, length, fall and connection to the stack of the waste pipe servicing the appliance

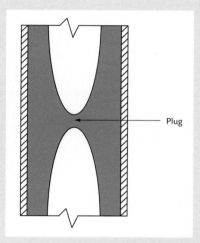

13-24 Flow in vertical pipe showing 'plug' formation

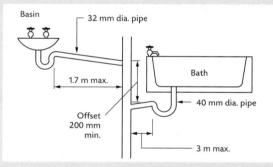

13-25 Regulations governing bath and wash basin connections to single stack system

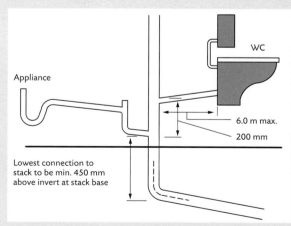

13-26 Regulations governing water closet (WC) branch connection to single stack system

Compliance with these guidelines will prevent pressure fluctuations and self-siphonage occurring from the use of other sanitary appliances (Figs. 13-25, 13-26).

The forerunner to the single-stack system was called the one-pipe system. This system was developed during the 1930s. Its use was almost exclusively limited to large multi-storey buildings.

With a one-pipe system the distinction between 'soil' and 'waste' appliances was abandoned. All wastes were connected to one main soil and waste pipe, at least 100 mm in internal diameter.

To guard against induced siphonage, all baths, basins, bidets and sinks connected to it had to have deep seal traps (75 mm) and the trap of each appliance had to be ventilated into a main vent pipe (Fig. 13-28).

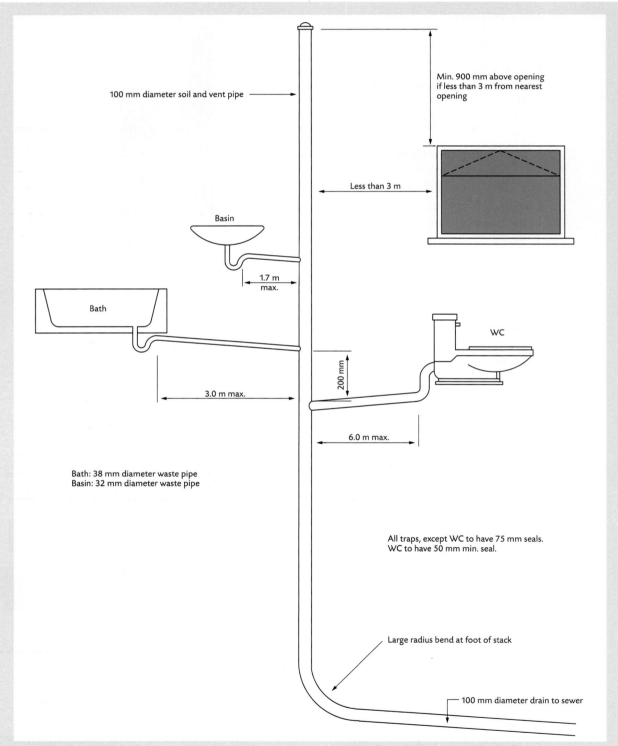

100 mm diameter soil and vent pipe

Min. 900 mm above opening if less than 3 m from nearest opening

Less than 3 m

Basin

1.7 m max.

Bath

3.0 m max.

200 mm

WC

6.0 m max.

Bath: 38 mm diameter waste pipe
Basin: 32 mm diameter waste pipe

All traps, except WC to have 75 mm seals.
WC to have 50 mm min. seal.

Large radius bend at foot of stack

100 mm diameter drain to sewer

13-27 The single-stack system

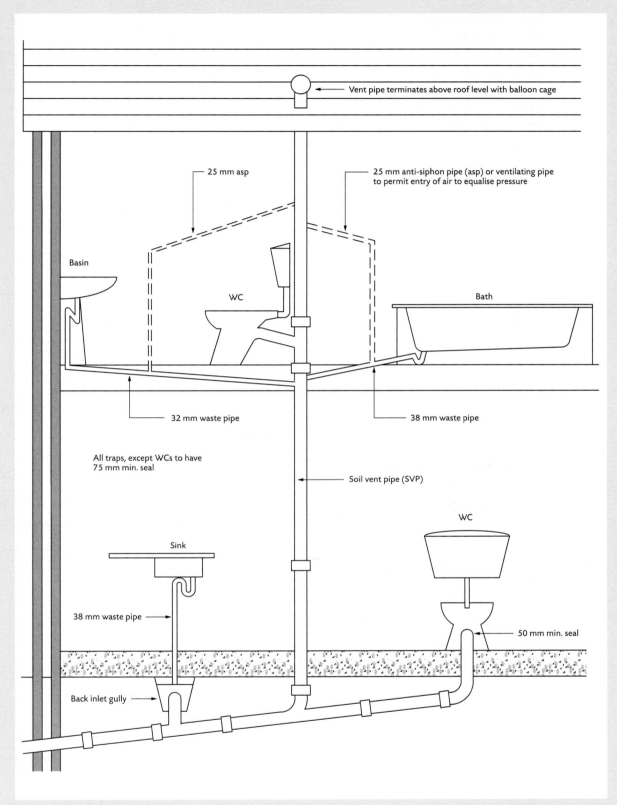

Vent pipe terminates above roof level with balloon cage

25 mm asp

25 mm anti-siphon pipe (asp) or ventilating pipe
to permit entry of air to equalise pressure

Basin

WC

Bath

32 mm waste pipe

38 mm waste pipe

All traps, except WCs to have
75 mm min. seal

Soil vent pipe (SVP)

Sink

WC

38 mm waste pipe

50 mm min. seal

Back inlet gully

13-28 **The one-pipe system**

THE TWO-PIPE SYSTEM In the two-pipe system, found in homes built before the 1930s, soil and waste discharges are piped separately to the ground drain (Fig. 13-29).

Soil describes waste from the WC; **waste** describes water not contaminated by soil (discharge from wash basins, sinks, baths etc.).

The two pipes may or may not be provided with ventilation pipes to balance out pressure in the system depending on its size. A variation of the two-pipe system is still occasionally used for bungalows, but seldom on two-storey houses as the amount of pipe work is considered extravagant.

The hopper head used in this system for collecting bath and basin waste can become foul smelling in hot weather, and its waste pipe may become blocked by dead leaves at other times. This causes the hopper to overflow, leaving stains on the wall of the building.

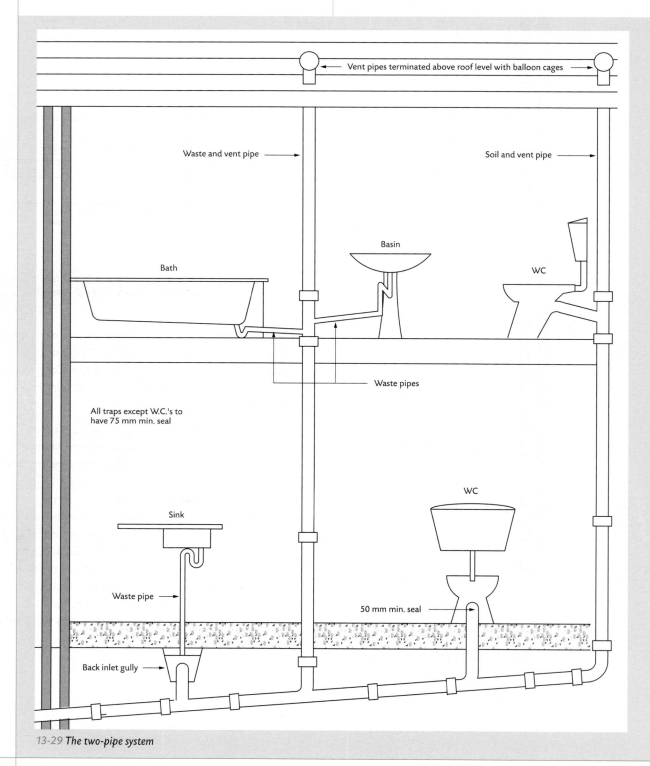

13-29 The two-pipe system

Siphonage and compression

The design of household drainage systems is a complicated business, governed by strict rules. The most important of these specify sizes and maximum and minimum lengths for the discharge pipes joining outlets to the waste or soil stacks. Other rules specify the correct fall for each type of discharge pipe and state where pipes can join the stacks in relation to one another. Once these rules are obeyed, the drainage should function satisfactorily as long as it is not blocked.

SIPHONAGE When the discharge pipe from an outlet is too small, too long or at too steep a slope, wastewater passing down it can create a vacuum and suck out the water in the trap beneath the unit. A gurgling noise results when the outlet is drained and the net result may be foul air entering the room because there is no longer a water seal to prevent this.

Similar problems can occur if two discharge pipes are connected opposite each other at exactly the same point on the stack; water leaving one sucks out the water in the trap of the other.

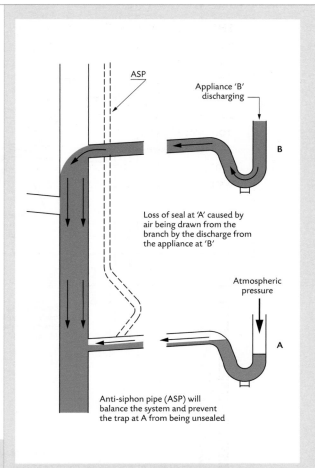

13-31 Induced siphonage: unsealing of the trap at 'A' due to air pressure changes in the pipes caused by discharge flow from 'B'.

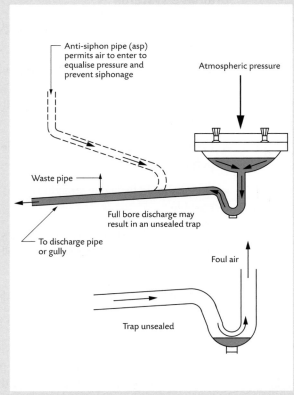

13-30 Self-siphonage: full-bore discharge may result in an unsealed trap.

The practical solution to the problem of siphonage is to dismantle the offending pipe work and re-assemble it according to proper design rules. An alternative solution is to fit an anti-siphonage trap to the particular outlet.

COMPRESSION is simply the build-up of abnormally high pressure somewhere in the discharge system. It can manifest itself in a number of ways:

If a discharge enters the stack high up and another one enters lower down at the same time, the air between the two is compressed. This could result in one discharge 'blowing back' through the discharge pipe of another outlet. Alternatively the pressure may prevent the upper discharge from leaving the outlet (Fig. 13-32 overleaf).

The solution to compression is to fit a vent pipe to the afflicted discharge pipe.

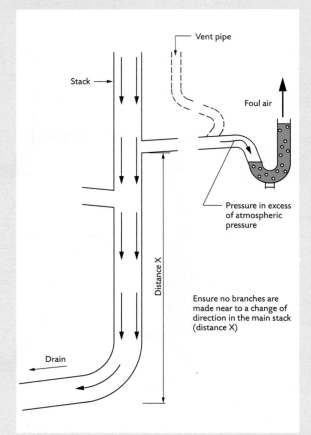

13-32 *Compression or back-pressure. Pressure build up by compression at foot of stack causes air to be forced into the lower branches and may bubble through the lower trap seals.*

Below-ground drainage

Foul water is the discharge from WC pans, basins, baths and sinks. Surface water is rainwater from roofs, paths and paved areas.

In a 'separate drains system', foul discharge and surface water each have separate underground drains leading to separate sewers.

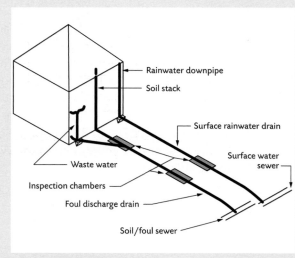

13-33 *The separate drains system*

In a 'combined drains system', foul and surface water are discharged to a common or combined drain system that in turn discharges to a combined public sewer. Combined drain systems are seldom used as they put too much strain on the sewage system during heavy rainfall. Some local authorities insist that surface water is drained to a soak way.

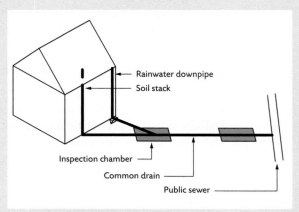

13-34 *The combined drains system*

Design principles of underground drainage systems

- Materials should have adequate strength and durability.

- Diameter of drain to be as small as practicable. For soil drains the minimum diameter allowed is 100 mm and for surface water drains the minimum allowed is 75 mm.

- Every part of a drain must be accessible for the purposes of inspection and cleaning.

- Drains should be laid in straight runs as far as possible.

- Drains must be laid to a gradient that will render them self-cleansing. **Maguire's rule** will give a gradient with a reasonable velocity:

  gradient = diameter of pipe (mm) / 2.5

  therefore for a 100 mm diameter pipe the gradient is 1 in 40.

- Every drain inlet should be trapped to prevent the entry of foul air into the building, the minimum seal required is 50 mm. Rainwater drains need not be trapped unless they connect with a soil drain or sewer.

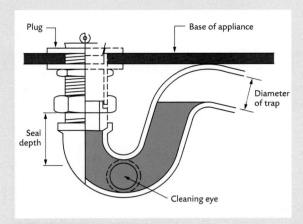

13-35 *Typical trap*

- Inspection chambers or manholes should be placed at changes of direction and gradient if these changes would prevent the drain from being readily cleaned.

- Inspection chambers must also be placed within 12.5 m of a drain junction, the maximum distance allowed between manholes is 90 m.

- Junctions between drains must be arranged so that the incoming drain joins at an oblique angle in the direction of the main flow.

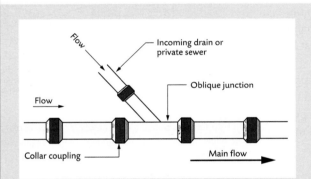

13-36 *Incoming drain connected obliquely to main drain*

- Avoid drains under buildings if possible. Where they occur they must be protected to ensure water tightness and to prevent damage. The usual methods employed are: (i) encase the drain with 150 mm (min.) of mass concrete and (ii) use cast iron pipes under the building.

- Drains that are within 1 metre of the buildings and below the foundation level must be backfilled with concrete up to the level of the underside of the foundations.

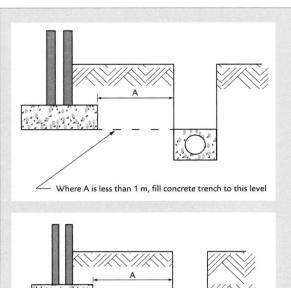

13-37 *Pipe runs near buildings*

- Where possible the minimum invert level to a drain should be 450 mm to avoid damage by ground movement and traffic. The invert level is the lowest level of the bore of a drain.

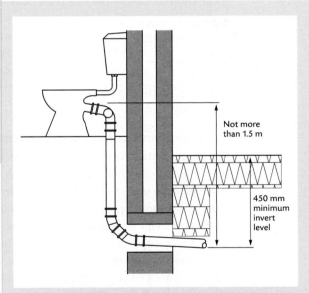

13-38 *The minimum invert level to avoid damage. The maximum drop for discharge from a ground floor WC is also shown.*

Layout of drains

The layout of drains should be as simple as possible and the runs as short as possible, this reduces costs and minimises the effort involved in laying.

Pipes should, where possible, be laid in straight lines from the building. If a change of direction cannot be avoided and the angle exceeds 45°, two bends should be used. All junctions should be oblique and the contained angle not more than 45°.

Pipes should not be planned for under new buildings. Where this is necessary the pipe work must be cased in a concrete sleeve. A pipe diameter of 110 mm is normally sufficient for domestic purposes and is also suitable for the soil stack connection.

Pipes should be laid to a gradient of at least 1:70. Where the rate of flow is likely to be small, as in a pipe length connecting a gully trap with the inspection chamber, the gradient should be steepened slightly to at least 1:40.

Too steep a gradient should be avoided, as it will cause water run-off, leaving the solids behind to cause a blockage. Suitable access points must be provided for maintaining and testing the system. Rodding eyes (cleanouts), access gullies, inspection chambers, or person access chambers can all be used. In a u-PVC system, rodding points can be incorporated instead of costly inspection chambers. A minimum of one inspection chamber must be used for inspecting flow, etc.

For good drainage it is essential to maintain pressure equilibrium between the inside and the outside of the system. Providing ventilation pipes along the system does this. Branches over 6 m in length require a vent pipe.

Inspection and person access chambers

The proper distinction between an inspection and person access chamber is that the latter is a deeper chamber, large enough for a person to climb down and into for the purposes of clearing blockages.

It is important to provide access to any point where a blockage might occur, including bends of 45°, at the junction of two or more pipes, at changes in gradient, at sharp bends and junctions where cleaning is not otherwise possible.

Severe changes of gradient in a pipe work run creates lips, which may cause build-up of deposits and eventual blockage. Access must therefore be provided at backdrops and ramps. Other access points should be within 12 m of the drain and sewer connection and at the head of each length of drain.

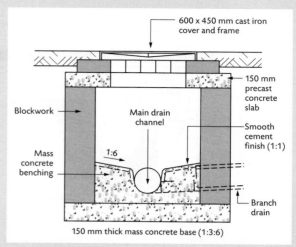

13-39 *Shallow inspection chamber*

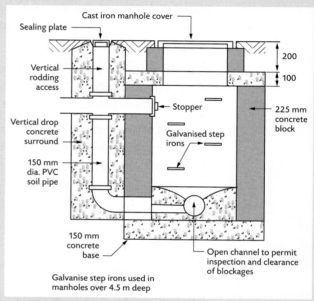

13-40 *Construction of a drop manhole (person access chamber) to allow shallow branch at high level to join a main drain at lower level.*

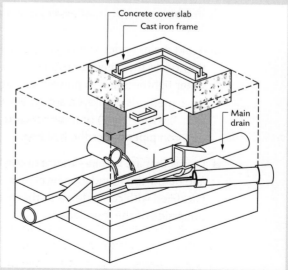

13-41 *Cut-away view of typical construction for a shallow brick manhole*

The size of these chambers will be determined by the size and angle of the main drain, the position and number of branches and the depth. Person access and inspection chambers are usually constructed in blockwork, but are also available in pre-cast concrete sections, glass fibre reinforced polyester (GRP), u-PVC, and cast iron. A reinforced concrete slab, approx. 150 mm thick is used for the roof of chambers.

Drain testing

The main purpose for testing drains is to ensure that they are watertight. This should be done after the trench is back-filled. Preliminary testing should take place by the contractor before back filling as mistakes or problems are easily identified and solved at this stage.

There are three types of test used:

1 **Water test.** This is the most common test used and it is carried out by filling the drain with water under pressure and observing if there is any escape of water.

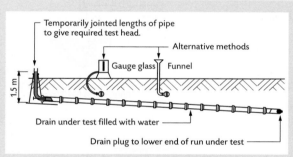

13-42 *Water test details*

2 **Air test.** This is also a pressure test, but it is not as reliable as the water test. It is used where a large volume of water would be required due to large diameter pipes. Where a drop in pressure results from carrying out this test, a water test should follow to confirm that there is a problem.

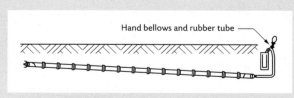

13-43 *Air test details*

3 **Smoke test.** Smoke is pumped into the sealed drain under pressure by a smoke machine. Any drop in pressure is recorded on the smoke machine.

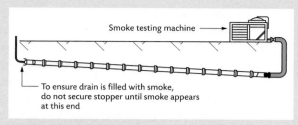

13-44 *Smoke test details*

Drainage materials and components

Several different materials can be used in a drainage system. Pre-formed concrete, stoneware and plastic components take the hard work out of constructing inspection chambers.

The choice of material for pipe work should be based on the type of effluent and the chemical and physical nature of the ground through which it passes.

Vitrified clayware pipe, sometimes called 'stoneware', is widely used because of its strength and low cost, but it is weak at the joints.

Clay pipe is now available with plain ends that are joined with a flexible joint consisting of a polypropylene slave (Fig. 13-45). This is easier than the traditional spigot and socket piping, where joints are made using 1:2 mortar and a tarred gaskin seal.

Pipes in various lengths and diameters are available, as are bends, junctions and taper pieces to match the more commonly used sizes.

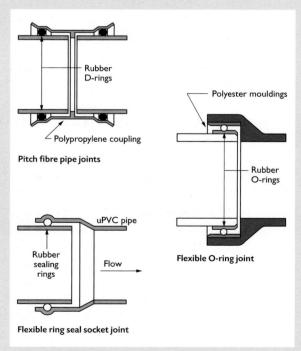

13-45 *Pipes and joints*

Cast-iron pipes are used where greater strength is required, though these suffer greatly from acid wastes and from corrosion resulting from soil conditions. To improve durability a bitumen coating must be applied to all surfaces. The pipes are joined by filling the spigot/socket with caulked lead and an inner seal of tarred hemp.

Pitch-fibre and u-PVC pipes can withstand considerable directional strain without rupturing and are usually laid directly on a suitable bed.

u-PVC joints are sealed by a system of neoprene O-rings within the spigot/socket. Push-on joints such as this speed up assembly procedures and permit slight movement without leakage.

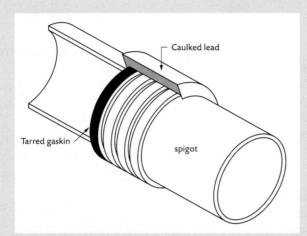

13-46 Method for joining cast-iron pipes

Pipes of asbestos-cement, pitch-fibre and u-PVC are now more popular.

Asbestos-cement pipes must be laid on a bed of concrete. They are sealed and joined using a sleeve of the same material in conjunction with a rubber O-ring arrangement.

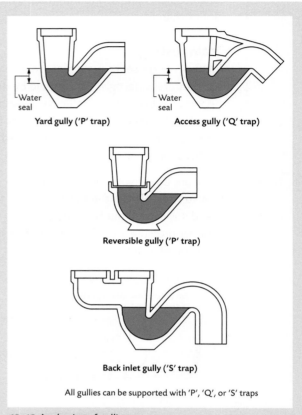

13-48 A selection of gullies

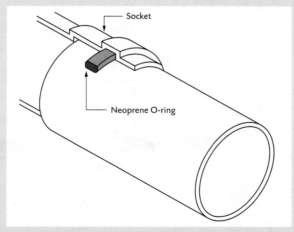

13-47 Neoprene O-ring used in u-PVC joints

Materials & Processing

Concrete blocks are key components of modern buildings, providing strength and stability, weather and fire resistance with good sound and thermal insulation.☞

☞ The Irish Cement Producing Plant, in Limerick

Irish Cement

Cement production involves the fusing together at high temperature of a precisely controlled blend of finely ground limestone and shale. The resultant clinker is then refined and blended with gypsum to the appropriate strength defined by international standards. Irish Cement Limited is Ireland's number one manufacturer of cement at its two plants near Drogheda and Limerick.

Roadstone

Roadstone has developed a ready-to-use mortar under the brand Flomix®. Flomix® is a ready-to-use premixed dry mortar, manufactured in state of the art computerised production facilities and stored on site in silos for ease of application.

John A. Wood Ltd.

John A Wood Ltd. is a major supplier of stone, readymixed concrete, concrete products and bituminous materials to the building and construction industry in the south of Ireland. The company operates limestone and sandstone quarries, gravel pits, blockyards, readymixed concrete and asphalt plants and is serviced by a fleet of over two hundred vehicles.

Chapter 14

Materials – properties and characteristics

Wood

Introduction

Wood is one of the most abundant natural materials on Earth. Unlike resources such as coal, ores, and petroleum, it is renewable. It has been used since the earliest days of human existence, first as a source of fuel and later for an enormous variety of uses. Despite the widespread use of metals and synthetics in modern society, the demand for wood products continues to increase annually.

> **Wood**
> may be defined as the hard fibrous substance consisting of xylem tissue that occurs beneath the bark in trees. In construction terms wood comes from the trunks of trees that have been cut and prepared for use as a building material. Wood as a building material is referred to as timber.

Hardwoods and softwoods

Woods come from two groups of trees: the conifers, or softwoods, and the broadleaves, or hardwoods.

Trees classified as hardwoods are not necessarily harder than softwoods: balsa, for example, is a hardwood but is in fact one of the softest woods.

Hardwoods and softwoods differ in their cellular form and structure.

Hardwoods

Hardwoods (*angiosperms* – flowering trees) are from broad-leaved trees, most of which are deciduous (they shed their leaves in winter).

Holly, some oaks and the majority of tropical trees are hardwoods. Tropical hardwoods (e.g. mahogany, teak, ebony) are the exception to the deciduous rule, they are evergreen.

Commonly available hardwoods include red and white oak, beech, ash, elm, sycamore, birch and walnut.

Hardwoods include the densest, strongest, and most durable timbers. Some hardwoods contain resins and/or oils which may interfere with the hardening of paints, and others such as teak include materials like silica which make working difficult.

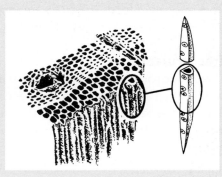

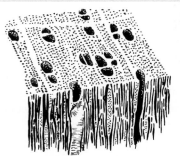

14-1 *Cell structure of softwoods (top) showing tracheids, and cell structure of hardwoods (bottom) showing vessels and fibres*

Most hardwoods occur randomly and are naturally growing. This makes felling and collection difficult, which results in higher prices.

The main feature of the structure of hardwood is the presence of large cells or vessels that transport moisture from the roots. Hardwoods also have parenchyma cells and fibres. The fibres give strength to the tree.

Softwoods

Softwoods (*gymnosperms*) are from coniferous trees, which have spiky leaves and are mainly evergreen (larch is an exception as it is the only coniferous tree in Ireland to lose its leaves in autumn).

The softwood most commonly used is *Pinus sylvester*, more commonly known as red deal. Other names for this include redwood, yellow deal, and Scots pine.

Common softwoods include cedar, Douglas fir, larch, Paraná pine, Quebec yellow pine, and Sitka spruce. Softwoods are now specifically grown and forested in managed forests.

Softwood timber consists of many tubular cells, called tracheids, cemented together. Tracheids transport moisture drawn up from the roots and give strength to the tree.

Another series of cells, called parenchyma rays, are located from the outside of the tree towards the pith. These are shorter than the tracheids and store reserves of food. These rays are sometimes used as a means of identifying timbers.

Tree structure

Three basic parts of a tree that can be seen in cross-section are the bark, the wood and the pith. Between the bark and the wood is the cambium, a thin layer of living cells where tree growth takes place.

The wood forms around the pith (the central core) in a series of concentric layers, called growth rings, which usually represent the yearly or seasonal cycle of growth.

Each ring is composed of two parts. The inner part, called early wood, or springwood, is lighter and softer and is produced in the spring. The outer part, called latewood, or summerwood, is added later in the growing season.

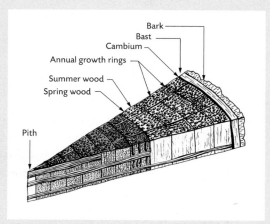

14-2 *Cross-section of a tree trunk*

After 10–20 years in most trees heartwood forms in the centre of the trunk. This is surrounded by sapwood. The distinction is clear in cross-section.

- **Heartwood**, the central portion of the tree trunk, is darker in colour and composed of inactive cells that do not participate in the life processes of the tree.

- **Sapwood**, the lighter area surrounding the heartwood, contains cells that conduct water and dissolved minerals up to the leaves and store food after photosynthesis.

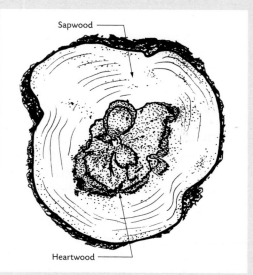

14-3 *Heartwood is the central core of nonfunctional xylem and is darker than sapwood. Sapwood is the soft wood, just beneath the bark in tree trunks, that consists of living tissue.*

The wood in most trees exhibits a radiating pattern from pith to bark, with rays varying in size from species to species.

Other physical characteristics of wood include:
- **colour**, varying from the white of a holly tree to the red of a redwood or the black of an ebony;
- **odour**, especially noticeable in such trees as the cedar but indiscernible in others;
- **texture**, the uniformity of a wood's surface; and
- **grain**, the direction of the wood fibres.

Wood properties

DENSITY AND SPECIFIC GRAVITY

Density is the weight or mass of a unit volume of wood, and specific gravity is the ratio of the density of wood to that of water. In the metric system, density and specific gravity are numerically identical. For example, the average density of the wood of Douglas fir is 0.45 grams per cubic centimetre and its specific gravity 0.45, because one cubic centimetre of water weighs one gram.

The density of wood varies from about 0.1 to 1.2 grams per cubic centimetre (specific gravity 0.1 to 1.2).

Determination of the density of wood in relation to that of other materials is difficult because wood is hygroscopic. Both its weight and volume are influenced by moisture content.

Most mechanical properties of wood are closely related to density and specific gravity. It is possible to learn more about the nature of a wood sample by determining its specific gravity than by any other simple measurement.

HYGROSCOPICITY

Wood is hygroscopic (i.e. exhibits an affinity for water) and can absorb water as a liquid, if in contact with it, or in the form of vapour from the atmosphere. Because of its hygroscopicity, wood, either as a part of the living tree or as sawn timber, always contains moisture. (The terms water and moisture are used without distinction.)

Although moisture affects all wood properties, note that only moisture contained in cell walls is important; moisture in the cavities of cells merely adds weight.

The amount of moisture held in cell walls varies from about 20 to 35 per cent. The theoretical point at which cell walls are completely saturated and cell cavities empty is known as the **fibre saturation point**. Beyond this point, moisture goes into the cavities, and when these are completely filled, the maximum moisture content of the wood is reached.

The moisture content of green wood gradually decreases when it is exposed to the atmosphere. Moisture in the cell cavities is lost first. The average moisture content of sawn timber is between 12 and 15 per cent. Local conditions of air temperature and relative humidity dictate the final moisture level.

Hygroscopicity is important because moisture content affects all wood properties, including weight of logs, dimension change, and resistance to decay and insects infestation. Processing, such as drying, preservative treatment, and pulping is also affected, along with gluing and finishing and the mechanical, thermal, and acoustical properties of wood.

STRENGTH

Density is a good indicator of the strength of clear wood. Higher density indicates greater strength.

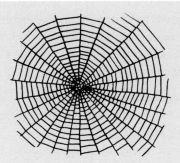

14-4 *A spider's web is three times as strong as steel of equivalent thickness.*

Moisture content influences the strength of wood when it fluctuates below the fibre saturation point. A decrease in moisture content is accompanied by an increase in most strength properties.

Temperature and duration of loading affect strength. Strength falls as temperature rises. Wood loaded permanently will not support the loads indicated by short-time tests in the laboratory. The most important strength-reducing factors are wood defects, such as knots, abnormal anatomy resulting from compression and tension, and grain deviations. Their adverse effect depends on the kind and extent of the defect, position, and manner of loading.

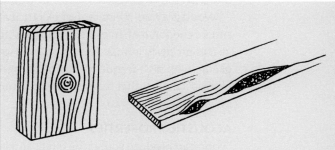

14-5 *Some common strength-reducing defects in wood include knots (left) and waney edge (right).*

Anisotropic *may be described as having different physical properties in different directions. It is the opposite of isotropic.*

Wood has different strength properties parallel to the grain than it does across the grain. Wood is therefore anisotropic.

THERMAL PROPERTIES

Wood expands and contracts with varying temperature. These dimensional changes are small in comparison to the shrinkage and swelling caused by variation of moisture content.

In most cases expansion and contraction are negligible and without importance. Only temperatures below 0°C may cause surface checks, and in living trees, unequal contraction of outer and inner layers may result in frost cracks.

This low thermal expansion and contraction, in conjunction with low heat conductivity, give wood an advantage when it is exposed to fire. The low heat conductivity of wood (high insulating value) makes it desirable for building construction.

Wood burns when exposed to high temperatures (about 400°C).

ELECTRICAL PROPERTIES

Very dry, especially oven-dry wood, makes an excellent insulator. However, electric conductivity increases as moisture content increases, and the behaviour of saturated wood approaches that of water.

The electrical resistance of wood decreases significantly when moisture content increases from zero to fibre saturation point. Within this range, electric resistance decreases about 10,000,000 times, whereas from fibre saturation point to maximum moisture content it decreases only about 50 times or less.

Factors such as species and density have little effect on the electrical resistance of wood.

Wood is a non-conductor of electricity but will sustain the force of an electric field passing through it. This property is important in relation to drying, gluing (with high-frequency electric current), and to electrical meters that measure the moisture content of wood.

ACOUSTIC PROPERTIES

Wood can produce sound (by direct striking) and amplify or absorb sound waves originating from other sources. This makes it a unique material for musical instruments and other acoustic purposes.

The pitch of sound produced depends on the frequency of vibration and the dimensions, density, moisture content, and modulus of elasticity of the wood. Larger dimensions, lower moisture content, and higher density and elasticity produce sounds of higher pitch (more acute in tone).

Sound waves originating from other bodies and striking wood are partly absorbed and partly reflected; hence wood may be set in vibration (resonate) by sound. The sound may be amplified, as in violins, guitars, organ pipes, and other musical instruments, or absorbed, as in wooden partitions.

Wood absorbs only a small portion of acoustic energy (3–5 per cent), but special construction techniques with empty spaces and insulation boards may increase this capacity up to 90 per cent. Defects such as decay affect acoustic properties.

Wood processing

SEASONING

Wood is dried (or seasoned) in the open air or in kilns in order to reduce shrinkage, swelling, and weight and to better prepare it for finishing. Unseasoned (green) wood is subject to attack by fungi and insects, and shrinks as it dries. It is likely to split and warp because it does not shrink evenly in all directions.

The most common seasoning methods are air seasoning and kiln seasoning. In air seasoning, the boards are stacked and divided by narrow pieces of wood called stickers to allow air to circulate freely about each board. The stack is slanted to facilitate drainage of rain.

In kiln seasoning, the wood is placed in a structure in which heat, humidity, and air circulation is carefully controlled by fans and steam pipes.

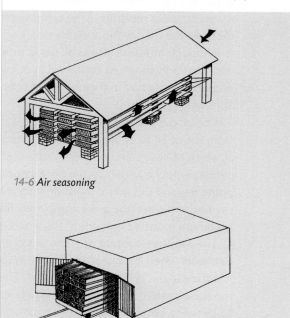

14-6 Air seasoning

14-7 Kiln seasoning

PRESERVATION

In order to attack timber, both insects and fungi need favourable conditions of food, moisture, air and temperature. By controlling any one of these factors timber may be rendered immune to attack. The food supply area is the easiest to control.

Wood can be treated easily with substances that are poisonous to fungi and insects. The preservative does not have to penetrate the wood completely, but only needs to form a continuous outer layer. This outer layer must be sufficiently thick to cover any slight cracks or mechanical damage so as not to expose the core of untreated wood.

Requirements of good preservatives:

- toxic to fungi and insects (but not to humans or domestic animals)
- permanent, stable for a long period and not liable to leach out

- cheap and plentiful
- safe to handle
- easily applied
- not corrosive to metals
- capable of good penetration
- fire-resistant
- capable of subsequent painting or finishing
- colourless and odourless

No single preservative will possess all of the above properties, but this list will serve as a guide for specific applications.

TYPES OF PRESERVATIVE

There are three categories of preservative: tar oils, organic solvents and water-borne preservatives.

1. **Tar oils** (creosote is the best example of this category).
   - very resistant to leaching, which makes them suitable for treating timbers for use externally.
   - not corrosive to metals
   - difficult to paint over
   - tend to 'creep' in plaster
   - strong odour, which may be picked up by foodstuffs

2. **Organic solvent types.** Various chemicals dissolved in an oil solvent make up this category. After application the solvent evaporates and leaves the preservative in the wood. This category has the following properties:
   - resistant to leaching, which also makes them suitable for exterior use
   - may be painted after the solvent has evaporated
   - do not stain and are usually non creeping
   - non-corrosive to metals
   - penetrate the wood better than other types
   - suitable for brush application, spraying or cold dipping
   - more expensive than other types

3. **Water-borne preservatives.** This category consists of chemicals such as certain salts of copper, zinc, sodium, potassium, mercury and chromium dissolved in water. This category has the following properties:
   - Less viscous than creosote, thereby giving good penetration
   - usually odourless
   - may be painted when the treated wood is dry
   - do not stain and are usually non creeping

- cheaper and easier to transport than other types of preservative.
- tendency for some types to leach out of the wood when in contact with the ground or in water
- the treated timber must be re-dried

METHODS OF APPLYING PRESERVATIVE

Non-pressure methods

Non-pressure methods are usually less effective than pressure methods. Nevertheless, the hot and cold tank treatment can achieve satisfactory results, for most purposes.

1. **Brush application** – this method gives very little penetration, usually 1–2 mm deep. Only well seasoned wood should be treated this way. The preservative should be applied generously and brushed into cracks and checks.

2. **Dipping** – this method consists of submerging timber into a bath containing the preservative for about 15 minutes. If creosote is used, better penetration is achieved by heating it. This method is only slightly better than brushing.

3. **Hot and cold steeping** – this method gives good protection to permeable timbers and to sapwood. It is not a substitute for pressure treatment, which is necessary for timbers resistant to penetration. The timber is submerged in a tank of preservative, which is heated for several hours. The preservative is then allowed to cool while the timber is still submerged. The total operation takes about 24 hours.

   Almost all the absorption takes place during the cooling period. The hot liquid heats the wood, causing the expulsion of some air from the wood cells. On cooling, the air remaining in the wood cells contracts, creating a partial vacuum. The preservative is then forced into the wood by air pressure.

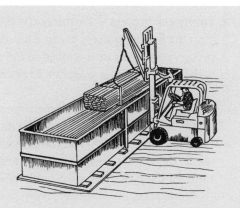

14-8 Hot or cold steeping

Pressure methods

Pressure application is the most effective way of applying preservatives. The procedure involves the use of a special pressure plant, which consists of a steel cylinder with tightly fitting doors at one or both ends.

The timber is loaded onto trolleys that are pushed into the cylinder on special rails. The length of the cylinder normally varies from 10–30 m long and the diameter from 2–3 m.

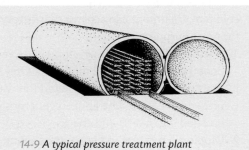

14-9 *A typical pressure treatment plant*

There are two main types of pressure treatment:

1. **Full-cell process** – the timber is placed in the cylinder, which is then sealed.

   A vacuum of up to 700 mm of mercury is created by a vacuum pump. This is maintained for between 15 minutes and several hours, depending on the permeability and the size of the timber. This vacuum is necessary to remove air from the cells of the timber in order to minimise resistance to the entry of the preservative. The preservative is introduced at a temperature of 60–80°C. A pressure pump then builds up pressure, and this may be maintained from 1–5 hours.

   Following the required pressure period to suit the timber, the surplus preservative is allowed drain back to the storage tank and a final vacuum is applied to remove preservative from the surface of the wood. The wood cells are, however, full of preservative.

2. **Empty-cell process** – this method is cheaper than the full-cell process because it uses less preservative. Pressure is applied to the cylinder without first creating a vacuum to remove air from the cells.

   The preservative is then forced into the timber at a higher pressure until the required absorption takes place. The compressed air within the wood cells then expands and expels much of the preservative from the cells.

   As the pressure is reduced, more preservative is removed from the cells. This results in the cell walls being well coated, while the cells themselves are empty.

WOOD FINISHES

Bare wood will absorb liquids, but if given a protective finish, liquids will not penetrate. Wood finishes are designed to:

- Protect the surface from liquids, heat, stains and insect attack
- Improve the appearance of the wood

The type of finish is determined by the end use of the wood.

PREPARING THE SURFACE

Plane solid wood with a fine-set smoothing plane. Use a cabinet scraper for patches of difficult grain and finish with abrasive paper. Sand down large areas with an orbital finishing sander.

Veneered boards require little if any sanding with fine abrasive paper.

Filler is used to fill the grain of some hardwoods so that a perfect surface can be obtained. Wood stopping is used to fill checks in the wood and gaps in the joints.

SURFACE FINISHES

Paint

The characteristics of the main types of paint are:

- **Oil/resin paint** tends to flake with age. Synthetic paints are now more common.
- **Polyurethane paint** is a one-pack finish that dries on exposure to air in about 2 hours – hardening continues for several days.
- **Cellulose paint** is a highly inflammable mixture that dries quickly when the solvent evaporates. The best finish is obtained when applied in several layers with a spray gun.
- **Acrylic/resin paint** is a synthetic water-borne mixture that spreads easily and dries quickly into a tough, water- and steam-resistant, non-fade finish.

Consider the surface of the material and the wear that it must withstand before selecting paint.

Wax

The resistance of wax finishes to heat and moisture partly depends on the wood sealer that is applied before the wax. Common sealers are brush polish, polyurethane varnish, acid-catalysed lacquer. Types of wax include:

- **Beeswax**: a pure wax dissolved in a petroleum mixture.
- **Furniture polish**: a synthetic mixture containing silicones.

Oil

All oils require regular maintenance. The different types are:

- **Linseed oil**: gives a dull finish. It dries slowly and tends to collect dust.
- **Teak oil**: dries more quickly. Additives increase resistance to heat.
- **Vegetable/olive oil**: used on wood products that will come into contact with food.

Polyurethane

Varnish dries on exposure to the air to give a hard, durable finish. Types include:

- **One pack varnish** – commonly available.
- **Two pack varnish** – normally used by furniture manufacturers.

Varnish may be applied with a brush, spray gun or aerosol, to dry surfaces that are free from grease and dirt.

Acid-catalysed lacquer

A hardener must be added to the lacquer before application. The two liquids must be mixed to the proportions recommended. This is the clearest finish available and will withstand hot water and hot objects such as hot plates.

Dyes (stains)

Wood dyes give permanent colour to the wood fibres, do not fade when exposed to the sun and can be covered with all types of wood finish. Modern wood dyes dissolved in spirit or alcohol do not raise the grain of the wood as did the traditional water and oil stains. Stained polishes do not dye the wood fibres and are not permanent.

Care of brushes

Best quality brushes give the best results. Clean the brushes immediately after use. Following is a list of brush cleaners appropriate to the type of finish used:

Type of finish	Brush cleaner
Oil paint	White spirit
Polyurethane paint	White spirit
Cellulose paint	Cellulose thinners
Acrylic paint	Water
Preservatives	White spirit
Creosote	Paraffin
Brush/French polish	Methylated spirit
Polyurethane varnish	White spirit
Acid-catalysed lacquer	Special thinners

Metals

Metals are derived from ores that occur naturally under the Earth's surface. To extract metal from an ore, the ore is removed from the Earth, crushed and then smelted until only the metal remains. Each metal has its own unique properties, but there are some that are common to most metals, including:

- they are solids (except mercury)
- have a shiny appearance (except mercury)
- expand when heated
- conduct electricity and heat
- can be stretched when heated (ductile)
- can be moulded into different shapes (malleable)
- can be mixed together to form new metals (alloys).

Mechanical properties

When a metal rod is lightly loaded, the strain (measured by the change in length divided by the original length) is proportional to the stress (the load per unit of cross-sectional area).

This means that, with each increase in load, there is a proportional increase in the rod's length, and, when the load is removed, the rod shrinks to its original size. The strain is said to be elastic, and the ratio of stress to strain is called the elastic modulus or Young's modulus of elasticity (see page 94).

If the load is increased further, a point called the **yield stress** will be reached and exceeded. Strain will now increase faster than stress, and, when the sample is unloaded, a residual plastic strain (or elongation) will remain. In other words, the rod will be bent.

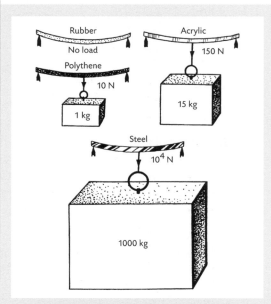

14-10 *Four bars made of different material but the same size would require different loads to cause the same amount of deflection on each.*

The most important mechanical properties of a metal are its **yield stress**, its **ductility** (measured by the elongation to fracture), and its **toughness** (measured by the energy absorbed in tearing the metal).

Electrical properties

The electrical conductivity of a metal is determined by the ease of movement of electrons past the atoms under the influence of an electric field.

This movement is easy in copper, silver, gold, and aluminium, all of which are good conductors of electricity. The conductivity of a metal increases with falling temperature.

Magnetic properties

When an electric current is passed through a coil of metal wire, a magnetic field is developed around the coil. When a piece of copper is placed inside the coil, this field increases by less than 1 per cent, but, when a piece of iron, cobalt, or nickel is placed inside the coil, the external field can increase 10,000 times. This strong magnetic property is known as ferromagnetism, and the three metals listed above are the most prominent ferromagnetic metals.

When the piece of ferromagnetic metal is removed from the coil, it retains some of this magnetism (that is, it is magnetised). If the metal is hard, as in a hardened piece of steel, the loss, or reversal, of magnetisation will be slow, and the sample will be useful as a permanent magnet. If the metal is soft, it will quickly lose its magnetism. This makes it useful in electrical transformers, where rapid reversal of magnetisation is essential.

Chemical properties

Most metals, except gold, will oxidise in air. At room temperature a clean metal surface will oxidise very little, since a thin oxide film forms and protects the metal from further oxidation. At elevated temperatures, though, oxidation is faster, and the film is less protective. Many chemicals accelerate this corrosion process (that is, the conversion of a metal to an oxide in air or to a hydroxide in the presence of water).

There are two main groups of metals:
- **Ferrous metals** – those that contain iron.
- **Non-ferrous metals** – those that do not contain iron.

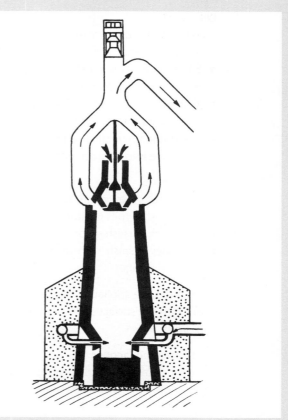

14-11 *A blast furnace is used to convert iron ore into iron. The furnace is fed at the top with a mixture of iron ore, coke and limestone. Blasts of hot air pass up the furnace, causing chemical changes to take place in the materials. The iron and a waste product, slag, are removed separately at the bottom.*

Ferrous metals

Ferrous metals contain iron and carbon in varying amounts and all of them are likely to rust when exposed to the weather. Rust is reddish-brown in colour and cannot exist unless water and oxygen are present. The application of a zinc coating (galvanising) is regarded as the best method of rust prevention. The main types of ferrous metals are:
- **Grey cast iron** – is an alloy of iron and about 3.5 per cent carbon. It is a brittle material that cannot be forged, but the high carbon content makes it melt and pour easily.
- **Malleable cast iron** – has a less brittle surface. Malleable cast iron is heat treated to remove some of the carbon from the surfaces to be machined.
- **Wrought iron** – is almost pure iron and is both malleable and ductile. The lack of carbon means that it cannot be melted into a liquid state for casting, but it is excellent for forging. Wrought iron develops an iron oxide surface, which gives it self-protection against rust.

- **Mild steel** – contains 0.15–0.35 per cent carbon and is three times more ductile than high-carbon steel. It is used for nuts, bolts and tubes.
- **Black mild steels** – is coated with a grey scale from oxidation during the process of hot rolling.
- **Medium-carbon steel** – contains 0.35–0.65 per cent carbon. The springs in exercise equipment are an example of its use.
- **High-carbon steel** – often referred to as tool steel, contains 0.65–1.15 per cent carbon. It is at least twice as hard as mild steel.

Steel alloys

Adding small quantities of pure metals to produce alloy steels can change the quality of steel. Metals that may be added include tungsten, nickel, chromium and manganese.

Tungsten is used to tip cutting tools such as drills and the woodworker's circular saw. At high speed the tips become hot, but the tungsten retains its cutting edge. Chromium is present in large quantities in good-quality cutlery and is about 13 per cent of stainless steel.

Non-ferrous metals

Non-ferrous metals do not contain iron or carbon and do not rust. Some are elements such as aluminium; others are alloys such as brass. Some of the more common types, their properties and uses follow.

- **Copper** – a reddish-brown metal, which is malleable and ductile. Used in the home for water pipes, electrical wiring and high-quality cookware. Copper is also used for making alloys such as brass. Copper hardens as it is worked.
- **Zinc** – a bluish-grey metal used mainly as the corrosion-resisting material of galvanised steel. It is mixed with copper to produce both brass and gilding metal. It has a relatively low melting point (420°C), which means that it is ideal for pressure die-casting. Zinc, with small amounts of aluminium, magnesium and copper added, produces an alloy used for casting carburettors and washing machine components.
- **Lead** – a bluish-grey, heavy and extremely malleable metal. It was once used for household plumbing. As it can cause lead poisoning, its use in the home is now limited to waterproof flashings for slate and tile roofs.
- **Aluminium** – a bluish-white metal, which is malleable and ductile. It is weak in its pure form so it is usually alloyed with other metals.

Aluminium alloys combine strength with lightness, making them ideal for working castings such as engines. Aluminium is used as a cheap alternative to copper in some electrical work. It is also a good conductor of heat.

- **Tin** – a silvery, malleable and ductile metal. Mainly used as the thin rust-resistant coating of tinplate.
- **Brass** – a mixture of 60 per cent copper and 40 per cent zinc. It is hard and brittle with a shiny appearance that tarnishes easily. Brass is a good conductor of heat and electricity. It is used for door handles, hinges, screws and electrical plug pins.

Finishes and rust preventatives for metals

Some metals need protective finishes to prevent corrosion. Other metals such as copper, silver, aluminium and stainless steel may be either resistant to staining and corrosion or may need only occasional polishing with metal polish. When left to weather, some metals are better left unfinished – the attractive green patina that forms on copper roofs is an example.

Where appropriate, metal surfaces are given a finish that will improve their appearance. Surface coatings are applied that will protect the metal from corrosion. Corrosion is a chemical reaction between oxygen and the metal. On steel this appears as blue-black oxidisation when joints are welded. A surface scale forms on copper that has been heated. Corrosion is increased by the presence of moisture. Moisture causes steel to rust and copper to turn green.

Metals are finished or prepared for a surface coating using abrasives and/or degreasing fluids.

METAL PRIMER

Primer with a zinc chromate base is best used before finishing with oil-based paint. Apply it by brush to steel that has first been de-greased and rinsed. Aluminium and zinc-coated steel, such as that used for seaside railings, must first be coated with an etching primer.

> *Etching primer* is a two-part water sensitive paint. It must be applied in dry conditions.

QUICK-DRY ENAMEL

This is a popular metal finish for machinery, equipment and fittings that is to be used indoors. Machine oils, battery acid or cutting fluids do not affect it.

ALUMINIUM PAINT

This gives an exotic finish that will resist high humidity and condensation. Pure aluminium is contained in 'Hammerite' paint, a one-coat finish. The paint dries in 15 minutes.

PAINT SPRAYING

This works by using the energy supplied by compressed air or electrically operated pistons. It is a superior method to brushing when used on flat surfaces such as car panels. The unit must always be held vertically. Spray only in a well ventilated area.

LACQUERING

Lacquer will preserve the surface finish of any metal, but it is most effective in preventing non-ferrous metals from tarnishing. A colourless lacquer may be used on trophies and jewellery made from silver. The work must be heated if hot lacquer is to be applied.

PLASTIC COATINGS

These coatings are a good finish for metal which must be kept hygienic or handled, but which will not suffer from direct heat or abrasion.

Plastics

Many everyday objects that were once made of wood or metal are now made of plastic. The manufacture of all plastics has one thing in common, i.e. processes involving pressure, heat or both shape them.

Plastics are used instead of conventional materials because they are easier to manufacture, are tougher, and provide thermal and electrical insulation. Other characteristics include their wide range of rigidity/flexibility, adhesion/self-lubrication/non-stick behaviour, their transparency/opacity and colour possibilities, and their resistance to water, rust, and rot.

Manufacturers of plastic products refer to plastics as either **commodity resins** or **speciality resins**. Commodity resins are plastics that are produced at high volume and low cost for the common disposable items and durable goods.

Some typical commodity resins are:
- polyethylene
- polypropylene
- polyvinyl chloride
- polystyrene

Speciality resins are plastics whose properties are tailored to specific applications. They are produced at low volume and higher cost. Engineering resins fall into this catetory. These are plastics that can compete with die-cast metals in plumbing, hardware, and automotive applications.

Important engineering plastics are:
- polyacetal
- polyamide (particularly those known as nylon)
- polytetrafluoroethylene (trademark Teflon)
- polycarbonate
- polyphenylene sulphide
- epoxy
- polyetheretherketone

Polymers

Most plastics are chemicals called **polymers** (substances made from molecules joined in chains). Polymers such as polythene and nylon are synthetic (artificial) materials; others occur in nature.

Cellulose, for example, is a polymer that is found in the cell walls of plants, and is a major constituent of wood. Cellulose consists of groups of 6 carbon, 10 hydrogen and 5 oxygen atoms, joined to form long chains. Most polymers are organic (carbon-based) materials, but others, such as asbestos, are inorganic.

Leo Baekeland produced the first completely synthetic polymer in 1908. His plastic was named **Bakelite** and was widely used for ornamental articles and electrical fittings.

Polymers are formed when molecules called monomers become linked together. A physical process such as the application of heat, pressure or mechanical agitation may start the transformation of a monomer into a polymer. A catalyst may be used in some cases.

Synthetic polymers can be divided into three groups – thermoplastic polymers, thermosetting polymers and elastomers.

Thermoplastics, such as polystyrene and PVC (polyvinyl chloride), can be repeatedly softened by heat. This is because their molecule chains can move relative to each other.

In **thermosetting polymers**, such as Bakelite and epoxy resin, cross-links between the chains prevent this from happening. This prevents thermoset polymers from softening when heated.

Elastomers include rubber-like plastics and natural and synthetic rubber. These materials are treated to produce a controlled amount of cross-linking between the molecule chains. Elastomers can therefore be stretched, but will return to their original shape when the stretching force is relaxed.

Plastics manufacture

The manufacture of plastic and plastic products involves sourcing the raw materials, synthesising the basic polymer, compounding the polymer into a material useful for fabrication, and moulding or shaping the plastic into its final form.

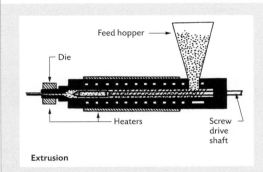

Extrusion

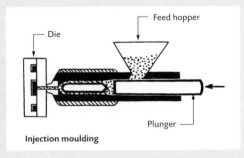

Injection moulding

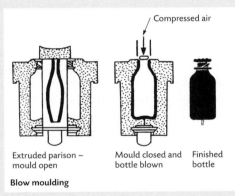

Extruded parison – mould open

Mould closed and bottle blown

Finished bottle

Blow moulding

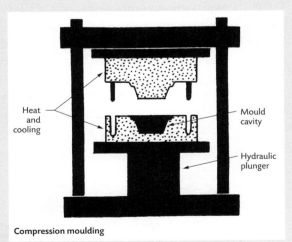

Heat and cooling

Mould cavity

Hydraulic plunger

Compression moulding

14-12 Methods of forming and shaping plastic include extrusion, injection moulding, blow moulding and compression moulding.

RAW MATERIALS

Originally, most plastics were made from resins derived from vegetable matter, such as cellulose (from cotton), furfural (from oat hulls), oils (from seeds), starch derivatives, or coal. Casein (from milk) was among the non-vegetable materials used.

Although the production of nylon was originally based on coal, air, and water, and nylon 11 is still based on oil from castor beans, most plastics today are derived from petrochemicals. These oil-based raw materials are relatively widely available and inexpensive. However, because the world supply of oil is limited, other sources of raw materials are being explored.

ADDITIVES

Chemical additives are often used in plastics to produce particular characteristics. For instance, antioxidants protect a polymer from chemical degradation by oxygen or ozone, and ultraviolet stabilisers protect against weathering. Plasticisers make a polymer more flexible, lubricants reduce problems with friction and pigments add colour. Flame-retardants and antistatics are other additives.

Antistatic.
A substance that is antistatic retains sufficient moisture to provide a conducting path, thereby avoiding the effects of static electricity.

COMPOSITES

Many plastics are manufactured as composites. This involves a system where reinforcing material (usually fibres made of glass or carbon) is added to a plastic resin matrix.

Composites have strength and stability comparable to that of metals but generally with less weight. Plastic foams, which are composites of plastic and gas, offer bulk with low weight. (Composites are dealt with in greater detail at the end of this chapter.)

Uses of plastics

PACKAGING

The packaging industry is a leading user of plastics. Much LDPE (low-density polyethylene) is marketed in rolls of clear-plastic wrap. High-density poly-ethylene (HPDE) is used for some thicker plastic films, such as those used for plastic waste bags and containers. Polypropylene is often used in house wares and as a fibre for carpeting and rope.

CONSTRUCTION

The building industry is a major consumer of plastics, including many of the packaging plastics mentioned above.

HDPE is used for pipes, as is PVC. PVC is also used in sheets for building materials and similar items. Many plastics are used to insulate cables and wires, polystyrene and polyurethane in the form of foam serves as insulation for walls, roofs, and other areas. Other plastic products are roofing, door and window frames, mouldings, and hardware.

JOINING

Dielectric refers to a substance of very low electric conductivity (insulator) that can sustain an electric field.

Welding can join some plastics, such as PVC and polyethylene tanks. It is more common for surfaces to be joined by being brought into contact with one another and heated by conduction or by dielectric heating.

MACHINING

Conventional processes such as drilling, sawing, turning on a lathe, sanding, and other operations can be performed on rigid thermoplastics and thermosets.

Glass-reinforced thermosets are machined into gears, pulleys, and other shapes, especially when the number of parts does not justify construction of a metal mould. Various forms can be stamped out (die-cut) from sheets of thermoplastics and thermosets.

In the case of a thermoplastic such as polystyrene, the scrap sheet left over can be reground and remoulded.

Mastics

The term **mastic** is used for various pasty materials used as protective coatings (for example, in thermal insulation and in waterproofing) and as cements (for example, in setting tile or wall panels).

Silicon sealant is the most common mastic used. It consists of a high performance, one-part, atmosphere-curing silicone joint sealant.

The physical properties of silicon sealant make it ideal for sealing joints between materials that expand and contract with temperature change, such as precast concrete panels, metal panels and window perimeters.

Adhesives

An adhesive is a substance that is capable of holding materials together in a functional manner by surface attachment that resists separation. 'Adhesive' as a general term includes cement, glue, and paste. Inorganic substances such as Portland cement can be considered adhesives, in the sense that they hold objects such as bricks and beams together through surface attachment.

Adhesives range from natural plant and animal glues to synthetic materials capable of bonding the massive structures of bridges.

Natural adhesives

Natural adhesives are mostly of animal or vegetable origin. The demand for natural products has declined since the mid-20th century, although some continue to be used with wood and paper products, particularly in corrugated board, envelopes, bottle labels, bookbindings, cartons, furniture, and laminated film and foils.

Owing to various environmental regulations, natural adhesives derived from renewable resources are receiving renewed attention. The most important natural adhesives are described below.

ANIMAL GLUE

The term animal glue usually is confined to glues prepared from mammalian collagen, the principal protein constituent of skin, bone, and muscle. When treated with acids, alkalies, or hot water, the normally insoluble collagen slowly becomes soluble. If the original protein is pure and the conversion process is mild, the high-molecular-weight product is called gelatin and may be used for food or photographic products.

The lower-molecular-weight material produced by more vigorous processing is normally less pure and darker in colour and is called animal glue.

Animal glue traditionally has been used in wood joining, bookbinding, sandpaper manufacture, heavy gummed tapes, and similar applications. In spite of its advantage of high initial tack (stickiness), much animal glue has been modified or entirely replaced by synthetic adhesives.

14-13 *Animal glue granules are heated in a special kettle-type container*

CASEIN GLUE

Casein glue is made by dissolving casein, a protein obtained from milk, in a water alkaline solvent. The strength and type of alkali influences product behaviour. In wood bonding, casein glues generally are superior to true animal glues in moisture resistance and aging characteristics. Casein also is used to improve the adhesion characteristics of paints and coatings.

BLOOD ALBUMEN GLUE

Glue of this type is made from serum albumen, a blood component obtained from either fresh animal blood or dried soluble blood powder to which water has been added. Addition of alkali to albumen-water mixtures improves adhesive properties. A considerable quantity of this glue is used in the plywood industry.

STARCH AND DEXTRIN

Starch and dextrin are extracted from corn, wheat, potatoes, or rice. They make up the principal types of vegetable adhesives, which are soluble or dispersible in water. They are obtained from plant sources throughout the world. Starch and dextrin glues are used in corrugated board, packaging, and as a wallpaper adhesive.

NATURAL GUMS

Substances known as natural gums, which are extracted from their natural sources, are used as adhesives. Gum arabic is harvested from acacia trees that are artificially wounded to cause the gum to exude. Natural rubber latex is harvested from Hevea trees. Most gums are used in water-remoistenable products.

14-14 Natural gums are extracted from trees

Synthetic adhesives

Although natural adhesives are less expensive to produce, the most important adhesives are synthetic. Synthetics can be produced in a constant supply with uniform properties. They can be modified in many ways and are often combined to obtain the best characteristics for a particular application.

The polymers used in synthetic adhesives fall into two general categories, thermoplastics and thermosets.

- **Thermoplastics** provide strong, durable adhesion at normal temperatures, and they can be softened for application by heating without undergoing degradation.

  Thermoplastic resins employed in adhesives include nitrocellulose, polyvinyl acetate, vinyl acetate-ethylene copolymer, polyethylene, polypropylene, polyamides, polyesters, acrylics, and cyan acrylics.

- **Thermosetting adhesives**, unlike thermoplastics, form permanent, heat-resistant, insoluble bonds that cannot be modified without degradation.

  Thermosets include phenol formaldehyde, urea formaldehyde, unsaturated polyesters, epoxies, and polyurethanes.

Elastomer-based adhesives can function as either thermoplastic or thermosetting types. The characteristics of elastomeric adhesives include quick assembly, flexibility, variety of type, economy, high peel strength, ease of modification, and versatility. The major elastomers employed as adhesives are natural rubber, butyl rubber, butadiene rubber, styrene-butadiene rubber, nitrile rubber, silicone, and neoprene.

Elastomeric adhesives, such as synthetic or natural rubber cements, are used for bonding flexible materials to rigid materials.

Adhesives are usually applied as thick, viscous liquids, which set to a solid, or to a near-solid form called a gel.

An important challenge facing adhesive manufacturers is the replacement of adhesive systems based on organic solvents with systems based on water. This trend has been driven by restrictions on the use of volatile organic compounds (VOC), which include solvents that are released into the atmosphere and contribute to the depletion of ozone.

In response to environmental regulations, adhesives based on aqueous emulsions and dispersions are being developed, and solvent-based adhesives are being phased out.

Damp-proof course and damp-proof membrane materials

A damp-proof course must be impermeable and durable, in order to last the life of the building without allowing moisture to penetrate. A DPC should also be reasonably flexible to prevent fracture with movement of the building.

Other properties of a DPC material include ease of application, ability to withstand loads, and readily available in thin sheets. There are three categories of damp-proof course.

Flexible

Flexible DPCs are suitable for most locations and they should be used over openings and for bridging cavities. They are the most satisfactory for stepped damp-proof courses and they can be shaped without damage. Materials in this category include sheet lead and copper, bitumen, polyethylene and pitch/bitumen polymer.

Semi-rigid

Semi-rigid DPCs are suitable for thick walls and the resistance of high water pressure. Mastic asphalt is the best example of a semi-rigid DPC.

Rigid

Rigid DPCs are suitable where high bond strength is required, such as in free-standing walls. They only provide a barrier to the capillary rise of moisture. Dense rock and slates are examples of rigid DPCs.

Damp-proof membranes must also be impermeable to water. In addition they should be continuous with the DPC in adjoining walls and be tough enough to remain undamaged when the finished floor screed is being laid. Suitable materials for damp-proof membranes include mastic asphalt, bitumen sheets, hot-applied pitch or bitumen, cold-applied bitumen and polyethylene film sheets.

Cements

Cements are finely ground powders that, when mixed with water, set to a hard mass. These cements are hydraulic, i.e. they depend on water rather than air for strength development.

When water is added to cement a chemical reaction begins immediately and continues while water remains. At first cements stiffen and later develop strength.

Only a small quantity of water is required to hydrate cement, any additional water evaporates, leaving voids. These voids reduce the density and therefore the strength of the products.

Strength is therefore related to the water-cement ratio. Water-cement ratio may be expressed as the total weight of water/weight of cement.

The lower the water-cement ratio the higher the strength of the concrete. The typical range of values for the water-cement ratios is between 0.4 and 0.7 for ordinary Portland cement. Strength development stops at freezing point and is reduced at higher temperatures.

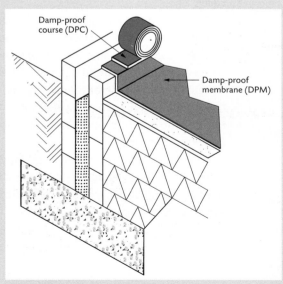

14-15 *Relationship between DPM and DPC*

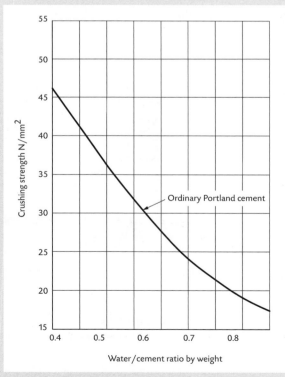

14-16 *Relationship between water/cement ratio and strength*

Portland cement is the most common cement used. It is available in the ordinary variety and in a rapid hardening category.

The rapid-hardening variety sets at the same rate as ordinary Portland cement but because it is more finely ground it develops strength more rapidly. This makes it suitable where early stripping of formwork or loading of structures is required.

Other types are the slag-containing cements and high-alumina cement. Cements may be used alone (i.e., 'neat' as grouting materials), but the normal use is in mortar and concrete in which the cement is mixed with inert material known as aggregate.

Mortar is cement mixed with sand or crushed stone that must be less than 4.8 millimetres in size. Concrete is a mixture of cement, sand or other fine aggregate, and a coarse aggregate that for most purposes is up to 19 to 25 mm in size, but the coarse aggregate may be as large as 150 mm when concrete is placed in large masses such as dams.

Mortars are used for binding bricks, blocks, and stone in walls or as surface renderings. Concrete is used for a large variety of constructional purposes.

Because concrete is the most widely used of all construction materials in the world today, the manufacture of cement is widespread.

Cement raw materials

Portland cement consists of compounds of lime (from limestone and chalk) mixed with silica, alumina, and iron oxide (from clays, shales and slates).

Additional raw materials such as sand, iron oxide, and bauxite may be used in smaller quantities to achieve the desired composition. Another raw material is blast-furnace slag, which consists mainly of lime, silica, and alumina and is mixed with a calcareous material of high lime content.

> **Calcareous** resembles calcium carbonate, chalky.
> **Kaolin** is a fine white clay.

Kaolin, which contains little iron oxide, is used as the fine-grained material component for white Portland cement.

Gypsum is another essential raw material; approx 5 per cent of gypsum is added to the burned cement clinker during grinding to control the setting time of the cement.

Cement manufacture

There are four stages in the manufacture of Portland cement:

1. **crushing** and grinding the raw materials
2. **blending** the materials in the correct proportions
3. **burning** the prepared mix in a kiln
4. **grinding** the burned product known as cement clinker together with approx. 5 per cent of gypsum.

There are three processes by which cement may be manufactured: the wet, dry, and semi-dry processes.

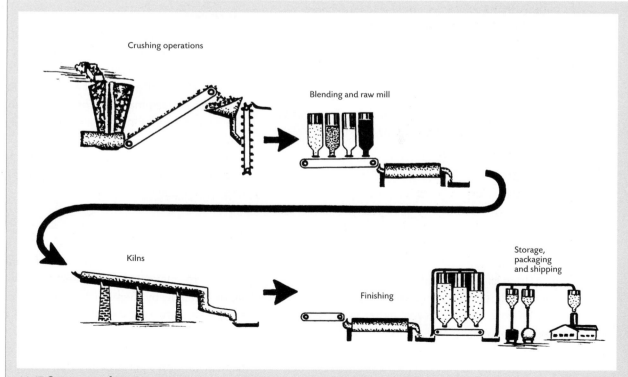

Crushing operations

Blending and raw mill

Kilns

Finishing

Storage, packaging and shipping

14-17 Cement manufacture

In the wet process the raw materials are ground wet and fed to the kiln as slurry. In the dry process the raw material is ground dry and fed to the kiln as a dry powder.

In the semi-dry process the raw material is ground dry and then moistened to form nodules that are fed to the kiln.

CRUSHING AND GRINDING OF RAW MATERIALS

All except soft materials are first crushed, often in two stages, and then ground, usually in a rotating, cylindrical ball, or tube mills containing a charge of steel grinding balls.

This grinding is done in wet or dry conditions according to the process in use, but for dry grinding the raw materials may first need to be dried.

Vigorous stirring breaks down soft materials with water in wash mills, producing fine slurry, which is passed through screens to remove oversize particles.

BLENDING

Selective quarrying and control of the raw material fed to the crushing and grinding plant obtain a first approximation of the required chemical composition.

The finer control is obtained by drawing ground material from two or more silos containing raw mixes differing slightly in composition in the dry process and from slurry tanks in the wet process.

Thorough mixing of the raw materials in the silos in the dry process is ensured by agitation and vigorous circulation induced by compressed air.

In the wet process, mechanical means or compressed air or both stir the slurry tanks.

The slurry, which contains 35 to 45 per cent water, is sometimes filtered; reducing the water content to 20 to 30 per cent, and the filter cake is then fed to the kiln. This reduces the fuel consumption for burning.

BURNING

The earliest kilns in which cement was burned in batches were bottle kilns, followed by chamber kilns and then continuous shaft kilns. The shaft kiln in a modernised form is still used in some countries, but the dominant means of burning is the rotary kiln.

These kilns consist of a steel, cylindrical shell lined with refractory materials. They measure up to 200 metres long and seven metres in diameter in wet process plants and are shorter for the dry process. They rotate slowly on an axis that is inclined a few degrees to the horizontal. The raw material feed, introduced at the upper end, moves slowly down the kiln to the lower or firing end.

Pulverise means to reduce to fine particles, as a result of crushing or grinding.

The fuel for firing may be pulverised coal, oil, or natural gas injected through a pipe. The temperature at the burning end ranges from about 1300° to 1500°C, according to the raw materials being burned.

Some form of heat exchanger is commonly incorporated at the back end of the kiln to increase heat transfer to the incoming raw materials and so reduce the heat lost in the waste gases.

The burned product emerges from the kiln as small nodules of clinker, which then pass into coolers where incoming air is heated and the product is cooled.

Dust emission from cement kilns can be an environmental nuisance. In populated areas it is usual and often compulsory to fit cyclone arrestors, bag-filter systems, or electrostatic dust precipitators between the kiln exit and the chimney stack.

Modern cement plants are equipped with elaborate instrumentation for the control of the burning process. Raw materials in some plants are sampled automatically, and a computer calculates and controls the raw mix composition.

The largest rotary kilns have outputs up to 3,000 tonnes per day. The clinker may be immediately ground to cement or stored in stockpiles for later use.

GRINDING

The clinker and the required amount of gypsum are ground to a fine powder in horizontal mills similar to those used for grinding the raw materials. Sometimes a small amount of a grinding aid is added to the feed material. For air-entraining cements, the addition of an air-entraining agent is similarly made.

Finished cement is pumped pneumatically to storage silos from where it is packed in paper bags or dispatched in bulk containers.

Concrete

Concrete is a manufactured mixture of cement and water, with aggregates of sand and stones, which hardens rapidly by chemical combination to a stone-like, water- and fire-resisting solid of great compressive (but low tensile) strength.

In the mix, water combines chemically with the cement to form a gel structure that bonds the stone aggregates together. In proportioning the mix, the aggregates are graded in size so the cement matrix that joins them together is minimised.

The upper limit of concrete strength is set by that of the stone used in the aggregate. The bonding gel structure forms slowly, and the design strength is usually taken as that occurring 28 days after the initial setting of the mix.

There is a one-month delay between the time in situ concrete is poured and the time it can carry loads. This can significantly affect construction schedules. In situ concrete is used for foundations and for structural skeleton frames.

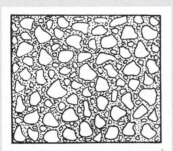

14-18 *Concrete sample*

Reinforced concrete

Reinforced concrete was developed to combine the tensile strength of steel with the compressive strength of mass concrete. Reinforcing metal is embedded in the concrete by being set as a mesh or as steel bars into the forms before pouring. In the hardened material the two act as one. The combination is much stronger than either product on its own.
Concrete has a limitless variety of uses, some of which include rigid frames, foundations, columns, walls, and floors.

Precast concrete structural members are fabricated under controlled conditions in a factory. Members that span floors and roofs are preten-sioned. The reinforcement is steel wire. The wires are put into tension (stretched) on a fixed frame, formwork is erected around the taut wires, and concrete is poured into it.

After the concrete has set and gained its full strength, the wires are cut loose from the frame. This gives the precast members a slight upward arch, which reduces deflection.

In industrialised countries the mixing and delivery of liquid concrete to building sites has been mechanised with the use of central plants and

mixing trucks, and this has substantially reduced its cost. In barely 100 years, reinforced concrete has progressed from being an experimental material to the most widespread form of building construction.

Concrete decay

Concrete is a manufactured construction product made by combining cement, sand, gravel and water. As these components begin to cure, the water is expelled during dehydration, leaving pores in the concrete. It may be described as a porous mass held together by the embedded steel, in the case of reinforced concrete.

Unfortunately these pores allow water and many other pollutants to penetrate into the concrete, which in time destroy the concrete and corrode the steel. If the liquid pollutant freezes, the expansion will split the mass or spall (splinter or chip) the surface, weakening and/or destroying the structure.

The pores set up a strong capillary action, which absorbs water and minerals from the ground (up to a depth of 7 metres). As the water passes through the concrete, it picks up the free lime and alkali in the concrete that was left over from the concrete curing process. The alkali reacts with any surface sealant such as polyurethane, epoxy, oil-based paint, and adhesives and causes 'saponification' – i.e. it forms a thin layer of soap. This then causes the surface sealant to separate, leaving the concrete exposed to the decaying effects of pollutants that will absorb into the concrete.

H Concrete additives

Additives (also referred to as admixtures) are additional materials that are added to the mix constituents to improve the properties of the concrete.

Additives are essential if optimum concrete performance is to be achieved. Additives are recognised for the important gains they provide in terms of cost savings on cement, higher produc-tivity levels due to improved workability and greater durability in the finished product.

Damp-proofing agents prevent water movement by capillary action, although additives cannot prevent entirely the passage of water vapour.

Additives and agents are intended to modify the properties of concrete. They should be used as recommended by the manufacturers. A selection of additives and their uses follow.

SUPERPLASTICISERS give a high workability concrete without the need for excess water in the mix – very good in applications where placing of the concrete is difficult, i.e. heavily reinforced areas etc. Plasticisers improve workability of mixes by reducing the surface tension of water and by trapping small air bubbles. Most plasticisers reduce strength.

RETARDERS are particularly useful for hot weather concreting because they delay the initial set of the concrete. A normal application will retard the concrete for 2–4 hours. Retarders are used to produce an exposed aggregate finish on concrete surfaces.

ACCELERATORS increase the rate of chemical reaction, which aids the development of early strength in concrete. Accelerators are particularly useful in the winter where conditions often require rapid strength in concrete in order to withstand effects of low temperatures.

AIR ENTRAINING AGENTS improve workability of concrete. Cohesion is also increased which reduces the risk of segregation and bleeding. Trapping up to 3 per cent of air increases workability.

Plastic settlement cracks form while concrete is still plastic, i.e. has not yet set.

EXPANDING AGENTS are used to avoid cracking and to compensate for water loss and plastic settlement.

FIBRES assist in crack control and increase durability.

WATERPROOFERS reduce the rate at which water can penetrate into or through concrete.

COLOUR PIGMENTS produce decorative coloured concrete and are available in a variety of colours.

Workability test for concrete

The slump test is used to establish the workability of concrete. Workability is important for correct placing and compacting of concrete.

Workability tests are used as indirect checks on the water/cement ratio of the concrete.

The equipment required to carry out this test consists of:

- a truncated conical mould, 300 mm high, 100 mm diameter at the top and 200 mm diameter at the bottom

14-19 *The conical mould used for the slump test*

- a steel tamping rod, 600 mm long and 16 mm in diameter, with both ends hemispherical
- a measuring rule
- a smooth, rigid and impervious surface

The **test procedure** is

- Check that the inside of the mould is clean and damp before each test.
- Place the mould as shown in Fig. 14-19, on a smooth, rigid and impervious surface.
- Fill the mould with concrete in three layers of approximately equal depth. Tamp each layer to its full depth 25 times with the tamping rod. Allow the concrete to be heaped above the mould before the top layer is tamped.
- Remove the excess concrete level with the top of the mould and clean any spillage from around the base.
- Lift the mould vertically from the concrete.
- Turn the mould upside down and place it beside the slumped concrete.

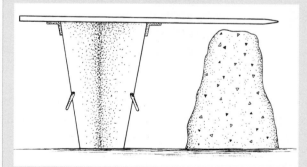

14-20 *The 'slump' is measured by placing the tamping rod across the inverted mould and measuring the distance from the mould to the concrete.*

- Lay the tamping rod across the mould and measure the slump from the top of the mould to the highest point on the concrete.

SLUMP RESULTS

- 0–50 mm slump = low workability
- 50–75 mm slump = medium workability

Strength test for concrete

The concrete cube test is used to check the strength of hardened concrete. The purpose of the test is to check that the concrete is above the minimum strength specified. It acts as a useful check on production control of concrete.

The equipment required to carry out the test consists of:

- cube moulds with base plates made of steel or cast iron (150 mm cubes are used for the test)
- mould oil
- spanners
- scoop for filling the mould
- steel float
- standard compacting bar, 380 mm long with a 25 mm square cross-section
- damp sacks
- polythene sheeting
- waterproof marker

The **test procedure** is

- Oil the clean moulds lightly and tighten them to the base plate.
- Fill the mould with concrete in 50 mm layers (three layers).
- Compact the concrete using the standard compacting bar. 35 tamps are recommended for each of the three layers.

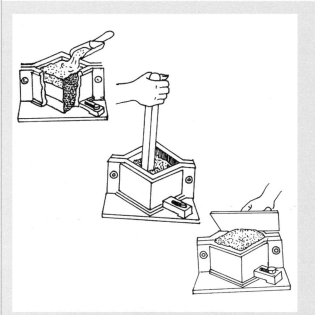

14-21 *Fill the cube in three layers for the concrete cube test. Tamp each layer 35 times and smooth surplus concrete with a steel trowel.*

- Remove surface concrete and smooth the top with a steel float.
- Clean the mould edges.
- Number the mould for identification.
- Cover the mould with a damp cloth and plastic sheet and store it in a dry cool location (15° to 25°C).

The moulds are removed between 3 and 7 days and are tested to destruction in a laboratory. This crushing test determines the strength of the sample of concrete.

Glass

Glass is an inorganic solid material that is usually transparent or translucent, hard, brittle, and impervious to the natural elements. Glass has been made into practical and decorative objects since ancient times. It is still very important in applications such as building construction, household goods, and telecommunications.

Glass is made by cooling molten ingredients such as silica sand with sufficient speed to prevent the formation of visible crystals.

Glass is made from three main materials: sand (silicon dioxide, or SiO_2), limestone (calcium carbonate, or $CaCO_3$), and sodium carbonate (Na_2CO_3).

Properties of glass

Glass, at ordinary temperatures, is a nearly perfect elastic solid, an excellent thermal and electrical insulator, and resistant to many corrosive media. (Its optical properties, however, vary greatly, depending on the light wavelengths concerned.)

The more or less random order of atoms is ultimately responsible for many of the properties that distinguish glass from other solids. Glass is isotropic, meaning that properties such as tensile strength, electrical resistance, and thermal expansion are of equal magnitude in any direction through the material.

Density

In the random atomic order of a glassy solid, the atoms are packed less densely than in a corresponding crystal, leaving larger interstitial spaces, or holes, between atoms. These interstitial spaces collectively make up what is known as free volume, and they are responsible for the lower density of a glass as opposed to a crystal.

Elasticity and plasticity

Because of the isotropic nature of glass, only two independent elastic moduli are measured: Young's modulus, which measures the ability of a solid to recover its original dimensions after being subjected to lengthwise tension or compression; and shear modulus, which measures its ability to recover from transverse stress.

A diamond micro indenter measures the hardness of glass.

Strength

Glass is much stronger than most metals when tested in the pristine state (pure state following correct manufacture).

Thermal properties

Glass expands when heated and shrinks when cooled. This thermal expansion of glass is critical to its thermal shock performance (that is, its performance when subjected suddenly to a temperature change).

When a hot specimen of glass is suddenly cooled, considerable tension may develop in the outer layers owing to their shrinking relative to the inner layers. This tension may lead to cracking. Resistance to such thermal shock is known as the thermal endurance of a glass.

Electrical properties

While most glasses contain charged metallic ions capable of carrying an electric current, the high viscosity of glass impedes their movements and electrical activity.

Therefore, glass is an efficient electrical insulator, but the electrical conductivity of glass increases rapidly with temperature.

Optical properties

Because electrons in glass molecules are confined to particular energy levels, they cannot absorb and re-emit photons (the basic units of light energy) by skipping from one energy band to another and back again.

As a result, light energy travels through glass instead of being absorbed and reflected, making glass transparent.

Glass to which certain metallic oxides have been added will absorb wavelengths corresponding to certain colours and let others pass, thereby appearing tinted to the eye. For example, cobalt

gives an intense blue tint to glass, chromium gives a green tint, and manganese purple.

Forming glass

Glass objects such as tableware, containers, flat glass, and fibreglass are formed of glass made by the melting process. Viscosity is the important property in glass forming.

After melting and conditioning, glass is transported to a forming machine in a manageable shape. The glass can be worked on, in this low viscous state, to form the desired object and then released in a near-solid condition. All through the process, heat is extracted in a controlled manner in order to allow the viscosity to increase from the levels of a liquid to those of a solid.

Flat glass

The float process is the method used to produce glass for such products as windows and mirrors.

A glass ribbon, soft enough to be workable, is fed from a glass-melting furnace and passed between rollers into the float bath. There it floats on molten tin under a controlled atmosphere of nitrogen and hydrogen (N_2/H_2) that prevents oxidation of the tin.

As the bulk of the glass begins to cool, the surface is heated and polished in order to remove surface blemishes and then allowed to cool. The ribbon leaves the float bath and passes through the annealer, where it is cooled uniformly in order to prevent the formation of internal stresses that may warp the glass. Diamond-tipped cutters then score the cooled glass, and individual sheets are separated and stacked.

Glass may be made in thickness of 2 to 25 millimetres and in widths up to 4 metres.

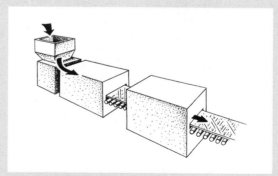

14-22 *The float glass process. Molten glass is poured on to the surface of molten tin. It is then cooled and cut into sheets.*

Fibreglass wool

Fibreglass (also known as glass-fibre) wool for insulation is produced by allowing a molten glass stream to drop into a spinning cup that has numerous holes in its wall. Glass fibres extrude through the holes under centrifugal force and meet a high-velocity air blast that breaks them into short lengths. On their descent to a travelling belt below, the fibres are bonded together with an adhesive spray. The binder is cured, and the wool is gently packed into rolls.

Fibreglass wool is an excellent sound and thermal insulator and is commonly used in buildings, appliances, and plumbing.

Treating glass

ANNEALING

Glasses may develop stresses during the glass-forming process. The process of annealing reduces these stresses. Annealing removes internal stress, crystal defects, and dislocations by heating.

STRENGTHENING GLASS

Strengthening by overlay glazing is carried out by firing onto the glass product a thin layer of another glass that has lower thermal expansion properties than the substrate.

THERMAL TEMPERING

Thermal tempering is achieved by quenching (or rapid-cooling) the glass.

The outer layers of the glass are cooled faster than the inner layers. The outer layers shrink at a higher rate and are compressed (in effect strength-ening the glass), while the inner layer is stretched.

Thermal tempering can strengthen many commercial glass products. Such glass may break, or dice, into a large number of pieces. As diced glass is unlikely to cause serious injury, building regulations may require that tempered glass is used in certain applications, such as in bathroom shower doors.

LAMINATED GLASS

In laminated glass, the mechanical energy associated with applied stress is absorbed by successive layers of glass and laminate, leaving less energy for crack development. Glass products are laminated by bonding sheets of tough polymers. A very tough interlayer of polyvinyl butyral, which does not suffer from optical ageing defects, is used in laminated glass.

Ceramics

Industrial ceramics comprise all industrially used solid materials that are neither metallic nor organic. The properties of ceramics that account for their enduring qualities include mechanical strength in spite of brittleness, chemical durability, hardness, ability to resist erosion, and the ability to be decorated.

Ceramic raw materials are classified as aggregates, plasticisers, binders, fluxes, and modifiers (chemical, thermal, physical, electrical, colour).

Traditional ceramic materials were largely derived from the elements most common in the Earth's crust – oxygen, silicon, aluminium, iron, and so on – but modern ceramics draw upon nearly every element.

Most ceramics are brittle at room temperature, i.e. when subjected to tension, they fail suddenly, with little or no plastic deformation prior to fracture.

Sanitary ware and glazed tiles represent the largest architectural uses of ceramics. Other uses include garden flower pots and lamp posts.

Composite materials

Most products in everyday use are made from monolithic materials. That means the individual components consist of a single material (an unreinforced plastic), or a combination of materials that are combined in such a way that the individual components are indistinguishable (a metal alloy).

Composite materials consist of two or more materials combined in such a way that the individual materials are easily distinguishable. The constituents retain their identities in the composites and do not dissolve or otherwise merge completely into each other, although they act together.

Reinforced concrete is an excellent example of a composite material in which the concrete and steel still retain their identities. The steel reinforcing bars carry the tension loads and the concrete carries the compression loads.

In aircraft construction the term composite structure refers to fabric resin combinations in which the fabric is embedded in the resin but still retains its identity.

The individual materials that make up composites are called constituents. Most

H

composites have two constituent materials: a binder or matrix, and a reinforcement. The reinforcement is usually much stronger and stiffer than the matrix, and gives the composite its good properties. The matrix holds the reinforcements in an orderly pattern. Because the reinforcements are usually discontinuous, the matrix also helps to transfer load among the reinforcements.

Cob
consists of a clayey soil and straw or fine roots, shaped in place, to make the walling of an earth building.

Many natural materials like wood, bone and muscle can be described as composite, although their properties cannot be engineered. Traditional building materials like wattle and daub, cob and concrete are examples of 'large scale' composites.

Conventional composites resemble plywood in that they are built in thin layers, each of which is reinforced by long fibres laid down in a single direction.

Modern engineering composites usually rely on the exceptional properties of fibres (e.g. glass, carbon and aramid), in combination with a suitable matrix. Most commercial composites use thermosetting or thermoplastic polymers in their construction.

Composite materials containing fibres are used in applications in which high strength and low weight are needed.

Building stone classification

Building stone or rock is classified into three major types according to origin. They are igneous, sedimentary, and metamorphic.

Igneous rock
Igneous rocks are those that solidify from a volcanic melt called magma. Igneous rocks are formed at high temperatures. They originate from processes deep within the Earth, typically at depths of about 50 to 200 kilometres, in the mid to lower crust or in the upper mantle.

The principal stones in this category are **granites** and **basalt**.

Granites consist of quartz, felspar and mica. Granite is a durable, hardwearing rock.

Basalt is black or greyish-black in colour. It weathers to a reddish or green crust. Most basalt occurs as lava flows.

Sedimentary rock
Sedimentary rocks are those that are deposited and lithified (compacted and cemented together) at the Earth's surface, with the assistance of running water, wind, ice, or living organisms. Most are deposited from the land surface to the bottoms of lakes, rivers, and oceans.

Sedimentary rocks are generally stratified, i.e. they have layering. Layers may be distinguished by differences in colour, particle size, type of cement, or internal arrangement.

The principal stones in this category are **limestones** and **sandstones**.

Limestones consist of calcium carbonate and small quantities of clay, silica and magnesia.

Sandstones are compacted sands ranging from grey to red in colour. They are harder and have rougher surfaces than limestones.

Metamorphic rock
Metamorphic rocks are those formed by changes in existing rocks under the influence of high temperature, pressure, and chemically active solutions. The existing rocks may be either igneous or sedimentary.

The principal stones in this category are **marbles** and **slates**.

Marble is limestone that has been transformed by heat and pressure, deep within the Earth's crust.

Slate is a fine-grained rock with perfect cleavage that allows it to split into thin sheets. Slate usually has a light to dark brown streak. It is considered the lowest grade of metamorphic rock.

Bricks

The process of brick making has not changed since the first fired bricks were produced thousands of years ago. The steps used then are still used today, but with refinements. The various phases of manufacture are as follows: sourcing the clay, raw material preparation, mixing and forming, drying, firing, and cooling. Brick manufacture is covered in Chapter 6, page 100.

Chapter 15

Materials processing

Introduction

This chapter concentrates on the skills and techniques required for processing materials. Chapter 14 gave an understanding of the properties of the various materials. The properties of materials are important when selecting the correct skills and techniques for processing.

Wood
Sawing and sanding
The most commonly used saws in woodwork are tenon saws and handsaws.

Handsaws can be broken down into **rip saws**, **crosscut saws**, and **panel saws**, all of which cut at different speeds and varying degrees of roughness. This is due to the size and distance between the teeth on the saw blade.

The rip saw has 4–8 teeth per 25 mm, the cross-cut saw has 6–8, and the panel saw has 10–12 teeth per 25 mm.

15-1 The main straight cutting saws are the dovetail saw (top), the tenon saw (middle) and the hand saw.

Saw on the waste side of the cutting line. The correct stance is important when sawing for balance and control. Make sure the workpiece is firmly held either on a bench hook or in a vice.

Use a cross-cut or panel saw for boards up to 15 mm thick, including plywood and MDF, and use a rip saw for heavier timber. Should the timber begin to bind on the saw blade open up the kerf using wedges.

Use a **cork sanding block** for hand sanding wood. Woodworking abrasive paper is available in garnet paper, glasspaper and silicon carbide. Each type carries a grading number, which refers to its grit size. Always sand with the grain and use long, uniform strokes.

Wood
Nailing and screwing
Nails and screws are the two most important fastening devices used to fix wood to wood. The two most commonly used hammers are the claw hammer and the cross-pein, or 'Warrington'.

Nail punches are used to bury nails below the surface of the wood and they come in different sizes to suit different nail sizes.

The claw hammer is used to remove partially driven nails.

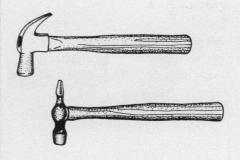

15-2 The claw hammer (top) and the cross-pein hammer

Screws are generally driven with a variable-speed power drill, which may be mains or battery powered. Cabinet screwdrivers with blades of approx. 300 mm are used for straight slot screws.

Screwdrivers with the appropriate tips must be used for crosshead, Phillips or Pozidriv screws.

It is good practice to drill pilot holes before screws are driven. A bradawl is used to start screws entering softwood smaller than No. 6 gauge. Two pilot holes are required for screws into hardwood and screws into softwood larger than No. 6 gauge. One is for the thread and one is for the shank.

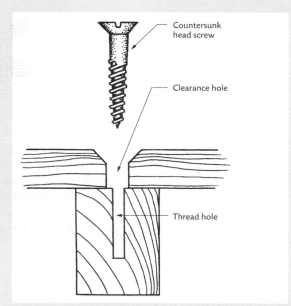

Countersunk head screw

Clearance hole

Thread hole

15-3 Types of holes required when screwing wood to wood

Pilot holes are not required when using 'superdrive' screws. These are self-tapping screws that are threaded the full length of the shank. They are used with cordless screwdrivers.

Countersinking is the easiest way to recess screw heads flush with, or below, the surface of the wood, using a countersink bit. Ensure that the tip of the screwdriver fits exactly into the slot in the screw head.

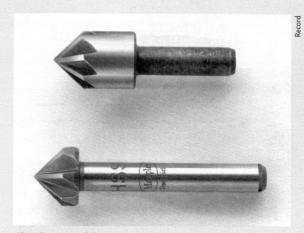

15-4 Countersink bits are used for widening the tops of holes to suit screw heads. (Record)

Wood
Gluing and cramping

The term **glue** correctly refers to pure animal or vegetable glue. Other types, which are resin based, are known as adhesives. Adhesives need clean dry surfaces and a warm atmosphere in which to set.

ADHESIVES

The most commonly used wood adhesives include:

- **Polyvinyl acetate (PVA).** PVA adhesive is available ready-mixed in easy-to-use containers. The setting time varies from 30 minutes to 3 hours depending on the brand used. PVA is a strong adhesive. It does not stain timber but, if smears are left on the surface, it will show through varnish as a light patch. Any smears should be wiped away quickly using a damp cloth. It is not suitable for outdoor use because it is not completely waterproof

- **Urea formaldehyde adhesive** is suitable for resinous woods. It resists moisture better than PVA.

- **Resorcinol formaldehyde** is the strongest and most water-resistant adhesive, making it ideal for outdoor use and boat building. Urea or resorcinol formaldehyde may be used on timber treated with a preservative.

- **Animal glue (Scotch glue)** is made from animal pelts and bones. It is available in cake, granular or liquid form. The cake or granular varieties need to be melted down in a glue pot with water at a temperature of 65°C and used while still hot. Animal glue does not stain wood and it dries to a medium brown colour. It is not waterproof. Liquid animal glues can be used cold, and unlike other forms, they stain the wood.

- **Synthetic resin cement** is almost completely waterproof and comes in a variety of forms – powder, semi-liquid or two-part (adhesive and hardener). It is suitable for outdoor use and small boat building.

- **Impact (or contact) adhesives** are used mainly for fixing laminates and tiles. The surfaces to be bonded are both coated with the impact adhesive and are then left to dry separately for a time. The two surfaces are then brought in contact with each other to make an instant strong bond. Impact adhesives are the only types that do not require cramping while they set.

- **Epoxies.** Almost any material can be bonded with epoxy adhesives. They are made up of two parts – a resin and a hardener – which must be mixed together. Setting time can vary between one hour and 24 hours.

- **Cyanocrylate adhesives ('super glues').** Great care is needed when using these because the manufacturers claim that one small drop of the adhesive and a little pressure will stick almost anything to anything (including fingers) in a few moments.

CRAMPING

The type of cramp to be used depends on the size of the wood to be glued.

- **G-cramp.** This cramp gets its name from its shape. G-cramps have a mouth capacity of between 25 mm and 300 mm and are used mainly for cramping pieces of wood to a bench and for holding down veneer or laminate while the adhesive dries.

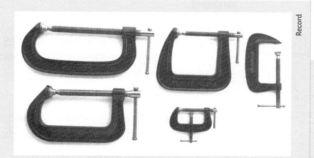

15-5 G-cramps are available in a variety of sizes.

- **Sash cramp.** These are used to cramp larger pieces of timber, such as carcasses and window frames. Sash cramps consist of two adjustable stops on a long bar, which come in different lengths up to 3 metres long with extensions.

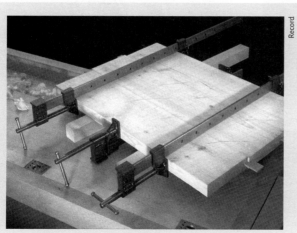

15-6 Sash cramps in use (Record)

- **Web cramp.** This consists of a 3.6 m loop of nylon webbing, running through a ratchet, which can be tightened and released using a spanner or a screwdriver. It is suitable only for light and medium weight gluing projects as it cannot apply as much pressure as a sash cramp.

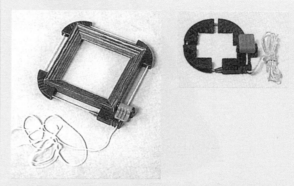

15-7 A web cramp is used where light pressure only is required.

It is good practice to 'dry assemble' the work before gluing to ensure that all joints fit correctly.

With the exception of impact adhesive, the wood should be cramped as soon as the joint has been made. Ensure that the surface of the wood is not damaged by the cramp while the glue is setting.

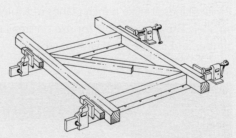

15-8 Check that the frame is square before final cramping. The diagonals must be the same length in order for the frame to be square.

Wood
Planing

A plane is used to remove unwanted wood, thereby reducing the wood to the required size and also leaving it smooth and flat.

Bench planes are the most commonly used planes and they come in four lengths. The jack plane is the type students would be familiar with and its length is between 350 and 375 mm. The plane blade has two angles forming the cutting edge – the ground angle of 25° and the honed angle of 30°.

15-9 *Jack plane*

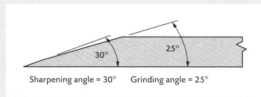

15-10 **The two angles that form the cutting edge of a plane blade**

Block planes are like bench planes but they are smaller. They are suitable for use on small pieces of timber and can be used with one hand.

15-11 **Block planes are used for more intricate work than bench planes. (Record)**

When using the jackplane hold it firmly but comfortably with both hands and with your body balanced over the top of the plane. Check with the try square that the edge being planed is at right angles to the other edges and use the edge of the try square, or a steel rule, to check that the edge is flat.

When planing end grain, place a piece of waste wood at the end and plane across both pieces. Any splitting will occur on the waste wood. An alternative is to plane from both ends towards the middle.

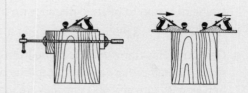

15-12 **Two methods of planning end grain**

Wood
Using a chisel

The chisel is one of the main wood-shaping tools and is used for paring, cutting joints and removing areas of wood for hinges and other fittings. The basic types of chisel are:

- **Bevel-edged chisel.** These have tapered edges which make them suitable for cutting dovetails and for shallow housings.

15-13 *Bevel-edged chisels (Record)*

■ **Firmer chisel.** These have strong blades of rectangular cross-section, which makes them stronger than bevel-edged chisels.

15-14 **Firmer chisels**

■ **Mortise chisels** are the strongest of the three types and are designed to withstand continual striking of the mallet and the levering action required when chopping a mortise. The heavy square section of the blade prevents the chisel from twisting in the mortise.

When working with a chisel always keep both hands behind the cutting edge. Do not try to remove large amounts of wood at once as trying to force a chisel will only lead to an accident.

Horizontal paring is a technique used for making housing or halving joints. Vertical paring is used to round off a corner or to make a curve in a piece of wood.

Wood
Halving joints

The halving joint is used in all kinds of framework. They are called halving joints because both members of the joint are halved in thickness so that the faces of the finished assembly are flush with one another.

The three basic types of halving joint are the tee halving, the cross halving and the corner halving. Variations of these three types are achieved by sloping one or both edges to give a dovetail halving.

The interlocking parts of a halving joint are known as 'pins' and 'sockets'. The tee-halving joint consists of a pin cut in the cross rail and a socket in the side rail. Corner halving joints consist of a pin in each member, and cross halving joints consist of two sockets.

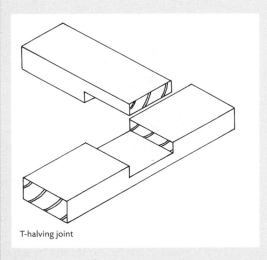

T-halving joint

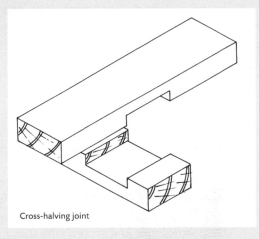

Cross-halving joint

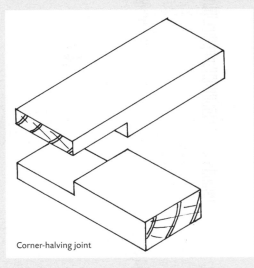

Corner-halving joint

15-15 **A selection of halving joints. Many more variations are possible.**

Wood
Mortise and tenon joints

The strength of a joint connecting two pieces of timber depends on three factors:

- the size of the gluing area
- the way in which one piece of timber encases the other
- the accuracy of the finished joint

A strong joint is one in which one member encases the other in such a way as to ensure a large gluing area without either member being weakened. The mortise and tenon joint satisfies all of these requirements best.

The four main types of mortise and tenon joint are the through, stub, through wedged, and fox wedged.

A haunched mortise and tenon is used to prevent the rail from twisting at the corner of a frame. A double tenon is sometimes used on large rails.

The thickness of the tenon should be approximately one-third of the thickness of the stile. The width of the tenon should not exceed five times its own thickness, this will determine whether a single or double tenon is required.

When the joint is at the top of the stile the tenon is divided into three parts – two for the tenon and one for the haunch.

When making a stub tenon the depth of the mortise should exceed the length of the tenon by 2 mm.

It is normal practice to leave waste material when making a mortise at the end of a stile. This waste is known as a 'horn'. The horn prevents the stile from splitting and protects the stile until it is trimmed off.

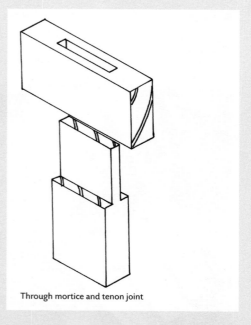

Through mortice and tenon joint

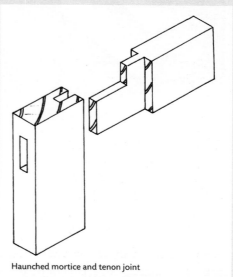

Haunched mortice and tenon joint

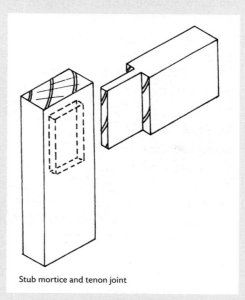

Stub mortice and tenon joint

15-16 **The common mortice and tenon joints**

Wood

Mitre joints

A mitre joint is a neat way of joining two pieces of wood at an angle. The simplest mitre joint uses wood of the same size, butt joined together with adhesives and pins. Its most common application is in picture frames.

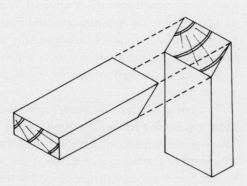

15-17 **A typical mitre joint**

It is possible to cut a mitre by holding the pieces at an angle in the vice and sawing them direct. But for greater accuracy a mitre block or a mitre box is used.

Use a picture framer's cramp to hold the mitres in position while the pins are driven home and use a fine pin punch to tap them below the surface. Larger frames can be cramped together using a web cramp. Check that the frame is square by checking the diagonals, which should be equal.

15-18 **A picture framer's cramp can be used for sawing and cramping.**

The **cross-tongued** or **feathered-mitre joint** provides greater gluing area and is therefore stronger.

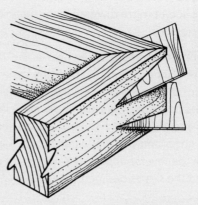

15-19 **Cross-tongues strengthen the mitre**

Keyed mitres are used to strengthen edge mitre joints.

Dowelled mitre joints are the neatest and strongest of the mitre joints discussed. Special dowel jigs are available, but the positions can be marked out without jigs if care is taken. The diameter of the dowel used should not be greater than one-third the thickness of the timber.

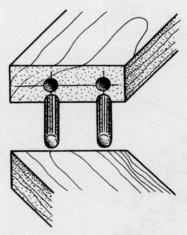

15-20 **Use either a dowelling jig or special dowel aids to mark the dowel positions.**

Wood

Dovetail joints

The dovetail is one of the most difficult joints to manufacture, but it is the best joint to use in traditional furniture and drawers. The dovetail is one of the most attractive joints. There are three main types of dovetail joint, through, lapped and secret mitre.

- The **through dovetail** shows both sides of the corner joint
- The **lapped dovetail** is used in drawers and shows on one side and is concealed on the other.
- The **secret mitre dovetail** hides the joint completely.

The component parts are known as the 'dovetail' (the female part), and the 'pin' (the male part). The slope of the dovetail is the angle, which gives the joint its strength. The usual slopes are 1 in 5, 1 in 6, 1 in 7 and 1 in 8. 1 in 5 is used where strength is more important than appearance, and 1 in 7 or 8 where the reverse applies. It is important not to exceed the slopes outlined.

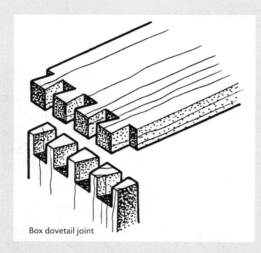

Box dovetail joint

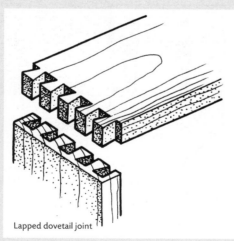

Lapped dovetail joint

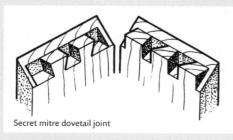

Secret mitre dovetail joint

15-21 **The three main types of dovetail joint**

Wood
Tool maintenance

Real excellence in woodworking is difficult to achieve unless the tools used are properly maintained. Damaged or blunt tools result in poor quality work and may cause accidents.

All cutting tools are ground but not honed when they are purchased. An oilstone is used to hone tools, which may be natural or artificial. Two types of natural stone are **Arkansas** and **Washita**. Two types of artificial stone are **carborundum**, which is fairly cheap, and **India**, which is more expensive.

Slip stones are used to sharpen hollow cutters such as gouges.

Traditional oilstones are being replaced by **Diamond honing stones**. Diamond honing stones combine the hardness of diamonds with the toughness of plastics to give excellent sharpening results. Fine monocrystalline diamond particles are permanently fixed to a flat plastic base in a unique screen pattern. Water is used as the lubricating wash for sharpening all tool steels. Stones are available in different sizes and in four grits.

14-22 **Diamond honing stones**

Water is used as a lubricant on coarse natural stone, and fine oil on the others. The whole surface area of the stone should be used to avoid localised wear. The most difficult part of learning to hone is getting the honing angle right. Several types of honing guide are available to make this task easier.

A **leather strop** is used to complete the sharpening process. The strop is soaked with light oil and impregnated with carborundum powder.

Gouges can be divided into 'firmer gouges', which are ground on the outside, and 'paring gouges' which are ground on the inside.

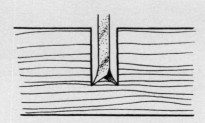

15-23 **An enlarged view of a saw showing the kerf generated by the set on the saw teeth**

A **saw** must be able to cut through a piece of timber without sticking. To allow this to happen the teeth are 'set' – this means that alternate teeth are bent outwards to make a cut, or 'kerf', which is slightly wider than the blade thickness.

A slotted piece of wood can easily be made up to protect the saw teeth.

Never force a saw when using it and always use firm, even strokes. Specific saw maintenance treatments include:

- **topping** – to ensure that the teeth are level
- **shaping** – to give the teeth the same profile
- **setting** – to offset the teeth at the right angle
- **sharpening**

A good saw can be sharpened several times before the set is worn away. Hard point saws are now available that are disposable.

Wood
Grooving and rebating

Simple grooves and rebates are used extensively in furniture using solid wood and manufactured boards. There are a number of specialised tools, both hand and power, used to cut grooves and rebates.

Rebates are common in simple drawer construction and at the corners of box carcass construction. Its main application is to provide a neat and solid fixing where a panel meets a frame. Rebates can be sawn, chiseled, planed or machined with a router. The main dimensions of a rebate are the depth and the width. For some applications the rebate will need to be stopped, that is, not run to the end of the board.

15-24 Rebate plane with a depth stop and a fence to control the two dimensions of the rebate

Grooving was used extensively before the advent of manufactured boards for edge-joining narrow timber to make up large sections with loose tongues. There are many other uses for this technique, for example, framed and panelled doors where the panel is grooved into the stiles and cross members. The main advantage of grooves is that the panel does not need to be rigidly fixed, and is therefore free to move should the frame shrink. Two cuts are generally required to make a groove with a saw. Electric routers cut grooves quickly and cleanly.

Wood
Woodcarving

A great deal of artistic skill is not necessary to begin woodcarving. Simple patterns can be copied from existing work or traced from books and transferred to the wood using carbon paper. Simple patterns are ideal for chip carving and when the skill of handling the carving tools has been mastered more artistic exercises can be attempted.

15-25 Examples such as the relief carving shown are easily mastered using the correct carving tools, the correct wood and some patience.

Beginners should select an even-textured and straight-grained piece of wood. The basic carving tools are straight gouges and chisels, which come in a variety of widths and sections. One or two firmer gouges and a veiner (for cutting narrow channels) are adequate to get started.

Woodcarving mallets have round heads, usually with a slight taper towards the handle.

The rasp is a multi-bladed plane that produces narrow shavings that come up through the body of the tool. It is commonly used in wood sculpture.

'Frosting punches' gives a pattern of dots, circles or crosses and is used for texturing the background of a carving.

Chip carving is the simplest form of carving in which hollows and channels are made in flat boards.

15-26 *Chip carving is used mainly on flat boards.*

Wood
Bending wood

There are four basic methods used to bend wood. These are:

- **Building-up or coopering.** Each section is made up of slats which are jointed and shaped on both sides. The slats can be coopered and then finished to a curve. A jig is usually required for cramping.

Coopering

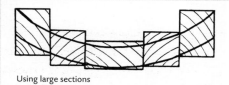

Using large sections

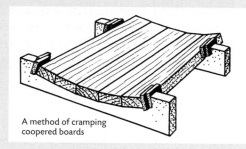

A method of cramping coopered boards

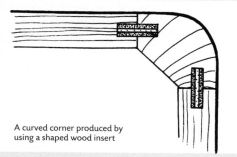

A curved corner produced by using a shaped wood insert

15-27 *Methods of producing built-up curves*

- **Kerfing.** This technique allows solid wood and plywood to be bent either across or along the grain. Making a series of parallel cuts (kerfs) partially through the wood reduces the strength of the timber and allows it to be bent.

   This technique should only be used where strength is not an important factor. The kerfs are usually cut to a depth equal to three-quarters of the stock thickness.

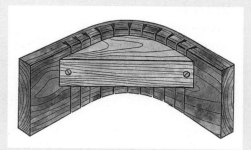

15-28 *Kerfs are used on the outside if the finished piece is to be veneered. Otherwise kerfs are cut on the inside.*

- **Laminating.** When a length of wood is bent it undergoes both tensile and compressive stresses. The degree to which wood will bend depends on the thickness of the piece to be bent and the nature of the wood. Hardwoods generally bend better than softwoods.

   It is possible to calculate the amount of cold bending wood will withstand before fracturing occurs. A rule of thumb ratio is 1:50, for example, a 25 mm thick section will form a curve of about 1200 mm radius.

   There are exceptions: Ash does much better at 1:38 (3 mm thick section will curve to 114 mm radius). Laminations should be of equal thickness ranging from 1.5 mm to 6 mm, depending on the degree of curve required.

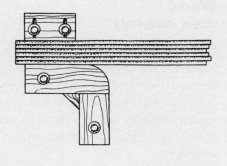

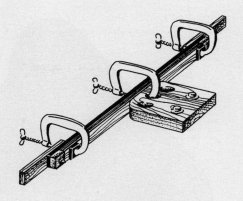

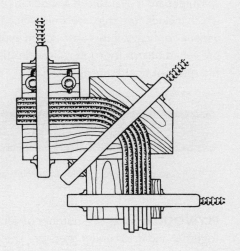

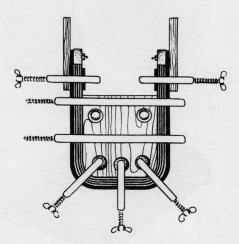

15-30 Bending steamed timber around a former
and holding with cramps

Wood
Working with veneer

Veneers are thin slices of wood, sliced with large, powered knives. The standard thickness for veneer is 0.8 mm but it can be as thin as 0.3 mm and as thick as 9.5 mm. The thickness depends on the type of timber and not the method of cutting. The three main methods of cutting veneer are: rotary peeling, half-round slicing, and flat slicing.

Cheap rotary peeling produces dull, unattractive veneers, which are mostly used in the manufacture of plywood.

Veneers are used as a means of protecting expensive and rare hardwood species. When carefully selected and applied to the right base or 'groundwork', veneers reduce the cost of finished artefacts and increase the scope of the designer to create fine furniture. Mirror-repeat patterns and other decorative effects are easily achieved with veneer, once it is cut correctly.

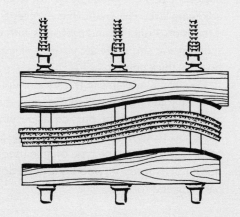

15-29 Two approaches to laminating. Bending a set of laminations and using a two-part former.

■ **Steam bending.** Steam bending is quicker and cheaper than laminating. The problem with steam bending is that solid wood rarely holds its shape for any length of time, so laminating is the better method. The most suitable woods to use are: ash, birch, beech, hickory, elm, horse chestnut, oak, yew and walnut.

Bends with a ratio of timber thickness to radius of curvature of more than 1:30 need external support to prevent the fibres from tearing under tension.

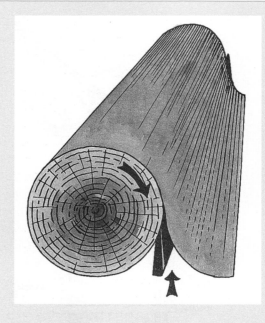

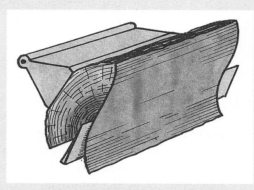

15-31 *Veneer is cut either by rotary peeling, flat slicing or half round slicing*

The finished product is only as good as the base or groundwork. Veneers can be glued to almost any wood as long as it is even grained, stable, knot-free and not resinous. Only top quality manufactured boards should be used as a base, such as plywood, MDF and blockboards. As it is difficult to veneer end grain, lippings are used to conceal the edges.

Wood
Sheet materials

CHIPBOARD (PARTICLE BOARD) is a cheap and versatile material. It is made by applying heat and pressure to wood chips which have previously been coated with a binder adhesive. The chips, which are usually softwood, make up about 90 per cent of the board. The balance comprises synthetic resin and additives.

Chipboard is available in a wide range of finishes, which include fine chip, melamine-faced and wood veneer. For heavy-duty construction applications, pre-felted boards for roofing, insect resistant and fire resistant boards are available.

15-32 *A cross-section through three-layer chipboard*

PLYWOOD consists of a number of veneers glued together and dried under pressure. The grain of each veneer is at right angles to the grain in the adjoining layer. Plywood offers excellent dimensional stability and problems with warping, splitting and shrinkage are virtually eliminated if the board is thick enough.

Plywood is available in thicknesses up to 25 mm. Three-ply can have layers of the same thickness, or a core thicker than the outside layers, which is known as **stout heart**. Plywood is graded according to its construction, the type of glue used and the quality of its faces. Plywood is used in flooring, paneling and roofing.

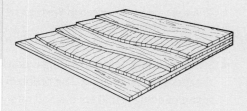

15-33 *Multiply has five or more layers*

MEDIUM DENSITY FIBREBOARD (MDF) belongs to a family of boards known collectively as fibreboards. Fibreboards are manufactured from wood fibres, with the main bond coming from the 'meshing' of the fibres and their natural adhesive properties. Fibreboard is stronger than chipboard.

MDF can be cut, chiselled and moulded like solid wood. Like plywood and chipboard it is available in a wide range of natural veneer surfaces.

OSB (ORIENTED STRAND BOARD) comprises softwood flakes/strands bonded together with phenolic resins, a binder and waxes. A consistent strand geometry results in a highly-engineered wood panel that achieves a reliable distribution of strength, stiffness and spanning capacity along and across the board.

Wood
Staining and finishing
Choosing the right finish for a particular wood is a difficult task due to the almost endless choice available. But take care – more projects are ruined by poor finishing than by any other factor.

Wood stains and varnishes allow projects to be finished to a select colour, and show off the natural beauty in grain pattern and configuration to its best advantage.

Stains
Stains are used in a variety of situations, for example, where mixed timbers are used and a uniform colour is required or where grain patterns need to be emphasised. Stains also have the effect of making cheap materials look more expensive.

The three commonly available types of stain are **water-**, **spirit-** and **oil-based**. Water stains are the cheapest but they can be difficult to apply.

Some typical dyes are described below:
- **Vandyke brown (walnut crystals):** this dye can give various shades of brown depending on the degree of dilution. It is usually used on oak and walnut and it will give mahogany a rich brown colour.
- **Potassium bichromate:** this chemical is most effective on wood containing tannin. The colour can vary from light orange to dark brown on mahogany. It can produce greenish-brown tones on oak.
- **Sulphate of iron (green copperas):** this dye turns oak and sycamore grey. If it is applied too strong it can stain oak bright blue. This dye is sometimes used on mahogany to make it look like walnut.
- **Ebony crystals:** this dye produces an almost black finish.

All these dyes may be categorised as analine dyes (chemically related compounds) and can be made into solutions using water, oil or methylated spirit. Analine dyes are available in a whole host of shades including purple, maroon, crimson, magenta, orange, yellow, brown, blue, green and black.

Water stains tend to raise the grain but this can be overcome by first dampening the surface with clean water after the wood has been thoroughly prepared. When it is dry, rub it down using very fine wet and dry paper. Any type of finish can be used over water stains and they do not need sealing.

Oil-based stains can usually be bought prepared and ready to apply. They do not raise the grain on timber surfaces, but they are not as transparent as water stains and therefore tend to hide the grain rather than enhance it.

Spirit stains are difficult to apply and may fade. They can be bought ready mixed or solutions can be made up using 25g of spirit soluble dye in 1 litre of spirit.

Fuming
Fuming is a traditional colouring process in which oak is darkened by the fumes of ammonia. This process turns oak a blue/grey colour, which turns to a rich brown when treated with an applied finish such as varnish or lacquer. Mahogany, walnut and chestnut are woods, which are also suitable for fuming. Trials should be carried out on test pieces in advance to ensure that the correct colour can be achieved.

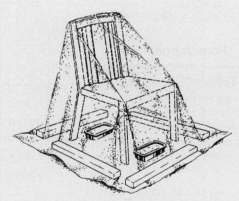

15-34 A DIY fuming chamber. Care is needed to seal the edges of the polythene.

Bleaching
Bleaching is another chemical process that can be applied to wood. This treatment is used to lighten colour, remove dark patches, even out the natural colour or prepare for staining with unusual colour. Oxalic acid is the simplest bleach to use. Oxalic acid is a poison and should be kept out of reach of children.

Wax and oil

Wax is the traditional furniture finish and beeswax is the best one to use. It varies in colour from brown to orange to pale yellow. Other waxes are 'carnauba' and 'cerestine' which are both hard, and paraffin wax, which is soft.

Oil-based finishes are probably the easiest of all finishes to apply, but time and patience are needed to get satisfactory results. The oil, usually linseed oil, is applied to the work and burnished every day for a period of four to six weeks. This process can be speeded up by first applying a sealer.

Lacquers

Synthetic materials called lacquers have superseded traditional varnishes, which are made from natural resin. Plastic lacquers are easier to apply, they are naturally rapid drying and they give an almost instant finish. They also offer excellent heat properties and provide greater resistance to chemicals than other traditional materials.

Polyurethane forms the base of the more commonly known plastic lacquers and offers a tough, hard-wearing surface. However, urea/melamine lacquer is a better product as it allows the wood to flex. Both types harden by chemical reaction and can be applied in thick coats initially. The one-pack lacquers, with the catalyst built in, are ideal for general purposes. Two-pack lacquers are used for specialist situations, like floor finishing, where the catalyst must be added just before application.

French polishing

Shellac is a yellowish resin secreted by the lac insect. A commercial preparation of this is used in varnishes and polishes.

French polishing is a traditional method of applying shellac.

A lot of skill, effort and patience is required to apply a French polish. If the wood is to be stained use only a water stain as the polishing process will rub off most other stains.

French polish is applied using a cloth pad or 'wad'. A ball of cotton wool, about 50 mm in diameter, is covered with cotton or linen fabric. A minimum of three pads is recommended for the process.

The pad is filled by pouring the shellac on the back of the pad. Do not pour liquid on the face of the pad or dip the pad into the liquid. The pad should be damp but not dripping.

Build up a film of shellac on the surface by working in a 'figure-of-eight' motion. Keep the pad in constant motion. If the pad is left stationary on the surface it will mark the work. Let the shellac dry for approximately 12 hours before applying another coat. A minimum of four coats are needed to build-up a high gloss finish.

Allow the last coat to dry for 24 hours. Use a new pad and fill it with alcohol only. Use less and less alcohol for each application until the pad is almost completely dry. Rub the pad in the direction of the grain across the surface. This process is called 'spiriting off' and produces the characteristic sheen of a French polish finish.

Metal
Basic metalwork

Metal is a versatile and useful material. This section will concentrate on a basic knowledge of the techniques and skills involved in metalwork. The areas that will be covered include measuring and marking, drilling, cutting and filing, folding and shaping, joining and finishing. The properties of the different metals are dealt with in Chapter 14 and in the Options.

Metal
Measuring and marking

Accuracy in measuring and marking is as important in metal as it is in wood. The basic measuring tools are a steel rule, calipers, vernier gauge and a micrometer. An engineer's try square or a combination square and a centre square are also important.

For marking, a centre-punch, a steel scriber and a set of dividers with steel points are recommended. A set of calipers is used to measure radial dimensions, such as the diameter of a tube.

A vernier gauge is used for more accurate work and if used correctly is accurate to 0.01 mm. A micrometer is even more accurate than a vernier gauge and is generally only used in precision engineering.

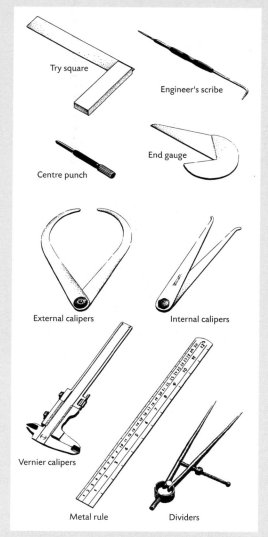

15-35 A selection of common metalwork tools

Labels: Try square, Engineer's scribe, Centre punch, End gauge, External calipers, Internal calipers, Vernier calipers, Metal rule, Dividers

Metal
Drilling

Ordinary twist drills should be used to make holes in metal. Do not use wood bits or flat bits. Drills are available in diameters ranging in size from 0.4 mm to 50 mm.

Before starting to drill, the position for the hole must be marked out. A centre punch is then used to give the drill a good start. For large holes a pilot hole is drilled first. If a high degree of accuracy is required, drill a hole slightly smaller than the required finished diameter, and finish the hole with a reamer.

All drill bits are hardened (tempered) and excessive heating, due to too much pressure being applied, causes a breakdown in their properties. It is therefore important that the drill bit is adequately cooled and lubricated. Soluble or cutting oil is used,

and this should be diluted with water to a concentration of 20:1.

If the correct drill speed is selected, overheating should not occur. Two rules for drill speed should be adhered to at all times:

The first is the harder the metal, the slower the drill speed, and vice versa. The second is the larger the drill bit, the slower the drill speed. This is because the outside cutting edge of a large drill will be rotating faster than that of a smaller diameter drill for a given speed.

Reaming: drill the hole smaller than the required finished size (0.3 mm smaller for holes up to 10 mm diameter, and up to 1 mm smaller for holes of 30–50 mm). A reamer should only be rotated in the cutting direction.

Metal
Cutting and filing

The hacksaw is the most widely used tool for cutting metal. Fine blades are used for hard metals, and coarse blades are used for softer metals to prevent the teeth from clogging. Blades should be fitted with the teeth pointing away from the handle and correctly tensioned. Apply pressure only on the forward stroke, when cutting.

Tin snips are used for cutting sheet material. Special purpose power machinery is available to cut metal: jig saws, bandsaws and circular saws can all be used in some circumstances.

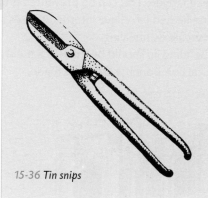

15-36 Tin snips

After sawing, the burred and pitted edges will need to be removed with a metal file. A wide range of files is available to cover a wide range of functions.

Files are classified according to their length, shape and type of teeth. There are four main types of teeth cuts: single cut, double cut, dreadnought (curved tooth) and rasp. Each type can be further graded from rough to dead smooth, depending on the finish.

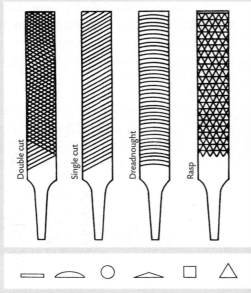

15-37 *The four main types of file*

Metal
Shaping

Unlike wood, most metals can be twisted, bent, beaten and folded into an almost infinite variety of shapes. Sheet steel, for example, can be folded like paper to make tool boxes. Wrought iron gates and furniture can be made from flat strips by heating and bending the metal, or welding the components together.

Metals 'work harden' as they are worked, that is they become brittle and suffer from what is known as metal fatigue. This can be prevented if the metals are first heated to relieve internal stresses in a process called annealing.

A bending jig should be made if a number of identical components are to be made.

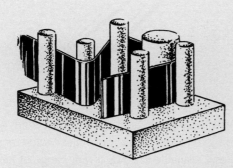

15-38 *Bending jigs are used when a number of identical components are required*

Beating metal is a process that can be applied to the manufacture of household items such as bowls, lampshades and ashtrays, as well as to the repair of car body parts. By beating the sheet over a former

it can be stretched and formed into a three-dimensional shape.

15-39 *Shaping metal using a planishing hammer and a mushroom stake*

Metal
Joining techniques

Screws, bolts and rivets are used to join metal items. In metalwork two basic types of screw are used: the self-tapping screw, which resembles the wood screw, and the machine screw, which resembles a bolt in its usual form.

Metalworking washers of various types can be used to lock screws and prevent them from coming loose due to vibrations, etc.

Machine screws require tapped (threaded) holes in the receiving piece of metal. A tap and a tap wrench is used to cut the threads.

Riveting is a means of joining sheets of metal together in a permanent manner. A rivet is a small plug of metal, which passes through the two components to be joined, the ends are then flattened and spread to prevent them from coming apart.

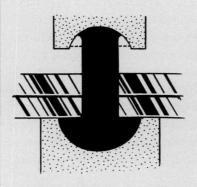

15-40 *Rivets formed using a rivet snap set*

Metal
Soldering and brazing

Soldering and brazing are the two methods of 'gluing' metals together. The 'glue' used is a soft alloy with a melting point lower than that of the two pieces to be joined. It is melted so that it flows into the joint between the two components and then cools and solidifies.

In **soldering**, solder is used, which is an alloy of lead and tin. In **brazing**, brass filler rods are used which are made of spelter. **Flux** must be used in both processes, this is a special compound which is mixed with the solder or the filler rod. The main purpose of the flux is to prevent oxides from forming on the metal, which would stop the solder or filler from adhering to it.

> **Spelter** is impure zinc, usually containing about 3% lead and other impurities.

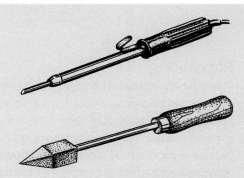

15-41 An electric soldering iron and a flame-heated soldering iron

Metal
Arc and gas welding

Welding is one of the most commonly used metal-joining processes. The welded joint is quick to make, strong, and easy to hide if ground down and painted over.

In arc welding, a high-energy spark melts the filler rod and the pieces of metal being joined so that they fuse together.

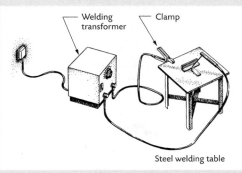

15-42 Arc welding equipment

In gas welding, an oxy-acetylene flame is used to melt the filler rod into the joint between the two components.

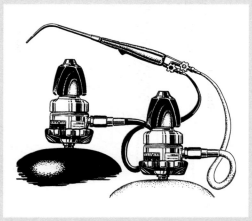

15-43 In gas welding a mixture of two gases, oxygen and acetylene, is burned through a torch.

Mild steel is the most common metal welded, but the process can also be applied to copper and aluminium, provided the correct filler rods are used. Dissimilar metals cannot be welded together.

Bricklaying/blocklaying
Basics

Setting out is an important task in brickwork or blockwork. It is essential to ensure that the main walls run in a straight line and remain level. A marker line or storey rod can be used. Bricks and blocks are bonded to create a rigid structure and to spread the load to the foundations. A builder's square is used to set out corners for a house, with sides in the ratio of 3:4:5.

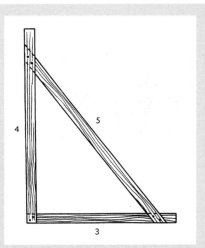

15-44 A builder's square uses the principle of the theorem of Pythagoras

Bricks cut to different sizes are given different names. A brick cut in half along its length is called a half-bat, and then there is a three-quarter bat and a quarter-bat. A brick cut in half along its width is called a queen closer.

The standard concrete building block is rectangular and measures 450 mm × 225 mm × 100 mm, other thicknesses include 150 mm, 200 mm and 250 mm. When building with blocks, normally only the half lap is used.

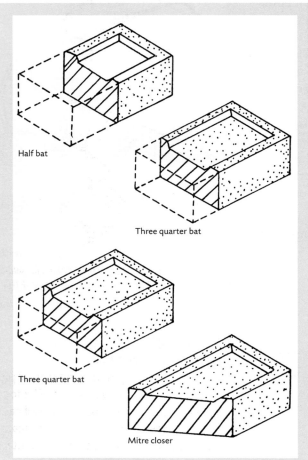

15-45 *Cut brick classifications*

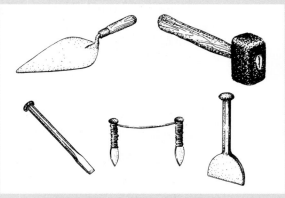

14-47 *A selection of blocklaying tools, clockwise from top left: trowel, club hammer, bolster, line and pins, and cold chisel.*

Blocks are laid using all the usual bricklaying tools and mostly the same techniques. Pre-cast concrete blocks are available in a variety of shapes and sizes.

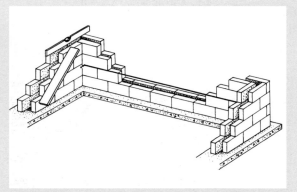

14-46 *The procedure when blocklaying is to build the two corners first. The blocks are raked back as shown. A guide string and pins are used when infilling the rows between the corners. A spirit level checks that the rows are level and a straight edge is used to ensure the walls are straight.*

Plastering

The main constituent of ready-mixed plasters is gypsum and calcium sulphate. Further constituents added during manufacture determine the type and grade of plaster. Gypsum plasters are only suited for internal work and should not be confused with cement render, which is a surfacing material made from sand, cement and lime and is generally used externally.

Render is used internally on block walls that have not been drylined. Render looks and feels like mortar because it has similar constituents.

Always store plaster in a dry place. If it comes into contact with water or moisture-laden air its properties will be altered.

Plumbing
Working with copper pipe

Copper has been the most widely used material for pipework and it is quite easy to work with. The rising main is normally 15 mm with a 22 mm indirect feed to the bath and wash hand basin. This is reduced to 15 mm for all other appliances.

New pipe fittings will be in metric sizes but existing pipework to which it is being joined may be in imperial sizes.

Copper pipe can be joined with either screw fittings or with soldered joints. Soldered joints are cheaper and have a neater appearance. Screw fittings are easier to use.

The two types of screw (or compression fittings) used in plumbing are known as manipulative or non-manipulative. The non-manipulative compression joint is most commonly used.

To make a compression joint, adjustable wrenches or open-ended spanners are used, and either a tin of jointing compound or a roll of PTFE tape. PTFE stands for PolyTetraFluoroEthylene, which is a plastic compound that is wrapped around the joint threads to make them watertight.

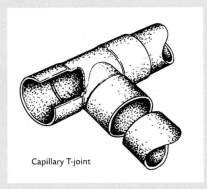

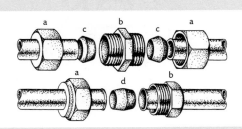

15-48 The two forms of compression joint for joining copper pipework. The non-manipulative (above) and the manipulative. Parts consist of (a) capnut, (b) coupler, (c) olive, (d) brass cone insert.

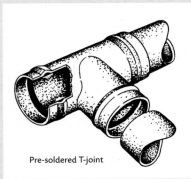

15-49 Two types of capillary fitting suitable for soldering: (a) the capillary T-joint and (b) the pre-soldered T-joint.

Plumbing
Soldering copper pipe

Soldering alloys fall into two groups: soft solders, and hard solders. Soft-soldering does not require high melting temperatures, but the use of a 'weaker' alloy for joining means that this method is suitable only for joints subjected to light loads. Most plumbing jobs fall into this category. Hard-soldering is known as 'brazing'.

Two basic types of flux are used in soft-soldering, and each is available in either liquid or paste form. Both types can be used for soft-soldering copper piping joints.

Mild, non-corrosive flux uses a resin base. It is used where it is not possible to 'clean-up' the joint area after soldering, as a non-corrosive residue remains.

Acid corrosive flux leaves a corrosive residue, which must be removed using soapy water along with a good brushing.

There are two types of capillary fitting, which all rely on the same principle. Capillary action draws the bonding material (molten solder) along the minute gap between the fitting and the pipe. In one type, the fitting is pre-soldered and requires little more than heating when joining. The other type requires solder to be applied at the edge of the assembled joint.

Plumbing
Bending copper pipe

One of the advantages of using copper pipe is the ease with which it can be worked. The forces involved in bending a copper pipe will cause the tube to collapse and flatten unless precautions are taken. This means that some form of internal support must be provided, unless a pipe bending machine is used. A bending spring provides the necessary internal support when bending by hand.

Annealing copper tube makes it easier to bend and this is done by heating the pipe to a dull cherry-red glow and then cooling it rapidly in a water bath or by pouring water over it.

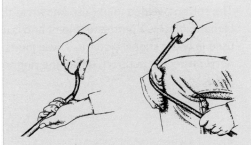

15-50 Use a bending spring to avoid kinking the pipe.

Plumbing
Working with plastic pipe

The plastic most commonly used in plumbing is PVC (polyvinyl chloride). PVC is an extremely hard and rigid material, but adding plasticisers during the manufacturing process can change these properties.

PVC is thermoplastic, which means that it softens and then melts on heating but will not support combustion. It is light but not weak, and rigid without being too brittle. PVC has an impact strength greater than cast iron, stoneware and concrete.

Special plastic pipes are now available for use with hot water supplies and central heating.

Plastic pipe is rapidly taking over from the more traditional forms of pipework in many areas of plumbing. This is because plastic is an easy material to work with, most forms are immune to chemical attack from the ground, and plastic piping is comparatively inexpensive and versatile in its application.

Two forms of joint are used for joining lengths of plastic pipe in the same material, the ring sealed joint and the solvent welded joint.

The ring sealed joint is a push-fit, semi-permanent connection. It is axially rigid enough for normal use, but capable of absorbing lengthways expansion.

15-51 The ring sealed joint. Insert the ring in the joint socket and apply petroleum jelly prior to pushing the two components together.

The solvent welded joint (also known as the solvent cement joint) is a permanent joint and is usually used in water supply systems. These joints do not need protective support, unlike the ring sealed joints.

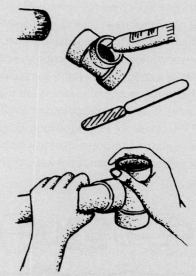

15-52 Making a solvent weld joint

Painting
Interior woodwork

Whether painting over new woodwork or a surface that has been painted previously, it is important to make sure that the surface is sound, clean and dry.

Smooth new woodwork with glasspaper, slightly rounding off any sharp edges. Treat knots or resinous patches with a knotting compound to prevent them from leaking sap through to the new paint.

Fill cracks and open joints with a cellulose filler such as Polyfilla.

New wood should be given a coat of primer to ensure that the undercoat (the next coat) will stick to the surface. Primer also helps to seal the surfaces. Remove dirt and grease by washing the surface with warm water and detergent or sugar soap.

An undercoat is applied after the primer or if wood is being painted a different colour. The undercoat provides a key for the final coat. Interior woodwork is usually painted with gloss or semi-gloss paint. Gloss paint is harder wearing than flat paints and is also easier to clean with a damp cloth.

Gloss paint is oil-based and includes resin to give it hard-wearing qualities. Acrylic paint is a water based gloss, which is jelly like in consistency and does not drip. It should not be stirred as this reduces its non-drip qualities.

Painting
Walls and ceilings

As with woodwork, a smooth, clean and dry surface is essential for a professional finish. Dry-brush plaster before painting to remove surface dirt and white fluffy alkaline crystals.

After preparation, the plaster must be sealed. When using emulsion paint, a coat of emulsion thinned with water is sufficient. Use an alkali-resisting primer for oil-based paints.

Wallpaper should be removed before painting. Painted surfaces should be washed to remove dirt and grease.

When painting ceilings, use an adequate scaffold arrangement. Remember not to let brushes and rollers dry-out during breaks, etc. Paint dries on rollers and brushes as easily as it does on walls and ceilings.

Primers and fillers

- **Knotting:** seals the wood and provides a key for the top coats of paint. It is not strictly a primer.
- **General purpose primer:** an oil-based primer that performs well on bare wood.
- **Lead primer:** available in red, pink and white. Rarely used nowadays since modern substitutes perform as well and are safer.
- **Acrylic primer:** this is a non-toxic primer suitable for internal use where the need is more to protect the wood from knocks than weathering. It works as both a primer and an undercoat.
- **Aluminium primer:** this is particularly good at sealing heavily resinous woods, such as pine.

Holes and cracks should be covered with an appropriate filler, once the wood has been thoroughly primed.

- **Cellulose/plaster filler:** this is the most common type of wood filler and is suitable for both interior and exterior use.
- **Plastic filler:** used only for large holes, these two part plastic fillers are expensive.
- **Fine surface filler:** is used for filling small dents or imperfections.
- **Natural wood filler:** these allow the wood to be stained or varnished afterwards.

Painting
Special effects

TEXTURE PAINTING involves brushing a thick compound on to a wall or ceiling and then rippling the surface with a special tool to create a pattern. As well as being decorative, it has the advantage of filling small cracks and faults. It is also cheap and easy to apply. Texture paints become semi-permanent when dry, so removing them is often difficult.

15-53 Regular and irregular comb textures are easily designed from plastic sheet blade

BRUSH GRAINING is where a woody grain is produced in the paintwork by applying a fairly light ground coat followed by a slightly darker topcoat. Before the topcoat dries, a brush is drawn across it to produce lines or streaks, which reveal the lighter colour.

MARBLING is the imitation of smooth polished marble on timber. For best results the ground coat must be completely smooth. A black or white ground coat is used for most types of marbling work.

SPONGE STIPPLING The surface is painted with a base colour and allowed to dry. A small amount of the glaze colour is placed in a container and the flat side of a sponge is dabbed in it. The sponge should be a natural sponge (not synthetic) and it should be slightly dampened. The sponge is first tested on paper and then dabbed on the wall.

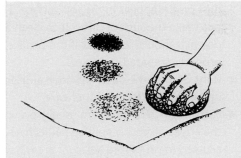

15-54 Sponge stippling

BAG GRAINING This effect is achieved by brushing a glaze coat over a base coat and then using a rag-filled plastic bag to create a pattern that allows the base coat to show through.

15-55 *Bag graining*

RAG ROLLING This effect is achieved by brushing a glaze coat of oil-based eggshell finish paint, thinned 50/50 with white spirit, over a base colour. Two people are required, one to brush the glaze colour and one to rag roll it off.

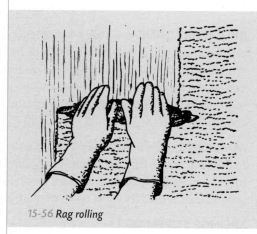

15-56 *Rag rolling*

Painting
Defects

Examining the finished surface will indicate where the failure occurred in the painting job.

- **Bittiness** occurs if any small particles of sand, dust or dirt appear in the top surface. The small bits make the surface difficult to clean and wash down. It should not occur if the surface has been properly prepared.
- **Runs** occur if the paint has been applied unevenly or without proper care.
- **Fatty edges.** This problem usually occurs where the edges of freshly applied paints have been allowed to set before adjacent areas have been covered. Fatty edges refers to thick, uneven lines of paint which build up on large areas as well as on edges.
- **Flashing** occurs on eggshell and sheen emulsion paint, which has been lapped and applied unevenly, resulting in areas, which are dull and patchy.
- **Ropiness** is the result of the paint not flowing evenly on to the surface, causing rough or heavy brush marks when the paint eventually dries. It can also be caused by using old paint, which has partially dried up, or by the misuse of thinners.
- **Bleeding** occurs when the newly applied coat of paint is discoloured or stained by ingredients from the underneath surface. Creosote, for example, will bleed through any oil-based paint applied on top of it.
- **Cissing.** Grease, polish or oil on the background surface causes cissing. Freshly applied paint breaks up and becomes patchy, exposing the surface underneath.
- **Non-drying paint.** Paint will not dry properly if applied in very low temperatures or in conditions of very high humidity. Check the paint manufacturer's instructions.
- **Lifting** occurs when the existing surface is soft, or covered with an undercoat, which has not dried. Wrinkles sometimes develop in advance of lifting.
- **Grinning** is when the topcoat of paint is so thin that the underneath surface is visible through it.
- **Blistering** is caused by moisture or moisture vapour trapped under the paint film. In time the moisture breaks the bond of the paint to the backing material.
- **Efflorescence.** White fluffy crystals form on the surface of brick, plaster or mortar. They come from alkaline salts, which are brought to the surface by dampness or moisture in the background material. All masonry should be brushed with a soft brush before painting.
- **Blooming** is caused by water or moisture settling on the paint film as it dries. A dull, milky film appears on the surface of gloss paint and lacquer.
- **Crazing.** A network of fine cracks appear over the surface. The fracturing occurs because of movements in the background or the undercoat.

Design

The refurbished Boland's Mill building in
Dublin, now the headquarters of the
National Treasury Management Agency

☞ Private residence using decorative concrete tiles and cladding, complementing the original clay facing blocks of the structure

Roadstone

Architectural products have an essential role to play in the achievement of versatile design concepts. Roadstone's Architectural Products Division manufactures and distributes a wide range of products used by specifiers and architects as well as private individuals, to enhance and complement their design concepts. These include concrete blocks, decorative stone, rooftiles, a wide range of paving and walling products, bricks, Forticrete® masonry and glass blocks.

Chapter 16

Design appraisal and processes

Introduction

There are many forms of design – dealing with both precise and vague ideas – that need both imaginative thinking and methodical calculation.

The three-dimensional nature of architectural design requires the designer to produce practical, aesthetic and well-functioning artefacts or end products. Designers in this category construct places or objects, which may have a major impact on many people's lives.

Design can be extremely varied and successful designers can employ very different processes in arriving at a solution. Designers must decide what effects they wish to achieve and how they plan to achieve them. For instance, a civil engineer must understand the structural properties of concrete and steel, and their understanding of technology has to be relevant to their design field.

For many types of design, designers must be technically competent and also have a well-developed aesthetic appreciation. Space, form and line, along with colour and texture, are important elements in the process of design.

The majority of items are designed for particular groups of users. Therefore, designers must understand the nature of these users and their needs.

One of the complexities of design is the need to embrace many different strands of thought and knowledge. It involves an advanced mental process capable of manipulating many different kinds of information, blending them into a coherent set of ideas, and generating some realisation of those ideas.

Design in this chapter will be discussed in the context of architectural design.

What is design?

The word design comes from the Italian verb *disegnare*, which means *to create*. Design is all around us, in man-made and natural forms and in the way we communicate and understand each other and our environment.

Design originates from basic human needs and desires. Since the beginning of history, humans have attempted to coexist with both the natural and man-made environment.

In the developed world, design has become a professional activity. There is now a wide variety of designers, all trained to design objects for specific purposes.

Design may be defined as the arrangement of visual elements that underlie the making of form, as well as the methods, theory and research that form making is based upon.

Design features and constraints

Form is the result of human or natural activity. It may be visual or it may lead to a visual outcome. All visual form is made up of three categories of components: elements, characteristics and interactions.

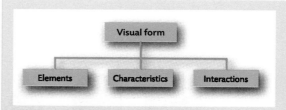

16-1 *Components of visual form*

Visual elements are dots, lines, planes, and volumes (Fig. 16.2). Each element possesses characteristics of size, shape, texture and colour. Position, direction and space are the principles of visual interaction, which direct these elements and characteristics.

Articles with two dimensions have **shape**; articles with three dimensions have **form** (Fig. 16-3).

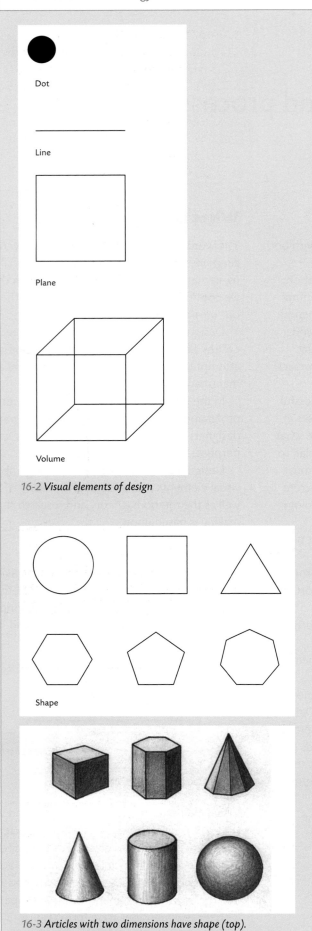

Dot

Line

Plane

Volume

16-2 *Visual elements of design*

Shape

16-3 *Articles with two dimensions have shape (top). Articles with three dimensions have form.*

Types of form

Geometric form has regular angles or patterns and is found in nature in the crystalline structure of rocks and snowflakes. It is also found in man-made form – in circles, triangles, squares, polygons, or combinations of these.

16-4 *A combination of geometric form is often found in architecture.*

Organic form is fluid in appearance and is predominate in nature.

Rounded

Conical

Pyramidal

V-shaped

Flat topped

16-5 *Organic form is found in trees.*

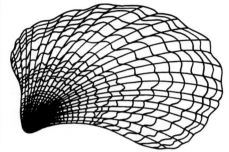

16-6 The shell is another example of organic or natural form. Organic form can be modeled in CAD.

- **Function** refers to a form's practical or personal use. It is generally part of three-dimensional design, such as architecture.
- **Meaning** is the message and use of form.
- **Interpretation** is the translation of a form's meaning. Rather than give factual information about the form's colour interactions, an interpretation might attempt to define its meaning and to explain how the colour interactions affect us.
- A form is **ambiguous** when it has two or more possible meanings or interpretations.
- **Appropriateness** is the suitability of a form, i.e. whether it is right or wrong for a particular purpose.
- **Colour** can help create meaning. Without light there is no colour, because objects have no colour of their own. Objects absorb or reflect particular light waves, which become visible to our eyes. Colour can create the perception of volume and depth.
- **Proportions** help describe the visual forms in every day use. Proportions can be compared, measured and analysed. The human body is the first reference point in finding and using proportions. A person's height and the length of their arms influence how they understand and interact with their environment.

The human body has served as a datum for measuring and understanding the world for centuries. The metric system, based on units of ten, relates to our ten fingers.

Geometry and ratios

The influence of ratios and geometry in design can be traced back to the origins of Greek architecture. With the aid of geometry, numerical ratios can be calculated and used to structure form.

The **Fibonacci series** is probably the best-known ratio. Each number in the series is the sum of the two previous numbers (1, 1, 2, 3, 5, 8, 13, 21, …). Any number in the series divided by the following is approximately 0.618, and any number, after 13, divided by the previous is approximately 1.618.

This ratio is more commonly known as the **golden section** and it has been the basis for geometric shapes used throughout history. The dimensions of a credit card conform to these proportions.

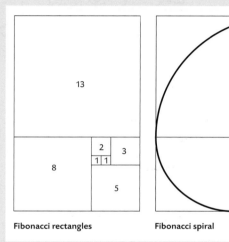

Fibonacci rectangles   **Fibonacci spiral**

16-7 The sides of the Fibonacci rectangles are two successive Fibonacci numbers in length. Quarter circles drawn within each square generates the Fibonacci spiral. Similar curves occur in nature, as in the shape of snail shells and some seashells.

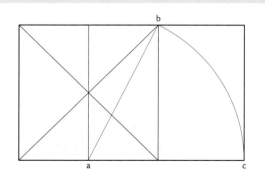

16-8 The golden section (also known as the golden mean or the golden rectangle) has a ratio of 1:1.618.

Divide a square to find the centre point 'a', from which length 'ab' is found. Swing the length 'ab' from 'a' to give point 'c'. This gives a rectangle of golden section proportions.

Aesthetics

While proportion is an integral part of good design, there are other aesthetic principles that need to be considered in architecture, including:

- unity
- balance and symmetry
- duality

These three factors affect the mass of the building.

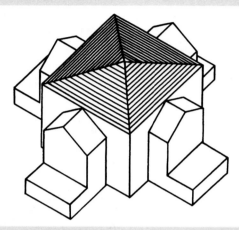

16-9 *Massing refers to a composition of two-dimensional shapes or three-dimensional volumes, especially if it gives the impression of density, weight and bulk.*

UNITY A sense of unity is achieved where the individual elements of a building contribute to the building mass. Unity of shape need not lead to monotony. A sense of completeness arises from consistency of shape and form.

16-10 *Unity may be referred to as the state of forming a whole from separate parts.*

16-11 *Uniformity refers to a state or condition in which everything is regular (identical).*

BALANCE AND SYMMETRY are achieved through a building having a focal point, i.e. a particular point that leads the eye to it, such as an entrance.

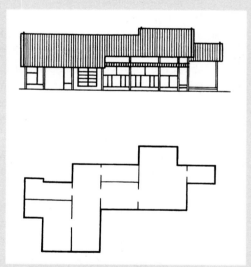

16-12 *Balance may be described as harmony or the pleasing arrangement of elements in a design.*

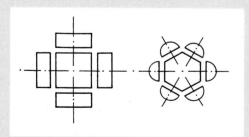

16-13 *Symmetry is the exact reflection in size, form and arrangement of components on opposite sides of a dividing line or plane.*

DUALITY refers to equilibrium of design. The arrangement of volumes and mass around the focal point creates balance. The visual impact as a result of the correct mass will emphasise the design concept.

Space

The single most important element of design is space. Spaces can be cheerful or depressing depending on the use the designer made of the design elements that form the whole.

Space is a costly commodity in modern times. Spaces tend to be smaller and less generous than in the past. Designers need to exercise great skill to give smaller spaces a particular atmosphere or character.

Space may be regarded as the raw material to be moulded and shaped with the designer's tools of colour, texture, light and scale. How space is manipulated is both an aesthetic and functional consideration.

A small entrance lobby in a building is needed to keep out wind and cold or heat and rain. This same lobby is equally important in providing a visual transition from outdoors to indoors.

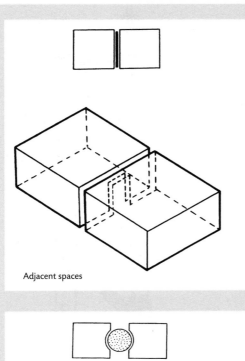

Adjacent spaces

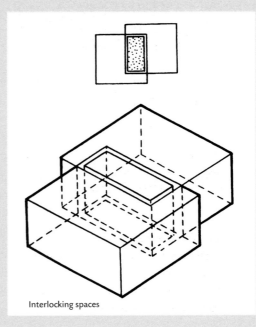

Interlocking spaces

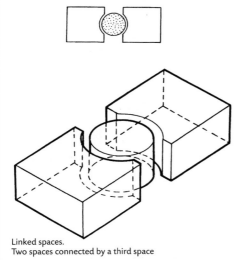

Linked spaces.
Two spaces connected by a third space

16-14 *Relationship between different types of space*

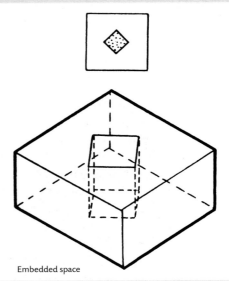

Embedded space

Ergonomics

Ergonomics is the study of the human form in relation to its environment. All design revolves around satisfying a need of human beings. Therefore, for the correct functioning of any design, the shape and size of human beings, the way they move, etc. must be considered.

Height, weight, sitting and lying positions, width, reach and hand sizes give a range of functional dimensions necessary for much design work. Many designs will require consideration of some or all of the senses hearing, vision, smell, taste and touch.

When designing for the senses, the following factors need to be considered:

TOUCH. As contact is made with many designed articles, attention must be given to:

- ensuring there are no sharp edges
- providing protection for very hot or very cold surfaces
- providing ventilation
- the design of hand-held components or parts
- inclusive design considerations

SIGHT. Visual communication is of great importance. Symbols, pictures, words and letters form the basis of graphical communication. Colours affect a person's psychological well-being.

HEARING. Loud noise can be uncomfortable and may even cause hearing damage. Special design considerations may be necessary to reduce the transmission of noise.

SMELL. Pleasant smells can be stimulating, while unpleasant smells can be annoying and irritating.

History of design

In the past many objects were made to very sophisticated designs without an understanding of the design's theoretical background. Undrawn traditional patterns were handed down from one generation to the next, as craftsmen designed objects while they were made. In this vernacular process designing is closely associated with the making. Design in the modern Western world is quite different.

The division of labour between those who design and those who make has now become a feature of our technological age. This separation of design from the making isolated designers, and made them the centre of attention. It also resulted in a central role for drawing.

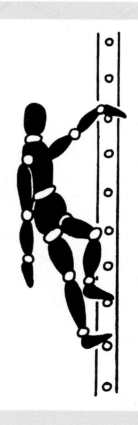

16-15 *Ergonomics is the study of the relationship between workers and their environment, especially the equipment they use.*

Because designers are no longer involved in the making, they must communicate instructions to those who are. Drawing has traditionally been the most popular method of communicating such instructions. Although design by drawing has many advantages, it also has some disadvantages. The designer can see from the drawing how the finished design will look, but not necessarily how it will work.

Design drawing can present a misleading appearance of the design. For example, architects tend to design with the plan, which is a poor representation of the relationship of rooms to each other in reality.

The shortcomings of the design by the drawing process became more obvious as designs became more revolutionary and progressive, especially in the field of architecture. It became obvious that if the making were to continue to be separated from the designing, and considering the rapid rate of change and innovation, then new forms of modelling the finished design would be required.

The design process

It is highly probable that the process of design involves generic skills that apply to all forms of design, and equally probable that certain types of design require specific skills. All designers need to be creative. Architects in particular need well-developed visualisation skills and the ability to draw well.

Many attempts have been made to specify the steps involved in the process of design, with the belief that the design process consists of a sequence of distinct activities, which occur in some predictable and logical order.

Concepts that arise in models of the design process

RESEARCH aids understanding of both the natural and man-made environment. Its main purposes are to search for and create new information, and to critically analyse existing information. Research may raise as many questions as it attempts to answer.

METHODOLOGY refers to the process of analysing, defining, evaluating or creating. Methodologies provide a structure for research.

ANALYSIS involves looking at relationships, looking for patterns in the information presented, and the ordering of objectives. Analysis involves understanding and structuring the problem.

SYNTHESIS is an attempt to come up with a solution to the problem.

APPRAISAL involves a critical evaluation of the proposed solutions when compared to the analysis.

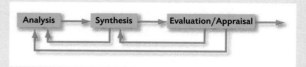

16-16 *A generalised plan of the key components in the design process*

PROBLEM SOLVING involves identifying a problem and then arriving at a solution to the problem. The design process is often referred to as a problem or a series of problems. There are four main steps in the process of problem solving:
1. Learn conditions.
2. Identify and define the problem.
3. Generate ideas and select solutions.
4. Implement solution and evaluate result.

Despite many attempts to map out the stages in the design process, there is no evidence to suggest that designers actually follow these stages in a logical order when designing. The design process, by definition, takes place inside our heads.

The design brief

The design brief is a problem set for the designer to work on and to solve. The designer must understand the requirements of the brief. The designer produces one or more solutions to the brief, which must then be tested to see if they fulfil the brief. Whether or not the steps occur in the order outlined is questionable.

The following three aspects must be considered for any design process:
1. **functional demands** of the building/artefact
2. **technical constraints**
3. **aesthetic considerations**

If the design process is to succeed, the architect must have detailed information on the following:
- durability of the project
- form of the building
- environment
- structure of the building
- ventilation and air movement
- water exclusion
- heat
- light
- sound
- security and privacy

The durability of each element can be established once the building's life expectancy is determined. Durability influences material selection and may also affect the form and shape of the building.

The form of the building will depend on the activities and the working environment set out in the design brief. The distribution of space is dependent on anthropometric data – i.e. the space required to perform human activities.

16-18 *A rectilinear form*

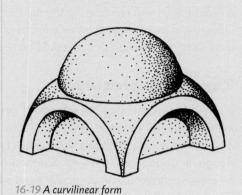

16-19 *A curvilinear form*

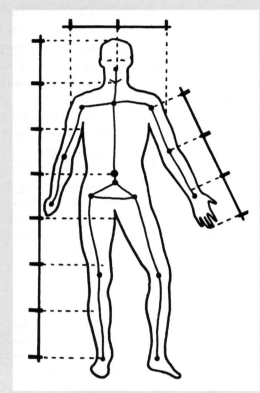

16-17 *Anthropometry relates to the comparative study of sizes and proportions of the human body*

The structural forms of buildings can be classified into rectilinear or curvilinear forms.

Rectilinear forms are those generated by beam, post and lintel structures. Traditional materials constrain the structural form. Aesthetics, such as proportions and unity are easily achieved.

Curvilinear forms are those generated by domes, arches or geodesic domes. The building shape in plan is constrained, as the dome form demands a square.

Design problems

A design problem usually originates with a client, someone who is unable to solve or perhaps understand a problem. It is highly unlikely that the client will present the designer with a complete brief where the problem is clearly defined and the constraints identified.

In many cases the client may not be the end user, for example, when architects design schools or public housing they have little contact with the end users of the building. This has led to the need for user requirement studies.

In the case of architectural briefs, a user requirement study involves identifying the purpose of the building in relation to activities and human needs, to determine its 'fitness for purpose'. This will result in the building allowing the occupants to carry out their activities conveniently and in a suitable environment.

The user requirement study will assist the design process by:

- clarifying the brief
- establishing performance standards for activities, area, cost and environment
- comparing alternative designs with the design brief

Legislators also create constraints within which designers must work. They issue standards for factors of safety, appearance, energy efficiency or utility, etc. The architect must also adhere to fire regulations and planning criteria.

The purpose of these constraints is to ensure that the designed object functions as efficiently as possible.

There is no definite end to the design process. It is very difficult to decide when a design problem has been solved. Designers stop designing when they feel they have reached a satisfactory solution to the problem or when they run out of time. It is difficult to know what information will be useful in solving a design problem until a solution has been attempted.

Design problems may have many facets to them. A designed object usually serves more than one purpose.

> *"The American architect Philip Johnson is reported to have observed that some people find chairs beautiful to look at because they are comfortable to sit in, while others find chairs comfortable to sit in because they are beautiful to look at."*
>
> Lawson, Bryan. 1997 "How Designers Think", Architectural Press, page 56

Good design may be regarded as an integrated solution to a whole series of problems. It is often difficult to determine which part of the problem is solved by which part of the solution.

> *"Recognising the nature of the problem and responding with an appropriate design process seems to be one of the most important skills in design."*
>
> Lawson, Bryan. 1997 "How Designers Think", Architectural Press, page 109

Design drawings

The modern design process places a great deal of importance on the drawing, especially because design is separate from construction. Drawing has become a central activity in the design process.

The two main types of drawings used are presentation drawings and working drawings. Presentation drawings are usually perspectives and show the final solution for the clients. The working drawings explain how to construct the design for those who will build it. Once the design reaches this stage the design process is effectively complete.

Much has been written about computer-aided-design (CAD) and how it will either assist or replace the human designer. To date, what is called CAD is really computer-aided-drawing rather than computer-aided-design.

Computers, however, do have input in the design process. Architectural packages are now available for evaluating the thermal, lighting and acoustic environments of buildings. It is now possible to model and render three-dimensional designs and simulate lighting conditions, surfaces and colours of materials so as to give a very clear indication of the actual appearance of the object.

These packages allow shapes to be refined in the same way that model making allowed in the past, with obvious time and cost savings.

With the proper software, buildings can be erected in virtual reality before building them physically. This will enable the client to walk around and/or walk through the building and experience the relationship of rooms and the positioning of windows and doors etc.

Use of models

Models are a useful means of testing design ideas. Poor ideas will show up in a model. It is easier and cheaper to scrap a model than a finished piece of work. It is easier to judge proportions, stability and arrangement of components from a model than it is from a drawing.

As models are three-dimensional they can be viewed from all directions, unlike drawings, which are two-dimensional. Design problems can often be remedied in a model, and if necessary, new drawings can then be made.

TYPES OF MODELS The main types of models are:

1. **Full-size models.** These are very useful when testing ergonomics.
2. **Small-scale models.** The most common type.
3. **Larger than full size.** These models are used when designing small components such as jewellery.
4. **Cut-away models.** Used to show constructional details or working mechanisms, which cannot be viewed from the outside.
5. **Complex models.** Used to show only the complex parts of a design.

6. **Working models.** Not commonly used in architectural situations.
7. **Layout models.** Useful for room layouts and interior design situations.

Model-making techniques will be dealt with in Chapter 17.

Evaluating design

It is difficult to evaluate what is good design. The tendency is to categorise a design as good according to its appearance, our personal tastes and current styles and fashions. However, fashions change, especially in clothing and automobile design.

In deciding whether or not a design is good, it might be better rely on experience, learning and research to analyse if the design works in the context of the situation.

A building that is attractive, well proportioned and visually pleasing has an aesthetic design. The design evaluation of a building will highlight success and failure in location. The technical evaluation will show the durability and tolerance of elements to abuse and overload. The operational evaluation will show how the building is functioning under working conditions.

Examples of the design process

All designing is concerned with finding solutions to problems. When a design solution fully solves a problem it is said to be successful.

A **design brief** is a statement that clearly specifies what is to be designed. The purpose of the brief is to state exactly what the problem is and specify any constraints.

Investigation

Investigation follows from the compilation of the design brief. Investigation will lead to solving the problems set by the design brief. This whole process is easier if a logical sequence is followed, remembering that professional design may not follow such a sequence. A suggested sequence of investigation might be:

1. Function and ergonomics

List the functions the design is expected to achieve. Study the relationships of human beings to the design (ergonomics). Determine the key dimensions.

2. Shape and form

Study the possible range of shapes, proportions, colours, textures and forms, that may influence the design. Pleasing proportions are based on the human figure.

Three-dimensional shapes (3D) are referred to as form.

16-20 Form in an architectural context

Shapes and forms arranged around a focal point play an important part in some design work. Lines, shapes and forms can be arranged to give the impression of movement in a design.

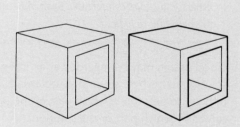

16-21 Some lines on a drawing are thickened to provide variation for the eye and to assist in understanding the form of the object.

Texture – soft, smooth surfaces are friendly and pleasing to touch. Rough, sharp surfaces are less friendly to touch but may produce interesting visual effects.

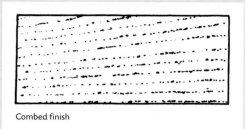

Combed finish

Daubing

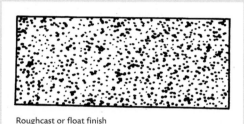

Roughcast or float finish

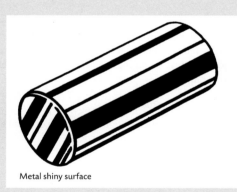

Metal shiny surface

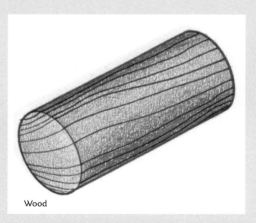

Wood

16-22 A selection of textures depicting plaster, shiny surfaces (metal) and wood.

Colours merit careful consideration in design work. Reds tend to make a design look warm and comfortable; blues have the opposite effect. Some colours, such as greys, some browns, greens and white are more neutral colours and are suitable for backgrounds.

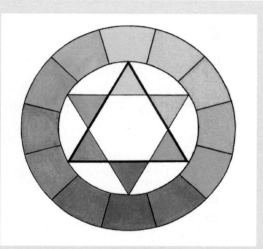

16-23 The colour wheel. Complementary colours are shown opposite each other. To designate a warm colour incline towards red, orange or yellow. To designate a cool colour incline towards green, blue or violet.

3. Materials

Are there any restrictions on the choice of materials available for the design? Which are the best materials? Justify the selection of materials for the particular design. Refer to Chapter 14.

4. Economics

Calculate the cost of the design in terms of materials and labour (time taken to complete the design), and sustainability of solution.

5. Processing

What methods of manufacturing, shaping and jointing will be used for making the design? Will permanent, temporary or moveable joints be used?

Permanent joints are expected to last throughout the life of the design without any movement taking place.

'Knock-down' jointing techniques fall in to the temporary category. They can be taken apart either with a screwdriver or a spanner or they can be pulled apart.

A moveable joint may be either permanent or temporary. Movement, such as sliding, rotating, bending, or moving along arcs, can occur even though the parts may be fixed to each other.

6. Strength

Is strength a primary consideration? Will it be necessary to test the materials, jointing methods and fittings for strength?

7. Surface finish

What are the considerations for the type of surface finish to be applied? What is the most appropriate finish for the article being made?

Appraisal/Evaluation

This consists of an assessment of the design after it has been made. The appraisal/evaluation usually answers the questions:

1. Does the finished design successfully meet the objectives set in the design brief?
2. Are all the requirements of the design brief fulfilled?
3. Does it function properly?
4. Are the materials appropriate?
5. Is the quality of workmanship satisfactory?
6. Have appropriate fittings been used?
7. Is the quality and type of surface finish satisfactory?
8. Are all aspects of the design safe?
9. Have suggestions for improvements or alterations been made?
10. What do test results in relation to the design say?

A typical representation of the design process follows:

Typical design process

Brief

A written statement of the problem to be solved including any constraints.

Research/investigation

Data collected in relation to function, shape, form, etc. Measure existing items of a similar design. Consult catalogues, Internet, etc.

Ideas/sketches

Sketch solutions to the problem as ideas are arrived at.

Select a solution

Decide which idea best satisfies the brief. Retain the other ideas until the chosen one has been tested.

Working drawing

Create a working drawing, which will help to refine proportions and dimensions.

Model/prototype

Make a model (prototype/mock-up) of the solution using dimensions from the working drawing. Refine the solution, if necessary, to improve proportions etc.

Materials selection

Select the most appropriate materials for the design. Carry out all necessary tests to determine strength requirements and jointing techniques.

Realisation

Make the design using the most appropriate processing skills and techniques. It may be necessary to make practice joints to test for strength and/or to practise new techniques.

Appraisal/evaluation

Assess the finished design against the original brief by answering a number of questions.

Chapter 17

Communication of design

Graphicacy is now accepted as an important means of communication in this 'technological age'. Along with numeracy and literacy it forms a tripod of thinking, recording and communicating.

This chapter deals with the various graphical methods of communicating design in an architectural context.

Stages in the design process

The design process consists of a number of stages. These provide a structure for the designer to progress from an initial idea to a finished artifact.

Designers use freehand sketches and technical drawings to communicate design ideas. Technical drawings may be produced by hand or by CAD.

In the past physical models were created either from technical drawings or before technical drawings were produced. Physical models are still employed in architecture. However, computer modelling is gaining in popularity as it allows the design to be created and visualized in advance of producing technical or working drawings. One of the main attributes of computer modelling is the ease of modification.

The design process was dealt with in Chapter 16. Figure 17-1 shows an adaptation of the design process with an emphasis on communication of design.

Freehand sketching

Sketching or freehand drawing is used in architecture to quickly communicate ideas or designs. The sketch can be used as a foundation for other work.

It is important to retain sketches, as evidence of the thought process, no matter how insignificant they may appear to be.

Some points to remember when sketching:
- Draw objects in proportion.
- Place an object on the sketch to give an idea of scale.
- If working in black and white prior to working in colour, take colour notes.
- Include notes on the sketch to describe additional elements.

Sketching techniques
- Record the bare essentials of the object. Concentrate on the basic component shapes. To achieve this be economical with the number of lines used to define the object.

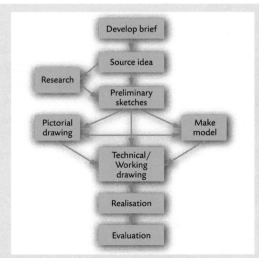

17-1 *The main stages in the design process*

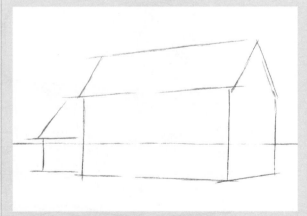

17-2 *Basic sketched outline of a building*

- Carefully select the view of the object you plan to sketch. Ensure that it shows the main features of the object.
- Get the proportions of the object right. Figs. 17-2 and 17-3 show how this is achieved.
- Add shade and texture if it helps to enhance the object.
- Colour gives a sketch a professional presentation, but it must be applied with skill and care.

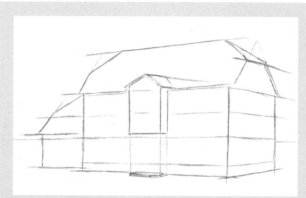

17-3 *Add additional features to the outline*

17-4 *Pencil shading gives a sense of depth to the object.*

17-5 *The complete solution in colour, including landscape details*

Presentation of design

LINE EMPHASIS

All lines, with the exception of lines that represent texture or pattern, indicate a change of direction. Some lines are thickened to make them stand out. The use of thick and thin lines produces a shadow effect, which makes the drawing clearer.

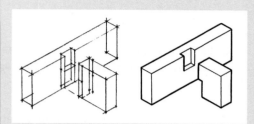

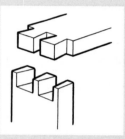

17-6 *Sketched lines on the left are allowed overrun the corners. Clarity is achieved by applying line weighting to the images on the right and below.*

Line weighting introduces contrast. Contrast creates visual interest. Thick and thin lines cannot be drawn just anywhere. The rules for drawing thick and thin lines are as follows:

- **Thin lines** are drawn where two surfaces meet and where both surfaces are visible.
- **Thick lines** are drawn where two surfaces meet and where only one surface is visible.

These rules apply to curved lines as well as straight lines.

CURVED SURFACES

Communicating information on irregular three-dimensional curved surfaces is reasonably complex but can be achieved in a number of ways.

The most common method used involves the use of plans and elevations. The elevations are divided into horizontal sections (planes). The information from each section is transferred to the plan view.

This process generates a number of layers (or templates) for setting up the drawing (or the model if an artifact is being produced). The layers are set up in a crate. They are drawn lightly with pencil so as not to interfere with the finished drawing.

The 3D outline is penciled in and finally shading is applied to the finished view.

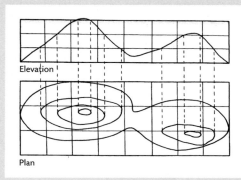

Elevation

Plan

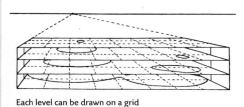

Each level can be drawn on a grid

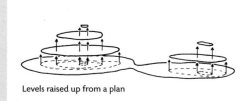

Levels raised up from a plan

Finished view

17-7 Steps involved in modelling curved surfaces

LIGHT AND SHADE

Line drawings give outlines of shapes and objects. These lines give enough information to indicate what the object is. How the object looks in reality is usually very different. One surface usually appears darker than another due to the effects of light and shade.

The side of an object close to a window will appear brighter than the side that is in shade. Lighter and darker versions of the same colour are referred to as tones.

Applying tones to a drawing through shading makes it look more solid.

Contrast refers to the difference between light and dark tones. An object with only one tone all over has no contrast.

17-8 An object with no tone looks flat and dull.

Pencil shading is the most common method used to produce tones on a drawing. Many different tones, from light gray to dense black, can be achieved from one soft grade pencil. The most suitable grades are 2B, B and HB.

The effect of light must be considered for shading to look realistic. Surfaces reflect different amounts of light, depending on the position of the light source in relation to the position of the object

17-9 Consider the effect of light when shading.

TONE WITH LIGHT AND DOTS

This technique is useful for creating sketches. Fine-line markers and ballpoint pens can be used.

Grouping the dots close together creates dark areas of tone. Light tone is created when more space is left between the dots.

17-10 Adding tone with lights and dots

SHADOWS

Shadows occur when objects block the path of light. Rays of light bounce off the object and an area of shadow is produced at the back of the object.

Guidelines for drawing shadows

- The shape of the shadow is linked to the shape of the object blocking out the light.
- The position of the shadow is related to the position of the light. The lower the angle of the light the longer the shadow.
- The shadow follows the form of the background. For example, if the background is curved then the shadow cast on its surface will also be curved.
- Shadow is a darker tone of the surface on which it falls. For example, a shadow falling on a green background (grass) will be a dark green.

TEXTURE AND MATERIALS

Texture refers to the representation of the nature of a surface. How the surface of a material is displayed is determined by how it is perceived by the sense of touch.

Texture helps to convey the form of an object and the material from which it is made. Words used to describe texture include shiny, smooth, rough, soft.

Texture is visible due to the effect of light and shade on the object. Applying texture to design drawings makes them look interesting and shows the materials from which different components should be made.

Coarse textures or rough surfaces in Architectural Technology include concrete, plaster, and polystyrene. Surfaces that are shaded from the light are textured the most. Surfaces that face the light have little or no texture applied to them.

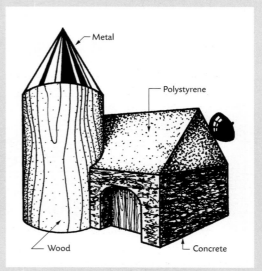

17-11 Line art representation of some common architectural material textures

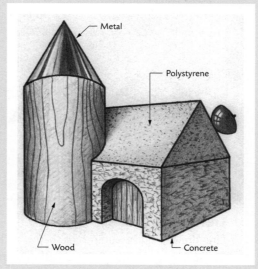

17-12 Pencil shading of some common architectural material textures

Smooth shiny textures include plastics, metal and glass. The shiny appearance results from the highlights and reflections on the materials.

One method of suggesting a reflection is to draw a number of short parallel lines across the surface. When representing glass, which is transparent as well as shiny, it will be necessary to draw the shapes that can be seen through it.

Matt surfaces are smooth and may only have a dull surface sheen. Wood is a good example of a matt surface. Other materials include paper, card, rubber, some metals and plastics. Tone is applied evenly to achieve a matt surface. Lines representing wood grain are a common technique of showing wood on a drawing.

Colour

Colour is a very important aspect of design communication. It influences choice in the purchase of items. It transforms bland objects into lively and exciting ones.

Colours affect our moods and feelings. Blue, for example, is a cold colour and can give a feeling of loneliness. Orange-red colours generate a feeling of warmth and comfort. Strong reds, on the other hand, can cause irritation and restlessness.

The primary colours of red, yellow and blue are used by designers to shock and gain attention, as they are strong and outstanding colours.

Colour used on a drawing will become the focus of that page. It is important that the colour does not detract from or obscure the design idea. Colour is a means of improving communication on a drawing. It is not a means of communication in itself.

In a design drawing colour is used to:
- suggest a colour scheme for the design
- suggest the materials from which an object is made
- highlight a sketch on a design sheet
- make the background to a drawing stand out
- show recognised colour standards, as in the case of wiring a plug top, wiring on a diagram or circuit
- help show different components in a multi-part object
- draw attention to the most important part of the drawing

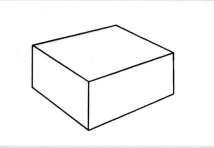

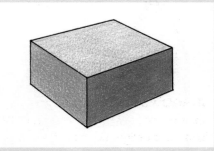

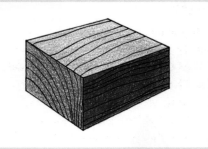

17-13 Different techniques used in applying colour

Colour terms

The colour wheel (see Fig. 16-21) shows how colours relate to each other. The wheel is based on the principle that all colours can be made from the three primary colours of red, yellow and blue.

Colours that agree together (harmonise) are found next to each other on the colour wheel.

Contrasting colours are found opposite each other and are referred to as complementary colours.

Secondary colours are violet, green and orange. Mixing two primary colours together makes secondary colours:

- Red + yellow = orange
- Red + blue = violet
- Blue + yellow = green

Tone refers to lighter or darker versions of the same colour.

Methods of applying colour

COLOUR PENCILS are excellent for applying colour to design drawings or sketches. They are easy to use and control. They involve no mess and they are inexpensive. Mixing the colours produces new shades and colours.

17-14 *Colour pencils were used to enhance this drawing.*

17-15 *Material textures are further enhanced by the use of colour.*

Guidelines for the use of colour pencils include:

- Keep a sharp point on the pencil.
- Continue using the pencil in the same direction.
- Colour up to the edges of shapes and objects.
- Apply the same pressure on the pencil to obtain a flat, even colour.
- Do not overuse colour.
- Mix pencils to produce different colours.

COLOURING WITH MARKERS. Felt-tipped markers or pens are used for colouring in. They produce bright colours and are often unsuitable for design drawings. Changing the pressure on the marker will have no effect on the colour produced. Bar shading has been used on the cylindrical form in Fig. 17-15. The bars are narrower and spaced further apart the closer they are to the highlighted area.

17-16 *Colouring with markers produces a harsh look, which can be overpowering.*

WATER-COLOUR WASHES Applying colour with water-based paints is the traditional method of colouring design drawings. Some people avoid using paints on design work as they find them difficult to control. However, if they are used with care and in an organised manner, very effective results can be achieved.

When colouring dark areas mix the paint with very little water so that it is quite thick. For brighter areas the paint can be thinned down until it is transparent enough to allow the lines on the drawing to show through the colour. This technique is known as watercolour wash.

To ensure that the linework will not smudge before applying this technique:

- Produce the sketch in pencil.
- Colour the drawing using the watercolour wash technique.
- Add the linework when the drawing is dry.

The paper can become very wet with this technique and may stretch and buckle. To prevent this happening pre-stretch the paper before the colour wash is applied. Wet the paper (using a damp sponge). Fix it to a flat wooden surface while it is still wet using strips of gummed paper. The paper will contract as it dries and pull taut against the gummed strips. When fully dry the paper will remain flat when paint is applied.

Always use special watercolour paper and pre-stretch it.

17-17 Interesting results can be achieved by using water-colour washes.

Architectural drawing

Oblique projection

Oblique projection is a form of pictorial drawing. The front elevation of the object is drawn as a true view. Any angle can be used for drawing the sloping lines, but 45° is the norm.

Although the front views of objects can be drawn to scale, the depth lines need to be scaled down to prevent the object appearing distorted. Generally the depth is scaled down by half.

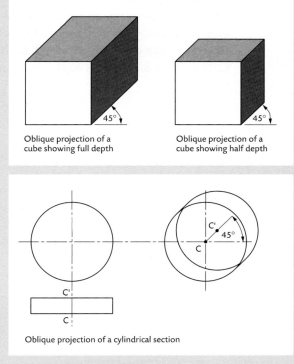

Oblique projection of a cube showing full depth

Oblique projection of a cube showing half depth

Oblique projection of a cylindrical section

17-18 Principles of oblique projection

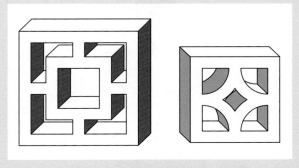

17-19 Two decorative concrete blocks drawn in oblique projection. The block on the right shows how curved surfaces are treated in oblique projection.

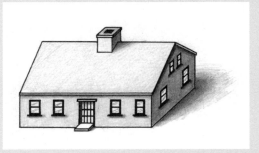

17-20 Model of a house drawn using oblique projection

Isometric projection

Isometric drawing or projection is a more realistic method of pictorial representation than oblique projection. The object appears tilted so that no surface of the drawing will appear as a true shape.

True distances can be measured accurately along three different axes. The axes make an angle of 120° to each other. More complicated shapes are drawn in isometric using a technique called 'crating' or boxing-in.

In isometric projection the circle appears as an ellipse in any of the three surfaces. The circle is first drawn true. It is then boxed in a square and divided using a number of ordinates. The ordinates with the positions of the circle are transferred to the correct surface on the isometric drawing. The circle (ellipse) is drawn freehand on the isometric drawing.

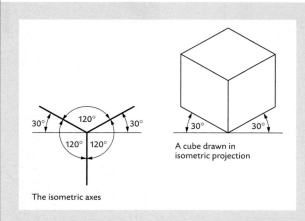

The isometric axes

A cube drawn in isometric projection

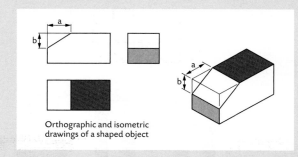

Orthographic and isometric drawings of a shaped object

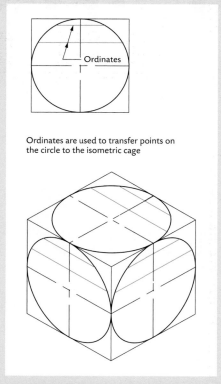

Ordinates are used to transfer points on the circle to the isometric cage

17-21 Principles of isometric projection

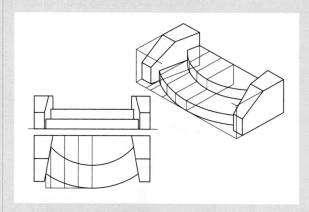

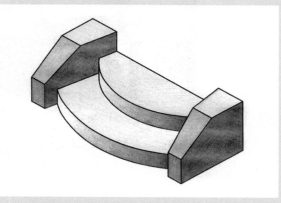

17-22 Details of concrete steps drawn in isometric projection

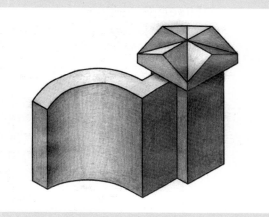

17-23 Light and shade used to enhance a finished isometric drawing

Orthographic projection

Orthographic projection is a method of drawing an object, model or house by producing 'flat' views of the different sides. This allows all of the object's features to be shown.

Each side is viewed as a true shape, unlike pictorial projection, which distorts the view. There are six possible views of any object but three views will generally show all the details. The three views are called the front elevation, the side or end elevation, and the plan.

Architects, engineers and designers use orthographic projection to show details of an object to allow it to be reproduced exactly. Detailed drawings of this nature are often referred to as working drawings.

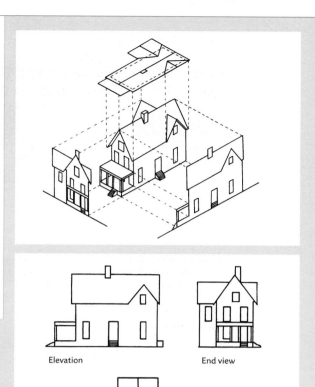

17-24 (right) Principles of orthographic projection (top), showing how the flat views are generated from the 3D model. The bottom view shows how the views are laid out following the rules of orthographic projection.

Elevation   End view

Plan

17-25a (below) Typical working drawings for a dormer bungalow

FRONT ELEVATION   SIDE ELEVATION

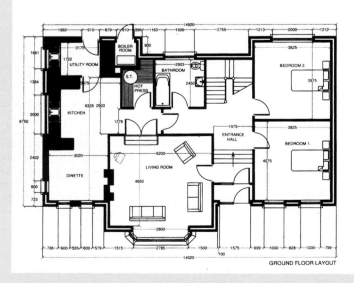

GROUND FLOOR LAYOUT

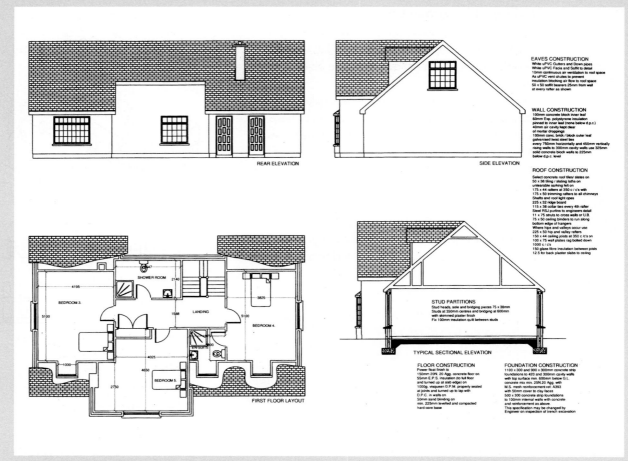

REAR ELEVATION

SIDE ELEVATION

EAVES CONSTRUCTION
White uPVC Gutters and Down pipes
White uPVC Facia and Soffit to detail
10mm continuous air ventilation to roof space
As uPVC vent chutes to prevent
insulation blocking air flow to roof space
50 x 50 soffit bearers 25mm from wall
at every rafter as shown

WALL CONSTRUCTION
100mm concrete block inner leaf
60mm Exp. polystyrene insulation
pinned to inner leaf (none below d.p.c.)
40mm air cavity kept clear
of mortar droppings
100mm conc. brick / block outer leaf
galvanised twist steel ties
every 750mm horizontally and 450mm vertically
rising walls to 300mm cavity walls use 325mm
solid concrete block walls to 225mm
below d.p.c. level

ROOF CONSTRUCTION
Select concrete roof tiles/ slates on
50 x 38 tiling / slating laths on
untearable sarking felt on
175 x 44 rafters at 350 c / c's with
175 x 50 trimming rafters to all chimneys
Shafts and roof light opes
225 x 32 ridge board
115 x 38 collar ties every 4th rafter
Steel RSJ purlins to engineers detail
11 x 75 struts to cross walls or U.B.
75 x 50 ceiling binders to run along
bottom edge of hangers
Where hips and valleys occur use
225 x 50 hip and valley rafters
150 x 44 ceiling joists at 350 c /c's on
100 x 75 wall plates rag bolted down
1000 c / c's
150 glass fibre insulation between joists
12.5 for back plaster slabs to ceiling

SHOWER ROOM

BEDROOM 3.

LANDING

BEDROOM 4.

ENSUITE

BEDROOM 5.

FIRST FLOOR LAYOUT

TYPICAL SECTIONAL ELEVATION

STUD PARTITIONS
Stud heads, sole and bridging pieces 75 x 38mm
Studs at 350mm centres and bridging at 600mm
with skimmed plaster finish
Fix 100mm insulation quilt between studs

FLOOR CONSTRUCTION
Power float finish to
150mm 20N. 20 Agg. concrete floor on
55mm E.P.S. insulation (to full floor
and turned up at slab edge) on
1000g. visqueen D.P.M. properly sealed
at joints and turned up to lap with
D.P.C. in walls on
50mm sand blinding on
min. 225mm levelled and compacted
hard-core base

FOUNDATION CONSTRUCTION
1100 x 300 and 900 x 300mm concrete strip
foundations to 420 and 350mm cavity walls
with top surface min. 600mm below G.L.
concrete mix min. 25N.20 Agg with
M.S. mesh reinforcement ref. A393
with 50mm cover to clay faces
500 x 300 concrete strip foundations
to 100mm internal walls with concrete
and reinforcement as above.
This specification may be changed by
Engineer on inspection of trench excavation

17-25b Typical working drawings for a dormer bungalow

Orthographic drawings have been in use since about 1800 as the standard means of communicating information about a design. Designers and architects frequently used colour to distinguish between different parts of a drawing. Coloured drawings disappeared with the need to reproduce drawings in quantity. Instead blueprints were used, which showed the drawing as a white line on a blue background.

Computer graphics have reintroduced the possibility of producing drawings in colour.

Perspective projection

Perspective projection is a method of drawing objects to make them look realistic. Perspective attempts to reproduce real and representative information in a drawing. Photographs may be regarded as perspective views.

Perspective is the best method of 3D communication and presentation. Architects use it to communicate design information to clients. Clients easily understand it because it looks realistic and an understanding of the 'graphics code' is not required.

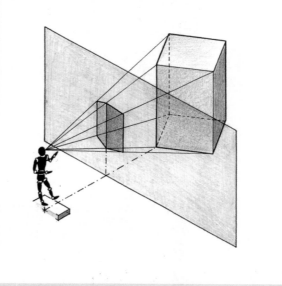

17-26 Principles of perspective projection. If a window pane (picture plane) is positioned between the observer and the object, the lines of sight will pass through the window pane in the same proportion that they reach the eye. The two-dimensional perspective image is traced on the window pane.

In perspective drawings parallel lines converge to a vanishing point as they recede into the distance. Perspective drawings will vary depending on the number of vanishing points used. One-point perspective is used for interior views in architecture. Two-point perspective is used for buildings. The object/building can be drawn at an angle to the viewer.

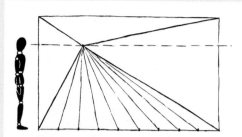

Select an eye level line and a vanishing point (not all in the center or too close to either wall).
Connect the corners of the room to the vanishing point.

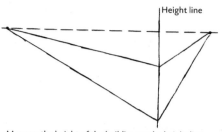

Measure the height of the building on the height line. Draw lines from the top and bottom points to the vanishing points.

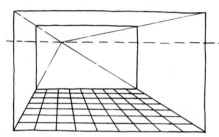

Draw in floor squares to give the room depth

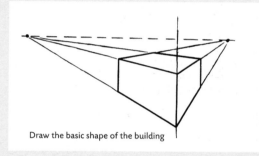

Draw the basic shape of the building

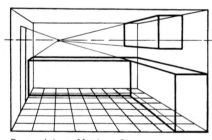

Draw end views of furniture. Connect corners to vanishing point.

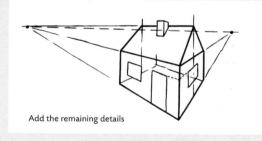

Add the remaining details

Add details and colour.

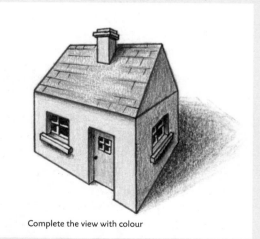

Complete the view with colour

17-27 Steps involved in producing a one-point perspective drawing

17-28 Steps involved in producing a two-point perspective drawing

RULES OF PERSPECTIVE

- Parallel lines converge towards a vanishing point where they disappear.
- Equal lengths foreshorten more the further they are away from the observer.
- In one-point perspective the only true surface is the one closest to the viewing point.
- In two-point perspective the vertical edge closest to the viewing point is the only true edge.
- A view with two vanishing points will have them positioned on the horizon line. The horizon line is always horizontal.

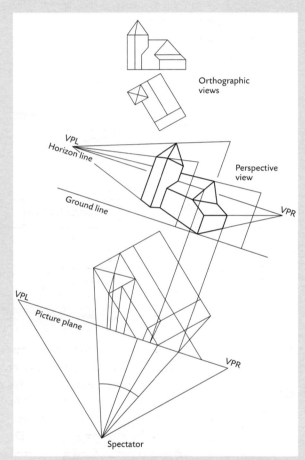

17-29 *A perspective view of a building with a square turret*

17-30 *The same building as in Fig. 17-29, but with details and colour added*

Cutaway drawings

Cutaway drawings are used by all types of designers, including architects. Part of the wall or building is removed to show the interior. Make sure the cut surface is clearly identified, otherwise it may lead to confusion.

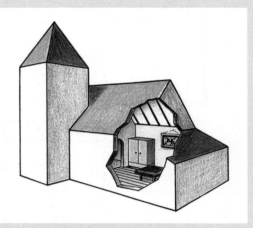

17-31 *An example of a cut-away drawing*

Exploded views

Exploded and cutaway drawings are used to give a more visual and easily understood view of a component or assembly.

In exploded views the spaces between the various parts is increased in the direction of the explosion. They are used to show the relationship between the various parts. The drawing of the light switch below illustrates this point.

Exploded views are used to show how things come together and how they come apart. They are generally drawn in isometric projection.

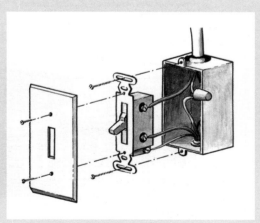

17-32 *An example of an exploded view*

Sequence diagrams

Sequence diagrams are used to show how something should be done. The various stages are shown visually in the correct order. A good diagram will show the information clearly. Decide on the information to be presented and the number of stages required to show the information.

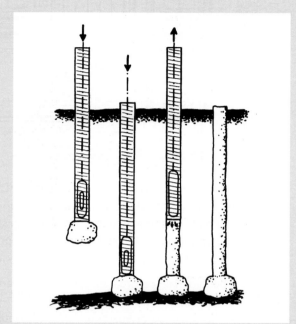

17-33 *A sequence diagram showing the steps involved in pouring uncased piles. A concrete plug is driven into the ground until it meets the required resistance. The pile is formed by ramming concrete into place as the casing is withdrawn.*

Computer aided design (CAD)

Computers have been used to produce architectural drawings since the early 1960s. The technological advances since then have provided the architectural sector with more efficient, powerful, reliable and cheaper systems.

The term CAD can mean computer aided draughting (drawing) or computer aided design.

Computer aided draughting is the production of drawings that were traditionally created using the drawing board and T-square.

Computer aided design involves using the computer as an aid to the design process. The computer's attributes that aid the design process include calculation capabilities, analysis, evaluation and modelling.

Combining computer aided design and draughting is sometimes referred to as CADD. This text will refer to CAD in the context of computer-aided design.

Computer aided manufacture (CAM) involves using computers to assist manufacture involving computer numerical controlled (CNC) tools and equipment.

Interaction takes place between the CAD and CAM systems. This is provided in a geometric database, which contains all the stored data generated by the drawing procedure.

CAD systems

A CAD system consists of a number of computer elements linked together to produce some function, such as design, drawing or manufacture.

All computer systems consist of the following:
- input devices
- processor
- storage devices
- display devices
- output devices

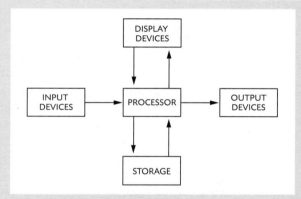

17-34 *Basic elements of a CAD system*

Input devices allow the computer operator to communicate with the computer. They are used to make selections from a menu. In CAD systems menus may be displayed in a variety of forms. The most common form is on the computer screen, generally in the form of graphic icons. Digitising tablets, which are flat surfaces connected to the computer, with the menus laid out externally, are also used.

CAD input devices include:
- **keyboard**
- **mouse**
- **trackball**
- **puck or stylus** – used in conjunction with the digitising tablet.
- **light pen** – the required position is selected by pointing the pen directly at the screen.
- **thumb wheels** – one wheel controls vertical movement and the other controls horizontal movement.

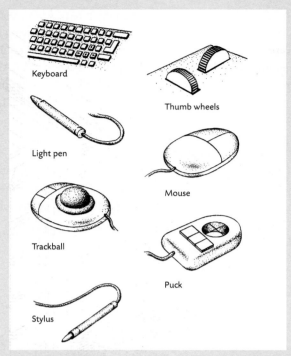

17-35 *Input devices*

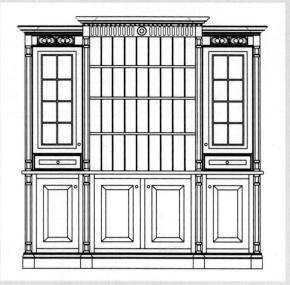

17-36 *2D CAD drawing of a pine dresser*

Output devices receive data from the computer and produce a hard copy. Printers and plotters are the two main types of output devices.

The two main types of printers in use are ink-jet and laser printers. Ink-jet printers direct a jet of ink at the paper to create the required output. Laser printers use a fine beam of laser light to create the required output.

Plotters are now available using the same technology as printers, i.e. ink-jet and laser types. The main difference between printers and plotters is the size of paper that each can handle. Printers are generally limited to A3 paper size while plotters can handle A0 paper size.

CAD software

There are many CAD packages available. The most popular package used in education and industry is AutoCAD. AutoCAD allows 2D draughting, 3D draughting and solid modelling. AutoCAD is limited as a design tool. Solidworks and AutoDesk Inventor are examples of software that currently offer design capabilities.

2D draughting

The screen is used in the same manner as paper when using the drawing board and T-square. Each view of the artifact must be drawn individually. The views are drawn in one plane only, without any depth. Additional views cannot be automatically generated.

There are four basic elements of a 2D CAD drawing: points, straight lines, arcs and curves.

Points on the screen can be located by selecting the position with the cursor, snapping to preset snap points or by using the co-ordinate systems.

The two main co-ordinate systems are: Cartesian and polar co-ordinates.

■ Cartesian co-ordinates use the horizontal distance x and the vertical distance y from the fixed origin to locate the required point.

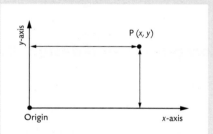

17-37 *Cartesian coordinates*

■ Polar co-ordinates use the length of the radius r and an anticlockwise angle measured from due east to locate the required point.

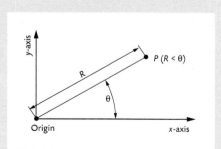

17-38 *Polar coordinates*

Examples of CAD functionality not available in manual draughting:

- **Scaling** – increasing or reducing the size of an object without changing its shape.
- **Zooming** – enlarging or reducing a selected area of the drawing.
- **Rotation** – objects or entities rotated about a selected centre point and redrawn in the new position.
- **Mirroring** – the ability to create a reverse image of an object about a chosen line of symmetry (otherwise known as axial symmetry).
- **Duplicating** – also known as copying or arraying. Copying is used to make one or multiple copies of an object. Arraying makes copies of an object in an orderly manner either linearly or rotationally.

The following automatic features are available with most CAD systems.

- **Fillets** – arcs are formed from two intersecting lines or curves.
- **Chamfers** – corners are beveled at equal or unequal amounts.
- **Tangents** – lines drawn to touch circles and arcs at the points of contact.
- **Hatching** – shading an area to represent different materials.
- **Dimensioning** – adding dimensions to the object.
- **Text** – similar to a word processor, text can be added using any size or style and can be placed on the drawing at any angle.
- **Trimming** – an excellent editing tool that allows parts of entities that intersects other entities to act as cutting edges. The unwanted elements are easily removed.

Isometric drawings

Isometric drawings are referred to as 3D drawings in the context of manual drafting. However, in CAD isometric drawings are not regarded as 3D drawings because they have no depth and cannot be viewed from different angles. Isometric drawings in CAD are best described as a 3D representation of a solid model.

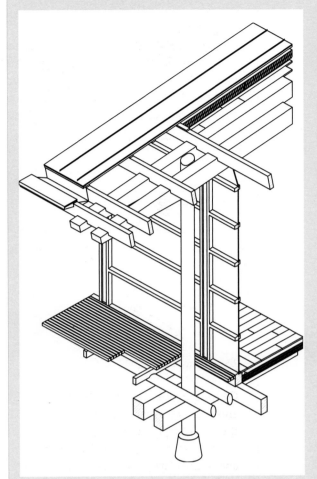

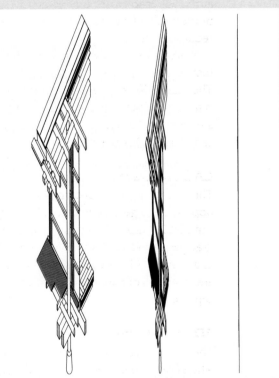

17-39 This decking model looks convincing as a 3D model but is in fact a CAD isometric drawing. This is evident when the drawing is viewed from a different angle and the drawing appears 'flat'.

Three-dimensional modelling

The object is drawn in a pictorial projection using *x-y-z* co-ordinate geometry. It can be rotated and viewed from a number of preset 3D viewpoints. Orthographic views of the object can be captured from the model without the need to draw them.

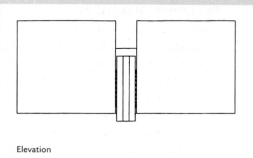

Elevation

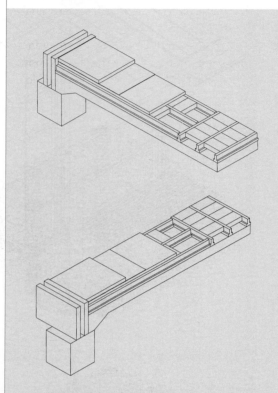

17-40 **A 3D solid model of beam and block construction**

Solid models give true representation of an object, using colour if desired. It is possible to achieve very realistic looking images. The model can be used for the calculation of volume, mass, moment of inertia, centre of gravity, etc.

Solid modelling uses the principles of Boolean geometry. 3D solids of different standard geometrical shapes are linked together to form the required model. The three Boolean processes of constructing solids are union, difference and intersection.

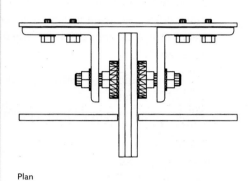

Plan

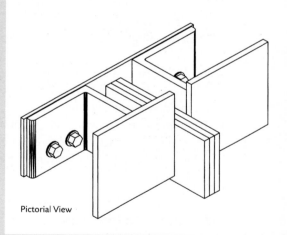

Pictorial View

17-42 **Solid model of a glass structure detail. The orthographic views are 'captured' from the solid model.**

Drawing a profile of the shape and then extruding the shape in the *z*-axis direction produces solid models of irregular shaped objects.

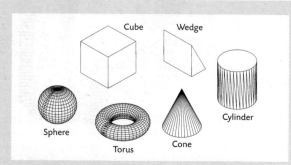

17-41 **Construction solids (primitives)**

Parametric modelling

Parametric modelling is the controlling, modifying or manipulation of graphical entities using mathematical variables (parameters). By creating CAD models using parameters, the user is able to adjust or update the attributes of an entity by changing a parameter.

Entities such as lines, circles and squares are used to describe real world objects. By making entities parametric, the model may be tailored to meet a design for multiple situations and/or design requirements without the need to generate an entirely new model.

AutoCAD is essentially a 2D drafting package with some 3D modelling capability. Inventor is an example of a parametric solid modeler. It uses sketches that are controlled by dimensions and constraints.

Inventor opens AutoCAD drawings and will convert them to 'sketches' or convert the dimensions to parametric driving dimensions. By changing a dimension, the geometry it is tied to will change accordingly.

Transitional constraints allow one component of an assembly to be constrained to an entire group of surfaces. An example of this constraint is a cam and a follower. Constraints can be applied to follow lines, faces or edges, smooth or spline edges or sharp corners.

Constraints in an assembly can be set up to control a part. For example, if you need a shaft to span a gap between two parts it is possible to constrain the length of the shaft within the assembly so that it will always be long enough, no matter how big the gap becomes.

Simply describing the cuts required creates section views.

Dimensions can be linked to views so that when a dimension is changed in one view, the projected view automatically changes.

Production drawings for parts and assemblies are quickly created from the 3D designs. This is the major difference between 2D drafting and parametric modelling. Parametric modelling allows concept designs to evolve from the sketch phase to the finished constrained model. Orthographic drawings are automatically produced. Changes to the model are reflected in the production drawings.

Parametric architectural modelling

Traditional architectural design and documentation methods using conventional CAD emulate an electronic drafting pencil. This results in digital drawings that are no more than a collection of lines and arcs. They do not represent real-world equipment and materials that make up a design. It is very difficult to change such designs, analyse them or get accurate take-offs.

New parametric building information modelers are available that change this design approach. Revit from AutoDesk is currently one example.

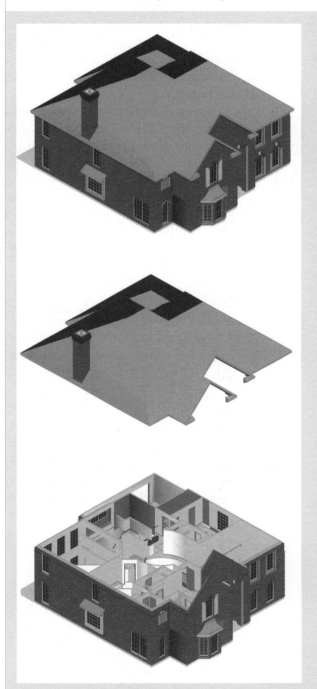

17-43 An example of a building produced using a parametric building information modeler

Revit automates design documentation, preparation of deliverables and tedious coordination chores. The software is built on a database designed to integrate design and documentation with coordination and change management.

Accurate and coordinated sets of drawings and schedules are produced. Equipment and fixture take-offs are always up-to-date. Consultants and contractors have access to up-to-date and complete digital design models. This greatly reduces errors and time chasing problems during the construction process.

Conventional CAD makes the user responsible for something the computer should be naturally adept at. Each change must be made to every sheet in the drawing set. This introduces errors and creates a time consuming cycle of checking and corrections.

Parametric building information modelers offer a new approach to prototype design. The designer can quickly create a complete parametric digital model of the building. Designers can work in whatever view they feel comfortable, designing in plan, elevation, section, 3D or even in live schedules. Each view is a window into the building information model, always updating and coordinating each of the associated views and drawings as the prototype design progresses.

A full photo-realistic rendering system is integrated into the parametric modeler. Animated walkthrough capabilities allow the designer simulate the client's experience of the current prototype. 'What if' analysis can be performed by switching one material type for another either on the building exterior or interior.

The Revit building information modeler allows the designer to lock specific design intent into the model. For example, if the building requires a corridor 3 metres wide, this is established as a fixed relationship in the model. Once the design intent is locked in, other changes to the design respect this decision, until the designer decides to change or relax this constraint.

Modelling techniques

Architects are sometimes referred to as spatial engineers. Buildings define space, and the best way to understand and solve spatial problems is by making models. But there are many types of model, so it is important to select the one that is the most suitable for your brief.

- **Presentation model:** this represents the complete solution. It is generally produced for promotional purposes and for a non-technical audience. They are popular with professional designers (Fig. 17-45 opposite).
- **Soft or sketch models:** these are produced early in the design process. They are made from readily available materials such as card and expanded polystyrene. Sketch models do not usually show detail, but give an impression of the possible design solution (Fig. 17-46 opposite).
- **Small scale models:** these models are smaller than life size. They are used when designing large items such as furniture. They are useful in interior design situations to give an idea of room layouts, etc.
- **Full size models:** also referred to as a 'mock-up', these are valuable in making decisions about dimensions and ergonomics.
- **Large scale models:** this is when the model is larger than the actual design such as a detailed mechanism or a locking device.
- **Cutaway models:** a section of the model is removed in order to expose the inside. These are useful to show details of the design or construction that cannot be seen from the outside.

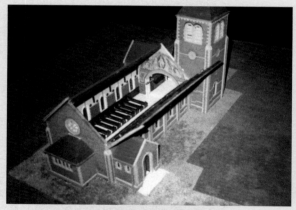

17-44 *A cut-away model or a model with an opening section reveals internal detail.*

- **Working models:** these usually have a mechanism and are intended to operate just like the finished design.

17-45 **A completed block model. Scale 1:750**

17-46 **A card model of a proposed design for a library in Sligo**

17-47 This apartment model is at a scale of 1:250. notice the increased detail compared to the block model in Fig. 17-45

17-48 This cresent model is at a scale of 1:200. The detail in this model is so realistic it could be mistaken for an aerial photograph of the finished estate.

Scale

The appropriate scale for houses and domestic buildings is 1:20 or 1:50. It is advisable to stick to these scales as architectural model suppliers work to them. At the largest scale, 1:20, the average person is 90 mm high (Fig. 17-47 opposite).

Consider the following points before making a model:

- Decide on the exact purpose of the model.
- Decide on the level of detail required.
- Use the most appropriate materials to make the model.
- Select a suitable scale for the model.
- Plan the method of construction.

Model making materials

Select a material that suits the type of model. Paper, card and foam are ideal for quick model making, but may not be suitable for obtaining the required amount of detail for a presentation model. Models should be made from material that has similar properties to the materials planned or in use in the final solution. For example, if the final design is to be constructed using acrylic, use sheet material such as card for the model.

Keep the variety of materials in any one model to the minimum. Too many different materials can spoil the appearance of a model. Following is a selection of materials suitable for modelling.

- **Paper and card** – available in a variety of colours and thickness. Cardboard and mounting board are extremely suitable.
- **Kappaboard** – this consists of two sheets of thin card with a layer of foam between them. It is available in two sheet sizes and in thickness of 3 mm and 5 mm.
- **Plastic sheet** – sheet polystyrene and rigid PVC.
- **Wood** – MDF, plywood, OSB. These are used as the base for the model. MDF can also be used for the model, as it is available in a variety of thickness.

  Red deal and **white deal** can be machined to specific sections for particular purposes. **Balsa wood** is available in thin sheets and in sections from 1 x 1 mm to 50 x 50 mm. Balsa wood is light, easy to cut and finish and looks well in models. Timber dowels are available in diameters of 6 mm, 9 mm, 12 mm, 15 mm, 18 mm, 21 mm and 25 mm, and are useful for making columns and pillars.

- **Polystyrene insulation board** – this is cheap and light but tends to crumble at the edges. A hot wire cutter should be used for really clean cuts.
- **Polyurethane insulation board** – is dense and fine-grained and cuts easily with a blade or a fine saw. It is available in different thickness.
- **Paper maché** – this is useful for creating irregular shapes, such as landscapes. It is strong when several layers are built up. Cork flooring tiles serve a similar purpose.
- **Plastic foams** – styrofoam, expanded polystyrene. Useful for taking up irregular shapes. A mould may be required.
- **Plasticine and clay** – easy to sculpt and form. Individual blocks can be shaped to make the building more authentic looking.
- **Plaster of Paris** – it can be cast. It is quick setting and easy to carve.

OTHER MATERIALS
Any scrap materials can be used in model making.

ADHESIVES
- **PVA adhesive** – use for paper, card and wood.
- **Contact adhesive** – use for plastic, metal and wood.
- **Balsa cement** – use for wood, card, metal and glass.
- **Polystyrene cement** – use for hard plastic materials.

Suggestions for modelling a building in card

A development of the sides of a building can be easily produced and details can be drawn on it directly.

- Add all decorative features to the development before assembly.
- Keep a photocopy of the development.
- Score all joints before folding to obtain crisp corners.
- If using flaps always glue them inside.
- Cut out all windows and openings before folding and insert transparent material for glass in the windows at this stage. (Use transparency film for copiers or overhead projectors.)
- Always cut with the finished surface uppermost.
- Include as many clues about scale as possible, e.g. people, cars, trees, etc.
- If using modelling paper to indicate textures such as bricks, make sure the correct size is available.
- Use available textures, for example, emery cloth is ideal for flat roofs and asphalt. Paint abrasive paper green and it resembles a well-mown lawn.

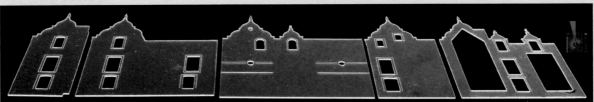

Modelworks.ie

17-49 *A model of a house with its component parts. In a professional modelmaking workshop the architect's drawings are used to generate the required part profiles. The CAD data is sent to the CNC router, which cuts the parts. The parts are assembled using a solvent to 'weld' the joints. Joints are sanded to a smooth finish. Roofs are fabricated by hand. The model is spray painted. Once painted a sheet of plastic containing the window frames and doors is assembled behind the walls and a layer of clear or opaque Perspex is laid behind the frames to model the window glass.*

- Sprinkling sand, gravels, etc. over a glued surface can also create textures.
- Create water using any transparent reflective material.

Finishing models

Models are sometimes best left in a single uniform colour. It is best not to add too much detail and to keep colours toned down unless a very precise presentation model is being produced.

Index

Index